PRAISE FOR
Michael Kimmel's *Angry White Men*

"Kimmel, a sociologist at Stony Brook University in New York, is unusually adventurous for an academic. . . . Kimmel maintains a delicate balance when handling his sources. . . . In one fascinating chapter Kimmel explores the changing nature of school violence. . . . Kimmel's balance of critical distance and empathy works best in his chapter on the fathers' rights movement, a subset of the men's rights movement."

—Hanna Rosin, *The New York Times Book Review*

"[*Angry White Men*] delivers . . . a lively, frequently scary look at a group of people who are trying, ever more desperately, to hang onto a world that no longer exists."

—*Booklist*

"Kimmel's writing is open and engaging, reminiscent of a conversation with friends in a bar. . . . Another worthwhile examination of important issues affecting men and, by extension, everyone else, from an author known for his insight into the subject."

—*Kirkus Reviews*

"[Kimmel's] book exposes an urgent need for a strong, appealing, sensible Left movement that addresses the dispossession of America's angry men and replaces it with a movement that respects our needs emotionally, politically and economically."

—*Truthout*

"An interesting and ranging discussion of the dark side of modern manhood with America's best expert on the topic. That quality is what makes the book so special, interesting, and easy to read. Kimmel blends personal stories with careful, journalistic study; he shifts between accessible academic and wide-ranged social commentarian; he explains complex sociology with the accessibility of a fun high school teacher in a small seminar class. . . . Whether you care about men, boys, masculinity, gender, feminism, violence, prejudice, post-industrial economics, or the frustrating, never-ending catastrophes that seem to make up modern American political life, *Angry White Men* is worth a read."

—The Good Men Project

"Being white and male has brought unfair power for so long that some think it's natural, both among those claiming it and those suffering from it. Michael Kimmel has done us the life-saving favor of naming this delusion that may endanger us more than any other. From executives for whom no amount of money is enough to white supremacists for whom no amount of power is enough, from U.S. wars in which men die to U.S. domestic violence in which even more women die, this illness is lethal for us all. *Angry White Men* is a brave, sane, compassionate, and rescuing book."

—Gloria Steinem, feminist activist and author

"White men still have most of the power and most of the money, so why do so many of them feel so victimized? In this fascinating guided tour of the world of angry white men—Glenn Beck fans, white supremacists, school shooters, men's rights activists—pioneer sociologist of masculinity Michael Kimmel shows how 'aggrieved entitlement' leads them to blame people of color, immigrants, liberals, intellectuals, the government, and above all, women, for a society that is changing fast and, they fear, leaving them behind. No dry academic study, *Angry White Men* is full of shrewd political analysis, empathy, and humor."

—Katha Pollitt, columnist for *The Nation*

"Michael Kimmel has written a comprehensive study of working and middle-class white men and described their collective grievances with insight and compassion. In regard to those among them who ally with the Far Right, he is equally insightful but justifiably more critical; his analysis of their misdirected rage at minorities and women is entirely persuasive. I enthusiastically recommend *Angry White Men* to the wide readership it has amply earned."

—Martin Duberman, professor of history emeritus at the Graduate School of the City University of New York

"Men and women should read *Angry White Men*. Women will gain insights into the sources of male anger and men will learn that increasing gender equality does not pose a threat to their masculinity. Rather, in this rapidly changing society, Kimmel believes that women and men will be able to lead more satisfying lives."

—Madeleine Kunin, former governor of Vermont,
author of *The New Feminist Agenda: Defining
the Next Revolution for Women, Work, and Family* and
Pearls, Politics, and Power: How Women Can Win and Lead

"In this timely book, Kimmel shows us that in these times, even those who have historically been powerful and dominant are becoming victims as they find themselves slipping between the cracks and falling behind. Kimmel has his finger on the pulse of their anger and by revealing their fears and growing desperation, he reminds us that their problems are ours as well."

—Pedro Noguera, Peter L. Agnew Professor
of Education at New York University

ANGRY WHITE MEN

Also by Michael Kimmel

The Guy's Guide to Feminism (with Michael Kaufman)

Misframing Men: The Politics of Contemporary Masculinities

Guyland: The Perilous World Where Boys Become Men

The History of Masculinity: Essays

The Gender of Desire: Essays on Masculinity and Sexuality

The Gendered Society

Manhood in America: A Cultural History

The Politics of Manhood

Against the Tide: Pro-Feminist Men in the U.S., 1776–1990

Men Confront Pornography

Men's Lives (with Michael Messner)

Changing Men: New Directions in the Study of Men and Masculinity

Absolutism and Its Discontents: State and Society in 17th Century France and England

Revolution: A Sociological Interpretation

ANGRY WHITE MEN

AMERICAN MASCULINITY AT THE END OF AN ERA

Michael Kimmel

NATION
BOOKS
New York

Hardcover first published in 2013 by
Nation Books, A Member of the Perseus Books Group
116 East 16th Street, 8th Floor
New York, NY 10003

Paperback first published in 2015 by Nation Books
Revised paperback published in 2017 by Nation Books

Nation Books is a co-publishing venture of
the Nation Institute and Perseus Books.

Books published by Nation Books are available at special discounts
for bulk purchases in the United States by corporations, institutions,
and other organizations. For more information, please contact the
Special Markets Department at Perseus Books, 2300 Chestnut Street,
Suite 200, Philadelphia, PA 19103, or call (800) 255-1514, or e-mail
special.markets@perseusbooks.com.

Designed by Pauline Brown

Typeset in ITC Giovanni Std

The Library of Congress has cataloged the hardcover as follows:
Kimmel, Michael S.
    Angry white men : American masculinity at the end of an era /
by Michael Kimmel.
        pages cm
    Includes bibliographical references and index.
    ISBN 978-1-56858-696-0 (hardback) — ISBN 978-1-56858-964-0
(e-book) 1. Men—United States—Attitudes. 2. Whites—
United States — Attitudes. 3. Masculinity—United
States. 4. Equality—United States. 5. Civil rights—United
States. I. Title.
    HQ1090.3.K55175 2013
    155.3'320973—dc23
                                                    2013025872

ISBN 978-1-56858-513-0 (2015 paperback)
ISBN 978-1-56858-961-9 (2017 paperback)
ISBN 978-1-56858-962-6 (2017 e-book)
                        LSC-C
            10 9 8 7 6 5 4 3 2

For
Amy and Zachary,
always

CONTENTS

Preface   ix

Author's Note: American Masculinity
at the End of an Era   xvii

Acknowledgments   xxv

Introduction: America, the Angry   1

1   Manufacturing Rage: The Cultural
Construction of Aggrieved Entitlement   31

2   Angry White Boys   69

3   White Men as Victims:
The Men's Rights Movement   99

4   Angry White Dads   135

5   Targeting Women   169

6   Mad Men: The Rage(s) of
the American Working Man   199

7   The White Wing   227

Epilogue   279

Notes   287

Index   301

PREFACE

The name Donald Trump does not appear in the index of *Angry White Men*. Nor does it appear anywhere else in the book, for that matter. This is not a book about Donald Trump. It's a book about his followers.

When I interviewed the white men whose stories formed the basis of the research, I picked up a sentiment among them, a feeling. They told me they felt pushed aside by Washington insiders, ignored by callous bureaucrats, and undone by a parade of others who challenged their previously unfettered access to the American Dream. Theirs were stories of being marginalized, "kicked to the curb by a Washington elite," as one of them put it. In this sense, *Angry White Men* is a book about Trump's followers, who were waiting for their leader to show up—even if they (and I) didn't know it at the time.

Like many Americans, I didn't see Trump's victory coming. I underestimated the depth of angry white men's rage and how others, including plenty of angry white women, might find it resonant as well.

I missed how a steady parade of events and statements that might have easily disqualified anyone else—anti-immigrant stances, confessions of sexual assault, racist statements about Latinos, coded racist remarks about African Americans—barely made a dent in Trump's appeal. Indeed, it only solidified their conviction that this was a guy who felt their pain.

Trump's election underscores the argument of the book: that white men's anger comes from the potent fusion of two sentiments—entitlement and a sense of victimization. The righteous indignation, the anti-Washington populism, is fueled by what I came to call "aggrieved entitlement"—that sense that those benefits to which you believed yourself entitled have been snatched away from you by unseen forces larger and more powerful. You feel yourself to be the heir to a great promise, the American Dream, which has turned into an impossible fantasy for the very people who were *supposed* to inherit it.

As I listened to these men, their anguish and despair turning to righteous rage at their downward trajectory in a country they found increasingly unrecognizable, I felt myself empathic. They were right: they had lost something. As they saw it, they'd lost some words that had real meaning to them: *honor, integrity, dignity*. They'd lost their autonomy, their sense of themselves as "somebody." And, as I heard them say it, they'd lost their sense of themselves as men. Real men. Men who built this country and who, in their eyes, *are* this country.

The unifying theme that runs through so many of the chapters of this book is, in fact, this notion of aggrieved entitlement. Whether it's men's rights activists fulminating about how feminist women have inverted the scales of gender justice, or the men who interpret their failures in the dating world to be the fault of gold-digger harpies, inspiring them to mass murder, or, finally, the denizens of the extreme Right, all these men feel furious that they are not getting what they feel they deserve. In every case, it's men who see themselves as having been cheated out of something valuable.

It wasn't my intention in the book to pass judgment on that feeling of aggrieved entitlement, or to try to convince these men that their feelings are somehow "wrong." It's hard to tell anyone that their feelings are wrong. Their feelings are *real*. They cannot be dismissed with a casual wave of the hand. But at the same time, their feelings may not be *true*—they may not provide an accurate assessment of their situation. I may feel, based on my perception, that the earth is flat. It is my experience. It just may not be a sound basis for developing navigational technology. With angry white men, we need to understand their feelings and perhaps offer an alternate way to understand their situation.

It is less about being white or male, in that sense, than about being angry. This is an emotional moment, a moment in which logical weighing of qualifications is dispatched by a cascade of outrage and entitlement. The men I spoke with in this book did not share a political position, a worldview, an analysis. They shared sentiments.

Populism is not a theory, an ideology; it's an emotion. And the emotion is righteous indignation that the government is screwing "us." There have been populisms of the Left (the anarchists of Spain) and populisms of the Right (Italian fascists). And in 2016, there were two populist movements: the left-wing populism of Bernie Sanders and the right-wing populism of Donald Trump. It's pretty likely that the standard-bearer of left-wing populism—a seventy-six-year-old Jewish democratic socialist—was not going to get anywhere near the White House in this election. But populism rode a tsunami of righteous entitled rage.

In her book *Strangers in Their Own Land*, sociologist Arlie Hochschild describes the emotions with a stark image, most applicable to policies about immigration: Imagine you are standing in line. You've been waiting hours, patiently. Then, suddenly, all these people you don't recognize cut in front of you in line. "Hey," you say, "I've been waiting in line like everyone else! Wait your turn!" Then a bunch of politicians show up and tell you to shut up, that these people have been historically shut out of even getting to stand in line, and now they get to cut in front of you.[1] That's how these guys feel.

Real feelings, yes. True facts? Not so much. After all, the states in which Trump scored his most lopsided victories—and even the counties in which he won handily—are precisely those states and counties that have the lowest rates of immigration in the nation. Those places that actually have experience with large numbers of immigrants were decidedly more welcoming to them.

That world in which white men grew up believing they would inevitably take their places somewhere on the economic ladder, simply by being themselves, is now passing into history. Yes, it's true they stood in line, played by the rules, and paid their taxes. It is the American Dream, the ideal of meritocracy. But that ideal misses how the deck was stacked in their favor for generations. They feel that anything even remotely approaching equality is a catastrophic loss.

The downwardly mobile lower middle class bought into the American Dream. They are true believers. To hear them tell it, if they worked hard, played by the rules, and paid their taxes, they, like their fathers and grandfathers before them, could buy a home and provide for a family. (Actually, they just needed to show up. They worked, yes, but on an uneven playing field.) But as I learned interviewing many of these men, that dream became a nightmare of downsizing, job loss, outsourcing, plant closings, shutting down the ma-and-pa store when Walmart moved in, losing the family farm. These men feel like they are seen as failures; they are humiliated—and that humiliation is the source of their rage.

This humiliation is deeply gendered, because when I say they wanted to support their families, they wanted to do it *by themselves*. The downwardly mobile lower middle and working classes are the last guys in our history to believe that they, alone, should support a family and that their wives "should not have to work." Like their moms and grandmothers, women were to be "exempted" from the work world. The core feature of American manhood has always been as "breadwinner."

They can't do it anymore. A generation ago, in 1974, the median income (in 2014 dollars) for a family of four in the United States was $48,497. Forty years later, in 2014, it was $53,057, less than $5,000 more. And what is the difference between that family of four in 1974 and 2014? Mom's working.

Of course, women have always worked. But we're talking ideology here, not history. And that helps explain why so many women ended up voting for Trump. Many of them voted not as "women," but as "moms"—working mothers who didn't want to be working. They were true believers also, and they believed that their role was to raise the kids and keep the home. When I interviewed Tea Party women a few years ago, many spoke of wanting their men to be the traditional heads of households, able to support their families. They wanted to live in a 1950s-era sitcom, a simpler time before zombie apocalypses and games of thrones. That white working women in the suburbs preferred a man who boasted about committing sexual assault, who held women in such contempt, suggests how deeply resonant this fantasy of that bygone *Father Knows Best* era remains today.

Social scientists often use the theory of "relative deprivation" to explain revolutions. It's rarely the poorest of the poor, those at the lowest rungs of society, who rebel, but rather it's those with something to lose. Middle-level peasants in Mexico, France, China, Cuba, Russia. Artisans, small independent farmers, and highly skilled workers in twentieth-century Russia, seventeenth-century England, and the American colonies. Relative deprivation describes the way that these groups look upward, at those rungs above them on the ladder of mobility, and realize that the ossified system is a permanent barrier to their upward mobility, for their chance at the dream. Their revolutions are, thus, aspirational, optimistic. They want to move up, but can't.

The angry white men I talked with in this book experience that same relative deprivation, but instead of looking upward at the rungs they are yet to climb, they look downward, at those below them, the people to whom these white men have always felt superior, to whom they have been taught to feel superior. It's not that their path upward is blocked; it's that the downward pressure from above is pushing them downward into the ranks of the marginalized. "They" might deserve to be down there, but "we" do not. Their revolt is, therefore, nostalgic, pessimistic, reactionary. They just want to prevent their being pushed down.

Listen to their language: "Make America great again." "Take our country back." And when they speak about manhood—or of identity more generally—they speak about what they must "retrieve," "reclaim," or "restore."

So, where to from here?

Maybe first a glance backward. In the late nineteenth century, a populist movement spread across the Midwest and the South, in areas that are now called "red states." Fueled by rural outrage at callous banks foreclosing on farms, on bankers and railroads destroying the small town as the center of the American landscape, populism nearly captured the presidency in 1896. Unable to make common cause with urban workers, however, the movement fragmented, and one leader, Thomas Watson, spiraled into racist, anti-Catholic, and anti-Semitic nativism. Only the Minnesota Farmer-Worker Party tried to bridge this gap.

Today those farmers and workers vote as reliably red as a fire truck. But if the rural population is unreachable, white urban workers in the

Rust Belt may still come around—if they can attend to their economic distress without condescension. Few recall today that one of President Obama's first proposals (instantly shot down by obstructionist Republicans) was to make community college tuition free, to help these guys, among others, retrain for the sorts of jobs that will be populating the economy of the twenty-first century.

Populisms of the Right always fail. Nostalgic longing for a lost Eden cannot restore what has been forever lost. Populisms of the Left may go too far, sweeping out the entirety of the regime that preceded it, often with cataclysmic violence. But they can triumph because they look to the future.

And that future is already here. The demographic trends that have been set in motion will not end. The year 2042 remains on the horizon as the time we become a majority-minority nation. The generation that will be majority nonwhite in America has already been born. Here, in America. They cannot be sent anywhere. They're here. They're ours. They're us.

The subtitle of this book is "American Masculinity at the End of an Era." When I wrote it, I predicted that the legions of angry white men would soon decline, though they'd become increasingly voluble—on the Internet. I did not expect this last stand, this valedictory lap around the field. I discounted the sentiments of their wives, for whom the traditional patriarchal bargain—he works and supports the family, she stays home and raises the children—was still a desire, if no longer a safe bet.

The end of that era of assumed entitlement will take a little longer to arrive. But the arc of history—and the teeming energy of demography—still points toward greater justice. It's just going to take a little longer, and we're going to have to fight a little harder to protect those who are now vulnerable.

Angry white men are hurt and angry and bewildered. They're right to be angry. They've been screwed. Heck, I'm angry too. But in the countless interviews I've given since the election, I'm always asking the same questions: Was it immigrants who issued those predatory loans that lost them their homes? Was it feminist women who outsourced their jobs and created deals that let billionaires pay no taxes? Did LGBT people embark on ruinous trade deals? Of course not. America's angry white men are right to be angry, but they are delivering their mail to the wrong address. That mail is now a letter bomb, and it will take a nation to defuse it.

Angry White Men concludes by recalling a 1932 speech by President Franklin Roosevelt, as he announced the New Deal. He spoke of "the forgotten man," who was suffering in the Depression, losing his farm, his livelihood, and his way. Donald Trump uses the same phrase and evokes the same forgotten man. FDR promised "to build from the bottom up and not from the top down," as he implemented a massive government spending effort to put people back to work. Trump, by contrast, offers only the same failed trickle-down policies that enriched the few and impoverished the many.

Long after the smoke and mirrors of Trump's promised economic policies, and after this mass hallucination that has many believing that rolling back environmental regulations and imposing draconian immigration policies will somehow restore America to its former glory, there will still be a future to build and, I believe, a large number of white men who will roll up their sleeves, alongside their neighbors, and, once again, put their massive shoulders to the wheel.

January 2017

AUTHOR'S NOTE

American Masculinity at
the End of an Era

That bawl for freedom in their senseless mood,
And still revolt when truth would set them free.
License they mean when they cry liberty . . .

—JOHN MILTON, SONNET XII (1645)

Whenever people have asked me about the subject of my new book, I've barely managed to tell them the three words of the title before they've regaled me with stories of blind rage being directed at them, daily incivility witnessed or experienced, outrage they've felt, heard, or expressed. I've heard so many recountings of the shouting across the aisles of Congress, the TV talking heads, or the radio ragers. They've talked of being enraged at demonstrations, confronted by equally enraged counterdemonstrators. I've heard of people behaving murderously on freeways, of my friends being frightened to sit in the stands at their children's hockey games or on the sidelines of their soccer matches. And nearly everyone has complained about Internet trolls who lurk on news websites and blogs ready to pounce viciously on anyone with whom they might disagree.

And they've told me that they've found themselves angrier than they'd been. Some were concerned that they're far angrier than they remember their parents being. Others have tried to maintain a boundary between political anger and raging against their families, though even there the boundary seems, to some, elusive. "The national blood pressure is elevated," said my friend Dan, a doctor given toward physiological metaphors. "It's at a frighteningly high level. Cultural beta blockers are in order."

This rise in American anger has been widely—and angrily!—noticed. Pundits lay the blame on greedy corporations, gridlocked legislatures, cruel and angry local and state governments, demographic shifts that infuriate the native born, and special interest groups promoting their special interest agendas. Mostly, they blame "them"—some group, organization, or institution that has acted so egregiously that outrage feels justified, righteous. The groups or individuals change; the scapegoating has become a national pastime.

And I admit, I've been angry too. I'm outraged by the arrogant religious sanctimoniousness of churches shielding pedophiles. I get impatient waiting on the telephone talking to yet another "menu of options," righteously indignant when crazed drivers swerve across three lanes of traffic to gain one car length, and aggravated by political gridlock and smarmy politicians. I'm easily ired when receptionists in offices or hosts in restaurants sigh loudly at my innocent request that they actually do their jobs and call the person I'm meeting or find me a table at which to eat. I'm generally not a grumpy person, but sometimes it feels that every other person is either smug, arrogant, infuriating, incompetent, or politically inane—sometimes all of the above.

Often I get angry about politics. How can I not? I'm incensed by intransigent, obstructionist Republicans in Congress who won't admit the mandate that the president received in his trouncing of Mitt Romney and irritated by a feckless and spineless Democratic majority that can't seem to seize that mandate. I fume about the inordinate influence a bunch of highly organized gun advocates have over public policy, even when popular opinion swings the other way.

There are other emotions besides anger, of course: anguish when I read of young black boys shot by the police; heartsick for gays and lesbians still targeted for violence by hateful neighbors for loving whom they love; torn apart at stories of women raped, beaten, and murdered, often by the very men who say they love them; horrified when people are blown up simply for running in a race or children are massacred simply for being at school.

On the other hand, I'm also aware that despite all, it's probably never been better to be a person of color, a woman, or LGBT in the United States. Yes, old habits die hard, and assumptions may die harder. But it's a pretty easy case to make that whether by race, gender, or sexuality, America has never been more equal. (Class is another story—and one I will tell in this book.) So I'm also thrilled that I've lived long enough to see a black man in the White House, women heading national governments and major corporations, lesbians and gay men proclaiming their love for the world to see.

Let me be clear: I am in no way saying we have "arrived" at some postracial, postfeminist, post–civil rights utopia; and even less am I saying that some switch has been thrown and now men or white people or straight people are the new victims of some topsy-turvy "agenda." I'm simply saying that women are safer today than they have ever been in our society, that LGBT are more accepted and freer to love whom they love, and that racial and ethnic minorities confront fewer obstacles in their efforts to fully integrate into American society.

To be sure, I'm temperamentally an optimist. As both an academic and an activist, I often think of optimism as part of my job description. As an activist, I believe that through constant struggle, our society can, and will, be shaped into a society that better lives up to its promise of liberty and justice for all. And as an academic, I believe that if I can inspire my students to engage more critically with their world, and help them develop the tools with which they can do that, their lives, however they choose to live them, and with whatever political and ethical orientations they may have, will be better as a result.

Surely, the arc of history points toward greater equality. Slowly, yes, and fitfully. But definitely.

And that comment leads me to a discussion not of the book's title, but of the book's subtitle. If this is a book that is about American masculinity "at the end of an era," what era, exactly, is it that is ending? And why is it ending? And is ending a good thing or a bad thing?

In a sense, these latter questions are too late. I am not chronicling a change that is coming. I'm describing a change that has, in most respects, already happened. It's a done deal. The era of unquestioned and unchallenged male entitlement is over. This is a book about those men who either don't yet know it or sense the change in the wind and are determined to stem the tide.

The end of that era leaves those of us who have benefited from the dramatic social inequality that has characterized American society for so many years—we straight white men—with a choice to make. We know what the future will look like twenty years from now: same-sex marriage will be a national policy (and neither heterosexual marriage nor the traditional nuclear family will have evaporated), at least one-quarter of all corporate board members will be women, universities and even the military will have figured out how to adjudicate sexual assault, formerly illegal immigrants will have a path to citizenship, and all racial and ethnic minorities (except perhaps Muslims, who will still, sadly, be subject to vitriolic hatred) will be more fully integrated.

So our choice is simple: we can either be dragged kicking and screaming into that future of greater equality and therefore greater freedom for all, or go with the tide, finding out, along the way, that the future is actually brighter for us as well. (Data here are plentiful that the greater the level of gender equality in a society—whether in a relationship or marriage—the lower the rates of depression and the higher the rates of happiness.)

This is a book about those men who refuse to even be dragged kicking and screaming into that inevitable future. They are white men who aren't at all happy about the way the tides have turned. They see a small set of swells as one gigantic tsunami about to wash over them.

It's about how feeling entitled by race or gender distorts one's vision.

Racial and gender entitlement knows no class system: working-class white men may experience that sense of entitlement differently from upper-class white men, but there are also many commonalities, many points of contact. White men of all classes benefit from a system based on racial and gender inequality. Whether we are working-class plumbers or corporate financiers, we're raised to expect the world to be fair—that hard honest work and discipline will bring about prosperity and stability. It's hard for us to realize that we've actually been benefiting from dramatic inequality.

Think of it as if you were running in a race. You'd expect that everyone plays by the same rules—start at the starting line, and run as best you can, and that the fastest runners win the race. You'd bristle if some groups had a different starting point, were allowed to enter where they pleased, or were allowed to tie others' feet together—or if some people ran in one direction with the wind at their backs, while the rest of us had to run into a strong headwind.

It may be hard for white men to realize that, irrespective of other factors, we have been running with the wind at our backs all these years and that what we think of as "fairness" to us has been built on the backs of others, who don't harbor such illusions as "meritocracy" and "fairness," who have known since birth that the system is stacked against them. The level playing field has been anything but level—and we've been the ones running downhill, with the wind, in both directions.

Efforts to level the playing field may feel like water is rushing up-hill, like it's reverse discrimination against us. Meritocracy sucks when you are suddenly one of the losers and not one of the winners. In fact, it doesn't feel like a meritocracy at all.

We didn't just inherit privilege as an unexamined birthright. It's less about the "having" and more about a posture, a relationship to it. Even if we didn't think of ourselves as privileged, we thought of ourselves as *entitled* to privilege, entitled to occupy the leadership positions.

Just because those in power are straight and white and male doesn't mean that every straight white man feels powerful. That's a logical fallacy as well as politically inaccurate. (The compositional fallacy holds that if all As are Bs, it is not necessarily the case that all Bs are As. The classic example: all members of the Mafia are Italian; all Italians are not members of the Mafia.) But just because straight white men don't feel powerful doesn't make it any less true that compared to other *groups*, they benefit from inequality and are, indeed, privileged.

That is the era that is coming to an end, the "end of an era" to which the subtitle of this book refers. It's not the end of the era of "men"—as in the misframed debate recently over "the end of men." It's the end of the era of men's entitlement, the era in which a young man could assume, without question, it was not only "a man's world" but a straight white man's world. It is less of a man's world, today, that's true—white men have to share some space with others. But it is no longer a world of unquestioned male privilege. Men may still be "in power," and many men may not feel powerful, but it is the sense of entitlement—that sense that although I may not be in power at the moment, I deserve to be, and if I'm not, something is definitely wrong—that is coming to an end. It is a world of diminished expectations for all white men, who have benefited from an unequal system for so long.

There are still many in this generation of men who feel cheated by the end of entitlement. They still feel entitled, and thus they identify socially and politically with those above them, even as they have economically joined the ranks of those who have historically been below them.

This is a book about those angry white men, men who experience a sense of what I here call "aggrieved entitlement"—that sense of entitlement that can no longer be assumed and that is unlikely to be fulfilled. It's about rear guard actions, of bitterness and rage, about fingers shoved in the crumbling dikes, trying, futilely, to hold back the surging tide of greater equality and greater justice.

But if this is the end of one era, the era of men's sense of unquestioned entitlement, it is the beginning of another, the beginning of the end of patriarchy, the unquestioned assumption men have felt to access, to positions of power, to corner offices, to women's bodies, that casual assumption that all positions of power, wealth, and influence are reserved for us and that women's presence is to be resisted if possible, and tolerated if not.

There is a way out for white men, I believe, a way for us to turn down the volume, redirect our anger at more appropriate targets, and find our way to happier and healthier lives. The data are persuasive that most American men have quietly, and without much ideological fanfare, accommodated themselves to greater gender equality in both their personal and their workplace relationships than any generation before them. And those who have done so are actually happier about it—happier about their lives as fathers, partners, and friends. It turns out that gender and racial equality is not only good for people of color and women, but also good for white people and men—and, most of all, for our children.

Perhaps that's what the Greenwich Village writer Floyd Dell was thinking as he sat at his desk on the eve of one of the great woman suffrage demonstrations in New York City in 1916. A well-known bohemian writer, Dell was also one of the founders of the Men's League for Woman Suffrage, who marched with women in support of their right to vote. In an article published in the *Masses*, called "Feminism for Men," he came up with a line that I think captures my argument. "Feminism will, for the first time, allow men to be free."

Perhaps today we might qualify it a bit and say "freer"—but we'd also add happier, healthier, and a lot less angry.

Brooklyn, New York
May 2013

ACKNOWLEDGMENTS

This book, like all my work, is part of a conversation, among colleagues, friends, allies, and adversaries who have pushed me to clarify, change, refine, and abandon my arguments. I'm happy to acknowledge them here, sure that they'll know where they fall on the adversary-to-ally continuum: Harry Brod, Richard Collier, Martin Duberman, Warren Farrell, Debra Gimlin, Donald Huber, Jackson Katz, Mike Messner, Rob Okun, and Sophie Spieler. And I'm grateful to Lillian Rubin and Michael Kaufman for arguing with me about everything, reading every word, keeping me honest, and pushing me beyond where I often felt like going. None of them will agree with everything I've written, but I hope each feels I made my case honestly and honorably.

My agent, Gail Ross, and my editor at Nation Books, Ruth Baldwin, have been amazing to work with, offering just the right amount of support and criticism, knowing when to push and when to back off.

I'm also grateful to Bethany Coston, Randi Fishman, Charles Knight, and Grace Mattingly for their support of the research.

I'm grateful always to my family and friends, who never seem to tire of conversations about neo-Nazis, rampage school shootings, Rush Limbaugh, or antifeminist men's rights guys. (If they do tire, then I thank them for faking it so well.) Mitchell and Pam, Shanny and Cliff, Marty and Eli, Mary and Larry, thank you for so many years.

What enables me to delve into topics that make me so angry, sad, and frustrated is how stable and grounded I feel in my private life. I often feel like I'm in the center of one of those busy street scenes in a digitized movie, where I move slowly and deliberately while the rest of the world rushes by frantically in a sped-up time-lapse framing. Amy and Zachary anchor me, give me a place to stand, and thus a place from which to move. I could not be more grateful, nor love them any more. This is for them.

ANGRY
WHITE
MEN

Introduction

America, the Angry

What happened to the country that loved the underdog and stood up for the little guy? What happened to the voice of the forgotten man? The forgotten man is you.

—GLENN BECK, INTRODUCTION TO
GLENN BECK SPECIAL, MARCH 13, 2009

PROLOGUE

"What's a nice Jewish boy from Brooklyn doing in a place like this?" I ask myself as I slide into my booth at the roadside diner. I'm right off Interstate 81, near Chambersburg, Pennsylvania, along the southern tier of that state's border with Maryland, near the actual Mason-Dixon line. I'm here to meet "Rick," a thirty-two-year-old father of three from Shippensburg. I had met him yesterday, and I invited him to meet me for breakfast at the diner so I could interview him.

I had driven to Shippensburg to attend a gun show that was held, as many are these days, in the gymnasium of the local high school. (The schools rent out their facilities to local merchants to raise extra funds.) At the entrance to the show, a long table was filled with literature— some advertising circulars for gun merchants and army/navy supply stores, a couple of catalogs of survivalist gear, and some pamphlets from Patriot groups, some anti-immigrant organizations, and even a single photocopied informational sheet from David Duke and "today's Ku Klux Klan" (KKK). "How the government is taking away your rights!" announces one pamphlet.

Rick was standing behind the table, talking with a few other guys. "Is this your stuff?" I asked, picking up the leaflet. The guys turned and looked at me. No one looked especially hostile, though they certainly didn't look friendly, either. More like "Do I know you?" Like "You're not from around here, are you?"

"I'm a writer, and I'm on a research trip, and wanted to talk to you."

They eye me suspiciously. I am not very tall, obviously "ethnic," older, balding, and wearing a button-down shirt. "What are you writing about?" "Who the fuck are you?" "You Jewish?" "How'd you hear about this?"

"Wait," I said. "I'll answer your questions. Yes, I'm Jewish. I'm a sociology professor from New York. I am writing a book about what is happening to white guys like you in our country. I'm really concerned about it."

"*You're* concerned about it!" snorts one guy. "We're livin' it. We're concerned about it."

"I hear you, really. I'm trying to figure it out. With all the economic changes in our country, and the social changes, I want to understand what's happening to guys like you. Guys like Joe the Plumber," I say citing a name that's now familiar to every American since the 2008 election. (Chambersburg is along that long industrial corridor from Chicago to Harrisburg that flows through Gary, Toledo, Akron, Cleveland, Pittsburgh—and Holland, Ohio, where Joe Wurzelbacher is actually from.)

"Ha!" one guys laughs. "You just try getting a job as a plumber around here these days! There are no fuckin' jobs at all, 'cept for Walmart hostess."

"That's what I'm trying to understand," I say. "I want to know how America's changed and what direction we're going in."

"Oh, I'll tell you," says the guy I eventually come to know as Rick. "We're going down the fucking toilet, that's what. I mean, just look around. There's illegals everywhere. There's Wall Street screwing everybody. And now there's a goddamn . . . " He pauses anxiously, a grimace on his face. Another second goes by; he's obviously sizing me up. "Oh, fuck it, I don't care if it is politically incorrect. We got a fucking nigger in the White House. We're all screwed. Nobody gives a shit about us guys anymore. It's all over."

"That's what I want to write about!" I say. "I'll listen to you. Seriously. I won't agree with you, but hey, that's not my job. I'm not here to convince you of some blue-state liberal agenda. My job is to understand how you see all this. I promise that I will listen to you. Would you be willing to talk to me?" I say, directly, to Rick.

His pals now look at him. "Yeah, Rick, you go talk to this guy." "Yeah, I sure as shit don't want to talk to no Jew." "Yeah, Rick, go ahead, make his day."

Rick, now seemingly put up to it by his pals, agrees to meet me the next morning for breakfast.

He arrives on time. (I've arrived a half hour early and parked my car a few blocks away.) He slides into the booth across from me. He wears a weathered Pittsburgh Pirates hat, a flannel shirt, open to expose a Confederate flag T-shirt—"I wore this special for you," he says, laughing at his own joke—jeans, and work boots. He has not shaved. Actually, neither have I.

He orders his breakfast; his coffee arrives. Milk, two, no, three, sugars. I take out my tiny portable tape recorder.

"Oh, shit," he says. "Are you a fed? I can't talk to you."

"No, no, not at all," I say. I take out my wallet, show him my university ID card. I put away the tape recorder. We begin to talk.

MEET AMERICA'S ANGRY WHITE MEN

Rick is one of the men you will meet in this book, men who feel they have been screwed, betrayed by the country they love, discarded like trash on the side of the information superhighway. Theirs are the hands that built this country; theirs is the blood shed to defend it. And now, they feel, no one listens to them; they've been all but forgotten. In the great new multicultural American mosaic, they're the bland white background that no one pays any attention to, the store-bought white bread in a culture of bagels, tortillas, wontons, and organic whole-grain designer scones. They're downwardly mobile, contemptuously pushed aside by fast-talking, fast-driving fat cats and bureaucrats. And they're mad as hell.

You see them pretty much everywhere these days—yet they're often invisible. They patrol America's southern border, determined to keep out Mexican immigrants. They tune in to venomous talk-radio hosts who translate economic anguish, psychological distress, and political confusion into blind rage. They swarm into populist Tea Party rallies, hoping to find like-minded kinsmen willing to join with them to turn the country around. Some even take up arms against their own country, establishing semiautonomous enclaves and blowing up federal buildings. And, of course, when threatened by external forces, they muster up their coldest steel-eyed Dirty Harry imitation and say, "Make my day."

In suburbia, they're the ones who cut you off on the freeway, screaming with rage if you dare to slow them down. If their kid doesn't make that suburban soccer team or that heartland hockey team, they're the ones who rush out onto the field to hit the coach or strangle the referee—or start a fight with another equally enraged dad. They hiss with rage at their ex-wives (and their ex-wives' lawyers) in family court. Further up the economic ladder, they're the guys seething in the corner of the corporate "diversity training" workshop, snarling that they are now "walking on eggshells" around the office, or stewing when their company hires a woman or a minority, because, they say, affirmative action is really reverse discrimination against white men. And some of their teenage sons are strolling through deserted suburban train stations at night with a bunch of friends, looking for immigrants or gay men to beat up—or kill.

They are America's angry white men. Actually, one might say more simply that they're just America's white men—they just happen to be angrier than ever before in our recent history. Journalists duly record the decrease in compassion and the increase in untrammeled selfishness, and pundits decry the collapse of civility in political discourse, even as they shout at each other at the top of the best seller lists. One guy's a big, fat idiot! The other is a big, fat liar! The current political atmosphere in Washington has been called the nastiest and angriest in our history.

The past two decades have witnessed mainstream white American men exploding like never before in our history. They draw their ranks from the middle class (office workers, salaried salesmen) and the lower middle class (the skilled worker, small farmer, or shop-keeper). They're the "pa" in the ma-and-pa store, Richard Nixon's "silent majority," and "Reagan Democrats." They're "Joe Lunch-bucket," and "Joe the Plumber," and just plain Joe. They feel they've borne the weight of the world on their backs, and they can't hold it up any longer. And now, suddenly, some of these regular guys are re-inventing the American Revolution with Tea Party, Minutemen, and Patriot organizations, while others are further out there, organizing militias and joining survivalist cults, waging war on "feminazis," rampaging through their workplaces, promoting protectionist and anti-immigrant policies.

They're listening to angry white men like Rush Limbaugh, Mike Savage, and a host of other radio hosts who lash out at everyone else as the source of their woes. They're trying to roll back the gains made by women and minorities in corporate and professional life and resisting their entry into the ranks of soldier, firefighter, and police officer. And their sons are either busy destroying the galaxy in their video games or actually opening fire on their classmates.

Some explode at work, "going postal" as they slaughter coworkers, supervisors, and plant managers before, usually, taking their own lives. You've heard of "suicide by cop," where a perpetrator pretends to go for his gun and the police open fire? These guys commit "suicide by mass murder": intent on dying, they decide to "take some of them with me."

And when they're not exploding, they're just plain angry and de-fensive. They're laughing at clueless, henpecked husbands on sitcoms; snorting derisively at clueless guys mocked in ads and reality-TV seg-ments; and snickering at duded-up metrosexuals prancing around ma-jor metropolitan centers while they drink cosmos or imported vodka. They sneer at presidential candidates like John Kerry who speak French, eat brie, and drink Chardonnay. They see nothing but feminized wusses who actually support global environmental policies and negotiation and diplomacy instead of "my way or the highway" unilateralism.

Unapologetically "politically incorrect" magazines, radio hosts, and television shows abound, filled with macho bluster or bikini-clad women bouncing on trampolines. These venues are the new "boys' clubs"—the clubhouse that once said "No Gurls Allowed." These moments allow these guys, who otherwise feel so put down, so "had," a momentary feeling of superiority.

Yet few observers notice the *gender* of these vitriolic legions. Few, if any, couple the increase in American anger with the growing gulf between women and men. The gender gap—politically, socially, and economically—is as large as it has ever been. It's not "Americans" who are angry; it's American *men*. And it's not all American men—it's *white* American men. This is a phenomenon so visible, so widespread, that were it happening with any other group (say, black men or Asian women), it would be discussed incessantly. But precisely because it's so ubiquitous, so visible, it has received hardly any serious discussion.

Now, it is true, one must say at the outset, that some of the most visible angry Americans these days are women, especially those parading at Tea Party rallies. And the patron saint of American anger at the moment is not former vice president Dick Cheney, sneering arrogantly at all potential opponents, but his daughter Liz, and the seemingly omnipresent Sarah Palin. Palin has become a poster girl for right-wing rage—and I mean that more than metaphorically. She is the Betty Grable of the political Right and the fantasy ideal of thousands, perhaps millions, of red-blooded American men. She's salty and sexy, vampy and folksy, strong yet slightly slutty.

And the Tea Party, at 59 percent male, is somewhat anomalous on the political landscape. While the men who overwhelmingly populate the ranks of rage rely on some amount of women's backstage support, the theme of their agitation, the motivation for their mobilization, is a desire to restore or retrieve a sense of manhood to which they feel entitled.

And they're unmistakably white. Former MSNBC political show host Keith Olbermann called the Tea Party the "White People's Party," while Jon Stewart hailed it as "a festival of whites." It's ironic, since the election of Barack Obama, the first African American president of the United States, was meant to suggest that America was becoming a "postracial" society. Instead of the predicted "Bradley effect"—in which white voters told pollsters that they were going to vote for Mayor Tom Bradley of Los Angeles, but then, in the privacy of the voting booth, decided they just could not pull the lever for a black man—there was the "Obama effect," in which *more* people ended up voting for Obama than told pollsters that they would and afterward congratulated themselves on having transcended racism. (I call this "premature self-congratulation.")

But Obama's election and reelection have actually elicited the most viciously racist public discourse—only thinly veiled behind well-worn code words—in which Tea Partiers and other activists shout racial epithets at elected members of Congress, and half of those partiers believe that Obama has usurped the presidency, having been born outside the United States. Maybe we should call this version of the backlash the "reverse Bradley effect"—having now declared ourselves postracial, suddenly white people have given themselves *more* permission to express deep-seated racism. It's as if having a specific target for their rage enables their racism, because they have already congratulated themselves for not believing those racial slurs about "all of them."

And you'd see the same thing at all the other rallies across the country, rallies where newly formed groups of mostly white men evoke the spirit of the American Revolution—Minutemen, Patriots, Tea Party—to express their contemporary rage at immigrants, health care, and taxation. Populist movements have swept across America before—most notably at the turn of the last century, with similar contradictory politics, a combination of agrarian socialism and racist nativism. Then, as now, populism combined anti–Wall Street sentiment and anti-immigrant sentiment; together, they fueled an agrarian anger at their "enabling" government bureaucrats.

Populisms are always contradictory, because populism is more an emotion than it is an ideology. And that emotion is anger.

UNDERSTANDING AMERICAN ANGER

Why should so many white American men be so angry, anyway? After all, just being Americans, they are among the most privileged people on earth. Certainly, they are the most privileged group that isn't part of a hereditary aristocracy. For one thing, the United States is the world's wealthiest country, and we consume more than any other country. We're only 5 percent of the world's population, but we gobble up 40 percent of its resources. One American consumes as much energy as forty-one Bangladeshis. And although we are experiencing a significant tax revolt, the share of our gross domestic product that is accounted for by taxes is third lowest among all Organization for Economic Cooperation and Development (better known as OECD) countries, higher only than Turkey, Chile, and Mexico.

And in the United States, white men get the lion's share of that wealth. Between 1983 and 2009, the top 5 percent of Americans took home nearly 82 percent of all the wealth gain; the bottom three-fifths actually lost 7.5 percent of their income, according to the Economic Policy Institute. (Doesn't it seem sort of irrational for that bottom 60 percent to be angry at others in the same boat?)

But being white gives one a boost. In the United States, we get an additional bonus of 22 percent just for being white (compared with black men); compared with Hispanic men, white men's bonus is 37 percent. And we get a bonus of 28 percent just for being male, compared with white women; compared with black women, it's a bonus of 35 percent, for Hispanic women 47 percent. That's right—at least an additional 25 percent just for a Y chromosome and a shortage of melanin. (Ironically, this "masculinity bonus" is virtually invisible because when we calculate the wage gap, we calculate the wages of women or minorities as a percentage of white men's wages. So what we "see" is the discrimination; for example, white women make 72.2 percent of men's wages.)

Yes, it's true that the economic recession—caused by the *absence* of government regulation of banks making unwise predatory loans and the failure to fund the Iraq and Afghanistan wars, let alone No Child Left Behind (which ran up US debt)—has hit America hard. (It's equally true that the Angry Class has sided *with* those financial institutions in opposing the sorts of meaningful regulations that would actually help us.) And yes, it's true that many Americans have been fed a consistent set of distortions and outright falsehoods, designed to facilitate that bait and switch, exonerated those who got us into this mess, and excoriated those who have been trying to fix it.

Yet the truth is that white men are the beneficiaries of the single greatest affirmative action program in world history. It's called "world history." White men so stacked the deck that everyone else was pretty much excluded from playing at all. When those others did begin to play, the field was so uneven that white men got a massive head start, and everyone else had to play with enormous handicaps. Maybe actually having to play evenly matched, on a level playing field, is too frightening for a gender that stakes its entire identity on making sure it wins every time.

Don't believe me. Have you seen the brilliant comedian Louis C. K. talk about this? After describing how white people have a unique privilege of being able to travel to any time in history where they'll always have a table for you, he says, "And I'm a white MAN," noting it doesn't get much better that this. "How many privileges can one person have? . . . You can't even hurt my feelings!" he giggles.[1]

Angry is what white men seem to be. With whom are they angry? Why? And why now?

In this book, I try to answer those questions. I've traveled all over the country, all to take the pulse of angry American white men. I've sought to dissect their anger, their anxieties, the feeling they've been cheated out of their birthright. Regardless of their class position, American white men are a nation of Esaus, and we have the sense we've somehow been had. It's a story of the rage of the American "Everyman." And I try to take seriously the race and the gender of American anger, by examining several points along a continuum of class—that is, I look at the ways that middle-class suburban anger is beginning to converge with working-class resentment and the agonizing cry of a declining lower middle class. All of these groups of men, in different ways, are experiencing a rage at what they perceive as dispossession.

White men's anger is "real"—that is, it is experienced deeply and sincerely. But it is not "true"—that is, it doesn't provide an accurate analysis of their situation. The "enemies" of white American men are not really women and men of color. Our enemy is an ideology of masculinity that we inherited from our fathers, and their fathers before them, an ideology that promises unparalleled acquisition coupled with a tragically impoverished emotional intelligence. We have accepted an ideology of masculinity that leaves us feeling empty and alone when we do it right, and even worse when we feel we're doing it wrong. Worst of all, though, is when we feel we've done it right and still do not get the rewards to which we believe we are entitled. Then we have to blame somebody. Somebody else.

And that's typically what we do. Listen to Harvard political scientist Harvey Mansfield, in an op-ed essay in the *Wall Street Journal*. "The protective element of manliness is endangered by women who have equal access to jobs outside the home," he writes. "Women who do not consider themselves feminist often seem unaware of what they are doing to manliness when they work to support themselves. They think only that people should be hired and promoted on merit, regardless of sex." And anthropologist Lionel Tiger, known for his celebration of male bonding, argues that "the principal victims of moving toward a merit-based society have been male."

But even that doesn't completely explain things. All these processes were taking place before the current recession. Why? America stands alone as the most powerful country on earth. Prior to the Bush administration's economic free fall, we had an economic surplus, unemployment was at its lowest rate in decades, the stock and housing markets were booming. And even then, American white men were angrier than they'd ever been, a new, emerging, identifiable voting bloc.

Yes, it's true that they've taken some hits in recent decades, and not simply from the most recent recession. Real income has fallen since the 1990s for white middle-class men, and it's been pretty flat since the early 1970s. The median household income for a family of four (in today's dollars) in 1971 was $56,329. Exactly forty years later, in 2011, it was $50,054. That's right—in real income, the median income has *declined* by about $6,000. And the big difference between those median households in the ensuing forty years is that now the wives are working. It literally takes two incomes to earn what one income earned for a family forty years ago—and even then, not quite.[2]

One of the men who journalist Susan Faludi spoke with while researching her 1999 book on male malaise, *Stiffed*, told her, "I'm like the guy who is hanging from the cliff. I'm starting to lose my grip." Yet he was a middle manager at a large firm, made a very good living, and drove an expensive late-model car. The inequality gap has become an inequality gulf; the chasm of the 1960s is now a likely unbridgeable canyon. Can you blame men for being angry?

A lot of men seem to believe that their only alternative is to draw the wagons into a circle, hoping that a reassertion of traditional ideologies of masculinity—and a return to the exclusion of "others" from the competitive marketplace—will somehow resolve this present malaise. By contrast, I believe that the solutions to white men's anger lie beyond a psychological balm on their wounded egos. It requires that we both look into the hearts of regular guys, as well as those who feel marginalized, and that we examine the social and historical circumstances that brought them to this precipice. Only by fusing a psychological and a sociological analysis can we ever hope to break the cycle of anger that impoverishes men's lives—and endangers them, and everyone else.

ANGRY WHITE KIMMEL?
UNDERSTANDING MY POSITION IN THIS BOOK

I've spent the past several years talking to these guys. As I have criss-crossed the country, first interviewing younger men on college campuses for my book *Guyland*, and later while crisscrossing it again being interviewed about the book, I've also been interviewing these angry white men. I've met white supremacists, neo-Nazis, and Klansmen. I've talked to devoted followers of angry white male radio, been lectured to by Tea Party activists about a version of American history that bears no relationship to what is taught in school or written in standard textbooks, listened to men's rights activists rage against feminism, and shared the anguish of divorced dads agonizing over losing contact with their children. I've read diaries by and online reporting on the rampage shooters who ultimately took their own lives.

I've also logged more hours than is probably healthy reading their blogs, lurking in their chat rooms and following the comments threads on their blog posts, and listening to the collection of radio ragers, especially as they massage anguish and confusion into rage at the "other" and the government that enables minorities to take over "their" country. I've even appeared on some of their talk shows.

In this book, I try to look into the hearts and minds of the American men with whom I most disagree politically. I try to understand where their anger comes from and where they think it's going. I do so not with contempt or pity, but with empathy and compassion. Many of the men I interviewed for this book are not bad men; they're true believers in the American Dream, the same dream that I inherited, and in which I believe. It's the same American Dream that Bruce Springsteen sings about in "The Promised Land," where "I've done my best to live the right way / I get up every morning and go to work each day."

In my interviews with many of them—even Rick and some of his fellow white supremacists—I identified more with their knee-jerk belief in the American Dream than I do often with the detached cynicism of some of my hipster neighbors. I grew up proud to live in a country that had defeated Hitler and in that part of the country that had fought successfully against slavery. I was proud to believe, as I was taught in primary school, that "America had never lost a war, and never been the aggressor."

I do not consider myself a breed apart from these men, as if I were a scientist examining the specimens of some esoteric species. Many of us who line up on the other side of the political spectrum understand that anger at our government for failing to live up to its promise and, in fact, for actively enabling those who crush our dreams. I believe that the anger of the American White Man is misguided and misplaced, yes, but it is not blind rage, without reason. Good or bad, many of the men I will discuss in this book are True Believers, and as such they are vulnerable to manipulation. If, as Susan Faludi argues, they've been "stiffed," then they've also been had, duped. It is the corporate elites who fund the faux populism of hate radio, border patrols, Tea Partiers, and other groups who are, to my mind, the ones who have contempt for the simple working man.

And thus far, those elites have guessed right. Fed a steady diet of disinformation and misinformation, America's white men have lashed out at all the wrong targets. They've blamed women, minorities, gays and lesbians, immigrants. Some blame the Jews. Some have blamed them generally and joined political movements to close our borders, to set back women's progress, to oppose sexual equality. And others have lashed out more locally and individually, attacking or killing those who somehow come to personify their grievances.

But unlike those cynical elites, who try to steer them toward their own extinction, and would happily dance on their graves, I believe these men can turn it around. Make no mistake: the future of America is more inclusive, more diverse, and more egalitarian. The choice for these men is not whether they can stem the tide; they cannot. All the Limbaughs and Arpaios in the world cannot put the gender-equality genie back in the bottle. Their choice is whether they will be dragged kicking and screaming into that inevitable future or walk openly and honorably into it, far happier and healthier incidentally, alongside those they've spent so long trying to exclude.

UNDERSTANDING WHITE MEN'S ANGER

But first we have to understand that anger, get inside it. For one thing, it's an anger that knows no class nor originates in a specific class. Whether we're talking about the white working class—shorn of union protection, stripped of manufacturing jobs that once provided a modicum of dignity with a paycheck, not to mention the hale-and-hearty camaraderie of the shop floor, they've watched as "their" jobs disappeared with the closing of the factory gates. Or the lower middle class, that wide swath of small farmers, independent shopkeepers, independent craft workers—plumbers, electricians, contractors—and small businessmen whose livelihoods have been steadily eroded, as the farm crisis of the 1990s consolidated independent farmers into wage workers for agribusiness, as Walmart put local grocery and other retail stores out of business. Even upper-middle-class men, even those with jobs and pensions and health plans, feel ripped off—by affirmative action programs, immigration, welfare, taxation, and the general sense that they're being had.

What unites all these groups is not just the fact that they are men. What unites them is their belief in a certain ideal of masculinity. It is not just their livelihoods that are threatened, but their sense of themselves *as men*. Faludi observed in *Stiffed* that American men have lost "a useful role in public life, a way of earning a decent and reliable living, appreciation in the home, respectful treatment in the culture."[3] They're feeling emasculated—humiliated. The promise of economic freedom, of boundless opportunity, of unlimited upward mobility, was what they believed was the terra firma of American masculinity, the ground on which American men have stood for generations. Today, it feels like a carpet being snatched from under their feet.

And it's not really their fault. Faludi subtitles her book "The Betrayal of the American Man." Unlike many of her subjects, who cast their eyes down for enemies but their allegiances upward at fictive allies, Faludi is clear that the betrayal has not been the result of an indifferent government doing the bidding of hordes of undeserving "others"—whether women, gays, immigrants, or whomever; rather, it has been perpetrated by the rich, the powerful, the corporate magnates, the corporate lobbyists and their plutocratic sycophants in legislatures and state houses. Like Thomas Frank's *What's the Matter with Kansas?*, Faludi observes a paradox of these white men voting for, and identifying with, the very people who are doing them in.

Middle-class white American men were the nation's first, and remain its most fervent, believers in the American Dream: that anyone can rise as high as their aspirations, talents, discipline, and dedicated hard work can take them. In my earlier book *Manhood in America*, I charted this ideology of the "self-made man," the single defining feature of American masculinity, over the course of American history. No single group of Americans has clung so tenaciously to those beliefs. No single group has so ardently subscribed to the traditional definition of "what it takes" to make it in America. And no other group has felt so cheated.

Angry White Men tells the story of the other side of the American Dream: the futility, the dashed hopes, the despair, and the rage. It tells the story of the rich and famous wannabes, the ones who thought they could invent themselves, reinvent themselves, be even more successful than their fathers. It tells the story of how white American men came to believe that power and authority were what they were entitled to, by birth, and how that birthright is now eroding. Economic and social changes that are bewilderingly fast and dramatic are experienced as the general "wimpification" of American men—castrated by taxation, crowded out by newcomers who have rules bent for them, white men in America often feel like they are presiding over the destruction of their species.

In a sense, of course, they're right. Or, at least, half right. Although they may choose the wrong targets for their anger—gay men, immigrants, blacks, and women are hardly the cause of their anguish—white men have felt themselves to be falling in recent decades. That 1971 family income that was roughly the same as today's? Then, it would have bought you a nice house in a good neighborhood with a decent school system, with about half left over for food and clothing and savings. Today, that income buys . . . well, let's just say it buys a lot less. Most young men will never be able to afford to buy the very house they grew up in—and they know it.

Even more immediately, in the recent economic crisis, just about 80 percent of all the jobs lost since November 2008—a number in excess of 5 million—were jobs held by men. Economists have been calling it a "he-cession," since it is so gender skewed. (The Great Depression was equally gendered, incidentally, but with single-breadwinner families, the crisis was experienced quite differently.) There is no doubt that white men have taken a big hit. And they're more vulnerable: unions, which once offered a modicum of protection, have all but disappeared. Union membership has declined from about 40 percent after World War II to about 13 percent today, and if you remove federal employees, it's closer to 8–9 percent—which makes the tenacious clinging to traditional ideals of manhood that much more difficult.

An anguished letter to the editor of a small upstate New York newspaper written in 1993 by an American GI, after his return from service in the Gulf War, captured some of this sentiment. The letter writer complains that the legacy of the American middle class has been stolen, handed over by an indifferent government to a bunch of ungrateful immigrants and welfare cheats. "The American dream," he writes, "has all but disappeared, substituted with people struggling just to buy next week's groceries." That letter writer was Timothy McVeigh from Lockport, New York. (McVeigh's father was a union-protected worker in the steel plants in Lockport; Tim watched as the plants closed.) Two years later, McVeigh blew up the Murrah Federal Building in Oklahoma City in what is now the second-worst act of terrorism ever committed on American soil.

Their very adherence to traditional ideals of masculinity leaves so many white men feeling entitled to that dream—and so now they are feeling cheated, unhappy, and unfulfilled. American white men bought the promise of self-made masculinity, but its foundation has all but eroded. The game has changed, but instead of questioning the rules, they want to eliminate the other players. Instead of questioning those ideals, they fall back upon those same traditional notions of manhood—physical strength, self-control, power—that defined their fathers' and their grandfathers' eras, as if the solution to their problem were simply "more" masculinity. Yet few, if any, are kings of the hill, top guns, the richest and most powerful. They're passing on to their sons the same tired and impossible ideals of manliness and the same sense of entitlement. And they will spawn the same growing rage. The cycle continues—unless we recognize it and act both to defuse and to diffuse the anger.

Actually, most men don't want to be the king of the hill; they just don't want to be underneath the landslide they feel is about to descend on their heads. They crave the dignity of the successful breadwinner, the family provider, the man who measures success by the look of respect in the eyes of his family and friends. To be a "man among men" is to be a "real man." They don't need to be leading the parade; they just can't bear the idea that they've been tossed aside by history's inexorable march.

It's also true that many men spent the past two decades searching for some new definition of masculinity that would feel more emotionally resonant, more connected, more fulfilling. They felt lost, and so off they trooped to the woods with Robert Bly, or they filled football stadiums with the PromiseKeepers. They've claimed to rediscover timeless traditional verities and experimented with "new" involved fatherhood. There is definitely something happening with American men—they are searching for *something*, searching for some *place* where they can feel like real men again, a place unpolluted by the presence of those others, a pure homosocial clubhouse, locker room, or "talking circle." Where can a guy go these days to just be around other men, just to hang out, be a guy, and not have to worry about who won't like it, or having them wonder if he's gay or some political Neanderthal?

At the same time as white American men cling ever more tenaciously to old ideals, women and minorities have entered those formerly all-male bastions of untrammeled masculinity. Gender and racial equality feels like a loss to white men: if "they" gain, "we" lose. In the zero-sum game, these gains have all been at white men's expense. We employ what I call a "windchill" psychology: it doesn't really matter what the actual temperature is; what matters is what it feels like.

The combination of these two forces—clinging to these old ideals and the dramatic changes in the actual contours of our lives—has been explosive. Men are angry and restless because of what they experience as the erosion of their "rightful" privilege, and they have convenient targets for their rage.

They're angry at immigrants, who, they believe, are displacing them in the workforce. They're angry at fat-cat capitalists, who, as they see it, downsize and outsource them out of their jobs, demolish communities, and then jet off in their private planes, only to golden-parachute onto some tax-haven island. They're angry at feckless bureaucrats, who are deaf to their cries for help and in it only for themselves. They're angry at women, who, they argue, are beautiful, sexy, and sexually available—yet turn them down with contemptuous sneers. They say they're angry at wives (which is different from being angry at women), who keep men in harness as responsible breadwinners and providers, working in jobs they hate for bosses who are capricious morons, only to take them to the cleaners in the divorce, snatching the kids and leaving them penniless and childless. And finally, they say they're angry at a government that, at best, does nothing to help them and, at worst, exacerbates the problem through its policies.

Let me give an example of how this works. I first began to think about these issues several years ago, when I appeared on a television talk show opposite three such "angry white males" who felt they had been the victims of workplace discrimination. They complained that affirmative action was really "reverse discrimination" and that it had ushered in a "new" ideology of unfairness into economic life. (Remember, the reality that affirmative action was actually developed to remedy the unfairness that already existed is beside the point; it's how it feels.) The title of this particular show, no doubt to entice a potentially large audience, was "A Black Woman Stole My Job." In my comments, I asked the men to consider just one word in the title of the show: the word *my*. What made them think the job was theirs? Why wasn't the episode called "A Black Woman Got *the* Job" or "A Black Woman Got *a* Job"? Because these guys felt that those jobs were "theirs," that they were entitled to them, and that when some "other" person—black, female—got the job, that person was really taking "their" job.[4]

I've referred to this story many times since, because it stuck with me as an example of that sense of entitlement—a sense of entitlement that seems to be specific to middle- and upper-class white men. It exposes something important about these legions of angry white men: although they still have most of the power and control in the world, they feel like victims. Although it's true that everyone needs to be a victim to even stand a chance of being heard in today's political arena, the white-man-as-victim comes with a certain self-righteous anger that makes it distinct.

These ideas also reflect a somewhat nostalgic longing for that past world and explain why, whether they retreat to the woods as weekend warriors or to arm themselves for Armageddon, they speak of manhood—or of identity more generally—as something they have to "preserve," or "retrieve," or "restore." To them, something has truly been lost—and it is their job to restore men to their "rightful" place.

That world, now passing into history, is a world in which white men grew up believing they would inevitably take their places somewhere on the economic ladder simply by working hard and applying themselves.. It is the American Dream, the ideal of meritocracy. And when men fail, they are humiliated, with nowhere to place their anger.

And today, many white men feel that they know why their dream is being deferred. As Carly Fiorina, the former CEO of Hewlett-Packard and the first woman CEO of a major corporation in our history, put it, "There is no job that is America's God-given right anymore."[5]

It's that "God-given right" that seems to be evaporating. What links all these different groups—rampage shooters and the Patriots, the Minutemen and the vengeful dads, Rush Limbaugh and Joe the Plumber, and Tom Metzger and the neo-Nazi minions—is a single core experience: what I call *aggrieved entitlement*. It is that sense that those benefits to which you believed yourself entitled have been snatched away from you by unseen forces larger and more powerful. You feel yourself to be the heir to a great promise, the American Dream, which has turned into an impossible fantasy for the very people who were *supposed* to inherit it. And where did they get the idea that it actually *is* their "God-given right" to begin with?

"Is a dream a lie if it don't come true," asks Bruce Springsteen in "The River," perhaps his darkest song, "or is it something worse?"

FROM ANXIETY TO ANGER

In an earlier book, *Manhood in America*, I chronicled the history of American masculinity in the nineteenth and twentieth centuries as a history of anxiety. The most dominant masculine ideal, from around the 1820s, was the "self-made man." Henry Clay announced that "we are a nation of self-made men" on the floor of the US Senate in 1832. And that same year, the young French nobleman Alexis de Tocqueville, perhaps the greatest observer of the American character ever, worried that this self-making was leading to a chronic restlessness, which he saw as a defining psychological characteristic of the American self-made man: "An American will build a house in which to pass his old age and sell it before the roof is on; he will plant a garden and rent it just as the trees are coming into bearing; he will clear a field and leave others to reap the harvest; he will take up a profession and leave it, settle in one place and soon go off elsewhere with his changing desires." Tocqueville was awed by the sight: "There is something astonishing in this spectacle of so many lucky men restless in the midst of abundance."

So many lucky men restless in the midst of abundance—a phrase that defined the past two centuries of American life. A chronic restlessness, a constant hyperactive frenzy that has produced the most dazzling and miraculous of inventions, led to daring entrepreneurial risk taking, to a drive to expand, to conquer, to settle, that has produced the strongest economy and the most enviable political form in the world, and left a path of both the "creative destruction" that Schumpeter said defined capitalism and vicious rapacious devastation of lands and peoples in its wake.

To be a self-made man was the American Dream—that anyone could, with enough hard work and discipline, and just the right amount of what Horatio Alger called "luck and pluck," rise as high as his aspirations and talents and abilities and desires would take him. Rags to riches, from log cabin to the White House, the poor boy who "minds the main chance" and makes it big—these are distinctly American stories. No Julien Sorel or Barry Lyndon for us, not even Edward Ferrars, whose virtue is rewarded, but who has no ambition. And they are distinctly American *men's* stories—of shipping out on the *Pequod*, joining the army, leaving home and heading west in search of riches, of "lighting out for the territory," ahead of Aunt Sally's feminizing clutches.

These themes have long captivated American men's imaginations— leaving home and seeking one's fortunes in the ever-expanding West. It's as powerful a theme in those canonical works that celebrate it— countless westerns, adventure stories, heroic sagas—as those that suggest its darker side, the road not taken (Alaska, in *Death of a Salesman*), fraudulent grandiosity (*The Great Gatsby*), or the deep psychic and sexual wounds of a supposedly glorious war (Jake Barnes in *The Sun Also Rises*).

The American Dream of endless upward mobility was always shadowed by the American nightmare—just as you could rise as far as your aspirations and talents could take you, you could also fall off the cliff, and, unlike Europe, with its medieval villages and social safety nets, there would be no one there to catch you if you did. If America was the land of abundance, where anyone could go from rags to riches, then conversely you could blame only yourself if you didn't make it. And so it is a dominant theme among the American middle class that you may strive for "the thrill of victory," as the old *ABC's Wide World of Sports* had it, but what really motivated you was avoiding "the agony of defeat." American masculinity was thus chronically restless—energized, electric, entrepreneurial, and frightened, afraid of falling.

Such chronic, temperamental restlessness could be easily accommodated as long as America was expanding—westward, overseas, into space. The ever-receding frontier was a gendered safety valve, siphoning off those who hadn't yet succeeded and giving them a chance to start over. America is the land of the do-over, says Billy Crystal in *City Slickers*, a film about three middle-class white guys who try to reclaim their manhood on a late-twentieth-century dude ranch, playing cowboy on the frontier.

As a New Yorker, I used to discomfit my students at Berkeley when I was a professor there. "American history," I declared once in class, "is the story of the westward migration of losers." The students looked puzzled and sometimes distraught. But consider: if you were a self-made man and you were successful in New York, Philadelphia, or Boston, you stayed put. But if you failed, you could move to that first frontier, Pennsylvania, or Ohio, and if you succeeded there, you stayed. Failure would bring you to Chicago or St. Louis, and if you failed there, again, well, Houston and Denver beckoned. If you couldn't make it there, well, then, you came to California. After California—well, it was Alaska, the colonies, the colonies that we didn't call colonies, perhaps, in fantasy, space, the final frontier.

That frontier is closed; indeed, it has begun to loop back on itself. There are few places—perhaps cyberspace is the new frontier—where a man can start over and make it. And the competition has become increasingly fierce, both from others overseas as well as from those "others"—women, minorities, immigrants—who had been successfully excluded for decades.

As the competition has ramped up, and the frontier safety valve has closed down, American anxiety has morphed into anger, the specific type of anger that I address in this book. It's as though the emotional character, the American male temperament, has changed. Anxiety may be fraught, unstable, jittery, and fearful, but it was also generative, productive, entrepreneurial. America was a land of opportunity, and anxiety can also be optimistic. Self-making was at least *possible*—even if you spent most of your time warding off the specter of failure. It was possible. Anxiety may be based in the past, but it sets one's activities toward the future.

Not anymore. The new American anger is more than defensive; it is reactionary. It seeks to restore, to retrieve, to reclaim something that is perceived to have been lost. Angry White Men look to the past for their imagined and desired future. They believe that the system is stacked against them. Theirs is the anger of the entitled: we are entitled to those jobs, those positions of unchallenged dominance. And when we are told we are not going to get them, we get angry.

It is that sense of entitlement thwarted—what I will call *aggrieved entitlement*—that I believe characterizes America's new breed of Angry White Men.

THE POLITICAL PSYCHOLOGY OF AGGRIEVED ENTITLEMENT

Despite the romantic fictions of Victor Hugo, it's not typically *les miserables*—the poor, the desperate, the hungry or homeless—who rise up politically enraged to ignite a revolution. They're often too depleted and distracted by more immediate concerns about getting some food or shelter. What's more, the poorest of the poor often feel they deserve nothing more, resigned to their fate.

Rather, it's those just above the poor who compose the vast armies of revolution—the middle or even richer peasants in China or Cuba, the most skilled industrial workers in Russia.[6] Earlier it was the lower middle classes of artisans or small shopkeepers in the towns and the independent yeoman farmers in the countryside who made up the sansculottes in revolutionary France or the Levellers and other radical groups in mid-seventeenth-century England. Revolutions are made not by those with "nothing left to lose," in Kris Kristofferson's memorable phrase (and branded indelibly in memory through Janis Joplin's incomparable voice), but precisely by those *with* something to lose—and a fear that they are, in fact, about to lose it.

The great political scientist Barrington Moore understood this when he offered this rejoinder to Marx's theory that the most oppressed class is the revolutionary one: "The chief social basis of radicalism has been the peasants and the smaller artisans in the towns. From these facts one may conclude that the wellsprings of human freedom lie not where Marx saw them, in the aspirations of classes about to take power, but perhaps even more in the dying wail of a class over whom the wave of progress is about to roll."[7] The wellsprings of human freedom lie there, yes, but so perhaps do the origins of those groups who would take that freedom only for themselves and deny it to others. It is the declining class—the downwardly mobile lower middle class in particular—that has provided the shock troops of virtually every great social movement, whether they are on the Right (think of the Italian Fascists, the original Ku Klux Klan) or on the Left (think of the anarchist waiters in Barcelona in the 1930s, the American Populist farmers and workers in the 1890s). Political scientist Ted Robert Gurr called it "relative depravation"—that our sense of being deprived is measured not in an abstract calculus, but always in relation to those around us, those who are getting more but don't deserve it.

The downwardly mobile lower middle class has more than just its economic position at stake; the class is defined by its economic autonomy—they are the nation's small shopkeepers, independent craft workers, high-skilled union-protected manufacturing workers, independent small farmers. It is this group who has lost the most over the past half century, and particularly since the 1980s, when outsourcing of manufacturing jobs was paralleled by the most extensive farm crisis since the Dust Bowl years. Small farms were foreclosed, swallowed up by corporate agribusiness; ma-and-pa stores were forced to shutter when Walmart moved in; and small family businesses, passed on from generation to generation—and generation to generation of *men*, as in "Kimmel and Sons"—and unions were decimated, unable to protect workers from factory closings and offshore corporate moves.

The lower middle class has always defined itself by its fierce economic independence and by its sense of community belonging, of citizenship in a political community in which their voices would be heard. They are the heirs of the New England town meeting, that bulwark of American democracy so heralded by Thomas Jefferson.

Today, they feel their voices are silent, drowned in the din of other voices shouting to be heard by a federal government that seems increasingly hard of hearing. Maybe, they imagine, their voices are not even silent, but silenced—deliberately suppressed to give others a chance. We, who were raised to believe our voices would be heard, are actually being told to be quiet. Surely, that is not fair. Economically, their independence is vanishing as they are downsized, outsourced, and foreclosed into service-sector jobs where they spend their days having to follow the seemingly unintelligible demands of undeserving supervisors.

It's largely the downwardly mobile middle and lower middle classes who form the backbone of the Tea Party, of the listeners of outrage radio, of the neo-Nazis and white supremacists—in many cases literally the sons of those very farmers and workers who've lost the family farms or shuttered for good the businesses that had been family owned and operated for generations. It's this group—native born, white, middle class—that had bought most deeply into the American Dream of upward mobility, or at least of holding the line. And now they feel that they're treading water at best, and more likely drowning.

It is that spring—the belief in the system, having something yet to lose, and feeling that they're not getting what they deserve—that sources the rivers of rage that flow through America. Even before the anger is pain, the injury of losing something, something valuable, precious, something that your father may have entrusted to you, or, more likely, that you felt your father was supposed to entrust to you before he lost your birthright. "The hallmarks of loss are idealization and rage," writes Carol Gilligan, "and under the rage, immense sadness."[8]

Before the anger or sense of being aggrieved, psychologist Carol Tavris notes, they must both want what they don't have and feel that they deserve what they don't have. Their sense of grievance depends on their sense of entitlement. That sense of entitlement can come from many places. It can come from specific promises made and unkept, like campaign-trail promises that are not implemented after an election. It can come from more abstract promises—like the American Dream that if a man works hard, is an honest and upstanding citizen, he will be rewarded with a good job that will enable him to support a family and give his children a solid foundation for their future, and will have earned the respect and authority that come with it.

Ironically, that sense of being entitled is a marker not of depravation but of privilege. Those who have nothing don't feel they deserve anything; those who already have something believe they are entitled to it. When one feels that slipping, one may idealize, as Carol Gilligan says, that earlier time when privilege was unexamined and assumed and rage at those who seem to be taking what you thought was rightfully yours.

Aggrieved entitlement can mobilize one politically, but it is often a mobilization toward the past, not the future, to restore that which one feels has been lost. It invariably distorts one's vision and leads to a misdirected anger—often at those just below you on the ladder, because clearly they deserve what they are getting far less than you do.

Of course, blaming others for your plight is the essence of scapegoating.[9] Surely, it's not *my* fault that I don't have the things to which I am entitled! Scapegoating—whether of Jews, minorities, immigrants, women, whomever—directs the blame for your predicament away from the actual institutional sources of our problem and onto other groups who are less powerful. It grants them far more power—the power to take away from you that to which you are entitled—than they actually have; the "other" always looms large in the analysis of your own plight. "It's not surprising that they get bitter, they cling to guns or religion or antipathy to people who aren't like them or anti-immigrant sentiment or anti-trade sentiment as a way to explain their frustrations" is the way that then senator Obama understood this rise of rage.

Here's a good example of that political scapegoating. Remember Jim Sasser? This Republican senator from Tennessee, a reasonable "moderate" in the Senate—he'd voted for the Brady Bill, for example (even though his state had a longer waiting period than the Brady Bill mandated)—was targeted by Far Right proto–Tea Party extremists within his own party. Big corporations, the National Rifle Association (NRA), and other groups began a media war against Sasser. Here is how he now understands his defeat:

They wrap you in the liberal mantra. He's going to take away our guns and give women and blacks our jobs. In my campaign, it was the anger of the white male. The anger at Washington from unemployed trade union members who had lost their jobs on the assembly line and were now doing crummy service jobs. They blamed affirmative action; they blamed blacks. Most important, they blamed women. . . . During the Thomas hearings [the hearings to confirm Clarence Thomas to the Supreme Court] white men kept calling from the rural part of the state, which has a heavily black population, to support Thomas. Their accusations reaffirmed what was going on in their lives: women trying to run the show. Their masculinity is being threatened. I almost became majority leader. In ordinary times, people would have been proud. This year it worked against me. Public ignorance is the problem. Plus the skillful effort to manipulate that ignorance.[10]

Perhaps the dynamic of aggrieved entitlement is best described by psychiatrist Willard Gaylin. "We can endure the fact that we do not have something unless we feel that something has been taken away from us. We will then experience a sense of violation," he writes. "The smoldering rage which comes from being cheated [will be extended] to the society which allowed us to be so cheated."[11] It's misdirecting that anger to others that is the central dynamic of America's angry white men.

Ultimately, I argue that understanding white men's anger requires a focus on *class*—the ironic parallel that finds the United States more racially and gender equal than ever before in our history and more unequal in terms of class than at least the Gilded Age, if not ever. The tensions and anxieties produced by such dramatic increases in class inequality lead many to look at those who appear to have gained, while "we"—the white middle and working classes—have most assuredly been losing. While race and gender are certainly the defining features of today's angry American, it is the growing chasm between rich and poor that is the engine of that rage.

THIS BOOK

Angry White Men is thus the story of a wide swath of American men—mainstream, middle-of-the-road American white guys—who are feeling somewhat at sea these days. Some are looking for answers; others want payback. It's a book about the mobilization—and manipulation—of a wide range of emotions into a politically motivated anger. It's a book about how these normal, everyday guys—office workers and carpenters, firefighters and construction workers, sales clerks and skilled workers, handymen and hardware-store owners—are today also signing up for rural militias, opposing women's participation in the military, and shrugging off harassment and assault. It's about the guy who listens to the out-of-control fulminators and says to his wife, "Well, he does have a couple of good points there. Those feminists have gone too far." And it's about how these everyday guys are also raising sons who pick on weaker kids at school, cheer for performers who brag about attacking women or gays, idealize those miscreants who attack others and get away with it. And these sons are also staying up late at night, surfing the Web for enough explosives to blow up their schools. It's also a story of the margins—the right-wing militias, guys who go on murderous (and suicidal) rampages against young women, the office workers who "go postal," the raging divorced dads who rail against unfair child-custody arrangements.

Mostly, it's the story of the connections between the margins and the mainstream, between the victims of bullying who take matters into their own hands and the nearly 70 percent of kids who have either been bullied or bullied themselves. It's about the connections between the ultra-right-wing extremists, the skinheads and Aryan youth who strut through Southern California shopping malls looking for targets, and the millions who support closing America's borders to keep our country white and safe. It's about the connections between mainstream dads, eager to be involved fathers and trying valiantly to carve out more time for their families, and the furious fathers who blame feminism for their divorces and claim a feminist-enthralled judicial system deprives them of their rights to access to their children.

These connections are vital to our understanding of American anger. American men are, in my view, right to be angry. They have a lot to be angry about. Most American men live in a system in which they were promised a lot of rewards if they played by the rules. If they were good, decent, hardworking men, if they saddled up, or, even more accurately, got into the harness themselves, they would feel the respect of their wives and their children; if they fought in America's wars and served their country fighting fires and stopping crime, they'd have the respect of their communities. And, most important, if they were loyal to their colleagues and workmates, did an honest day's work for an honest day's pay, then they'd also have the respect of other men. "I grew up thinking that all I had to do was to sign up, you know, sign up to be a man the way they told me to be," says Al, a fifty-two-year-old divorced father of three, who's been downsized out of a good-paying sales job. "I mean, you know, suck it up, never show your feelings, be tough, strong, powerful—all that crap about . . . [grimacing, making air quotes] masculinity." Al is explaining this to me—to the entire group, actually—at a workshop I'm conducting on improving male-female relationships. He makes the air quotes and rolls his eyes, looking at me. Okay, I nod, I get it. He says:

> Look, I thought if I did it right, did everything they asked of me, I'd be okay, you know. Play ball and you'll get rich; you'll get laid. And I did, man. For thirty years, I've been such a good fucking soldier. And now these new laws about sexual harassment, about affirmative action? And now you're telling me, "Sorry, but you aren't going to get all those rewards." Is that what you're telling me? Jesus, I wouldn't have done it if I knew I wasn't going to get those goodies. How can you just take it away from us? We've earned it! We paid our dues! We did everything you told us, and now you're saying we aren't getting the big payoff? And they are?! Are you kidding me? And now we're the enemy? We are getting royally screwed, guys. [Now he is looking at the rest of the men in the room.] We are just so fucked. [softer] Seriously, I would never have said "Sign me up" if I knew I wasn't going to get to reap the same benefits my father and grandfather did. It all seems so unfair.

And he's right.

THE PLAN OF THE BOOK

The book follows a thematic unfolding. Most chapters begin with a particularly egregious set of claims or a heinously headline-grabbing event as a way to get inside that subject. The chapters then move from the extreme cases to the more commonplace, all the while describing how these more general patterns are links to the more horrific.

Chapter 1 explores what we might call the "social construction" of white men's anger. While I locate this rise in rage in the experiences of white men, whose sense of entitlement has begun to wane, their anguish and confusion are also being carefully manipulated into politicized rage. I look at the mean-spirited media, which tries to fan the flames of discontent already smoldering across America's suburban lawns, and consider those cynical marketers who are discovering that anger sells. I briefly discuss the Tea Party, Patriots and Minutemen, and the new suburban racism. This anti-immigrant and recharged racism and this virulent antigay rage are directed at anyone—a generalized ethnic and racial "other"—who is seen as threatening to transform America from a Christian (read: white) nation into a multicultural polyglot with no center of racial gravity and, of course, gays, who transform that multicultural polyglot into a "depraved and immoral" polyglot.

The next three chapters explore the anger of men and boys. Chapter 2 is about angry white boys—those boys who open fire, seemingly randomly, on their classmates and teachers. What, if anything, do these random school shootings and these boys who are committing suicide by mass murder tell us about what is happening not only in their heads, but in our culture more generally?

Chapter 3 examines the angry men who seek to restore men's rights. These men's rights activists, spurred by radio commentators and an active blogosphere presence, trumpet various disparities—health, longevity, putative discrimination against boys in school—to rectify the gender imbalance perpetrated by feminist women and their male lackeys. Some promote men's health initiatives, others educational reforms, but all see women as the cause of men's and boys' problems.

A subgroup of these men's rights activists are the fathers' rights groups, the subject of Chapter 4. Many divorced dads were involved fathers and good husbands, yet in the aftermath of bitter divorces, they become enraged as their children were snatched from them and their wages garnished by capricious judges and vicious divorce attorneys. Ironically, the changes inspired by feminist women—increased commitment to family life, greater time spent with children—now come back to bite these guys on their butts, as they invested so much more emotional energy on their families, only to lose what they feel is everything in the divorce. (You'll notice, then, that I focus primarily on the *white* fathers' rights movement. There is a significant fathers' *responsibility* movement among African Americans, which inspired comments from President Obama about black men being more responsible husbands and fathers. The fathers' rights movement spends virtually no energy on responsibility, which means that some of the efforts to bridge these groups have produced less than stellar results.)

Chapter 5 focuses on some extreme cases of what happens when women deny men what men feel entitled to. From the thousands of men who batter and murder their wives, ex-wives, and girlfriends every year to men like George Sodini, who embark on murderous rampages against random women at a local gym, some men blame women for their problems—with occasionally lethal results.

Chapter 6 shifts our attention away from America's shopping malls to its industrial mills, to the angry white guys who "go postal" in their workplaces, bringing lethal weapons to work and opening fire, often targeting their supervisors or bosses, but also taking out a few coworkers in the process. Like the school shooters and George Sodini, many of the guys who go postal also end up committing suicide by mass murder.

Finally, in Chapter 7, I turn to Rick and his fellow travelers on the extreme right wing, the White Wing. Among the white supremacists, neo-Nazis, and other hate groups, we can see most clearly the sense of outrage that unites all of America's angry white men.

In the Epilogue, I address anger as a form of resistance, not specifically its content. After all, anger can be hopeful, instrumental, a belief that with enough effort, change is still possible. Anger can be politically mobilized outrage, the emotional fuel of every popular social movement in history. But anger can also turn to bitterness, a sense of hopeless despair, that is the source of impotent nihilistic violence. Anger can temporarily relieve humiliation, but often only at the expense of another. Many of the Patriots and Tea Partiers believe they are fighting for the future of "their" country and that it is still possible to reclaim it. And some lone wolves, like George Sodini, are resigned to the impossibility of change and commit suicide by mass murder only to go out in a blaze of glory.

1 | Manufacturing Rage

The Cultural Construction of Aggrieved Entitlement

"Tom," from Wichita, Kansas, has been waiting on hold, he tells us, for two hours and twenty minutes. An army veteran, he lost his job earlier this year. For months, he's been looking for work, sending out hundreds of résumés. A few interviews, no offers. What will happen to his family when his unemployment insurance runs out? "We're into the red zone," he explains. "We're cutting essentials: food, laundry, clothing, shoes." He's worried, he says, "scared to death." Repeatedly, he insists he is "not a whiner."

What he wants to know, he asks Rush Limbaugh on his nationally syndicated radio show, is what President Obama is doing to turn the economy around. Why was he spending all this energy on health care when people are out of work? What has the stimulus plan done to create jobs for people like him, with families to support? Fortunately, he says, his wife has a job that provides health care for the family. But if he doesn't find something soon, he's considering reenlisting. He lost his own father in Vietnam, he says, softly, and he's afraid that at forty-three, he might leave his own children fatherless. "My self-esteem is right now at its lowest that I've ever had it," Tom says. "I'm getting choked up."

"I know," replies Limbaugh empathetically. "I've been there." Limbaugh recounts his own history of unemployment. But then, he transforms Tom's experience. "I don't hear you as whining," says Rush. "I hear you as mad."

Wait a second. Did you hear Tom as mad? I'm no expert in auditory interpretation, but what I heard was anxiety, vulnerability, and more than just a slight tremor of fear. I heard someone asking for help. In a revealing analysis of Limbaugh's radio persona, antiviolence activist Jackson Katz carefully parses this particular exchange as emblematic—how the talk-show host transforms this plaintive emotional expression into something else. What starts as sadness, anxiety, grief, worry is carefully manipulated into political rage.[1]

Rush Limbaugh is a master at this translation of emotional vulnerability or insecurity into anger. All that he needs is that shared sense of aggrieved entitlement—that sense that "we," the rightful heirs of America's bounty, have had what is "rightfully ours" taken away from us by "them," faceless, feckless government bureaucrats, and given to "them," undeserving minorities, immigrants, women, gays, and their ilk. If your despair can be massaged into this Manichaean struggle between Us and Them, you, too, can be mobilized into the army of Angry White Men.

Limbaugh is one of hundreds of talk-show hosts on radio dials across the nation—indeed, the AM radio dial seems to have nothing but sports talk, Spanish-language stations, and vitriolic white men hosting radio shows. Talk radio is the most vibrant part of the radio dial—thirty-five hundred all-talk or all-news stations in the United States—up from about five hundred two decades ago.[2] According to the Pew Research Center for the People and the Press, while the majority of radio, newspaper, and magazine consumers are female (51 percent), Limbaugh (59 percent), Sean Hannity (57 percent), and Stephen Colbert (58 percent) skew most heavily toward men. (So, incidentally, does Rachel Maddow, at 52 percent.) Limbaugh's audiences skew slightly older, less educated (only 29 percent are college graduates, compared to 39 percent and 35 percent for liberals Colbert and Maddow, respectively). Their income tends to be squarely in the middle—30 percent make more than seventy-five thousand dollars, 37 percent between thirty and seventy-five thousand dollars, and 21 percent below thirty thousand dollars a year. Obviously, more than seven in ten identify as conservative.[3]

Visitors to Limbaugh's website tilt even more rightward. It's visited by 1.1 million people a month—more than 94 percent white and 85 percent male, most are between thirty-five and sixty-five, with the biggest bulge at forty-five to fifty-four. Most (54 percent) do not have kids. Two-thirds have incomes below one hundred thousand dollars a year, though two-thirds also have at least a college, if not a graduate, degree. (That's an index of downward mobility; their educational achievements haven't paid off in better jobs.)[4] This would make the typical Limbaugh fan (enough to view his website) a downwardly mobile white male, whose career never really panned out (college or grad school but only modest income) and whose family life didn't either (majority childless). That is a recipe for aggrieved entitlement. Everything was in place to partake of the American Dream, and it didn't quite work out. Just whose fault is that?

Sociologist Sarah Sobieraj and political scientist Jeffrey Berry call it "outrage media"—talk-radio, blog, and cable news designed "to provoke a visceral response from the audience, usually in the form of anger, fear, or moral righteousness through the use of overgeneralizations, sensationalism, misleading or patently inaccurate information, ad hominem attacks, and partial truths about opponents."[5] Sobieraj and Berry trace this development through the technological shifts from radio and TV to cable news, the blogosphere, and talk radio as the news vehicles of choices and to the incredible consolidation of media companies, so that only a handful of companies control virtually all of America's airwaves. (Women own about three of ten businesses in America but own only 6 percent of radio stations. Racial minorities own 18 percent of all businesses, but only 7.7 percent of radio stations. Clearly, white men are being squeezed out, right?)[6]

But it's also linked to the displacement of white men from every single position of power in the country. Talk radio is the last locker room, juiced not on steroids but on megahertz. It's the circled wagons keeping out the barbarian hordes, who may be just a millimeter away on that dial. It's the Alamo on AM frequency.

The rise of outrage media is coincident with the erosion of white male entitlement. Outrage media generally begins with Peter Finch in the film *Network* (1976), exhorting his audience to go to their windows and scream, "I'm mad as hell, and I'm not going to take it anymore!" Finch's impotent outburst provides a heroic riposte to a film about the steamroller of corporate takeovers, the ethically rudderless drive for ratings trumping all other criteria, including quality. Like the tabloid newspaper or local newscast—whose motto is "If it bleeds, it leads"—the motto of outrage radio is closer to "If he yells, it sells."

Of course, one needn't be some academic postmodernist to understand how the catharsis of the experience is what enables us to take more of it. We feel outrage, and we're told it's not our fault and that we have plenty of company.

But it's more than just the cheerleaders of the angry mobs. Anger sells. It's become part of marketing strategies for products ranging from regular-guy cars and beer to defiantly politically incorrect items like Hummers and cigars. Anger, after all, implies some degree of hope, of "aspiration," which is a core element in advertising strategy. Anger implies commitment; if you're angry, you feel yourself to be a stakeholder. Anger is emotion seeking an outlet, an excited politicized electron seeking to connect with other atoms. (Contrast it with what happens to the anger that does not find a means of expression: it can become nihilistic, despondent, or resigned bitterness. The resigned and despondent do not buy products. They sulk. They give up.)

You could hear that anger, the aggrieved entitlement, on election night 2012, as President Obama handily defeated Mitt Romney for president. Romney, the unfathomably wealthy corporate plutocrat, was unable to transform himself into a populist firebrand. Even though white men were the only demographic who went for Romney (although not decisively), it was too close in all those battleground states to offset the huge margins Obama racked up with African Americans, women, union workers, and Latinos.

The fact that white men are not a monolithic group—and that enough voted Democratic, especially in blue states—is, of course, an important empirical counterweight to the claims of many of the Angry

White Male choirmasters on talk radio and Fox News who say that they speak for all of "us."

But it hardly deters them. Do you recall the commentary on election night 2012? Rush Limbaugh said that he went to bed thinking "we'd lost the country." Bill O'Reilly quoted one of his listeners, mourning that "we have lost our American way of life." "I liked it the way it was," former *Saturday Night Live* news anchor Dennis Miller (now more of a self-parodying talk-show host) said about the country. "It's not going to be like that anymore."[7] And what was the single unifying campaign slogan the Tea Party had to offer? "We want to take back our country."[8]

When I read these comments, I was reminded of a joke from my childhood. It seems that the Lone Ranger and Tonto were riding across the plains when suddenly they were surrounded by ten thousand angry Indian warriors. (The word *savages* would likely have been used in those days.)

"We're in trouble, Tonto," says the Lone Ranger.

"What do you mean 'we,' kemosabe?" is Tonto's reply.

Tonto was right. Just what *do* they mean by "we"? Whose country is it?

One has to feel a sense of proprietorship, of entitlement, to call it "our" country. That sense has led millions of Americans, male and female, white and nonwhite, to feel like stakeholders in the American system and motivated millions to lay down their lives for that way of life. It's prompted some of the most moving stories of sacrifice, the most heroic and touching moments of connectedness with neighbors and strangers during crises. But it has its costs. That sense of holding on to what's "ours" can be turned into something ugly, sowing division where unity should be. Just as religiosity can motivate the most self-sacrificing charity and loving devotion, it can also be expressed as sanctimonious self-righteousness, as if a privileged access to revealed truth grants permission to unspeakable cruelties.

It's not the depth of those collective feelings that is troubling—obviously, love of country can inspire us to great sacrifice; rather, it's their direction. When threatened, that sense of entitlement, of proprietorship, can be manipulated into an enraged protectionism, a sense that the threat to "us" is internal, those undeserving others who want to take for themselves what we have rightfully earned. "We" were willing to share, we might say, totally inverting the reality that "they" ask only for a seat at the table, not to overturn the table itself; "they" want it all for themselves. According to these angry white men, "they" not only want a seat, but now they got a guy sitting at the head of the table itself.

Note, also, that I said "can be manipulated." The expression of emotion often leaves one also vulnerable, susceptible to manipulation. There's little empirical evidence for some biologically driven or evolutionarily mandated tribalism—at least a tribalism based on such phony us-versus-them characteristics. Sure, it's true that when threatened, we have an instinctive reaction to circle the wagons and protect ourselves against whatever threatens us. So, for example, the fierce patriotism that emerged after the 9/11 attacks was a natural, collective response to invasion, just as the mobilization of the entire nation's sympathies after Hurricane Katrina or Sandy; few Americans were inured to the outpouring of collective grief, anguish, and shared purpose.

But to fixate on Saddam Hussein and the invasion of Iraq? That had to be manipulated: Iraq had not invaded us; indeed, Saddam Hussein was antipathetic to al-Qaeda. There were no weapons of mass destruction—but even had there been, why was it necessary to try to divert the outpouring of grief and desire for revenge to a different enemy? That we feel collective sentiments tells us nothing about how those sentiments can be mobilized and manipulated. In the case of the Iraq War, there was no threat, just the raw sentiments ripe for exploitation by cynical politicians.

Angry white men are genuinely floundering—confused and often demoralized, they experience that wide range of emotions. But their anger is often constructed from those emotional materials, given shape and directed at targets that serve other interests. Angry white men are angry, all right, but their anger needs to be channeled toward some groups—and away from others.

OUTRAGEOUS RADIO

As an emotion, anger has a fairly short shelf life. It's a "hot" emotion, like sexual desire, not a cooler emotion like devotion to a loved one, or abiding love of country, or pride in one's child. Anger must be fed, its embers constantly stoked—either personally, by holding a grudge, or collectively, by having sustained the sense that you have been injured, wounded, and that those who did it must pay. Feeling like the wronged victim is a way to channel hurt into a self-fueling sense of outrage; a personal sense of injury becomes "politicized" as an illustration of a general theme.

The politicization of the countless injuries, hurts, and injustices is the job of the self-appointed pundits in the media. It is they who offer a political framework for the anguish that you might feel, suggest how it represents a larger pattern of victimization of "people like you," and then urge collective action to redress it. (The collective action can be simply tuning in to the same radio show every day, knowing that you are among friends and allies.)

As a result, Angry White Men are a *virtual* social movement. I don't mean that they are "virtually" a movement—as in "almost, but not quite." I mean that they organize virtually, that their social-movement organization is a virtual organization. They sit alone, listening to the radio, listening to Rush Limbaugh and Mike Savage and Sean Hannity. They meet online, in chat rooms and on websites, whether promoting antifeminist men's rights or the re-Aryanization of America. They troll cyberspace, the anti-PC police, ready to attack any blogger, columnist, or quasi liberal who dares to say something with which they disagree.

It is the task of the Angry White Male pundits in the media to act as the choirmasters of the Angry White Male chorus, to direct and re-direct that rage, to orchestrate it so that the disparate howls of despair or anguish, the whimpers of pain, or the mumblings of confusion can sound unified. They are the conductors; they believe that we are their instruments. It's their job to take the anger that might, in fact, be quite legitimate and direct it elsewhere, onto other targets.

Say, for example, you are an autoworker, and you've seen your wages cut, your benefits dismantled, and your control over your hours steadily compromised. You may well be a bit miffed. But at whom? Left to your own devices—and conversations with your friends—you might conclude that it is the fault of rapacious corporate moguls, who line their pockets and pay themselves fat bonuses and who squeeze every drop they can from America's working man. You might even list to the Left and make common cause with others in similar situations and try to get the government to regulate the industry, raise wages, protect benefits, and institute national health care. You might even work with your union.

So, if I were to try to channel Rush Limbaugh or Mike Savage, my task would be to redirect that anger onto others, those even less fortunate than you. Perhaps the reason you are so unhappy is because of all those immigrants who are streaming into America, driving the costs of labor lower and threatening "American" jobs. Or perhaps it's because women—even, perhaps, your own wife—want to enter the labor force, and that's what is driving down labor costs, as corporations no longer need to pay men a "family" wage, since they no longer support a family. Your grievances are not with the corporations, but with those just *below* you. In other words, as Thomas Frank points out in *What's the Matter with Kansas?*, it's the task of the pundits to create "a French Revolution in reverse—one in which the sans-culottes pour down the streets demanding more power for the aristocracy."[9]

Limbaugh and Savage are only two of the hundreds of angry white men who have staked out an angry white male club on radio waves. I'll focus on them briefly here not because they are any worse than any of the others, but rather because they are so similar—in that masculinity is so central in their radio ratings. They're among the most popular: *The Savage Nation* is heard on 350 radio stations and reaches 8.25 million listeners each week, ranking third behind only Rush Limbaugh and Sean Hannity. Limbaugh outpaces everyone else, heard on more than 600 stations, with a weekly audience of more than 20 million.[10]

Angry White Men dominate the American airwaves (even though their claim that the media tilt leftward enables them to both claim dominance and victimhood); their goal is to protect and preserve the dominance of American white men, even at the moment when white men, in real life, are actually accommodating themselves to greater and greater gender equality—and, actually, liking it very much.

What, though, are they actually so angry about?

Angry White Men exhibit what French social theorist Georges Sorel called "ressentiment"—a personal sense of self that is defined always in relationship to some perceived injury and whose collective politics mixes hatred and envy of those who we believe have injured us. That "creative hatred," Sorel argues, is anathema to serious collective action because it is so easily manipulated; it is more likely to spawn sporadic spasmodic violent eruptions than a serious social movement.

This sense of self, grounded in victimhood, both hating and envying others, can be a brilliant strategy, generating an audience of consumers. And it's not only these angry white men. Indeed, Oprah Winfrey's early television success involved constructing her audience as victims. In the early 1990s, I entered a discussion to appear on her show following the publication of my book *Men Confront Pornography*. When I spoke to the producer, she suggested that I appear alongside several women whose "husbands or boyfriends had forced them to do degrading sexual things after they'd seen them in pornography." I said no, that my book was a serious effort to invite men to take on the political debate that was, at the time, roiling feminism. I proposed being on with a few men who took the issues seriously. We went back and forth, up the ladder of increasingly senior producers. Finally, the very seniormost producer of the show, the one who talks directly with Oprah, admitted she didn't understand how my idea would work or what was wrong with her idea. "I just don't see it," she said. "I don't see who the victim is. You can't have an Oprah show without a victim."

What a revealing statement! As the producer saw it, the world was divided into two groups, viewers and victims. Viewers would tune in each day, perhaps feeling that their lives were miserable. And then they'd watch the show and exhale, and say, "Well, at least my husband doesn't force me to do degrading sexual things after he sees them in pornography! Maybe my life isn't so bad after all." And the next day, as the effects wear off, and viewers feel crappy again, they tune in to see someone who has it far worse, and they feel, temporarily, better. It's like *Queen for a Day*, a show I watched assiduously as a young child, in which three different women would tell of the terrible fates that had befallen them (husband injured on the job and unable to work, debilitating illnesses, and so on), and the studio audience would vote (by the loudness of their applause, registering on an "Applause-o-Meter") which one of the women would be crowned queen and receive gifts like a new refrigerator and other household appliances. (I ended up going on *The Phil Donahue Show* instead.)

Oprah's shows in her last years on the air were more inspirational—not necessarily a parade of victims, but more about people who had triumphed over adversity, who had fallen down seven times and gotten up eight. But the theme of viewers and victims resonates more now on talk radio. It's but a short hop from dichotomous viewers and victims to a more unified community of viewers as victims. The genius of Rush Limbaugh and the others is that they have appropriated a more commonly "feminine" trope of perpetual victimhood and successfully masculinized it. In fact, they claim, it's your very manhood that is constantly under threat!

As befits an industry leader, Rush Limbaugh's politics of ressentiment has been amply parsed for its racism and sexism—he's popped into national consciousness usually when he strays over a line already drawn far to the other side of decency and respect.

He defends white people against what Lothrop Stoddard and Madison Grant, early-twentieth-century racialists, called "the rising tide of color." Limbaugh's racism is as transparent as his nativism and sexism. Here's what he said after Obama was elected the first time: "It's Obama's America, is it not? Obama's America, white kids getting beat up on school buses now. You put your kids on a school bus, you expect safety, but in Obama's America, the white kids now get beat up with the black kids cheering, 'Yeah, right on, right on, right on,' and, of course, everybody says the white kid deserved it: he was born a racist; he's white."[11]

And how does one get ahead in Obama's America? "By hating white people. Or even saying you do. . . . Make white people the new oppressed minority. . . . They're moving to the back of the bus. . . . That's the modern day Republican Party, the equivalent of the Old South: the new oppressed minority."[12]

Poor white people, the victims of government-sponsored racial discrimination. And poor men, victims of reverse sexism as well. For example, when Sandra Fluke, a graduate student at Georgetown, testified in support of requiring all institutions receiving federal funds to actually obey the law and provide contraception, Limbaugh launched into a vicious *ad feminam* attack against Fluke personally, calling her a slut and a whore for having so much sex, and demanded, as a taxpayer, that she provide high-quality videos of her sexual escapades. "If we are going to pay for your contraceptives and thus pay for you to have sex, we want something. We want you to post the videos online so we can all watch."

It's easy to understand the sense of entitlement that this sixth-generation upper-class heir to a Missouri family of lawyers and politicians might feel. And it's not so very hard to understand how so many of his white male listeners might identify with him, even if they're more recent arrivals, and they've always held jobs for which you shower after work, not before it.

What binds this bilious martinet to his listeners, though, is that they are men, at least the overwhelming majority of them, and their sense of entitlement comes from their deep-seated feeling that they are the heirs to the American Dream that, as Woody Guthrie should have sung, this land was really made for them. Note that he assumes that his listeners are male—that "we" are entitled to see videos of Sandra Fluke or that it's a little white boy who is being harassed. "We" is white and male. Indeed, a cover story in *Newsweek* on talk radio called it "group therapy for mostly white males who feel politically challenged."[13]

Rarely, though, have commentators gone much further than noticing how these shows resonate with white men. It's as if noting the demographics explains the sociology. So they rarely discuss gender, discuss how masculinity is implicated. Nor do they see Limbaugh's rage as a particularly masculine rage, the "gender" of the pain he claims to channel into outrage. On the one hand, he's a real man, a man's man—"a cigar-smoking, NFL-watching, red-meat right winger who's offended by the 'feminization' of American society."[14] His sense of aggrieved entitlement is to restore not the reality but the possibility of dominance. It is simultaneously aspirational and nostalgic—he looks back to a time when it was all there, unchallenged, and forward to its restoration. Limbaugh's own public struggles with his weight, his failed childless marriages, his avoidance of military service, his addiction to OxyContin (surely the wimpiest addiction possible; real men smoke crack or shoot heroin), and his well-known need for Viagra all testify to a masculinity in need of propping up, in need of reconfirmation. In Limbaugh's case, right-wing racist and sexist politics is the conduit for the restoration of his manhood—and for the manhood of other fellow sufferers of aggrieved entitlement. Limbaugh offers a prescription for political Viagra, designed to get that blood flowing, reenergize a flagging sense of white American manhood.

But if the elite-born Limbaugh plays in the populist sandbox, Mike Savage is both the real deal and even more a poseur. At least he's a working-class guy—born Michael Alan Weiner, the son of Russian Jewish immigrants who settled in the Bronx during World War II. But then, why would such a nice Jewish boy, whose own mother and father were the beneficiaries of the American Dream of immigration, now want to slam the door on the faces of everyone else?

Limbaugh is positively tame compared to Savage, who seems to believe that the higher the decibels of his denunciations, the more persuasive they will be. And like Limbaugh, he's interested in reversing the very multicultural trends that he represents. Like Limbaugh, he's immensely popular, and like Limbaugh, he engages in a conspiratorial Us-Them framing, in which "we" are the enlightened few and "they" are the dupes of the government-inspired hijacking of freedom. He calls illegal immigrants and their allies "brown supremacists" and accuses activists for sexual equality of "raping" children through media campaigns for tolerance.

But ultimately, it all has to do with masculinity. Savage alternates between Limbaugh's conspiratorial outrage—can you believe what they are doing to us?—and chastising his audience for allowing this all to happen under their very noses. The campaign for so-called civil rights is a "con," and affirmative action stole his "birthright." What you have now, he claims, is "the wholesale replacement of competent white men." And what has been our reaction? We've become a "sissified nation," a "sheocracy." Part of "the de-balling of America," "true red-blooded American types have been thrown out of the—out of the government."[15]

Part of this is women's fault, of course—feminist women who have become more masculine. Here's what he said on his show: "Particularly today, the women are not, you know, what they were thirty years ago. The women have become more like guys, thanks to the hags in the women's movement, and the white race is dying. That's why they won't reproduce, because the women want to be men. They want to behave like men, they want to act like men, they've been encouraged to think like men, act like men, be like men. Consequently, they don't want to be women, and they don't want to be mothers."[16]

Were you to ask Limbaugh and Savage, and the others who aspire to their seats of influence, they'd likely tell you that they aren't really antiwomen but antifeminist, and specifically promale, more about legitimizing the anger of white men. Feminism comes under attack—after all, it was Limbaugh who popularized the term *feminazi*—phantasmagorically linking campaigns for wage equality, or safety from battery and rape, to the organized, methodical genocide in the Third Reich.

Now, why has this resonated? Because the defensiveness of white men is so narcissistic that any criticism of masculinity and male entitlement is seen as the effort to leverage the apparatus of the state in the service of the destruction of an entire biological sex. But these guys aren't really interested in women. They're interested in promoting the interests of white men.

In a particularly revealing rant, Savage links racism, sexism, and anti-immigrant nativism in his pitch to fellow angry white men:

> Many of you have been hoodwinked into believing that we are a multicultural nation, which we are not. We're a nation of many races and many cultures, that is true, it has been true from the beginning, but in the past people would come over and become Americans. Now they come over, and they want you to become them. . . . We're going to have a revolution in this country if this keeps up. These people are pushing the wrong people around. . . . If they keep pushing us around and if we keep having these schmucks running for office, catering to the multicultural people who are destroying the culture in this country, guaranteed the people, the white male in particular . . . the one without connections, the one without money, has nothing to lose, and you haven't seen him yet. You haven't seen him explode in this country. And he's still the majority, by the way, in case you don't know it. He is still the majority, and no one speaks for him, everyone craps on him . . . and he has no voice whatsoever. . . . And you're going to find out that if you keep pushing this country around, you'll find out that there's an ugly side to the white male.[17]

Outrage media is not, however, a one-way street. The audience is an active participant; together with the host, they produce the rage of the day and direct it toward the issues on which the free-floating rage will land. Each day offers no shortage of the horrors of what "they" are doing to "us"—"they" being government bureaucrats in thrall to the feminist cabal, implementing the gay agenda, illegals, and minorities guided by sinister Marxian forces. (They often come perilously close to denouncing their Zionist puppeteers of the International

Jewish Conspiracy. Indeed, were it not for the convenience of stoking anti-Muslim sentiment since 9/11, we'd hear quite a bit more anti-Semitism from some of these hosts. Generally, the right wing loves Israel, but hates Jews.)

Angry White Male Radio is the New England town meeting of the twenty-first century. The participatory experience, with its steady stream of callers, ups the emotional ante. Sure, there's plenty of defensive anger to go around. But the tone expresses a sense of aggrieved entitlement. Rush's followers call themselves "dittoheads," echoing every sentiment. "What Rush does on his shows is take frustration and rage and rearticulate and confirm them as ideology," writes Sherri Paris, after listening nonstop for several weeks. "Limbaugh's skill lies in weaving political alienation and anger into the illusion of common political ground." He's creating a community out of people's individual frustrations, giving them a sense of "we-ness."[18]

"I love it," says Jay, a twenty-six-year-old Nebraskan with obvious self-consciousness. Jay was one of several dittoheads I talked with around the country. Actually, he drove the taxi from the university where I'd been lecturing to the airport. Rush was on in the cab. "I mean, all day long, all I get is multicultural this and diversity that. I love it because I can let off steam at how stupid the whole thing is. I can't stop it—there's no way. But I get all these other guys who remind me that it's not right, it's not fair, and the system's out of control. And I'm the one getting screwed!"

Jay was among the more articulate when it came to discussing substantive issues like affirmative action or race and gender preferences in admissions. Most of the guys I spoke with whose analysis came from Limbaugh and Fox News merely mouthed platitudes they took directly from the shows, without so much as actually thinking if they applied to their situations. I cannot count the number of times I heard lines like "It's not the government's money, it's the people's money" in response to tax policy.

You'd think that after nearly a half century of sustained critique of racial and gender bias in the media, of the most convincing empirical social and behavioral science research imaginable, of civil rights, women's, and gay and lesbian movements, white guys would have finally understood how bias works and would have accommodated themselves to a new, more egalitarian, more democratic, and more representative media. Or at least you'd think they'd be less vocal in their resistance. But as far as they're concerned, the world hasn't merely changed—it's been upended, turned upside down into its perverse mirror image. "It's completely crazy," says Matt. "The inmates are running the asylum. They're completely in power, and they get anything they want. And us regular, normal white guys—we're like nothing. We don't count for shit anymore."

Outrage media offers a case of what Frankfurt School philosopher Herbert Marcuse called "repressive desublimation." Although not exactly the catchiest of phrase makers, Marcuse was on to something that, as a refugee from Hitler's Germany, he found so scary: how the ability to sound off angrily, to express all your pent-up rage (the "desublimation" part), could actually serve the interests of those in power. Being able to rebel in these impotent ways actually enables the system to continue (hence, the "repressive" part). You think you're rebelling by listening to jazz, or punk rock, or even angry rap music, having a lot of sex, drinking and screaming your heads off about how the system is oppressing you. You find common cause with others who are doing the same thing: instant community. And, after desublimating, you go back to work, a docile, sated drone, willing to conform to what the "system" asks of you because the system also lets you blow off steam. Bread and circuses. Participatory entertainment. (Instead of worrying, for example, that an excessive diet of violent video games would make a young guy more likely to commit an act of violence, the Frankfurt School would have been more worried that he'd be more docile, that he'd never rebel socially, collectively, because he got all that rebellion out of his system on a machine created by one of the world's largest corporations.)

Yet, ironically, the very medium that provides the false sense of community of Limbaugh's dittoheads can also be, simultaneously, isolating. "People tend to be less angry when they have to interact with each other," writes journalist and media commentator Joe Klein; they become afflicted with "Information Age disorder"—the "product of our tendency to stew alone, staring into computer screens at work, blobbing in front of the television at home." Perhaps we're not bowling alone, but fuming alone. Together.[19]

So American white men, still among the most privileged group of people on the face of the earth—if you discount hereditary aristocracies and sheikdoms—feel that they are the put-upon victims of a society that grows more equal every day. It's hard if you've been used to 100 percent of all the positions of power and privilege in the world to wake up one morning and find people like you in only 80 percent of those positions. Equality sucks if you've grown so accustomed to inequality that it feels normal.

Listen to the words of one leader, defending the rights of those disempowered white men: "Heaven help the God-fearing, law-abiding Caucasian middle class, Protestant or even worse evangelical Christian, Midwest or Southern or even worse rural, apparently straight or even worse admittedly [heterosexual], gun-owning or even worse NRA card-carrying average working stiff, or even worst of all, male working stiff. Because not only don't you count, you're a downright obstacle to social progress."[20] That leader was, incidentally, Charlton Heston, acting less like Moses and more like an angry Pharaoh, feeling powerless as he watches his slaves disappear.

These are not the voices of power but the voices of *entitlement* to power. The positions of authority, of power, have been stolen from them—handed over to undeserving "others" by a government bureaucracy that has utterly abandoned them. If listening to Guy Radio and watching Guy TV is about blowing off steam, this is what that steam smells like.

Far from fomenting a reactionary revolution, Limbaugh and his ilk are the Peter Finches of the twenty-first century, screaming about how they are mad as hell and not going to take it anymore—which is the very thing that enables them to take far more of it.

A GLANCE BACK: A BRIEF HISTORY OF AMERICAN ANGRY WHITE MEN

Of course, this isn't the first time that Americans have been treated to a chorus of complainers that rail against the "masculinization" of women and the "feminization" of men.[21] A century ago, pundits across America bemoaned what they saw as a crisis of masculinity. They bemoaned the loss of the hardy manly virtues that had settled the country, harnessed its natural resources toward amazing industrial breakthroughs, "tamed" a restive native population, and fended off external threats. Men were becoming soft, effeminate. Ironically, it was the somewhat effete novelist Henry James who captured this sentiment most eloquently in the character of Basil Ransome, the dashing southern gentleman in *The Bostonians* (1885):

> *The whole generation is womanized; the masculine tone is passing out of the world; it's a feminine, nervous, hysterical, chattering, canting age, an age of hollow phrases and false delicacy and exaggerated solicitudes and coddled sensibilities, which, if we don't soon look out, will usher in the reign of mediocrity, of the feeblest and flattest and most pretentious that has ever been. The masculine character, the ability to dare and endure, to know and yet not fear reality, to look the world in the face and take it for what it is . . . that is what I want to preserve, or, rather, recover; and I must tell you that I don't in the least care what becomes of you ladies while I make the attempt!*[22]

Where these critics disagreed was over the source of this emasculation—and, therefore, of course, what solutions might be helpful to restore American men's manly virtues. Most agreed that modern urban civilization had a feminizing effect: instead of working in the fields, or in factories, or as artisanal craft workers, American men now sat in stuffy offices, in white-collared shirts, pushing paper around desks. Instead of being apprenticed to older, seasoned male workers, young boys were now taught by female teachers, by female Sunday-school teachers, and, most of all, by their mothers, as fathers were away all day at work. (The separation of work and home may have meant that women were "imprisoned" in the home, as Betty Friedan would later argue, but it also meant that men were exiled from it, away all day, and returning to an increasingly feminized Victorian living space.) Even religion had become "feminized," as Protestant ministers spoke of a beatific and compassionate Christ, who loved his enemies and turned the other cheek.

Not only were women demanding entry into the public sphere—going to work, joining unions, demanding the right to vote and go to college—but native-born white men were facing increasing competition from freed slaves migrating to northern industrial cities and waves of immigrants from Asia and southern and eastern Europe, moving into tenement slums and creating a vast pool of cheap labor.

Everywhere men looked, the playing field had grown increasingly competitive and uncertain. Just as Horatio Alger was celebrating the "luck and pluck" that would enable young men of modest means to make their way to the top, native-born American white men were becoming far less concerned with how to make it to the top and far more anxious about sinking to the bottom. Restoring or retrieving a lost heroic manhood was less about the thrill of victory, as television announcers might have said, had there been *ABC's Wide World of Sports* in 1900, and far more about forestalling or preventing the agony of defeat.

Actually, there was the equivalent of Jim McKay, host of that iconic TV show. Or, rather, a lot of equivalents. It was at the turn of the last century that all the modern sports we know and love today—hockey, football, baseball, basketball—were organized into leagues and prescribed, especially, for schoolboys to promote a healthy, hardy manliness. Following on the heels of the British elite private schools and the success of *Tom Brown's School Days*, American reformers were quick to point out the restorative qualities of athletic prowess and the tonic virtues of the outdoors. Baseball, for example, was trumpeted by Theodore Roosevelt, himself the epitome of manly triumph over aristocratic weakness, as a "true sport for a manly race." "All boys love baseball," wrote the western novelist Zane Grey in 1909. "If they don't, they're not real boys."[23]

Getting in shape was a manly preoccupation at the turn of the last century, as urban men fretted about the loss of manly vigor. In studying the late nineteenth and early twentieth centuries, I discerned three patterns of response to this mounting crisis, three avenues in which American men were counseled to restore the manhood that seemed so threatened.

First, they sought self-control. Believing that American men had grown soft and indolent, they sought to demonstrate greater amounts of self-control. Believing that the body was an instrument of their will, American men at the turn of the twentieth century bulked up, pumped up, and worked out as never before. As famed psychologist G. Stanley Hall put it, "You can't have a firm will without firm muscles."[24] Gyms sprouted up all over the country, especially in large cities where middle-class white-collar office workers followed athletic regimens offered by scions of "physical culture" (like Bernarr Macfadden) and admired the physique of bodybuilders like Eugen Sandow. By the

1920s, they'd begun to follow a young, scrawny, Italian American immigrant who'd been unsuccessful at picking up a girl at the beach at Coney Island, Brooklyn. Ashamed of his physique—he called himself a "97 Pound runt . . . skinny, pale, nervous and weak"—young Angelo Siciliano developed a muscle-building regime that became the most successful body-transforming regimen in US history. Along the way, Siciliano changed more than his physique, becoming the "world's most perfect man." He also changed his name, to Charles Atlas.

The biceps weren't the only muscles over which American men felt they needed to exert greater control. They were equally concerned that they'd grown soft and weak because of their sexual profligacy. Masturbation not only threatened a man's healthy development, but was also a moral threat to the nation. Reformers utilized what one historian labeled the language of a "spermatic economy" to discourage it. Sperm were a resource, not to be squandered or "spent," but rather "saved" and "invested" in the future. Other health reformers like Sylvester Graham, C. W. Post, and J. H. Kellogg experimented with different whole grains and flours in their crackers and cereals to help keep men regular and thus prevent the blockages that pollute the body, and thus the mind, and lead to solitary vices. It's one thing to prescribe graham crackers or Post Toasties, or even Corn Flakes, and quite another to prescribe suturing the foreskin closed without anesthesia as a way for parents to ensure that their sons didn't masturbate. But that is what Kellogg did in his efforts to treat all sorts of male malaise in his sanitarium in Battle Creek, Michigan (Kellogg's own hysteria was held up to hilarious ridicule by novelist T. Coraghessan Boyle in *The Road to Wellville*).

These efforts represented only one of the three major patterns of solutions to the "crisis" of masculinity that were offered to American men at the turn of the last century. A second strategy was "escape." Boys needed to escape the feminizing clutches of women; they had to run away, ship out on the *Pequod*, join Henry Fleming in the army, or otherwise be "lighting out for the territory," in the immortal last words of Huckleberry Finn, "because Aunt Sally she's gonna adopt me and sivilize me, and I can't stand it." Modern society had turned "robust, hardy self-reliant boyhood into a lot of flat-chested cigarette smokers with shaky nerves and doubtful vitality," according to Ernest Thompson Seton, who founded the Boy Scouts of America in 1910 to turn the tide of feminization. Other clubs and organizations followed, including the Boone and Crockett Club, and later the YMCA (Young Men's Christian Association) itself, proclaiming itself a "man factory," providing a homosocial haven in an increasingly coeducational world.

Just as their sons needed to be rescued from the feminizing clutches of mothers and teachers, American men, too, set off to retrieve their deep manhood. And while the boys were busy with Boy Scouts and the Boone and Crockett Club, college guys were joining Greek-letter fraternities and rowing and boxing. Middle-aged men were joining fraternal lodges (nearly one in four American men belonged to a lodge in 1900) or heading off on safaris and treks and military-inspired adventures in search of the ever-receding frontier, or creating the frontier itself at newly invented "dude ranches" where urban gentlemen could get their hands dirty learning to rope and ride and play cowboy. "The wilderness will take hold on you," wrote western naturalist George Evans. "It will give you good red blood; it will turn you from a weakling into a man." Or they could always read westerns, like *The Virginian* (1902), by Owen Wister, the story of an urban dude who encounters a real man of the West and devotes his life to recounting his exploits (written by a Harvard-educated upper-class dandy who, himself, was a convert to the vigorous virtue of the West).[25]

Or they were attending men-only religious revivals with itinerant preacher Billy Sunday (a former Chicago Cubs baseball player–turned-evangelist) whose "Muscular Christianity" was a riposte to the "dainty, sissified, lily-livered piety" of mainstream Protestantism. Jesus, Sunday thundered, was a scrapper, who kicked the money changers out of the Temple; Christianity was "hard muscled, pick-axed religion, a religion from the gut, tough and resilient."[26]

Finally, and most germane to our purposes here, men saw "exclusion" as a strategy to protect their ability to sustain themselves as men. If the playing field had now grown more crowded, and the cries for leveling it had grown more insistent, then one strategy was to kick them out. One can read American nativism, racism, anti-immigrant sentiment, and, of course, anti-feminism through this lens; movements to restrict immigration, to keep women out of college or the labor market, to maintain racial segregation were all efforts by white men to make the playing field smaller and therefore minimize the competition and maintain the opportunities that white men had earlier enjoyed. Then, as now, social Darwinism and the "natural" hierarchies of race and nation were useful fictions on which to base this exclusion. "How long before the manly warlike people of Ohio of fair hair and blue eyes," asked Ohio congressman Samuel Sullivan Cox, "would become, in spite of Bibles and morals, degenerate under the wholesale emancipation and immigration [of black slaves]?"[27]

Racists, nativists, and anti-Semites all made common cause: protecting the pure white race from degeneracy required keeping "them" out, away from "our" women, and from competing for "our" jobs. Anti-immigrant sentiment from the Know-Nothings of the 1840s to the present day has seen border closings as a win-win: we don't have to deal with "their" ways and accommodate ourselves to their needs for health care or education in their own languages, *and* we can eliminate the additional competition for jobs.

Interestingly, the grounds for exclusion were often gendered—that is, the "other" was simply not appropriately masculine. In what I have come to call the "Goldilocks Dilemma," the masculinity of the other was like the porridge—either "too hot" or "too cold," but never "just right." *They* were either "hypermasculine" (violent, out-of-control, rapacious animals) or "hypomasculine" (weak, effeminate, irresponsible, and dependent). *We*, by contrast, had just the right mixture of hardy self-reliance and community spirit: we had tamed our animal nature into civilized gentlemen, but not so much that we lost sight of our rugged side.

Jews were imagined as weak, effete, and bookish nerds, who were also so avariciously greedy that they controlled the economy of the entire world. Blacks were lazy, irresponsible, dependent, and also rapacious predatory sexual animals. Feminist women, for that matter, were more masculine than their men. Chinese men were slight, frail, and effeminate, were nonviolent, and wore women's clothing, and, at the same time, they were part of a yellow peril that was maniacally sweeping over California ports. One critic wanted it both ways; the Chinese were, he wrote, "a barbarous race, devoid of energy." This constant jumping between hyper- and hypomasculine, often in the same utterances, would be echoed by today's white supremacists, as we will see later in this book.[28]

Of course, these strategies for manly restoration are broad, and not mutually exclusive. For example, many of the fraternal orders were not only for men only, but also racially exclusionary. The Loyal Order of the Moose, Modern Woodmen, and the Order of the United American Mechanics were all white by charter; the latter could be relied on as a racist goon squad. And, of course, the resurgence of the fraternal order of the Ku Klux Klan in the first decades of the twentieth century, in border regions like southern Indiana, was dedicated to expunging "aliens" as well as resisting racial equality.

Several best sellers at the turn of the last century sounded an alarm that has echoed across the century into the voice of today's angry white men. Then, Lothrop Stoddard's *The Rising Tide of Color* (1920), Homer Lea's *The Day of the Saxon* (1912), and Madison Grant's *The Passing of the Great Race* (1916) prefigured contemporary warnings about the dangers of immigration, miscegenation, and interracial sex. At the turn of the last century, it bordered on hysteria. "The whole white race is exposed to the possibility of social sterilization and final replacement or absorption by the teeming colored races," wrote Stoddard; that would be "an unspeakable catastrophe." "The white man is being rapidly bred out by negroes," echoed Grant, resulting in an "ever thinning veneer of white culture." Grant was convinced that "the cross between a white man and a Negro is a Negro," and "the cross between a European and a Jew is a Jew." Race mixing was race destroying. (This last is a revealing insight into the fears of angry white men: that the sexuality of the other is imagined as both more predatory and rapacious, but also that the other is far more sexually capable, whether in stereotypes about black men's penis size, hot-blooded Italian ardor, Filipino alacrity, or Latino suaveness. Of course, such projections are far less about the feared and far more about the anxieties and insecurities of the fearful and their insecurities about their ability to satisfy increasingly sexually entitled women.)[29]

Women's and men's missions were clear. Women had to have babies—white babies—and a lot of them to avoid "race suicide" and ensure the perpetuation of the purity of the race. Men had to stand tall and determined against the rising tide of color, providing steadfast resistance to the promise of the Statue of Liberty. If the promise of America would be a welcome mat to new opportunities for the world's "huddled masses," angry white men would make sure they felt utterly unwelcome. There was no way they would let the welcome mat to others turn them, the Americans who were entitled to be here, into a doormat. It's a fine line, and they would not let it be crossed.

At the turn of the last century, that's how it sounded, how racism and nativism blended together in fears of loss and downward mobility and rage at a government that would so casually erode the inalienable rights of native-born white folk. And that's pretty much how it sounds today, along the fences that anti-immigrant groups patrol to make sure "they" stay out.

BORDER PATROLS

Old habits die hard. At the turn of the twentieth century, those angry white men sought to seal the borders and make sure that aliens did not overrun the country. Today, their grievances are no less palpable. Perhaps these are the great-grandsons of the Lothrop Stoddards and Madison Grants of the 1920s—still protecting their women from those bestial hordes, still furious at a government too enthralled with the ideals of multiculturalism, and beholden to corporations who like the wage suppression that invariably accompanies immigration, and terrified that the country they knew, "their" country, was becoming un-recognizable. They don't ride horses along those borders very much; now it's mostly pickup trucks with gun racks and high-beam lights. But their anger echoes their forebears, and their sense that "their" country is being taken away from them is no less tangible.

The sense of aggrieved entitlement is evident in the language of these contemporary nativists. It's not "immigration" but an "invasion" of "illegals" who are "alien" and unsuited for our way of life. "An invasion is spreading across America like wildfire, bringing gangs, drugs, and an alien culture into the very heartland of America" is how a video from the Voice of Citizens Together put it in 1999. Anti-immigration activists use the same language as Nazis or Hutus and others who promote genocide. They are a "cancer" threatening the healthy body from within, a foreign invading army, threatening from outside—often both. Immigrants are a "hostile force on our border" and a "cultural cancer . . . eating at the very heart of our nation."[30]

They come because they want what we have—which has always been one of the reasons for immigration to the United States, after all, the promise of a better life, of starting over in the land of the do over. The founding fathers remembered that America had been founded by illegal immigrants who had been hounded out of their own country for being too religiously rigid; they created an open society where, by the turn of the twentieth century, the world's "huddled masses, yearning to breathe free," came by the boatloads. Today's nativists have forgotten their own origins in another country and want to deny to others what they, themselves, found.

The mobilization to repel this invasion of illegals is justified by gender. "Their" women are hypersexual, reproductive machines, cranking out babies with utter disregard for propriety. They're unwashed, unclean, and unpleasant. Their men are sexually irresponsible, equally unwashed, and predatory. Listen to Joe Arpaio, America's nativist in chief, the racist, self-proclaimed "America's toughest sheriff," sheriff of Maricopa County, Arizona: "All these people that come over, they could come with disease. There's no control, no health checks or anything. They check fruits and vegetables, how come they don't check people? No one talks about that! They're all dirty. I sent out 200 inmates into the desert, they picked up 18 tons of garbage that they bring in—the baby diapers and all that. Where's everybody who wants to preserve the desert?"[31]

Arpaio is hardly an environmentalist, seeking to preserve the desert. He's far more interested in preserving white native-born entitlement to the desert. Perhaps the most visible public figure seeking to close the border to Mexican immigration, he seems to revel in accusations of racism (he is said to have found it "an honor" to be compared to the KKK, since "it means we're doing something"). He's been under federal indictment for racial profiling (which he admits), for setting up some of the most miserable jail conditions in America, including a tent city for overflow inmates (which he calls a "concentration camp"), feeding inmates surplus food, limiting meals to twice a day, and forcing inmates to wear pink underwear as a sign of their humiliation.

But Arpaio is also a figurehead in the anti-immigration movement and one of the more willing to see the battle as between "real men" and poseurs. While Mexican men are lazy, dependent on welfare, dirty, and clearly unable to maintain the necessary self-control to be real

Americans, they're also bloodthirsty soldiers in a war of reconquest. "My parents did not regard any inch of American soil as somehow belonging to Italy, so their arrival here never constituted a 'reconquest' of that land. A growing movement among not only Mexican nationals, but also some Mexican-Americans contends that the United States stole the territory that is now California, Arizona and Texas, for a start, and that massive immigration over the border will speed and guarantee the *reconquista* of these lands, returning them to Mexico."[32]

Arpaio is hardly alone. Take Harley Brown, a perennial candidate for office in Idaho. (He ran unsuccessfully for Congress in 2010.) In his campaign for the state's sole congressional seat, Brown, who bills himself as "A Real Man for Congress," outlined his policy positions:

> THE MIDDLE EAST: "Nuke Their Ass, Take Their Gas"
> GUN CONTROL: "Hitting Your Target"
> GAYS IN THE MILITARY: "Keep the Queens Out of the Marines"
> IMMIGRATION POLICY: "Adios, Amigos"

Sure, Brown is a life-size cartoon, a caricature of the crazed armchair warrior, a Duke Nukem who has never been to actual war. But Brown expresses the epigrammatic anger of a wide band of American men who are joining the Tea Parties, rural militias, Minutemen, and Patriot groups to patrol our borders. "The Zoo has an African lion and the White House has a lyin' African," commented one Tea Party placard.

As with Limbaugh's legions, it was difficult to get any of the Tea Party protesters I met at any of the sparsely attended rallies I observed to say anything of more substance than the aphorisms that were already on their placards. I'd ask what I thought was an innocent question, and I usually got puzzled looks, as though I might have been speaking a different language. For example, at one rally, I asked a nicely dressed older guy named Ralph, a former sales rep perhaps in his late sixties, who was wearing khakis, a plaid shirt, and a three-cornered hat, what about the original Boston Tea Party had proved so inspiring to him. "They revolted against taxation from an illegitimate government," he said flatly, as if he were reciting a catechism. "They were revolting against a government takeover." When I asked what he meant, he said—as did every single Tea Partier with whom I spoke—that Obamacare was socialized medicine that would raise taxes on the middle class. "It's part of the plan. They want to take over everything. But America was founded on the idea that the government couldn't tell you what to do. We need to get back to that."

Such contentless statements are what often passes for political discourse in America in 2013. When I tried, foolishly, as it turned out, to ask exactly how universal health care would raise taxes, or raise the cost of care, or how government spending on such things as education, highways, or the GI Bill augured a government takeover, or how government regulations to rein in corporate greed somehow hurt middle-class Americans—well, I got initially puzzled looks, followed pretty quickly by more hostile glares and a simple shrug as they walked off. Slogans are the Tea Party's version of political theory; oft-repeated falsehoods gradually become self-evident truths.

I heard the same thing when I talked with anti-immigrant groups. These groups see illegal immigration as an "alien invasion," as the Minutemen do. And most see the repulsion of this invading horde as akin to the colonials kicking out the British colonists in 1776. (It's one of the great ironies of the current nativist movement that it cloaks itself in the language of the founding fathers, but its politics are far more reminiscent of those of King George III. Well, except for that fact that he taxed the colonials to further his own ambition.) The Minutemen, another private paramilitary band of white middle- and working-class guys in border states who patrol the borders, doing the job that they believe our own immigration police fail to do, are most explicit in calling for a second American Revolution against a tyrannical King Barack. "Do the citizens of the United States view the Federal Government as an oppressive force occupying Washington? There came a point in American history—April 19, 1775—that the colonists could no longer tolerate oppression of the occupying forces that consumed their rights and led to the revolution. It was a moment in history, which not only shocked the Kingdom of Great Britain, but also set off a cascade effect that is still felt today."[33]

And these sentiments are not limited only to the southwestern border states. I talked to people who were demonstrating against the building of an interfaith Islamic community center in Lower Manhattan, who seemed to think that establishing a place for dialogue and day care was establishing a beachhead on Normandy Beach in preparation for the full-on assault on the capital of the world economy.

(These are the same people who complain that the "legitimate" Muslim world did not immediately condemn the terrorist attacks of 9/11. When a group actually does want to build a bridge, they're accused of refusing to design it properly.)

One of the most horrific cases happened, in fact, right around the corner from my campus on Long Island. Long Island is the quintessential American suburb—one of the first suburbs in the nation. Its demographic profile—largely white and middle class, with a significant influx of immigrants and minorities in recent decades—makes it a cauldron in which anti-immigrant sentiment bubbles up to unify disparate levels of discontent. Here, in those split-level houses atop those leafy front lawns, breathes the same rage that drives pickup trucks along the Texas-Mexico border, patrolling illegal immigrants and attacking their families.

Farmingville is a "typical" middle-class Long Island suburb. But in 2004 it erupted when two Mexican day laborers were attacked and nearly murdered by a gang of white male suburbanites. Not far away, in 2008 an Ecuadoran immigrant named Marcelo Lucero was attacked by seven white teenagers and stabbed to death simply because of his ethnicity. Lucero had been walking with a friend near the Long Island Rail Road station around midnight in November 2008 when they were confronted by the white teenagers who had gone out specifically looking for a Hispanic to attack. "Let's go beat up some Mexican guys," they had said. They found one, and they killed him. Four of the teenage boys pleaded guilty to the hate crime and testified against the other three.

Although we northerners are used to feeling horror, revulsion, and more than a little contempt for the white South when we hear about racist lynchings in the Jim Crow South, we don't really know how to absorb that such things are happening all over our country. The siege mentality, the defense against invasion—these are themes that echo across all classes and in every region.

This notion that America is under siege contains several layers of anxiety among white American men. The fear that "they" are taking over is an insult to "our" manhood—for they will take our jobs, our homes, and our women if we are not vigilant. The fear that they are taking what is rightfully ours—a government that serves *our* needs to be left alone, as opposed to *their* need to have everything handed to them on a silver platter. The fear that we are being emasculated—by these less than fully manly hordes and by a feckless government utterly in their thrall.

In a sense, the government that is imagined by Angry White Men embodies the same hyper- and hypomasculine qualities that the "other" embodies. On the one hand, the government is weak, having been invaded by all these special interests (like women or unions or minorities or gays and lesbians) and unable to resist being taken over by them. The "others" are the real men, more masculine than the government, which has become weak, a "nanny state," feminized.

On the other hand, the government is voracious, taxing and regulating, greedy beyond measure. Hypermasculine, it subdues the raw, noble masculinity of the heroic American white man and subordinates it to the ignoble, undeserving, unmanly hordes clamoring for what we have. This is a government that doesn't "permit" others to learn in their native language and thus become integrated; it's a government that will pretty soon require that everyone speak Spanish. Thus, "English only" is not arrogant and entitled but protectionist, just holding on to what we have.

Angry White Men are thus stuck—between a voracious state and the hypermasculine invading army, or between a feminized nanny state and these dependent, weak, and irresponsible masses. Or perhaps it's more of a mix and match: a hypermasculine alien force capturing the weakened state, or a greedy nanny state taking from us, from real men, and giving to those whining, victim-mongering wimps. The permutations are far less important than the result of the equation: we, we once-happy few, we American men, who built this country with our own hands, are now having it wrenched from us and given to these undeserving others. Right under our noses.

The thread that ties together these disparate and often contradictory strands is gender—masculinity. These tropes float, collide, contradict, but they fit together in an ever-shifting cosmology because they are bound together by codes of gender. "They" emasculate "us"—both by being more primally masculine than we are (and thus in need of control) and, simultaneously, by being dependent and weak (and thus needing the state to control "us" from succeeding). Only from the position of aggrieved entitlement can these various images be reconciled—irrationally, but viscerally.

ANGRY WHITE MEN AT THE MOVIES

Perhaps media will give us some relief. What if some white guys, moved to righteous anger, can single-handedly halt an alien invasion, a horde of zombies, a crowd of vampires, or a brilliantly coordinated band of terrorists? What if I play some first-person-shooter video game and can wipe out the entire terrorist conspiracy with only my biceps, an assault weapon that never runs out of ammunition, and the ability to jump onto roofs from a standing position three stories below? After all, it's a psychological axiom that what we lose in reality, we re-create in fantasy. If we feel ourselves losing, how will we get back what is rightfully ours to begin with?

American men have always flocked to action movies where the heroes rise victorious from the ashes, bloodied and battered, but always unbowed. Earlier films that attracted angry white male resentment saw heroic men constrained by institutional ennui or bureaucratic red tape—like GI Joe, or Dirty Harry. Sylvester Stallone in *Rambo* played a guy who single-handedly returned to Vietnam to win the war that the bureaucrats lost, a triumph of will over red tape and institutional corruption. Movies like the *Die Hard* and *Rush Hour* series have proved extremely versatile, as renegade cops prove themselves heroes, despite the doubting skeptics. (No other country produces guy flicks with such consistent themes.)

Of course, there are counterexamples of cross-racial pairings, like the black-white buddies in the *Lethal Weapon* series, or *Rush Hour* (black and Asian), or films of women who are as heroic as men, like Demi Moore in *GI Jane*. And they've become such a genre that they have spawned a subgenre of near-satiric films, in which the aging stars participate in their own self-parody, like *The Other Guys* or *Red* or *The Expendables*.

American films are among the most gendered in the world: men tend to like action movies in which, as one producer explained to me, they "blow shit up" (this was offered as a technical Hollywood phrase), and women tend to like chick flicks in which grown-up women try to navigate the thorny world of grown-up relationships despite the fact that most of the men in their lives are big babies.

Several films go further and have captured the zeitgeist of Angry White Men. A film like *Office Space* or *Horrible Bosses*, for example, provides a few comedic moments in its effort to show how white men who are trying to do the right thing and work hard to make a living are continually thwarted by arbitrary and cruelly sadistic bosses. For younger men, *Fight Club* has become the touchstone cinematic text of the guys in their mid- to late twenties that I interviewed for *Guyland*. The film, like the novel on which it's based, is a sustained assault on middle-class male existence, a critique of the life that men have to live these days. They live in boxes, work in boxes, drive to work in boxes, are utterly cushioned and protected and safe and driven mad by their things. As Chuck Palahniuk writes in the novel, "You buy furniture. You tell yourself, this is the last sofa I will ever need in my life. Buy the sofa, then for a couple years you're satisfied that no matter what goes wrong, at least you've got your sofa issue handled. Then the right set of dishes. Then the perfect bed. The drapes. The rug. Then you're trapped in your lovely nest, and the things you used to own, now they own you."

Modern men have no identity, no soul. They're lost, confused, aimless, adrift. In one of the film's most memorable soliloquies, Tyler Durden says, "You are not your job. You're not how much money you have in the bank. You're not the car you drive. You're not the contents of your wallet. You're not your fucking khakis." (I will return to this film in Chapter 6 when I discuss how middle-class white guys are coping with changing working conditions.)

No movie encapsulates this decline of the white-collar guy into the blind-rage angry white male politics of despair better than *Falling Down* (1993). The film, directed by Joel Schumacher and starring Michael Douglas, is an allegory of the besieged middle-class white man. Having bought into the American Dream, even after his layoff from an aerospace company in the Los Angeles area, William Foster, whose vanity license plate reads "D-Fens," becomes progressively unhinged as the traditional props of privileged white masculinity are shed. He's blindsided by his sudden unemployment and divorce—his wife wants greater independence also—and he's torn apart by his inability to get to his daughter's birthday party. (His wife has taken out a restraining order against him, and he is legally barred from seeing her.)

Determined to get to the party regardless, Foster's journey leads to an encounter with pretty much every single "other" that is perceived as threatening to white males in America today: young Latino men (here gangbangers); upwardly mobile, hardworking Asian immigrants (who own a deli); a beautiful policewoman—all of whom he blames for his inability to cling to both economic security and mental stability. He even scares a few fat-cat rich white guys on a golf course. In one scene, Foster explains a sort of moral economy to a Korean grocer: he is willing to pay for what he wants—but only at 1965 prices, the year that the immigration laws changed.

At one point, Foster enters an army surplus store. By now, he's beaten up Latino gang members and the Korean grocer and is wanted by the police. The store owner perceives him as a fellow white supremacist and shows him some World War II memorabilia, including some empty gas canisters used in the gas chambers at Auschwitz. This enrages Foster. He assaults the store owner, shouting, "You're not like me! I'm just a man who's trying to get home! You're insane!" Angry white men are *not* the lunatic fringe, Foster is saying, just guys trying to make their way home.

Of course, he has no home—no wife, no family, because he has already become somewhat unhinged. He's spiraling downward, and his impotent rampage leads inevitably to his death: traditional masculinity cannot be resurrected, and even the old pillars of white male entitlement—racism, sexism, nativism—cannot keep the edifice from falling down.

A similar theme is sounded in *Gran Torino* (2008), Clint Eastwood's ode to the sacrificial heroism of white working-class American men. The movie proceeds toward a similar, and equally inevitable, outcome. If William Foster is blindsided by his decline, Eastwood's character, Walt Kowalski, eventually accepts it elegiacally; his death is heroic and sacrificial, whereas Foster's is defiant and uncomprehending. It took fifteen years, but now the angry white man surrenders to his fate.

Kowalski evokes the pre-1960s white working class. A Korean War veteran, widower, and retired blue-collar Ford factory worker in Detroit, he's embittered and unbowed. All he wants is to be left alone. He fought a war in Asia, and now all he sees are Asians moving into his working-class neighborhood of small, clean homes and well-cut lawns. He's an equal-opportunity racist—he hates everyone, including "those jabbering gooks" (the Hmong who have moved next door). In one of the film's most strangely touching scenes, he teaches Thao, his young

Hmong neighbor, how to navigate acceptable racist put-downs in a barbershop. (It was Thao who had tried, on a dare, to steal Walt's car, the 1972 Gran Torino of the film's name, Walt's vintage prize automobile that he had, himself, helped to build.)

The film offers the viewer the same elegiac, sentimental pathos that his antiwestern *Unforgiven* (1992) offered—a sacrificial coming to terms with the new, multicultural world. Walt, like Moses, can see the promised land, but can't enter it. He realizes that these "gooks" are decent, hard-working Americans, like him, and in the end he not only sacrifices himself for them, but leaves his prized car to Thao as a parting gift—and a parting blow to his saccharine children and spoiled granddaughter.

The extreme Right did not appreciate Walt's sacrifice. In a review of the film in a white supremacist magazine, Stephen Webster calls it "dishonest," because it "convincingly portrays the dispossession of white, middle-class America . . . graciously giving way to its non-white future." At the end, Webster complains, "we are led to believe that although immigrants are alien to begin with, they will soon become good Americans—perhaps even better Americans than whites."[34]

What they miss, of course, is that Walt embodies the very masculine characteristics they claim to admire and the ones that are in such short supply these days among American men: honor, sacrifice, courage. Walt's self-sacrifice is not because "they" are better Americans than he is, but rather it's Walt who shows them—and shows us all—that heroic sacrifice is noble in the service of others. Now that he has understood that his stereotypes were wrong, and that the Hmong family is worthy and virtuous, his actions are the ultimate demonstration of heroic masculinity—a demonstration that the extreme right wing, blinded by racism and nativism, couldn't possibly see.

ANGRY WHITE WOMEN

Of course, by now most of you are ready to remind me that it's not just white men who are angry. Quite true. There are plenty of angry people of color—both male and female. And plenty of them feel some amount of aggrieved entitlement—feeling "entitled" to an even playing field in education, employment, or housing, to health care, to the right to vote without some arcane new law that throws up obstacles. And, to be fair, many poor and working people, of all races, feel entitled to government support for health care, for food and financial support if they are unemployed, for support to raise their children. That is, they tend to feel entitled while looking "up," looking at what their country tells them they are entitled to—equality, fairness, an equal chance at making it.

Angry White Men feel entitled while looking "down"—at the hordes of "others" who are threatening to take what they believe is rightfully theirs and are being aided in their illegitimate quest by a government that is in their thrall. It's ironic that the Angry White Men I am discussing in this book feel they can actually get what they are entitled to only if the government shrinks—nearly to the point of disappearing. By contrast, poor people should—I emphasize the normative—understand that they can get what they want only if the government expands to stimulate growth, promote consumer spending, and provide a social safety net.

This irony is resolved not by some abstract analysis of entitlement, but by a sense of historical context. Angry White Men tend to feel their sense of aggrieved entitlement because of the past; they want to restore what they *once had*. Their entitlement is not aspirational; it's nostalgic. Poor people and people of color, by contrast, feel entitled to what they *should have*, what others in fact do have. Angry white men feel entitled to restrict equality; people of color want to expand it.

And, of course, there are legions of angry white women. Since 2008 they've been mobilized through the Tea Party and its standard-bearers, former Alaska governor Sarah Palin and Minnesota congresswoman Michele Bachman. Angry white women are decidedly not upper-middle-class, Volvo-station-wagon-driving, Chardonnay-sipping soccer moms. They're hockey moms, drinking beer and driving Chevy pickups. (Palin famously explained the difference between a hockey mom and a pit bull: lipstick.) Now they've declared themselves "mama grizzlies."

At first glance, the presence of so many women in the Tea Party— surely, one of the angriest white people's organizations this side of the Klan—would tend to undermine my argument that the current political rage is such a gendered phenomenon. In addition to their femme fatale standard-bearers, many of the most visible leaders of the movement are also women, like Jenny Beth Martin of the Tea Party Patriots,

Amy Kremer of the Tea Party Express, and Tabitha Hale of Freedom-Works.[35] Keli Carender, then a thirty-year-old Seattle woman, is often credited with initiating the whole movement, even before CNBC host Rick Santelli famously used the phrase on the air (although his utterance was what mobilized the well-publicized and well-financed and male-backed events). According to *Slate* writer Hanna Rosin, six of the eight board members of Tea Party Patriots, their national coordinators, are women; fifteen of the twenty-five state coordinators are women.[36]

That's not, of course, to say that the Tea Party is a "women's movement." Its rank and file tend to be male: the typical Tea Partier, according to a *New York Times*/CBS poll, is white, male, married, and older than forty-five—similar to the typical Limbaugh listener.[37] But that is illusive, since nearly half of the Tea Party members are female. And yes, it's also true that the big money behind all these spontaneous eruptions of populist sentiment is male—in fact, the overwhelming amount of funding comes from the billionaire Koch brothers, fabulously wealthy right-wingers who want to foment the illusion of a populist groundswell.

As a result, it's been easy for some to write off the Tea Party as internally incoherent—epitomized by the "Keep the Government Out of My Medicare" placard—and often contradictory, with members perfectly happy with *their* benefits, but unwilling to extend them to anyone else. The Tea Party's been castigated as a fake populism, manipulated from outside by powerful corporate interests (which is, itself, ironic, since so much of their message is also tending toward the anticorporate). The male money financing the movement also leads many to dismiss the gender of so many of its followers. That's also a mistake. The Tea Party is a populist movement, a movement from below—it just happens to be directed at those even further below them (minorities, immigrants) and those in the government who are seen as supporting them.

Populism is an emotion, not a political ideology. And its dominant emotion is outrage at what is being done to "us," the little guy. This is true of populisms of the Left, like the American populists of the turn of the last century or the Spanish anarchists or even the Parisian mob so lovingly portrayed in *Les Miserables,* just as it is true of populisms of the Right, like the Italian Fascists or the violent anti-immigrant Know-Nothings of mid-nineteenth-century America (and equally lovingly portrayed in *Gangs of New York*).

So let's acknowledge that the anger of the Tea Party is real. It's just not true. That distinction is important for us: Tea Partiers are right to be angry. There is a lot to be angry about. But like all the other groups I describe in the book, they are delivering their mail to the wrong address.

So, what of the women of the Tea Party? What is the particularly gendered source of their anger?

In some cases, these angry white women of the Right are living lives very much like their leaders, who are making a career out of telling women they shouldn't pursue careers. But in other cases, as historian Ruth Rosen points out, the Tea Party acknowledges that these women need to work, that some even *choose* to work. Excluded from the Republican Party (GOP standing for Grand Old Patriarchs), these working women do not—*cannot*—embrace the traditional roles that the party might have envisioned for them.[38]

What Rosen misses, I think, is that they want to. The women of the Tea Party believe themselves entitled to live in a traditional, conservative household. Their sense of aggrieved entitlement runs parallel to the men's: they *want* their men to be the traditional heads of households, able to support their families. They want to be *moms*, not "women."

Look at how they describe themselves: hockey moms and mama grizzlies. "It seems like it's kind of a mom awakening," said Sarah Palin in a 2012 speech. It's "a lot of mama bears worried about their families," says spokeswoman Rebecca Wales.[39]

Listen to Debbie, a thirty-eight-year-old mother of three, whom I met at a Tea Party rally in Harrisburg, Pennsylvania. "I'm afraid. You know, I think I'm angry because I'm so afraid. I'm afraid that we're bankrupting our children. We're spending so much, in debt up to our eyeballs, and who's going to have to pay for that? My kids. Their kids. We're going to leave them a complete mess—a debt-ridden country where immigrants feed off our taxes like we're goddamned breast-feeding them. It's just wrong. It's all upside down."

Debbie's sentiments were echoed by pretty much every one of the Tea Party women with whom I spoke. Again, their statements were largely aphoristic and contentless. But their fears and their anger were real. In their view, the government is a misguided sponge, slurping up all the resources from hardworking "real" Americans and then squeezing it out all over the undeserving, unwashed, undocumented. "I can't believe we've gone so wrong," says Lucy, a forty-one-year-old bookkeeper and mother of two. "The way we tax and spend, we will have nothing left for our children. We're breaking open their piggy bank, instead of putting money into it!"

Tea Party women speak as mothers, not as women. Their language is more reminiscent of another "women's" movement at the turn of the last century: the temperance movement. They speak of caregiving, of mothering, of fixing the mess that men have made of things. They are going to clean up the national household—since women, the bearers of morality and sobriety, are better at cleaning up the messes in their own homes.

Feminist in practice, antifeminist in theory, conservative feminism hopes to secure the economy so that women can return to their families and their homes and leave the labor force. If liberal feminists are housewives who want to be working, these conservative feminists are working women who want to be housewives.[40]

Of course, there are class differences: when those liberal feminists are eager to enter the labor force, they're thinking not of being cashiers or secretaries or waitresses, but of being accountants and lawyers. Even in the labor force, Tea Party women think as women, not as workers. When they campaign against higher taxes or government intervention, it's less about the rights of entrepreneurs to keep their profits and more about balancing household accounts, shrinking family budgets, unsustainable spending. They're concerned about the economy this generation is leaving for its children. As one sign at a Tea Party rally put it, "My Kid Isn't Your ATM."[41]

That seems to be the particular genius of the Tea Party. Alongside traditionally libertarian slogans about smaller government and lower taxes—words like *autonomy, individual,* and *freedom*—the Tea Party has added words like *family, community, children,* and *mother.* The Tea Party mobilizes angry white women alongside angry white men, wannabe stay-at-home moms alongside wannabe domestic patriarchs, looking back to a long-gone era in which white men went to work, supported their wives and families, and all the government programs that enabled and supported that—the roads, the bridges, the schools, the training sites, the military—were paid for invisibly, so it appeared that they had built it all by themselves.

The future of the Tea Party is unclear. But one thing that is clear is that it's going to have fewer women. Women flocked to the Tea Party as a populist movement because the Republican Party had so long ignored them, especially as mothers. But the Tea Party has done little to address distinctively *mothers'* needs, either. Republican corporatist economic policies don't hold much appeal; corporations would prefer to staunch any trickle-down economics; they'd like tax policies and regulation to better turn the faucets upward in a reverse waterfall. The very programs that mothers need to have the lives they actually say they want—the *option* to work, with well-fed and -clothed children, who go to good schools, and remain healthy—require massive government expenditures.

Support among white women is waning; according to a *Washington Post* poll, white women were less interested in and less positive about the Tea Party in 2012 than they were in 2011, whereas rates of approval among white men have remained relatively stable. The Tea Party will, most likely, come increasingly to resemble all the other populist iterations of aggrieved entitlement: white, southern, midwestern and rural, lower middle class, overeducated, or underemployed—that is, downwardly mobile, if not from their family of origin, then at least downwardly mobile from the expectations they had about where they'd end up. And male. For women, aggrieved entitlement may be more of a fleeting emotional response to setbacks; for men, it may become more of a way of life.

2 | Angry White Boys

I am not insane. I am angry.

—LUKE WOODHAM (AGE SIXTEEN),
  PEARL HIGH SCHOOL, PEARL, MISSISSIPPI

We've always wanted to do this. This is payback.
We've dreamed of doing this for years. This is for
all the shit you put us through. This is what you
deserve.

— ERIC HARRIS (AGE EIGHTEEN) AND DYLAN KLEBOLD (AGE
  SEVENTEEN), COLUMBINE HIGH SCHOOL, LITTLETON, COLORADO

By now the story has been told so often it's begun to have the gloss of fable. On a sunny Tuesday morning in April 1999, two seniors walked calmly through the halls of Columbine High School, opening fire, seemingly randomly, on their fellow students. By the time the carnage was over, twelve students and one teacher lay dead, alongside the two troubled teenagers who had pulled the triggers. Another twenty-four were injured. More than a dozen years and several novels and movies later, a large security apparatus has appeared in suburban schools, the phrase "pull a Columbine" is uttered menacingly almost daily in countless high schools and middle schools across the country, and Dylan Klebold and Eric Harris have joined a parade of storied killers that includes Bonnie and Clyde, Billy the Kid, and Babyface Nelson. To some current high schoolers, they're Butch and Sundance; to others, they're Leopold and Loeb. (The rampage was the second-most-covered emerging news story of the entire decade of the 1990s, edged out only by the O. J. Simpson car chase.)[1]

In the immediate aftermath of that horrific day, there was no shortage of facile armchair explanations offered by observers. Some suggested Goth music and particularly Marilyn Manson. President Clinton thought it might be the Internet. Dr. Phil chimed in, blaming violent video games. Right-wing pundits like Newt Gingrich credited the hippie embrace of freedom of the 1960s, and Thomas Sowell argued that the '60s exonerated individuals from responsibility (it was "society's fault"). Speaker of the House Tom DeLay just blamed day care, the teaching of evolution, and "working mothers who take birth control pills."[2]

Then came the somewhat more reasoned academic explanations. Maybe, some thought, it's the media. "Parents don't realize that taking four-year-olds to *True Lies*—a fun movie for adults but excessively violent—is poison to their brain," noted educational avatar Michael Gurian. In her erudite warning on violence, Sissela Bok suggested that the Internet and violent video games "bring into homes depictions of graphic violence . . . never available to children and young people in the past," which undermines kids' resilience and self-control.[3]

Or perhaps it's guns. After all, firearms are the second-leading cause of death to children between ten and fourteen, the eighth-leading cause of death to those aged one to four. In 1994, 80 percent of juvenile murderers used a firearm; in 1984, only 50 percent did.[4]

But the amount of violent media content has surely been increasing, while at the same time youth violence generally and school violence in particular have actually been decreasing. Juvenile violence involving guns has also been in decline since 1994 (largely as a result of the decline of the crack epidemic). As liberal firebrand Michael Moore reminded us, there are more rifles per capita in Canada than in the United States, and there have been no Canadian rampage school shootings. (In both Britain and Australia, where there had been rampage shootings, intensified gun-control laws have ensured that there have been no repeats.)

Maybe it's both. Barry Krisberg, president of the National Council on Crime and Delinquency, said that "the violence in the media and the easy availability of guns are what is driving the slaughter of innocents," while then NRA president Charlton Heston believed the problem was actually not enough guns. Had there been armed guards in the schools, he argued, the shooting would have ended instantly— which is also what the current NRA executive vice president, Wayne LaPierre, said after the mass shooting at Sandy Hook Elementary School in Newtown, Connecticut. But boys everywhere are frustrated, abused, and saturated with media violence, although not all of them live in places where guns are so readily available.[5]

Some have proposed psychological variables as possible explanations, including a history of childhood abuse, absent fathers, dominant mothers, violence in childhood, unstable family environments, or the mothers' fear of their children. All possible. But empirically, it appears that none hold up. Most shooters come from intact and relatively stable families, with no reports of child abuse.

Subsequent government-supported investigations—such as the FBI report, the surgeon general's report *Youth Violence*, and the Bureau of Justice Statistics' "Indicators of School Crime and Safety, 2000," as well as a major study of bullying—all concentrated on identifying potential antecedents of school violence, such as media influence, drugs and alcohol behavior, Internet usage, father absence, and parental neglect.[6] But surely these influences are far too universal to predict why some kids who are subject to these large-scale influences pick up guns and others—the overwhelming majority, in fact—don't.

These large-scale cultural explanations got so vague, so grandiose, that they were utterly unpersuasive. We needed to get closer.

Since then, our tendency has been to abandon the search for bigger sociological interpretations, as if Columbine represented some frightening trend, and to look closer, a lot closer, at each individual event. Most recently, in *Columbine*, published on the tenth anniversary of that tragic day, journalist Dave Cullen completely jettisons a bird's-eye view of that tragic school shooting in favor of an extreme close-up psychological portrait of Eric Harris and Dylan Klebold. Like a pointillist painting, each dot of color is rendered in excruciating detail, as we read about Harris's deep-seated psychopathologies and Klebold's eagerness to be accepted by his sociopathic friend and mentor.[7]

Cullen's right, of course—as right as any analyst of those tiny dots of color can be. Any event, I imagine, looked at closely enough, ceases to resemble any other, as the existential uniqueness of the individuals involved makes comparison with other events impossible. It's no doubt true that Harris externalized his rage at the world and his contempt for those he considered inferior and that Klebold, depressed and suicidal, followed him like a lost puppy.[8]

Such an analysis begs several questions, however. How did such a decidedly disturbed kid manage to fool everyone who ever came into contact with him, as he glided under the radar of every parent, teacher, administrator, and guidance counselor? And why is that same phenomenon true of all the other school shooters—that few, if any, adults in their lives noticed just how disturbed they were? Are our schools so poorly run, or teachers and administrators so blind, or our nation's parents in such denial or so oblivious that they have no idea what is happening with their obviously psychotic children?

In one sense, Cullen is right. These boys acted because they were so psychologically troubled that they could have been diagnosed as psychotic. He also misses the point. After all, Klebold and Harris weren't the first school shooters. And as the multitude of subsequent shootings have tragically shown—from Santee, California, to Sandy Hook Elementary School—nor are they the last.

But what Klebold and Harris did represent was a new type of rampage school shooters; they finally forced us to notice something that had been happening for some time. Up until 1990 or so, school shootings fitted a certain profile. They took place in urban schools, where one boy, almost always a boy of color, would carry a handgun into school, looking for a particular target, either because of a romantic dispute, a drug deal gone south, or the escalation of group animosities. (In some cases, it's true that the shooter had been "dared" to do it, his masculinity relentlessly questioned, having been the target of gay baiting and bullying. But even then, he wasn't out to "show the world" he was a man; he was just confronting the guy who dissed him.)

By 1990 these school shootings had become rare, partly because metal detectors had been installed and police officers had been stationed in many high-risk urban schools. As a result, the number of such school shootings dropped dramatically. (This was also due to an artifact of the data collection. Since schools now had metal detectors and armed security personnel, it seemed much easier to wait just off school property for one's target to appear before opening fire. If the incident took place just off the formal boundary of the school, it was not counted in the category "school violence.")

But beginning in the late 1980s to early 1990s, the profile of the school shooter shifted dramatically. Now, the shooter was almost always white, from a suburban or rural school, using rifles or assault weapons, and opening fire seemingly randomly, killing teachers and fellow students. Since 1999 rampage school shooters have also committed suicide at the end of their rampages—sort of "suicide by mass murder": take as many of "them" with you as you can before you take your own life. And, it seems, they don't just want to get even with their tormentors any longer; they want to go out in a blaze of glory, to be remembered, to be "famous." (Harris and Klebold left a videotape; Cho sent one to the news media.) School shooters used to want to get even; now they want to be celebrities.

In fact, there was only one constant in those two profiles. They were all boys. All of them. Does that not merit attention? And should we not pay attention to race, now that virtually every single rampage school shooter since 1987 was also white? What about region—since all but a couple were in rural or suburban schools?

Take a little thought experiment. Imagine all the rampage school shooters in Littleton, Colorado; Pearl, Mississippi; Paducah, Kentucky; Springfield, Oregon; and Jonesboro, Arkansas; now imagine they were black girls from poor families who lived instead in Chicago, New Haven, Newark, Philadelphia, or Providence.

Can you picture the national debate, the headlines, the handwringing? There is no doubt we'd be having a national debate about inner-city poor black girls. The entire focus would be on race, class, and gender. The media would doubtless invent a new term for their behavior, as with *wilding* two decades ago. We'd hear about the culture of poverty, about how living in the city breeds crime and violence. We'd hear some pundits proclaim some putative natural tendency among blacks toward violence. Someone would likely even blame feminism for causing girls to become violent in a vain imitation of boys.

Yet the obvious fact that virtually all the rampage school shooters were middle-class white boys barely broke a ripple in the torrent of public discussion. This uniformity cut across all other differences among the shooters: some came from intact families, others from single-parent homes; some boys had acted violently in the past, and others were quiet and unassuming; some boys also expressed rage at their parents (two killed their parents the same morning), and others seemed to live in happy families.

But these categories—race, class, gender—provide the middle ground between the pointillism of David Cullen's myopic approach and the vague abstractionism of the government-sponsored studies, which paint on such a large canvas as to universalize the events out of any specificity.

A more comprehensive analysis of the school shooters stands further back from that pointillist painting, where the microdots of juxtaposed color actually form discernible patterns, where the minimalist details form recognizable shapes that make such individual psychologies comprehensible. That's why humans invented such concepts as categories in the first place, as cognitive devices that enable us to see such social patterns.

We need not ignore the individual pathologies of Eric Harris and Dylan Klebold; it neither diminishes the horror of their crime nor elevates them to some status as sublimely martyred victims to acknowledge that Harris and Klebold exhibited some similarities—and some differences—with Michael Carneal, Barry Loukaitis, Evan Ramsey, Gary Scott Pennington, Luke Woodham, Andy Williams, Kip Kinkel, and all the rest of the young suburban white boys who opened fire on their classmates and teachers.

To ignore these "categories"—all were boys, all but one were white, all but two were suburban or rural—is to have no sense of the forest in which these boys were lost, but a very good idea of the texture of any individual leaf. Race, region, religion—all these and more shape the social context in which school shootings take place.

There are discernible patterns that compose profiles of school shooters. Peter Langman, a researcher at KidPeace Children's Hospital, constructed a typology of shooters that ranges from "traumatized" boys (those, like Evan Ramsey or Jeffrey Weise, who came from broken homes and suffered sexual or physical abuse), "psychotic" boys (such as Michael Carneal, Kip Kinkel, and Seung-Hui Cho, who came from intact families but exhibited schizophrenic symptoms that might have included hallucinations, voices, and other ideations), and "psychopathic" boys (like Eric Harris and Andrew Golden, who were consumed by narcissistic rage and a lack of empathy). Such a model helps understand the psychological spectrum on which these boys might have fallen, though given the number of other boys who don't fit the model, it's of limited utility.[9]

School shootings are a psychiatric issue, to be sure, but they are also a community issue if no responsible adult notices the psychopaths in their midst. It's a sociological issue, given the eerie similarities among the shooters. And it's a cultural issue, an issue of how we educate our children and what sorts of differences we tolerate—and which ones we don't.

From an early age, boys learn that violence is not only an acceptable form of conflict resolution, but one that is admired. Four times more teenage boys than teenage girls think fighting is appropriate when someone cuts into the front of a line. Half of all teenage boys get into a physical fight each year.

These are not just misguided "kids," or "youth," or "troubled teens"—they're boys. All of them. They are a group of boys, deeply aggrieved by a system that they may feel is cruel or demeaning, or, in the case of Eric Harris's fraudulent reversal, beneath him. Feeling aggrieved, wronged by the world—these are boilerplate adolescent feelings, common to many boys and girls. What transforms the aggrieved into mass murders is also a sense of entitlement, a sense that using violence against others, making others hurt as you hurt, is fully justified. Aggrieved entitlement justifies revenge against those who have wronged you; it is the compensation for humiliation. Humiliation is emasculation: humiliate someone, and you take away his manhood. For many men, humiliation must be avenged, or you cease to be a man. Aggrieved entitlement is a gendered emotion, a fusion of that humiliating loss of manhood and the moral obligation and entitlement to get it back. And its gender is masculine. "Some young men experienced a sense of humiliation that emerged from perceptions of loss of privilege made evident in schools; and when merged with fantasies of retribution and images of a form of masculinity grounded in violent action, their sense of humiliation led some young men to open fire in schools."[10]

Humiliation is so injurious to the psyche, so threatening to the self, that it must be healed. When that sense of self is gendered, it is masculinity that must be restored. Anger and rage are the translation of that humiliation into the potential for action. And anger can mobilize the self to retrieve and restore the individual's sense of masculinity through any means possible, including violence.

PROFILING THE SHOOTERS

Random school shootings are extremely rare. More than 99 percent of public high schools have never had a homicide—and never will. Not only that, but their incidence varies widely. According to the National School Safety and Security Services website, the total number of school-related violent deaths varies from a low of eleven in 2009–2010 to a high of forty-nine in 2002–2003. Curiously, the numbers seem to vary in cycles—two to three years at low rates in the low teens, and then more than doubling for the next three or four years, only to drop back down again. Since the total numbers are so low to begin with, it's possible that these cycles are episodic and random, correlating with one or two well-publicized incidents in one year that led to a spate of deaths for a couple of years, only to return to preevent levels.[11]

Yet since 1999, virtually all the shootings—and, even more, the rampages that were planned but were thwarted by more alert parents, kids, or teachers who notified authorities—referenced Columbine as their template model of what a shooting should look like. Columbine is now more than a tragedy; it is also a trope, a cultural reference point. The history of school shootings is now demarcated by Columbine; rampages can be sorted into "pre-Columbine" or "post-Columbine."

Before Columbine, sociologist Ralph Larkin explains, shootings were more "personal"—focusing on specific perceived injustices, female rejections of male romantic interest, or personal revenge for bullying and humiliation. Since Columbine, rampages have generally moved upward in age, largely to college campuses where surveillance is more lax and access to weapons is easier, but also because the mental illnesses that produce these paroxysms of violence have had longer to develop and manifest. All have been boys, and all have been solo efforts. Of those that have been thwarted—there were at least thirty—several were pairs or groups, and one, in New Bedford, Massachusetts, involved a girl with three boys, but she eventually broke ranks and warned a teacher she particularly liked who had been marked for death.[12]

The post-Columbine pattern has been more "political," all targeting the supposed "jock culture" that, to the plotters, so dominated the school's culture as to make daily life a constant torture. Columbine has now become the single script upon which virtually every other shooter has drawn.

But what causes the unleashing of such homicidal rage? With my colleague Matt Mahler, I have investigated all the rampage school shootings that took place in the United States since 1987. Reading the press coverage of each of these cases, middle school, high school, or college, Matt and I began to notice another pattern. Virtually every one of the shooters described their school days as a relentless gauntlet of bullying, gay-baiting epithets, physical assault, and harassment until they "snapped." These boys spent a good part of every day fending off a constant barrage of criticism of their masculinity. They were desperate to prove their detractors wrong and to exact revenge against their tormentors and the other kids who laughed, went along with it, or said nothing and allowed it to continue. In his insightful book, psychiatrist James Gilligan suggests that violence has its origins in "the fear of shame and ridicule, and the overbearing need to prevent others from laughing at oneself by making them weep instead." Shame, inadequacy, vulnerability—all threaten the self. Violence is restorative, compensatory.[13]

The damage to these boys' sense of self was incalculable, their humiliation so severe that they felt they had pretty much ceased to exist. Going out in a blaze of glory becomes, ironically, the affirmation of that self through its annihilation—as long as you can take some of them with you.

The work of cultural anthropologist Katherine Newman and her students is illuminating. In *Rampage* and subsequent articles, Newman and her students identified five factors that together contributed to school shootings: (1) social marginalization (the incessant bullying or gay baiting), (2) individual predisposing factors (a catchall psychological category that led some boys who had been marginalized to lash out and others to find other coping strategies), (3) cultural scripts (some sort of cultural media that inspired or justified their actions), (4) failure of the surveillance system (both physical security and the mental health surveillance system so that shooters passed under the radar of those who might have picked up warning signs), and (5) the availability of guns. "It's the boys for whom a range of unfortunate circumstances come together," they write, "who constitute the likely universe of school shooters." All of these factors, from the individual psychological predisposition to the cultural and material apparatus, are necessary conditions for a rampage.[14]

Some interesting recent research by two psychologists compared the profiles of the rampage school shooters to volunteer suicide bombers in the Middle East. Rampage school shooters are irrationally acting out of pent-up rage; suicide bombers are rational, if fanatic, political actors seeking to further a cause. But Adam Lankford and Nayab Hakim find some interesting similarities: both groups were composed of young people who had troubled childhoods, suffered from low self-esteem, sought revenge from a precipitant personal crisis, were eager for fame and glory, and lived in what the authors call "oppressive social conditions."[15]

Rampage school shooters are the suicide bombers of the American educational system. Listen to the stories of a few of these boys.

Fourteen-year-old Michael Carneal was a shy and frail freshman at Heath High School in Paducah, Kentucky, barely five feet tall, weighing 110 pounds. He wore thick glasses and played in the high school band. He felt alienated, pushed around, picked on. Boys stole his lunch, constantly teased him. He was so hypersensitive and afraid that others would see him naked that he covered the air vents in the bathroom. He was devastated when students called him a "faggot" and almost cried when the school gossip sheet labeled him as "gay." On Thanksgiving 1997, he stole two shotguns, two semiautomatic rifles, a pistol, and seven hundred rounds of ammunition, and after a weekend of showing them off to his classmates brought them to school, hoping that they would bring him some instant recognition. "I just wanted the guys to think I was cool," he said. When the cool guys ignored him, he opened fire on a morning prayer circle, killing three classmates and wounding five others. Now serving a life sentence in prison, Carneal told psychiatrists weighing his sanity that "people respect me now."[16]

Luke Woodham was a bookish and overweight sixteen-year-old in Pearl, Mississippi. An honor student, he was part of a little group that studied Latin, read Nietzsche, and got fascinated by Satanism. Students teased him constantly for being overweight and a nerd and taunted him as a "fag." "People always picked on me," he said after the fact. "They always called me gay and stupid, stuff like that." Even his mother called him fat, stupid, and lazy. On October 1, 1997, Woodham stabbed his mother to death in her bed before he left for school. He then drove her car to school, carrying a rifle under his coat. He opened fire in the school's common area, killing two students and wounding seven others. After being subdued, he told the assistant principal, "The world has wronged me."[17]

A few minutes before he opened fire, he handed this message to a friend:

I am not insane. I am angry. I killed because people like me are mistreated every day. I did this to show society, push us and we will push back. . . . All throughout my life, I was ridiculed, always beaten, always hated. Can you, society, truly blame me for what I do? Yes, you will. . . . It was not a cry for attention, it was not a cry for help. It was a scream in sheer agony saying that if you can't pry your eyes open, if I can't do it through pacifism, if I can't show you through the displaying of intelligence, then I will do it with a bullet.[18]

The list goes on. Gary Scott Pennington, seventeen years old, who killed his teacher and a custodian in Grayson, Kentucky, in 1993, was labeled a "nerd" and a "loner" and was constantly teased for being smart and wearing glasses. Fourteen-year-old Barry Loukaitis, who killed his algebra teacher and two other students in Moses Lake, Washington, in 1996, was an honor student who especially loved math; he was also constantly teased and bullied and described as a "shy nerd." Evan Ramsey, age sixteen, who killed one student and the high school principal in Bethel, Alaska, in 1997, was also an honor student who was teased for wearing glasses and having acne.[19]

Then, of course, there's Columbine, the locus classicus of rampage school shootings. This connection between extreme homophobic bullying and Harris and Klebold's violent rampage was not lost on Evan Todd, a 255-pound defensive lineman on the Columbine football team, an exemplar of the jock culture that Dylan Klebold and Eric Harris found to be such an interminable torment. "Columbine is a clean, good place, except for those rejects," Todd said.

Most kids didn't want them there. There were into witchcraft. They were into voodoo dolls. Sure, we teased them. But what do you expect with kids who come to school with weird hairdos and horns on their hats? It's not just jocks; the whole school's disgusted with them. They're a bunch of homos, grabbing each other's private parts. If you want to get rid of someone, usually you tease 'em. So the whole school would call them homos, and when they did something sick, we'd tell them, "You're sick and that's wrong."

Athletes taunted them: "Nice dress," they'd say. They would throw rocks and bottles at them from moving cars. The school newspaper had recently published a rumor that Harris and Klebold were lovers.[20]

On the surface, both boys *seemed* to be reasonably well adjusted. Harris's parents were a retired army office and a caterer, decent, well-intentioned people. Klebold's father was a geophysicist who had recently moved into the mortgage-services business, and his mother worked in job placement for the disabled. Harris had been rejected by several colleges; Klebold was due to enroll at the University of Arizona that fall.

But the jock culture was relentless. One boy described what it was like to be so marginalized:

Almost on a daily basis, finding death threats in my locker. . . . It was bad. People . . . who I never even met, never had a class with, don't know who they were to this day. I didn't drive at the time I was in high school; I always walked home. And every day when they'd drive by, they'd throw trash out their window at me, glass bottles. I'm sorry, you get hit with a glass bottle that's going forty miles an hour, that hurts pretty bad. Like I said, I never even knew these people, so didn't even know what their motivation was. But this is something I had to put up with nearly every day for four years.[21]

"Every time someone slammed them against a locker and threw a bottle at them," another former friend said, "I think they'd go back to Eric or Dylan's house and plot a little more—at first as a goof, but more and more seriously over time."[22]

You know the rest. Harris and Klebold brought a variety of weapons to their high school that April morning and proceeded to walk through the school, shooting whomever they could find. Students were terrified and tried to hide. Many students who could not hide begged for their lives. The entire school was held under siege until the police secured the building. In all, twenty-three students and faculty were injured, and fifteen died, including one teacher and the perpetrators.

In the videotape made the night before the shootings, Harris says, "People constantly make fun of my face, my hair, my shirts." Klebold adds, "I'm going to kill you all. You've been giving us shit for years."

So the profile that gradually emerges is that of white boys who have been targeted, bullied, beaten up, gay baited, and worse— virtually every single day of their lives. They were called every homophobic slur in the books, and then some. They were mercilessly ridiculed, threatened, attacked, and tortured. Most strikingly, it was *not* because they were gay (none of them were gay, as far as I can tell), but because they were *different* from the other boys—shy, bookish, honor students, artistic, musical, theatrical, nonathletic, a "geek," or weird. Theirs are stories of "cultural marginalization" based on criteria for adequate gender performance—specifically the enactment of codes of masculinity.

And so they did what *any* self-respecting man would do in a situation like that—or so they thought. They retaliated. They knew they were supposed to be "real men," able to embody independence, invulnerability, manly stoicism. The cultural marginalization of the boys who committed school shootings extended to feeling that they had no other recourse: they felt they had no other friends to validate their fragile and threatened identities, they felt that school authorities and parents would be unresponsive to their plight, and they had no access to other methods of self-affirmation. It was not because they were deviants, but rather because they were overconformists to a particular normative construction of masculinity, a construction that defines violence as a legitimate response to a perceived humiliation.

In a sense, then, these boys were not simply "nonconformists"— by which we mean they were mentally ill, disturbed, or unbalanced. At the same time, they were "overconformists," clinging quite tenaciously to an ideal of masculinity that can be—and *must* be—proved by heroic deeds. They were not *either* mentally ill *or* rational but both: deeply disordered to the point of breaking and simultaneously convinced that they knew—from the assembly of cultural means available to men who seek to prove their manhood—how to remedy their situation. For some, it was a rampage itself that restored, at least to their troubled minds, their sense of themselves as men. For others, it was in their glorious suicide that they became martyrs, restoring their manhood in one defiant, glorious explosion.

But still, something is missing from this picture. It's as if we're looking at a painting, a group portrait of the boys, posed, armed to the teeth in front of their schools, and paying attention only to how different they are from other boys or even, in my case, to how similar they are to each other at the same time. But so many boys feel aggrieved, and many also feel that sense of aggrieved entitlement that might legitimate revenge—whether in fantasies of blowing up the galaxy or in being superheroes and taking one's vengeance against all who have wronged them, or in actually becoming bullies themselves and enacting on others what they, themselves, have endured. The roots of rampage murders lie perhaps in the story of the individuals who make those tragically fatal choices. But we need also to make the background present, to foreground it even, for a fuller portrait.

Looking at two more cases in a little more depth can illuminate this dynamic more fully. These two stories can enable us to see the connections between the profiles of the shooters and the profiles of the schools—and the importance of both levels of analysis. We need to reinstall these angry white men and boys in a cultural and social context in which that anger can find expression.

ANDY WILLIAMS "PROVES HIS POINT"

Consider first the case of Andy Williams, the shy, scrawny, fifteen-year-old new kid in town, a freshman at Santana High School in Santee, California. Not yet pubescent, Williams tried hard to fit in with his new neighbors when he went to live in this San Diego suburb, adopting a skate-rat affect and clothes and hanging around the local skate park, even though he was terrible at it and ached to return to South Carolina to live with his mother.

He never seemed to fit in, no matter how hard he tried. "His ears stuck out, he was small, skinny, had a high voice, so people always picked on him 'cause he was the little kid," one of his friends said. His nickname was "Anorexic Andy."

Daily life was a torment. "He was picked on all the time," remembered one student. "He was picked on because he was one of the scrawniest kids. People called him freak, dork, nerd, stuff like that." Another friend said, "They'd walk up to him and sock him in the face for no reason. He wouldn't do anything about it."

That wasn't the half of it. He was beaten up, taunted, locked in his locker, set on fire, his skateboard stolen, money taken, his skater clothes taken off his body, his skate sneakers ripped off his feet. His public defender listed eighteen incidents of bullying in the few weeks leading up to his rampage, including being burned with a cigarette lighter on his neck; sprayed with hair spray and then lit with a lighter; beaten with a towel, leaving large red welts on his body; and being slammed against a tree a couple of times, because of utterly unsubstantiated rumors about his sexual orientation. His father said the bullying was so severe that it was "bordering on torture."

On March 5, 2001, he walked into a school bathroom and opened fire, killing one boy, and then walked into the quad, at the center of the school, killing one more boy and wounding twelve others (two teachers and ten students). He then walked back to the bathroom and waited for the police to arrive. He was unarmed when they came through the door.

Why, we ask? Why did he do it? As expected, psychologists weighed in on how mentally unstable he was, which is no doubt true. Classmates had said that for weeks they'd heard him say he was going to "pull a Columbine." But those experts never seem to see the sources of that destabilization, that mental imbalance doesn't necessarily bubble up from within a troubled mind. It can be produced. With some pre-existing proclivity, circumstances can "unbalance" a mind, destabilize someone whose resilience is compromised. And that is clearly what happened to Andy Williams.

Two years prior to Williams's rampage, the school received a $137,000 grant from the US Department of Justice to study the causes and effects of school bullying. The school never conducted a survey, organized a focus group, or conducted a single interview with the students about the bully culture that permeated the school. They spent the money instead on computer equipment and software for the police, hiring consultants whose advice was promptly ignored.

Both the school administration and the prosecutor who took the case denied that bullying and torture might have had any impact on Williams's violent explosion. The district superintendent denied Williams had been bullied at all and thought it a distraction from the actions of the perpetrator. It's no wonder that, as journalist Mark Ames found, "Santana High School kids and parents both felt that there was no point in complaining to the administration because they wouldn't have done anything anyway." The parents and students were right. Indeed, after the shooting, the school hired a consultant who conducted interviews with students, parents, and teachers and provided a set of recommendations about how to change the school culture. The school board rejected every one of her recommendations.[23]

When this tragic rampage occurred, then president George W. Bush called it a "disgraceful act of cowardice"—which, given my analysis here, actually makes matters worse, decrying the boy's ostensible lack of manhood yet again.[24] Any effort to expose the toxic environment in which Williams suffered was met with a brick wall of denial. When you are tortured so relentlessly, and they don't seem to believe you, and you feel you have no hope of a remedy, you can hit your head against that wall for only so long before you decide, instead, to line your antagonists up against it and re-create the St. Valentine's Day Massacre. When Andy Williams explained why he had committed this terrible act, he was brief. "I was trying to prove a point."

THE AGGRIEVED ENTITLEMENT OF SEUNG-HUI CHO

Consider the case of Seung-Hui Cho, the disturbed Virginia Tech student who slaughtered thirty-two people and wounded many others before committing suicide in April 2007. Cho's hours of rage culminated in the deadliest shooting incident by a single gunman in American history.[25]

At first, Seung-Hui Cho seems the exception to the pattern I've described. The middle-class son of South Korean immigrants (his parents owned a set of dry cleaners), he's the only nonwhite rampage shooter in more than a decade. At twenty-three, he was older than the high school and middle school boys who had murdered their classmates over the previous decades. Cho, also, was clearly mentally ill; he'd been diagnosed but was largely untreated, meaning that there had been some warning signs, but that he continued to fly just under the radar. (Privacy laws actually hid Cho's diagnoses and treatment from Virginia Tech residential officials when they assigned dorm rooms and roommates.) Despite his diagnosis of a serious mental disorder, he had easy access to guns.

Being Asian American, of course, prompted all sorts of racially based explanations. (The fact that virtually *all* the other rampage shooters were white had never elicited any question of race.) Finally, after two decades of school shootings by white kids in which race was never once mentioned as a variable, suddenly the entire explanation centered on the fact that Cho was Asian American. Whatever happened, some asked, to the model minority? Perhaps being an Asian American came with so much pressure to perform, to be that model minority, that it was simply too much. Perhaps he simply cracked under the strain.

The psychological profile of Seung-Hui Cho suggests some bullying, to be sure, and some serious humiliation. In his video, he says that he'd been treated like a "pathetic loser" and had experienced such humiliations as being spat on in public and having garbage shoved down his throat. (It is not known if such statements were true.) He claimed that these other students had "raped" his soul and "torched" his consciousness.[26] Perhaps his life was not quite the same quotidian torture that high schoolers like Eric Harris and Dylan Klebold experienced. Perhaps he was less overtly bullied, but he was no less marginalized.

Awkward socially, Cho never seemed to feel that he fitted in. He was teased and dismissed as a nonentity. Former classmates of Seung-Hui say he "was pushed around and laughed at as a schoolboy" because of his "shyness and the strange, mumbly way he talked." Chris Davids, a Virginia Tech senior who graduated from the same high school as Cho, recalled that he almost never opened his mouth and would ignore attempts to strike up a conversation. Once, in English class, the teacher had the students read aloud, and when it was Cho's turn, he just looked down in silence, Davids recalled. Finally, after the teacher threatened him with an F for participation, Cho started to read in a strange, deep voice that sounded "like he had something in his mouth," Davids said. "As soon as he started reading, the whole class started laughing and pointing and saying, 'Go back to China.'"[27]

At Virginia Tech, he had no friends; rarely, if ever, spoke with his dorm mates; and maintained a near invisibility on campus. His web screen name was a question mark—he toyed with his invisibility. No one seems to have actually known him, although his teachers in the English Department said they thought he was strange and possibly dangerous.

Cho's marginalization also appeared cultural, class based, not entirely the result of his obvious overdetermining psychiatric problems. His videotape raged against the "brats" and "snobs" at Virginia Tech, who weren't even satisfied with their "gold necklaces" and "Mercedes." Apparently, too, some of it had a racist component. In addition, there was a deep alienation from campus culture. Few campuses are as awash in school spirit as Virginia Tech: the campus is festooned with maroon and orange everywhere, and the branding of the campus is a collegiate consumerist orgy of paraphernalia.

But what if one doesn't feel to be much of a citizen in "Hokie Nation"? What if one isn't much interested in football or in sports-themed, beer-soaked weekend party extravaganzas? It's possible that, to the marginalized, Hokie Nation doesn't feel inclusive and embracing, but instead feels alien and coercive. If one is not a citizen in Hokie Nation, one does not exist. And perhaps, for some, if *I* don't exist, then *you* have no right to exist, either.

Cho's marginalization must also have been gendered. After all, recall the way that race is "gendered," as discussed in the last chapter. Asian American men are stereotypically perceived as soft, almost feminine, both in body and in mind. Their bodies are often thin and hairless, unmuscular, their faces beardless and their features delicate. They are seen as robotically disciplined grinds, but not men of "action" or experience. They study extremely hard, perhaps too hard, a sure sign of gender nonconformity for males, since academic disengagement is so often heralded as a sign of masculinity. Unlike other ethnic or racial minorities, like Latino or African American males, Asian American males are perceived as *hypo*masculine, as insufficiently manly. What better way to prove them wrong?

Of course, not everyone who is bullied in school, nor even those whose masculinity is a big question mark because of race or ethnicity, picks up a gun and starts shooting. Indeed, there are kids who are bullied relentlessly, mercilessly, every day at probably most of America's high schools and middle schools. Bullying seems to have become such a national "crisis" that it has inspired countless policy programs, intervention strategies, and even presidential initiatives.

There has to be something more. His videotaped testament shows a young man enthralled with fantasies of revenge, in full-bore aggrieved entitlement, externalizing his inner torment on everyone around him. "You have vandalized my heart, raped my soul, and torched my conscience," he declares on his videotape. "You thought it was one pathetic boy's life you were extinguishing. Thanks to you, I die like Jesus Christ to inspire generations of the weak and the defenseless people." Cho was another suicide bomber; his self-immolation was intended to inspire others to destroy the oppressive systems arrayed against them.

But did he have to? Many have commented that no one in authority seemed to pay any attention to Cho, despite warnings from teachers and female students that they felt unsafe around him, that his fantasies expressed in class papers were disturbing enough to warrant attention. Nikki Giovanni, the celebrated feminist poet, refused to teach him because she said he was "mean." Diagnosed with mental problems, he was able to buy guns, attend classes, fantasize revenge, and eat in the dining halls—all, apparently, just like anyone else.

There are many Seung-Hui Chos out there, victims of incessant bullying, of having their distress go unnoticed. So many teen suicides have this same profile: they turn their rage on themselves. So many teenagers who fit this profile self-medicate, taking drugs, drinking, cutting themselves. There are so many of them, and virtually all fly just beneath the radar of teachers, parents, administrators.

They don't all explode. Is it possible that the environment in which Cho lived had anything to do with it? Is it possible that the elements of a rampage school shooting include access to firepower, an explosive young man who is utterly marginalized, humiliated and drenched in what he feels is righteous rage, as well as an environment that sees such treatment of its weakest and most marginalized as justified, as "reasonable"? Is it possible that it's not just the shooters that need profiling, but also the schools?

PROFILING THE SCHOOLS

What if we shift the lens through which we look at these cases of rampage school shootings to the widest-angle lens we can? What if we make the background the foreground for a moment? Is there something that distinguishes schools as well as the shooters? What makes a violence-prone school different from a relatively violence-free school?

Here's one way to do it. Here is a map of the United States, with thirty-two cases of school shootings marked on it. (I've omitted those where there was a specific target and included only those that could be coded as "rampage" shootings.)

Notice anything? For one thing, it's clear that rampage school shootings are *not* a national trend. Of thirty-two school shootings between 1982 and 2008, all but one were in rural or suburban schools (one in Chicago). New York, Boston, Minneapolis, San Francisco, Los Angeles—nothing. All but two (Chicago again and Virginia Tech) were committed by a white boy or boys. The Los Angeles school district has had no school shootings since 1984; in 1999 San Francisco, which has several programs to identify potentially violent students, had only two kids even try to bring guns to school.

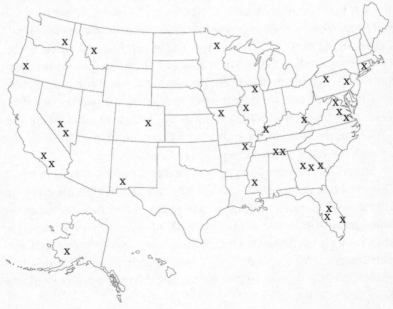

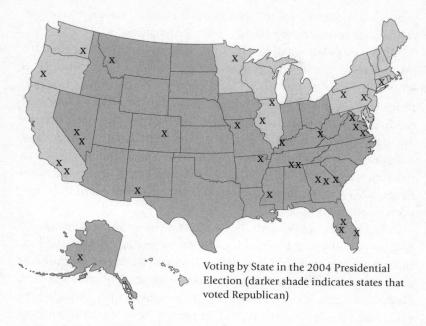

Voting by State in the 2004 Presidential Election (darker shade indicates states that voted Republican)

Now, here are that same data, superimposed on a map that might be more politically familiar.

Of the thirty-two school shootings, twenty-two took place in red states, by this map. Of the ten in the blue states, only two were in urban areas—one was in suburban Oregon, one was in rural (eastern) Washington, two were in Southern California, one was in rural and another in suburban Pennsylvania, one was in rural New Mexico, and one was in rural Illinois. Six of those eight took place in "red" counties (such as Moses Lake, Washington; Santee, California; Red Hill, Pennsylvania; and Deming, New Mexico). Even Springfield, Oregon, located in a blue county, is known as "Springtucky"—which gives you an idea of its political leanings.

What this suggests is that school violence is unevenly distributed. I am not suggesting that the sons of Republicans are more prone to open fire on their classmates than the sons of Democrats. But I am suggesting that different political cultures develop in different parts of the country and that those political cultures have certain features in common. (Most of the time, we celebrate these diverse political cultures.) Some of those features are "gun culture" (what percentage of homes have firearms, gun registrations, NRA memberships), local gender culture, and local school cultures—attitudes about gender non-conformity, tolerance of bullying, and teacher attitudes.

Here's one element of local culture that directly affects whether the psychological profile would show up on anyone's radar. Since local school districts are funded by local property taxes, some "violence-prone schools" may have been subject to a significant decline in school funding over the past two decades. Coupled with the curricular demands of the No Child Left Behind Act, which mandates performance outcomes that require increased attention to a set curriculum, schools have cut back significantly on after-school programs, sports, extracurricular activities, teacher training, remedial programs, and, most important, counseling.

One in five adolescents has serious behavioral and emotional problems, and about two-thirds of these are getting no help at all. In the average school district in the United States, the school psychologist must see ten students each day just to see every student once a year. In California, there is one counselor (not to mention psychologist) for every one thousand students, and 50 percent of schools do not have guidance counselors at all. It is likely that this paucity of funding for psychological services enabled several very troubled students to pass undetected in a way they might not have in past years.

In his exemplary analysis of the shootings at Columbine High School, sociologist Ralph Larkin identifies several variables that he believes provided the larger cultural context for the rampage. The larger context—the development of a culture of celebrity, the rise of paramilitary chic—spread unevenly across the United States; some regions are more gun happy than others. (Larkin credits the West; Cho's rampage implicates the South.) But more than that, he profiles both the boys and the school and suggests that the sociological and psychological variables created a lethal mixture.

It wasn't just that Harris and Klebold—and other eventual rampage shooters—were bullied and harassed and intimidated every day; it was that the administration, teachers, and community colluded with it. At Columbine, when one boy tried to tell teachers and administrators that "the way those who were 'different' were crushed . . . what it was like to live in constant fear of other kids who'd gone out of control," the teachers and administrators invariably turned a blind eye.

"After all," he says, "those kids were their favorites. We were the trou-blemakers." Thus, Larkin concludes, "By allowing the predators free rein in the hallways and public spaces and by bending the rules so that bad behavior did not interfere too much with sports participation, the faculty and administration inadvertently created a climate that was rife with discrimination, intimidation and humiliation."[28]

And sanctimony. Larkin also argues that religious intolerance and chauvinism directly contributed to the cultural marginalization of the boys. Jefferson County, where Columbine High School is located, is more than 90 percent white, 97 percent native born, and almost en-tirely Christian, with nearly 40 percent evangelical Protestants. (Indeed, it has one of the largest concentrations of Christian evangelicals in the country.) Whereas local preachers saw in Klebold and Harris the pres-ence of the devil, Larkin believes that evangelical intolerance of others is more cause than consequence. "Evangelicals were characterized," he writes, "as arrogant and intolerant of the beliefs of others." Evangelical students were intolerantly holier than thou—they would "accost their peers and tell them that if they were not born-again, they would burn in hell." In most cases, Larkin writes, this would be "merely annoying." But "in combination with the brutalization and harassment dished out on a regular basis by the student athletes, it only added to the toxicity of the student climate at Columbine [High School]."[29]

Columbine, like Virginia Tech, was a "jockocracy"—a place where the jocks ruled, the students adored and respected them, and the teachers, parents, and administrators enabled them by BIRGing in the glory of "our boys." (BIRGing is a well-known social psychologi-cal process of "basking in reflected glory," identifying with those who are perceived as heroes.) Jocks ruled; everyone else worshipped. Here's what two *Washington Post* reporters observed at Columbine:

> The state wrestling champ was regularly permitted to park his $100,000 Hummer all day in a 15-minute space. A football player was allowed to tease a girl about her breasts in class without fear of retribution by his teacher, also the boy's coach. The sports trophies were showcased in the front hall—the artwork, down a back corridor.
> Columbine High School is a culture where initiation rituals meant upper class wrestlers twisted the nipples of freshman wrestlers until they

turned purple and tennis players sent hard volleys to younger team-mates' backsides. Sports pages in the yearbook were in color, a national debating team and other clubs in black and white. The homecoming king was a football player on probation for burglary.[30]

After the shooting, a former student spoke about what had happened to him when he came out as gay in middle school (one of the schools that fed Columbine High School): "One year everyone loved me," he said. "The next year I was the most hated kid in the whole school." Jocks were his worst tormentors, he said. He described one in particular who pelted him with rocks, wrote "faggot" and "we hate you" on his locker, and taunted him in the hallway with "I heard the faggot got butt-fucked last night."

"It gets to the point where you're crying in school because the people won't leave you alone," he said. "The teachers don't do anything about it." The boy attempted suicide several times that year and eventually spent time in a mental hospital. "It can drive you to the point of insanity. What they want to do is make you cry. They want to hurt you. It's horrible. I hope that the one thing people learn out of this thing is to stop teasing people."

In the interview, the boy didn't condone what Harris and Klebold did, but said he understood what drove them over the edge. "They couldn't take it anymore, and instead of taking it out on themselves, they took it out on other people. I took it out on myself. But it was a daily thought: 'Boy, would I really like to hurt someone. Boy, would I like to see them dead.'"[31]

That toxic climate combined brutal harassment, sanctimonious superiority, traditional gender norms, and a belief in violence as restorative. It's a long-standing masculine trope. Cho and the others were, according to *New York Times* columnist Bob Herbert, "young men riddled with shame and humiliation, often bitterly misogynistic and homophobic, who have decided that the way to assert their faltering sense of manhood and get the respect they have been denied is to go out and shoot somebody."[32] In a 1994 study, sociologist Richard Felson and his colleagues found that regardless of a boy's personal values, boys are much more likely to engage in violence if the local cultural expectations are that boys retaliate when provoked. And their local gender culture certainly encouraged that.

In his book *No Easy Answers* (2002), Brooks Brown, a former Columbine student and childhood friend of one of the Columbine killers, explained how the rage-rebellion context reached his school:

> The end of my junior year (1998), school shootings were making their way into the news. The first one I heard about was in 1997, when Luke Woodham killed two students and wounded seven others in Pearl, Miss. Two months later, in West Paducah, Ky., Michael Carneal killed three students at a high school prayer service. . . .
>
> Violence had plagued inner-city schools for some time, but these shootings marked its first real appearance in primarily white, middle- to upper-middle-class suburbs. . . .
>
> When we talked in class about the shootings, kids would make jokes about how "it was going to happen at Columbine next." They would say that Columbine was absolutely primed for it because of the bullying and the hate that were so prevalent at our school.

Klebold and Harris, Seung-Hui Cho, and the other rampage school shooters experienced "aggrieved entitlement," that gendered sense that they were entitled—indeed, even expected—to exact their revenge on all who had hurt them. It wasn't enough to have been harmed; they also had to believe that they were justified, that their murderous rampage was legitimate. Once they did, they followed the time-honored script of the American western: the lone gunman (or gang) retaliates far beyond the initial provocation and destroys others to restore the self.

This belief that retaliatory violence is manly is not a trait carried on any chromosome, not soldered into the wiring of the right or left hemisphere, not juiced by testosterone. (It is still the case that half the boys don't fight, most don't carry weapons, and almost all don't kill: are they not boys?) Boys learn it.

And this parallel education is made more lethal in states where gun-control laws are most lax, where gun lobbyists are most powerful. All available evidence suggests that all the increases in the deadliness of school violence are attributable to guns. Boys have resorted to violence for a long time, but sticks and fists and even the occasional switchblade do not create the bloodbaths of the past few years. Nearly 90 percent of all homicides among boys aged fifteen to nineteen are firearm related, and 80 percent of the victims are boys.

Boys may also learn violence from their fathers, nearly half of whom own a gun. They learn it from media that glorify it, from sports heroes who commit felonies and get big contracts, from a culture saturated in images of heroic and redemptive violence. They learn it from each other.

REVISITING HOKIE NATION

To better understand the synergistic interplay between shooter and school, between a shooter's sense of masculinity, mental illness, and his environment, let's turn again to the case of Seung-Hui Cho and Virginia Tech.

Consider, first, the case of a young woman named Christy Brzonkala. In the first semester of her freshman year in college in 1994, Christy was viciously gang-raped by two football players at her school. Traumatized by the event, she sought assistance from the campus psychiatrist, who treated her with antidepressants. Neither the campus psychiatrist nor any other "employee or official made more than a cursory inquiry into the cause of [her] distress." Christy eventually recovered enough to bring charges against her attackers and, to her surprise, was successful in prosecuting the case through campus judicial channels. The fact that everyone testified that she repeatedly said no seemed to count! One of the players was suspended for a year. However, the judicial board soon reversed the decision, largely, it appeared, because the football coach pressured the administration to make the problem go away. The university restored his scholarship and postponed his suspension until after he graduated.

Shocked, humiliated, and outraged, Christy never returned to school, but eventually brought a Title IX suit against the university for creating a hostile environment. The Fourth Circuit Court found that the university had "permitted, indeed fostered, an environment in which male student athletes could gang rape a female student without any significant punishment to the male attackers, nor any real assistance to the female victim."[33]

What does Christy Brzonkala have to do with Seung-Hui Cho? In one sense, nothing. But ask yourself this: what sort of university was so in thrall of its football players that it would trample over an innocent young woman's feelings, let alone her rights, and create such a hostile environment?[34]

Or take another example. I lecture about issues such as sexual assault, violence against women, and date rape and, more generally, about why men should support gender equality. In twenty years, lecturing at about twenty to twenty-five colleges and universities every year, I have been physically harassed after a lecture at only one campus. There, members of some on-campus fraternities had been required to attend, after reports of some potentially actionable incidents on campus. As I walked to my hotel room—a hotel located on campus—a bunch of guys hanging off the back of a moving pickup truck threw a glass beer bottle at me, missing me by inches. The truck had decals from both the fraternity and the university on its rear window.

At what kind of university are the men so threatened by such a message, and so emboldened, to assault a visiting professor?

Virginia Tech.

Let me be clear: I am not in any way saying that Virginia Tech was itself to blame for Cho's enraged madness, or even that one might have predicted his horrifying explosion after the callous indifference of the administration to a young first-year student a decade earlier.

I am saying, however, that one of the things that seems to have bound all the school shooters together in their murderous madness was their perception that their school was a jockocracy, a place where difference was not valued, a place where, in fact, it was punished. Community is always about membership and belonging—and about exclusion and isolation.[35] There are students hovering on the precipice of murderous madness everywhere. But as with Klebold and Harris, the boys also have to feel that no one is paying attention, that no one in authority notices, that no one gives a damn at all. No one tried to stop Cho, either, and he believed that was because everyone—all those "brats" and "snobs"—was part of the problem.

Social science is a tricky predictive science, and one would have to go way out on a limb to hypothesize that despite there being plenty of disturbed young men at other schools—say, for example, at Vassar or Princeton or New York University or Williams or the University of California at Santa Barbara—those schools would be less likely to experience a rampage school shooting.

Such an argument would be tendentious, after all: it's a virtual certainty that none of them will, because such rampage school shootings are so unbelievably rare in the first place. Yet, on the other hand, those schools also do not extract such universal allegiance to campus culture, nor are they ruled by one impenetrable clique. Nor is the administration under relentless alumni pressure to maintain and build the sports programs at the expense of every other program—especially the campus-counseling program that might identify and treat such deeply troubled, indeed maniacally insane, students a bit sooner.

Rampage school shooters may be mad, but their madness must pass unseen, and their marginalization needs to be perceived as justified. And those dynamics have less to do with crazy individuals and more to do with campus cultures.

This emphasis on local school cultures must also be placed alongside what can only be called the globalization of media culture. Young boys with access to the Internet anywhere in the world have access to the same narratives of aggrieved entitlement. When, for example, Pekka-Eric Auvinen opened fire at his Tuusula, Finland, high school in November 2007, he used the same narrative repertoire as his American counterparts. Just before he embarked on his massacre of eight of his classmates, as well as taking his own life, Auvinen posted his intentions on YouTube.

The narrative may be global, but it is still an utterly gendered narrative as well, and that suicidal explosion remains a distinctly masculine trope. It may be necessary to shift our frame slightly, to implicate the more local cultures of schools, regions, the political economy of psychological intervention, the institutional complicity with bullying and harassment (as long as it's "our guys" who are doing it). Yet alongside these local iterations lies the possibility of an overarching global master narrative to which an increasing number of young boys might find murderous solace.

At the local level, schools that want to prevent such rampage school shootings in the future might do well to profile the shooters—identify those students whose marginalization might become entangled with such aggrieved entitlement—as well as conduct a profile of their school, to mediate the effects of that marginalization on all its students (including those who are suicidal, self-medicating, and self-harming). Thus far, we've focused solely on security and control:

Michael Carneal's high school in Paducah, Kentucky, was experienced by students as on permanent lockdown; students called it "Heatha-traz." (It was Heath High School.) Other schools have experimented with banning backpacks and book bags, prohibiting Goth clothing and accessories, requiring photo IDs to be worn at all times, and using computerized access devices, as well as metal detectors and security guards.

Local school culture and this globalized media culture form two of the three legs of a triangulated explanation of rampage school shootings; only placed in this "glocal" context will any psychological profiling make sense. "Good wombs" may have "borne bad sons," as Dylan Klebold said, quoting *The Tempest*. But there are bad seeds everywhere. They also need fertile ground in which their roots can take firm hold.

3 | White Men as Victims

The Men's Rights Movement

Roy Den Hollander doesn't exactly look like a revolutionary. He's a reasonably good-looking guy—nattily dressed, sort of preppy-corporate, Ivy League–educated, former New York corporate lawyer. He should be comfortable in his late middle age, approaching retirement at the top end of the top 1 percent. Yet Den Hollander is not only an angry white man; he is, as he told me, "incensed," furious at the ways that men like him, upper-class white men, are the victims of a massive amount of discrimination—as white men. In this self-styled revolutionary, the legions of oppressed men have found a self-proclaimed champion.

Men's oppression is not an accident, Den Hollander says. It's the result of a concerted campaign against men by furious feminists, a sort of crazed-feminist version of "girls gone wild"—more like "feminazis gone furious." And they're winning. Roy Den Hollander is one of the few who is standing up to them, or at least trying to. He suffers, he says, from PMS—"persecuted male syndrome." As he told a reporter,

"The Feminazis have infiltrated institutions and there's been a transfer of rights from guys to girls."[1]

A corporate attorney by training, Den Hollander has refashioned himself a civil rights champion, fighting in court for the rights of men that are being trampled by the feminist juggernaut. He's funded his lawsuits himself and fancies himself the Don Quixote of gender, tilting at feminist legal windmills, fighting the good fight. (This re-branding has brought him a lot of fame—he's been profiled in heaps of media, including a very funny and self-mocking takedown on *The Colbert Report*—even if he's had no legal success at all.) Over the past decade, Den Hollander has filed three different lawsuits (each seems to have had multiple iterations). He may sound like some masculinist buffoon, but I think his efforts, taken together, form a trinity of issues raised by the angry middle-class white guys who march under the banner for men's rights.[2] As he puts it, "This trilogy of lawsuits for men's rights makes clear that there are now two classes of people in America: one of princesses—females, and the other of servants—males. Governments, from local to state to federal, treat men as second class citizens whose rights can be violated with impunity when it benefits females. Need I say the courts are prejudiced, need I say they are useless, need I say it's time for men to take the law into their hands?"[3]

First, Den Hollander went after bars in New York City that offered ladies' night. You know, those promotional come-ons that offer women reduced or free admission to clubs, but require that men pay admission. Bars and clubs offer ladies' nights, of course, to entice men to come to the club; men are more likely to show up, and more likely to buy women drinks, if there are more women there—that is, if the odds tilt in the guys' favor.

Ladies' nights obviously discriminate against men, Den Hollander argued. They're supposed to; it's good for business. So, in 2007, he filed a federal lawsuit against six New York City bars and clubs (hoping they'd come to constitute a class for a class-action suit), claiming they violated the Fourteenth Amendment (specifically, the Equal Protection Clause). According to the suit, these bars "allow females in free up to a certain time but charge men for admission until that same time, or allow ladies in free over a longer time span than men."[4]

Nearly forty years after women had successfully sued McSorley's Old Ale House for the right to drink alongside men (a suit that is cited as some sort of antidiscrimination precedent here), is this what civil rights law has come to—infantile parodies of serious civil rights cases?[5] When asked by a reporter what would happen if he were to win, Den Hollander replied, "What I think will happen is that clubs will reduce the price for guys and increase it for girls. Every guy will have ten or fifteen more dollars in his pocket, which the girls will then manipulate into getting more drinks out of him. If they drink more, they'll have more fun, and so will us guys. And then when she wakes up in the morning, she'll be able to do what she always does: blame the man."[6] (Either way, according to Den Hollander, women win: they get lower prices, or they get more drinks, have more fun, and then still get to blame the men.) Den Hollander needn't have worried. The case was thrown out of court—by a female judge, of course.

The next year, he went after the Violence Against Women Act or, as he likes to call it, the "Female Fraud Act." VAWA is a favorite target for the men's rights movement, since they see its specific scrutiny of violence against women as both discriminatory toward men as well as failing to acknowledge, let alone minister to, the pervasive violence perpetrated by women against men. Den Hollander's logic is a bit more tortured—and more torturedly personal. In his view, VAWA provides legal cover for scheming, conniving non-US women to trap native-born American men. (This is, he claims, his own story.) If they have been the victims of violence, VAWA gives "alien females who married American guys a fraudulent track to permanent residency and U.S. citizenship." All she has to do is claim her husband battered her or subjected her to "an overall pattern of violence." So, he argues, the reason that the feminist establishment pushed for this law is to "intimidate American men into looking for wives at home," though it isn't entirely clear why feminists would promote this. Again, the judge (a man this time) dismissed the case as without merit.

Most recently, in 2009, Den Hollander brought a suit against Columbia University. Essentially, the case centered around the fact that Columbia has a women's and gender studies (WGS) program—a pretty good one, for that matter—but it doesn't have a men's studies program. According to Den Hollander, that qualifies as gender discrimination right there—failing to provide comparable services based on gender. What's more, the WGS program at Columbia promotes "feminism," which is, Den Hollander alleges, a religion—"a belief system that advocates an accident of nature, born a girl, makes females superior to men in all matters under the sun." Thus, Columbia University is violating not only the Fourteenth Amendment, but also the First Amendment, guaranteeing the separation of church and state. So men are doubly injured—by their absence from the women's studies curriculum and by the unfettered spread of feminism, the religion.

The judge—again, Den Hollander notes, surprised, a man—disagreed and called Den Hollander's case "absurd." "Feminism is no more a religion than physics," Judge Lewis Kaplan wrote, perhaps ignoring all those creationists and biblical literalists who believe that physics *is* also a religion. Although subsequent appeals were denied, Den Hollander is convinced that the judge ruled "with an arrogance of power, ignorance of the law, and fear of the feminists."[7]

Roy Den Hollander's men's rights legal trilogy makes for fascinating reading on his website.[8] Although not exactly Tolstoyan in the arc of its emotional compass, it captures both the spirit and the substance of the men's rights movement, a loose but loud collection of Internet blog sites, policy-oriented organizations, and legions of middle-class white men who feel badly done by individual women or by policies they believe have cheated them. These men don't generally do well with expressing pain—so they translate it into rage.

His cases perfectly illustrate their positions: men are the victims of reverse discrimination in every political, economic, and social arena; feminism has been so successful that men are now the second sex; and men have to stand up for their rights. In doing so, they believe, they strike a blow against the wimpification of American manhood: they get their manhood back by fighting for the rights of men. Who says the personal isn't also political?

Den Hollander's lawsuits may not have found sympathetic judicial ears, based, as they were, on the shakiest of legal and empirical foundations. But they provide a triumvirate of issues that incense the men's rights activists (MRAs): the putative institutional arenas of discrimination against men; the "special treatment" of women, especially around violence and in family life; and the dramatic tilt toward women in education. We'll look at each one, after I describe the historical emergence of the men's rights movement and its trajectory in the present. (I'll turn to the claims of discrimination in family life in the next chapter.) These issues also lay bare several contradictions that lie at the heart of the men's rights movement—contradictions so fundamental that it leaves them personally paralyzed and politically unpersuasive.

WHERE DID THE MEN'S RIGHTS MOVEMENT COME FROM?

Given Roy Den Hollander's characterization of feminism as a vicious, man-hating ideology—a sentiment shared by many in the men's rights movement—it might come as a bit of a surprise to know that the initial seeds of the contemporary men's rights movement were planted in the same soil from which feminism sprouted. When the "second wave" of feminism began to emerge in the 1960s, it was fed by two distinct streams of political outrage. (The first wave was, of course, the woman suffrage movement.) First were the women mobilized by Betty Friedan's scathing critique of domestic life in *The Feminine Mystique* (1963), that furious wake-up call from the somnambulant 1950s, which suppressed the ambitions of a generation of postwar women, swathing them in a midcentury cult of domesticity. These disappointed women were met by a second, younger, group, some their daughters, who had already been politically mobilized into the civil rights, student, and antiwar movements and who had also experienced not being taken seriously by men, being asked to suppress their ambitions in order to further the cause, and being made to serve the men who ran the movements. Both groups agreed that traditional notions of femininity submerged women's abilities and drowned their ambitions.

That critique of what became known as the female sex role, the traditional ideology of femininity, resonated for some men who by the early 1970s took the feminist call for women's liberation as an opportunity to do some liberating of their own. "Men's liberation" was born in a parallel critique of the male sex role. If women were imprisoned in the home, all housework and domestic drudgery, men were exiled *from* the home, turned into soulless robotic workers, in harness to a masculine mystique, so that their only capacity for nurturing was through their wallets. The separation of spheres was disappointing for men, too: women were demoted to the realm of feeling; men were relegated to a public persona where their success depended on the suppression of emotion.

Men's liberation posited a set of parallelisms. If men had, as writer Sam Keen would put it, "the feeling of power," then women had "the power of feeling." These were thought to be equivalent: women and men were equally oppressed by traditional sex roles. The early men's liberationists even claimed to be inspired by women's emancipatory efforts. But feminists moved from a critique of those sex roles—abstract ideological constructions—to a critique of the actual behaviors of actual men, corporeal beings who acted in the name of those antiquated roles. And once women began to make it personal, to critique men's behaviors—by making rape, sexual harassment, and domestic violence part of the gender dynamics that were under scrutiny—the men's libbers departed.

Instead, the men's liberationists stuck with the analysis of roles, which, they argued, were equally oppressive to men; they shifted their focus to those institutional arenas in which men were, they argued, the victims of a new form of discrimination—gender discrimination against men. Initially, these included the sites of gender discrimination like the military, where only eighteen-year-old males, and not females, were required to register for military service, an indication that men were considered "expendable." Traditional notions of masculinity were as toxic and outdated to these men as traditional notions of femininity were to feminist women.

For their part, those early feminist women managed to figure out how to be angry about men's behaviors, furious about their own subordinate position, incendiary about institutional discrimination in the workplace, yet retain their compassion for the not quite comparable, if parallel, experience of men. Here's Betty Friedan in 1973, in her epilogue to the tenth-anniversary republication of *The Feminine Mystique*:

> *How could we ever really know or love each other as long as we kept playing those roles that kept us from knowing or being ourselves? Weren't men as well as women still locked in lonely isolation, alienation, no matter how many sexual acrobatics they put their bodies through? Weren't men dying too young, suppressing fears and tears and their own tenderness? It seemed to me that men weren't really the enemy—they were fellow victims, suffering from an outmoded masculine mystique that made them feel unnecessarily inadequate when there were no bears to kill.*

By the 1980s, the dissatisfaction with the "male sex role," as they called it, had reached a crossroads. Yes, they agreed, men were unhappy, their lives impoverished by shallow friendships; fraught relationships with wives, partners, girlfriends, and potential girlfriends; and strained or nonexistent relationships with their children. Books proliferated, consciousness-raising groups formed, and folk songs bid good-bye to John Wayne. The question was *why* men were so unhappy. What *caused* the male malaise? The way different groups of men resolved this question provided the origins of the various men's "movements" currently on offer.

To these questions, there were essentially two answers, though one had two parts. Maybe one could say there were two and a half answers, roughly parallel to the two and a half male characters on the hit TV sitcom *Two and a Half Men*. The setup story, you'll recall, pivots on the triangle among Charlie Harper, a drunken skirt chaser with a heart of gold, and his brother, Alan, a divorced dad (his son, Jake, is the "half"), who's near-hysterically confused and emasculated.

Let's start with Jake, the pubescent, addled, and socially inept but perpetually wisecracking half man. There's one thing he knows for sure: the models of masculinity offered by his father and uncle are not for him; they're negative role models if anything. He's looking for something new, but he has no idea where to look or how to know he's found it. Although it's a bit of a conceptual stretch to link Jake to mythologists and poets like Robert Bly, the search for an authentic masculine identity brings them closer than either would be to traditionalists. Like Jake, a large number of men sustained their critique of traditional notions of masculinity, arguing that the John Wayne model, a sort of "male mystique" that paralleled the equally false "happy housewife" heroine, was ill-suited for today's men, who wanted emotional sustenance and deeper and more meaningful relationships with their children, their partners, and their friends. And just as countless women had joined the women's movement in an effort to expand their lives beyond the feminine mystique, many men trooped off to wilderness retreats, stadium rallies, and woodsy campfires to explore a deeper, more resonant masculinity. Jake, of course, joins the army instead of going to college—where, no doubt, he'll enjoy all the bonding rituals that will enable him to man up.

What became known as the mythopoetic men's movement is often attributed to the work of Bly and Michael Meade and writers like Sam

Keen (all of whom had best sellers in the early 1990s), who sought to enable men to search for some "deep" or "essential" masculinity. The movement's leaders claimed that the authenticity of the male experience had been both diluted and polluted by life in mass-consumer society. Mythopoets were largely gender separatists, neither feminist nor antifeminist in their politics; rather, they said, they were "masculinsts"— of men, by men, and for men. And, they claimed, rightly as it turned out, their efforts to enable men to experience that depth would only redound well for the women in their lives: men would be more nurturing, more emotionally responsive, and more reliable as men. (In my research, many mythopoets had far better second marriages than their first and reconnected with their grown children in ways they never did when their children were younger.)

Another group was more like Alan Harper, Jake's dad, the fey, ingratiating, Goody Two-Shoes, who always wants to do the right thing, but always seems to miss the boat. Utterly contradictory—he's both a perpetually broke, dependent freeloader and a professional (a chiropractor) who actually has several girlfriends—Alan is still emasculated, hypomasculine, afraid of his own shadow, perpetually anxious, a non-Jewish nebbish.

Like Alan, many men saw in feminism the critique not only of traditional femininity but also of traditional masculinity. Politically, they agreed with Friedan that men were "fellow victims." Social psychologist Joseph Pleck, for example, offered a scathing empirical critique of the male sex role, revealing its internal contradictions and unrealizable pretensions. Actor Alan Alda was more flippant, but no less perceptive; in an essay in *Ms.*, he quipped that men needed liberation because "a man isn't someone you'd want to have around in a crisis—like raising children or growing old together."[9]

To these profeminist men, women's demands to enter the labor force meant that men did not need to stake their identity solely in their workplace success. Women's efforts to balance work and family life enabled men to reconnect with their children and their partners. Feminist women's campaigns against violence, battery, sexual assault, and other harmful expressions of men's contempt and rage also enabled men to begin to unravel the tightly wound skein of manhood and violence. Feminist women sought solidarity with other women in a collective struggle, inspiring men to break down their own barriers that kept them feeling isolated and alone. It turned out to these "profeminist" men that the feminist vision of full equality and gender justice might not be such a bad thing for men—indeed, it might be the very political theory we (I count myself among them) had been searching for. Like Alan, profeminist men today also want to do the right thing; unlike him, though, we find ourselves grounded in more solid relationships with our friends, our children, and our partners and wives.

Finally, there's Charlie, the alcoholic, unrepentant womanizer, politically incorrect and loving every minute of it. Charlie simultaneously sees every woman as a potential conquest, but like many sexual predators, he actually holds women in contempt. Charlie thinks the only good thing about feminism is that it gave women permission to put out as a way to express their liberation. *That* part of women's lib he likes. But, in general, the source of his malaise is that he blames women for his predicament. So, too, does the men's rights movement. Like the movement, Charlie cannot figure out if he's a "liberated man" on the hunt for equally liberated women or a more traditional man looking for a more traditional woman—albeit one who puts out at the drop of a hat. (Of course, as life imitates art, the actor portraying Charlie, Charlie Sheen, whose real-life antics were so over the top, was eventually replaced by the sweetly naive Ashton Kutcher.)

Out of this amorphous men's liberation movement emerged a core group in the late 1980s and early 1990s that embraced what they called men's rights. They may have shared the initial critique of the oppressive male sex role, and the desire to free men from it, but for the men's rights activists, that critique morphed into a celebration of all things masculine and a near infatuation with the traditional masculine role itself. Men didn't need liberating from traditional masculinity anymore; now they needed liberating from those who would liberate them! Traditional masculinity was no longer the problem; now its restoration was championed as the solution.

The problem was, in a word, women—or, more accurately, women's equality, women's empowerment, and feminism. Feminism, men's rights activists argued, was both a political strategy to take power and an individual lifestyle that despised and denigrated men. It wasn't traditional notions of masculinity that made men so miserable;

it was women. Feminism was a hateful ideology; feminists were castrating bitches. (To them, the iconic feminist was more Lorena Bobbitt than Gloria Steinem—this despite the fact that neither Bobbitt nor her followers thought of themselves as feminists at all.) But here, also, that contradiction seemed to prevent the movement from ever articulating any coherent policy ideas. Feminism, they argued, has turned normal, healthy feminine women into a bunch of gold-digging, consumerist harridans; as one antifeminist men's rights magazine put it:

> Unlike Chinese women, for American women "every dollar earned is an opportunity for her to enjoy herself. The fruit of her labor is squandered on eating out, going to a spa, getting her hair done, working out at a gym, dancing or gambling. She goes into marriage without any sense of responsibility or duty to anyone but herself, and our society, based as it is on consumerism, celebrates and encourages this attitude. It is as though the American economy relies upon the production of lousy daughters and wives, good for nothing but selfish expenditures and entirely unable and unwilling to see any purpose to life beyond self indulgence."[10]

Just how different is this from 1950s guys complaining about their prefeminist wives or traditionalist guys who are seeking Asian mail-order brides on the assumption that they are more docile and obedient, unlike their wastefully spending American cousins? Not very. And, of course, feminism has provided the most coherent *critique* of consumerist femininity in history; feminists were the ones, you'll recall, who were shouted at for encouraging women to be productive, go to work, eschew economic dependency.

So men's rights activists hate those traditional women because they enslave men, gluing them to gold-digger trophy wives, who spend, preen, and otherwise ignore their hardworking husbands. No, wait. Men's rights activists love traditional women who won't compete outside the home for scarce jobs that should go to men anyway.

And men's rights guys are equally confused about their position on masculinity. Some want to embrace traditional masculinity; Alan Baron's "Men's Manifesto" (2001) urges men to "vigorously defend the concept that male domination/patriarchy is part of the natural order of things." Others want to reject the old John Wayne image entirely, casting it as a recipe for an emotionless automaton who slashes and burns his way through life like the Terminator, competitive and unfeeling, until he dies an early death of some stress-related disease, without ever knowing his family—or himself.[11]

See the confusion? Men's rights guys don't know if they want to be restored patriarchs or liberated men. And as a result, their websites and pamphlets are clogged with howls of anguish, confusion, and pain. (That confusion, I believe again, is real, but not necessarily true. These men feel a lot, but their analysis of the cause of their feelings strikes me as decidedly off.) Mostly, though, the men's rights movement has been an expressive movement, especially in cyberspace—a movement to help men get their balls back. Those howls of pain and anguish that men felt led many to wallow in self-pity before they turned it into rage. The men's rights movement became a movement of—and for—angry white men.

And angry they are. They are so angry, in fact, that the Southern Poverty Law Center, which monitors all sorts of "hate groups"—from paramilitary organizations to Klansmen and other neo-Nazi groups— recently started listing men's rights groups in its annual survey of hate, citing their "virulent misogyny, spreading of false anti-woman propaganda and applauding and even encouraging acts of domestic terrorism and extreme violence against women and children, up to and including murder."[12]

They are so angry that they're threatening violence (and cheering for it, as we'll see when we discuss the men who murder women):

> Who said I was interested in proving I wasn't violent? In point of fact, I continually warn people that if these issues are not MEAN-INGFULLY addressed, and soon, there will be a LOT of violence (see: Middle East) that we MRAs [Men's Rights Activists] won't be able to stop. And frankly, if it comes to that, society (and all the women in it along with the men) flat out DESERVES whatever is coming. Your hubris as a movement is causing a lot of men to be angry. You all vastly underestimate both the anger, and the ubiquitous nature of this anger. We MRAs do nothing except act as weather vane and map. That's why we have no central authority, or funding, or organization of any kind. We are average guys mad enough to stand up like we do. There are a LOT more guys that are just as mad, but content to let others lead. And there are a growing number of men that take

Feminist (and "official") dismissal of mens issues as indication that ONLY violent revolution will lead to change. And speaking for myself, if it ever comes to violence, I will stand aside, and feel bad while all manner of nasty things are done . . . but I won't lift a FINGER to stop it. Just like people like you are doing right now.[13]

Starting in the 1990s, the men's rights movement got angrier. Asa Baber, who wrote the "men's" column in *Playboy*, sounded the clarion call in *Naked at Gender Gap*, a collection of his columns gathered into a book in 1992. "Men have now had 25 years of sexists calling us sexists," he wrote about a feminism that was now "out of control" and had become "an attack on masculinity itself." Baber celebrated manhood. "It's fine to be male," he proclaimed, "a glorious, sexual, humorous thing to be male."[14]

Warren Farrell's career spans the arc from men's liberation to men's rights. His turn toward men's rights—and blaming feminists for men's problems—wasn't inevitable. In fact, early in his career as a writer and speaker on gender issues, Farrell's politics seemed to ally with feminism; he convened the National Organization for Women's Task Force on the Masculine Mystique and was twice elected to the board of New York's chapter of NOW. He believed that men could benefit from women's liberation: if she could refuse to be a "sex object," he could just as easily refuse to be a "success object." He sought to be "the liberated man"; he despised traditional masculinity, loathed competitive sports, and advocated sharing housework and child care.[15]

His 1993 book, *The Myth of Male Power*, has become something of the touchstone text to the men's rights crowd. Some of its inversions are worth noting, because they anticipate many of the more hyperbolic claims made by the MRAs today. According to Farrell, men's power is, well, a myth. (He prefers to see things as complementary roles.) "Power is not earning money that someone else can spend and dying earlier so they can get the benefits," he said.[16]

He has a point. When white men are cast as the oppressors, normal, everyday middle-class white guys don't often feel all that power trickling down to them. When informed by some earnest gender studies type of the amount of "privilege" or power they have, white male students often look puzzled. "What are you talking about?" they'll say. "I have no power!" (And they're half right, of course. They're *students*—

and their parents and professors and friends all tell them what to do. What they miss, on the other hand, are the ways that their race and class and gender confer on them all sorts of benefits that they neither asked for nor recognize.)

You can see where this is going with middle-aged white men. To the MRAs, the *real* victims in American society are men, and so they built organizations around men's anxieties and anger at feminism, groups like the Coalition for Free Men, the National Congress for Men, Men Achieving Liberation and Equality (MALE), and Men's Rights, Inc. (MR, Inc.). These groups proclaim their commitment to equality and to ending sexism—which was why they were compelled to fight against feminism. According to them, feminism actually gave women *more* freedom than men, while men were still responsible for initiating sexual relationships, fighting in wars, and paying alimony and child support. Feminism, they argued, was the most insidious and vexing form of sexism going. Feminist women were "would be castrators with a knee-jerk, obsessive aversion to anything male," wrote Richard Doyle, an administrator of the Men's Rights Association, in his 1986 book *The Rape of the Male*. Fred Hayward, the founder of MR, Inc., claimed that men were the most common victims of violence, rape, abuse, and battery and that "women are *privileged* because they are more frequently *allowed* to raise children, while men are being *oppressed* by denial of access to children"—and it was women who controlled this situation. Another advised men who felt powerless in the face of divorce-court proceedings to "fight dirty and win" by exploiting their wives' vulnerabilities.[17]

They may not feel powerful, but they do feel entitled to feel powerful. And it's this aggrieved entitlement that animates the men's rights movement. It's what links them to other angry white men, though they sometimes find themselves on the other side of the political spectrum (or so they'd claim).

At the very least, they argue, they should feel *necessary*. But with books like *New York Times* columnist Maureen Dowd's *Are Men Necessary?* and journalist Hanna Rosin's *The End of Men*, and seemingly countless others, MRAs are starting to wonder if men's power is more like the polar ice cap—once solid and fixed and today melting faster than you can say "declining sperm counts." Men seem to have gone from being "king of the castle," running virtually every single organization and institution in America, to "the end of men"—in one short generation! It's dizzying how quickly male supremacy—which we'd been told was encoded in our genes—has unraveled. Are men necessary? Well, yes. Is it the end of men? Hardly. But do those men who see the world as a global zero-sum game feel resentful, confused, and angry? As Sarah Palin would say, "You betcha!"

Politically, such resentment and anger have fueled a new gender gap, the preponderance of middle-class, middle-aged, straight white males who are now listing constantly to the right. Raised to feel "entitled" themselves, they resented any entitlement program that gave anything to anyone else. "If I can't have what I'm entitled to," they seemed to say, "then neither can you"—a new twist on the old exclusionary formula employed to retrieve a sense of manhood. One writer fumed that he "will have none of the nonsense about oppressed and victimized women; no responsibility for the conditions of women, whatever that condition might be; none of the guilt or self-loathing that is traditionally used to keep men functioning in harness." And another wrote that women "have always dominated me, directed me, intimidated me, loaded me with guilt, sometimes inspired me, oftentimes exploited or shamed me."

Such sentiments about entitlement reveal a curious characteristic of these new legions of angry white men: although white men still have most of the power and control in the world, these particular white men feel like victims. These ideas also reflect a somewhat nostalgic longing for that past world, when men believed they could simply take their places among the nation's elite, simply by working hard and applying themselves. Alas, such a world never existed; economic elites have always managed to reproduce themselves despite the ideals of a meritocracy. But that hasn't stopped men from believing in it. It is the American Dream. And when men fail, they are humiliated, with nowhere to place their anger. Some are looking for answers; others want payback. In that sense, men's rights activists are True Believers—but they believe in a world that was spectacularly unequal.

MEN'S RIGHTS TODAY

There men's rights might have remained—a fringe movement of sad and angry middle-class white guys, moaning about how hard they have it. Three social changes, however, catapulted the movement into a much angrier and more vociferous collection of disgruntled men.

First are the seismic economic shifts that have transformed America, in one short generation, from, say, 1980 to the present, from a nation of middle-class achievers with a small upper and lower class into an utterly bifurcated nation of the superrich and everyone else. Dramatic economic inequality and the redistribution of wealth upward have pulled the rug out from under formerly secure, comfortable middle-class men, whose identity had been tethered to being competent providers for their families, with a possibility of upward mobility in a more open society. The elimination of the middle rungs on the economic ladder, leaving an unbridgeable gulf between the gated communities and the apartments with bars on the windows, actually hit middle-class white men hard—at least psychologically. They believed themselves to be entitled to make a grab for that ring on the merry-go-round. They may not reach it, but they believed in the system enough to try. Many of these middle-class guys—outsourced, downsized, benefits slashed—are bitter and angry to begin with.

This stands next to an important change among the men themselves—one that I think is so politically significant that I'll discuss it more fully in the next chapter. Most simply put, despite the histrionics and hyperbole, the MRAs were right about one thing: fatherhood. Or at least partly right. Although the story is far more complicated than the fathers' rights movement would have it, there is some truth to their claims that the reason so many fathers feel utterly screwed by the divorce and custody proceedings is because the laws, and their enforcement, are woefully out of date and evoke a time in American family history that is long past. The story may not be as stark as the MRAs portray it, nor the villains some feminist-inspired cabal, but the fathers' rights movement does have a legitimate gripe. As long as they have that tenuous hold on credibility, their other, more unhinged, claims get a fuller airing.

The final change is easier to describe. The development of the Internet has fueled websites and blogs that keep the conversation going and the blood boiling. The emergence of what one writer calls the "manosphere" is a loose collection of websites that sustain the rage; even the most casual tourist will happen upon "a torrent of diatribes, invectives, atrocity takes, claims to entitlement, calls to arms, and prescriptions for change in the service of men, children, families, God, the past, the future, the nation, the planet, and all other things non-feminist." This makes sense; after all, cyberspace is a place of false power—of being able to mouth off and scream at those you don't like without actually having to hear any response to your ideas or to actually have to make much of a rational case. It's perfect for the less tethered.[18]

There are hundreds of men's rights sites, many simply consisting of one angry guy sitting in his basement, spewing out vitriolic posts that refuel day after day. Some sites get virtually no traffic and simply repost the day's supposed outrages from other sites. But a few larger sites get hundreds, if not thousands, of hits a day, aggregating these individual posts into what feels like a social movement.

Most of the excitement comes not from the blog posts, but in the fiery comment sections that follow. There, "commenters" let fly with a spiraling series of accusations, crazed conspiracy theories, and threats to their enemies. "It's ironic," says Amanda Marcotte, a feminist blogger, "that the very success of feminism has produced such disfigured spawn. It's so much less acceptable these days to be openly sexist, that men have been forced to retreat to such virtual havens."[19]

"You know," says Jeff, "once upon a time, every fucking place was a locker room, you know?" Jeff is a men's rights fellow traveler I met at one of my campus lectures—after he followed me back to my hotel, peppering me all the way with questions and challenges.

> I mean, the workplace was a locker room, just us guys. And the corporate boardroom and the law office and the operating room in the hospital, not to mention the foxholes and the police stations and the firehouses. Everywhere you went, there was that easy guy thing— you know, just hanging out, shooting the shit, being guys, and not worrying about being so politically correct all the time. I mean, you could do stupid shit, shit you wouldn't want the ladies to know about, and say stuff too, without everyone getting all so uptight about it. It was like the whole world was the locker room.

"Well, what happened?" I ask.

Feminism happened! Now the fucking locker room isn't even a locker room anymore! Women have invaded everyplace! There's nowhere a guy can go and just chill, you know, like those scenes in Knocked Up where the guys are sitting around, doing bong hits, and talking about porn? It's like the only place you can go these days is your man cave—and if you don't have one of those, well, there's the Internet, those free porn sites, the men-only places, the places where guys can bitch and moan and not get so screamed at by women all the time.

This sounded familiar to me, this idea that women's increased equality was experienced as an invasion of a previously pristine all-male turf. While researching my previous book *Guyland*, I happened on a Brooklyn bar that has been home to generations of firefighters and their pals. There's an easy ambience about the place, the comfort of younger and older guys (all white) sharing a beer and shooting the breeze—until I happen to ask one guy about female firefighters. The atmosphere turns menacing, and a defensive anger spills out of the guys near me. "Those bitches have taken over," says Patrick. "They're everywhere. You know that ad 'It's everywhere you want to be'? That's like women. *They're* everywhere *they* want to be! There's nowhere you can go anymore—factories, beer joints, military, even the god-damned firehouse! [Raucous agreement all around.] We working guys are just fucked."

The Internet provides just such a man cave, a politically incorrect locker room, where you can say whatever you feel like saying without having to back it up with something as inconvenient as evidence and still hide behind a screen of anonymity so that no one knows that you're the jerk you secretly think you might just be. That's a recipe for rage.

Yet there's even more. Some years ago, I was doing some research with a graduate student on the levels of violence in various pornographic media. We found—no big surprise—that videos were more violent than magazines and that the Internet chat rooms were more violent still. (This "some years ago" was the era of chat rooms and alt sites, the birth of the web era.) My colleague and I postulated that the chat rooms were increasingly violent because of an element of homosocial competition, a competition among the guys. One guy would claim he did such and such to some "bitch," and another would comment, "Oh, yeah? That's nothing. I did this and that to some slut—twice!" And then a third would chime in, "Oh, yeah? Well, I did so and so to this bitch and that slut and those whores . . . " And suddenly, the atmosphere got every violent, very dark—and all because the guys were competing with each other about how powerful and sexually aggressive they were.

The Internet has such a disinhibiting effect in many arenas that it's become a mini research area among psychologists. Researchers have especially noticed a dramatic and rapid escalation of both the romantic and the hostile—flirtations become steamily sexual, and arguments become murderously rancorous within minutes. You can say all kinds of stuff you'd never say in public; indeed, sometimes you wouldn't even think of the things you say until you read someone else saying something similar, and it triggers some emotion for you and you can instantly and aggressively reply. Instant, aggressive—and safe. You can scream all you want at people, call them all sorts of names, but no one ever shows up at your workplace or knocks on your door and calls you to account, calls you to demonstrate the validity of the assertion you made or challenges you in any way, except virtually. It's street noise, background rage, preserved forever in the ether.[20]

So what are they saying? Here's just a little sample. A recent column on the *Men's News Daily* site, an activist clearinghouse, captures both the rage and the rationale of these defenders of men's rights. It's a movement, says Paul Elam (the editor of the site), as he described the mounting pressure on men brought about by the waves upon waves of "misandrous" culture, generating a nation of ticking time bombs:

> *The misandric Zeitgeist, the system of feminist governance that most are still loath to acknowledge is about to head toward its inevitable and ugly conclusion, and the results of that will inflict another deep wound on the psyche of the western world.*
>
> *In the men's rights community, a minority in its own right, we have long lamented the cruel and destructive war that has been waged against men and boys for the past half century. We've shouted endlessly at a deaf world that we were on the path to destruction, and we have*

watched our predictions of men being reduced to indentured servants to a malicious matriarchy come true, even as society continues to dismiss and humiliate us for speaking

The comments came fast and predictably furious. Here's one guy: "We may well get to see how well the feminists fare when faced eyeball to eyeball with mobs of pissed off men."

And here's another:

Lets have 10 Million Man March! Lets Stand up to those feminist Natzis [sic] like Hillary Clinton!! Lets have it brothers I'm ready!!!! Lets go to Washington DC and stay there for a month let them know we mean it. We are not going back to our jobs till you don't change those nasty laws in this country. Lets see what they are going to do?? Arrest us all??? I don't think so. . . . there's no room in the jails for all of us. let's have a showdown. lets see what women are going to do with no cops, no electricians, no soldiers to go to stupid wars, with no mechanics to fix their cars, no cooks, no farmers ect., ect lets see!!!! Im ready! It's going to be lots of fun. We bring tents and barbys.

to all man from usa and canada! unite brothers! lets end the male-bashing culture!

And a third:

The Federal government is feminist. Our laws are feminist. Our educational institutions are feminist. There is a coordinated effort driving this and this ugly monster lives in the ivory towers of academia where this beast thrives in an environment separated from fiscal realities and peer reviewed accuracy. It is a giant, networked monster deeply embedded within the infrastructure of this country and it is spreading out into the rest of the world, and it is continuously at work rigging society against men and in favor of women on all levels of society.[21]

Sometimes the rhetoric gets violent, even if the men advocating it would never actually do the things they advocate. Here's Elam again, advocating violence against women:

There are women, and plenty of them, for which [sic] a solid ass kicking would be the least they deserve. The real question here is not whether these women deserve the business end of a right hook, they obviously do, and some of them deserve one hard enough to leave them in an unconscious, innocuous pile on the ground if it serves to protect the innocent from imminent harm. The real question is whether men deserve to be able to physically defend themselves from assault . . . from a woman. [22]

When a men's rights blogger wrote to me, asking what I thought of the "manosphere" that was developing, I replied that I was curious about why the guys he was writing about seemed so angry. Here's what he said:

Men are angry at losing their kids in the divorce and taking their dream of raising them and reducing it to a child support payment and every-other weekend. Men are angry that they are forced to compete at a handicap with women for the same jobs, and then get penalized for their success (I've seen that happen repeatedly). Men are angry that they have a higher chance of being audited than they do of finding a successful long-term relationship. Men are angry . . . and our anger is justified. It's not all directed towards women nor even at feminism, but we are angry nonetheless, and when men are angry things happen. [23]

Most of what constitutes men's rights activism is this sort of recitation, supported by a few anecdotes, and the occasional series of empirical inversions that usually leave the rational mind reeling. To hear them tell it, white men in America are steamrollered into submission, utterly helpless and powerless. They're failed patriarchs, deposed kings, and not only the "biggest losers" but also the sorest.

Women complaining about sexual harassment? Actually, it's *men* who are the victims of harassment. "The way young women dress in the spring constitutes a sexual assault upon every male within eyesight of them," writes William Muehl, a retired professor at the Yale Divinity School. Warren Farrell argues that "consensual sex among employees," as he euphemistically calls it, is "courtship" when it works and "harassment" when it doesn't. If there is a problem with employer-employee sex, Farrell argues, it's because it "undermines the ability of the employer to establish boundaries because the employer often feels needy of the employee."[24] See, the employee, the beneficiary of the sexual attention, is actually the one with the power.

It's the same with sexual harassment on campus and even at home. Sexual contact between professor and student may confer on the young woman "potential academic advantages over other students," Farrell writes. She's the one with the power, not him! And what he calls "workplace incest" is similar to at-home incest, which reverses family-authority dynamics, since "parental authority becomes undermined because the child senses it has leverage over the parent."[25] What a novel theory—incest afforded undue power to the young girl over her father's actions! Does this mean that those altar boys and other children abused by all those Catholic priests were the ones actually with all the power, able to get the priest to do such un-Christian things at their, the boys', whim?

How about rape and sexual assault? Rape, Farrell argues, is not, as feminists have argued, simply a crime of violence. It's about sex. Younger, more attractive women are 8,400 percent more likely to be raped than older women, we're told. The general point that rape has a sexual component is, of course, not entirely wrong, despite the hyperbolic statistics. But to suggest that rape is a crime of sexual frustration implies that if only women would put out a little more often, rape rates would go down. (The reason younger women are more likely to be raped is also because they are more likely to be unmarried and out in the public sphere "unescorted," going to parties and on dates—and, of course, because the vast majority of sexual assaults are committed by a boyfriend, date, or someone the young woman knows.)[26]

By now nearly everyone's heard the canard that men are battered and abused by their wives and female partners at least as much—if not much more—than women are by their husbands. It turns out, by the way, that this "gender symmetry" in domestic violence is empirically true—but only if you ask women and men if, during the past year, they *ever* used any one of a set of physically violent "tactics." But if you ask questions like "How often? How severe? Who initiated? Did you use violence to protect yourself? Were you protecting your kids?" then the rates of domestic violence come to resemble what we've known all along: that the overwhelming majority of violence is used by men— against both women and against other men.[27]

Of course, it's preposterous to suggest gender symmetry in rates of violence—especially when these same men argue that women and men are so fundamentally, biologically different and that men, propelled by testosterone, are driven to greater aggression. Even one of the two researchers on whose work the MRAs rely disavows their claims: "It is categorically false to imply that there are the same number of 'battered' men as there are battered women," writes Richard Gelles, careful even to put the word in quotations when discussing men but not when discussing women.[28]

If you argue for biological difference, it's pretty hard to claim also that women are equally violent. In fact, in the real world of empirical research, gender differences are few, and those small mean differences that one typically finds in, say, fourth-grade math scores are highly variable (girls score higher than boys in some countries, not in others). But the one single intractable gender difference that holds across virtually all societies is that the overwhelming majority—in the range of 90 percent—of the world's violence is committed by men. Except, of course, if you believe the MRAs that it's in a man's home, where somehow he becomes the victim.

But what if we take such ridiculous claims on their face? Here's a question I often ask MRAs about the claims they make about domestic violence. They claim that women hit men as often as men hit women, *not* that men don't hit women as often as feminist women claim they do. That is, their claim of "gender symmetry" is that women's rates of violence are equal to men's rates. What if we were to assume their claims are true? Then they should be advocating for more shelters for battered men—but not challenging the number of shelters for battered women. That is, domestic violence, by their logic, is not a zero-sum game. If these guys were really interested in serving these legions of battered men, they would *ally themselves* with feminist women in the antiviolence movement and advocate for greater funding for men's shelters in addition to maintaining the funding for women's shelters.

They're actually not interested in those legions of battered men, only in discrediting feminist women's efforts to protect women who have been battered. In 2000 eighteen men sued the State of Minnesota's commissioners of the Departments of Corrections, Human Services, Public Safety, and Children, Families, and Learning to end the granting of state money to shelters for battered women. Their lawsuit, *Booth v. Hvass*, argues that these shelters "publish fanatical, irrational, hysterical, sexist literature which maliciously and falsely defames and seeks to generate social and political hatred against men in general, portraying them as the basic cause of all domestic violence and associated acts of cruelty in American society."[29] (This is an example of what logicians call the "compositional fallacy": just because all As are Bs does not mean that all Bs are As. In this case, virtually all of those who commit acts of violence are men. Therefore, the fallacy would hold, virtually all men commit acts of violence. Of course, no sensible person, feminist or not, would make such a ludicrous claim.)[30] In case you're curious, the US District Court dismissed the case in 2001. The US Court of Appeals for the Eighth Circuit upheld the dismissal in 2002. The US Supreme Court refused to hear the case.[31]

MRAs also claim that men are discriminated against in the workplace—and in their efforts to balance work and family life. Women have far more choices than men do. Warren Farrell observes that women have three choices: they can work full-time, stay home full-time, or balance work and family. Men, he says, also have three options: they can work full-time, work full-time, or work full-time. See how oppressed men are?[32] But for the most part, it is other men who have outsourced the jobs, cut wages and benefits, and so corrupted the industry that so many men, firm believers in their role as family providers, are losing their homes to foreclosure, sinking underwater on their home values, and struggling to keep their jobs. (In fact, the financial meltdown of 2008 was a dramatically "gendered" crisis, engineered entirely by guys being guys.) Yet, to the MRAs, it's "a black woman stole my job."

Finally, there's sex. Although some women may complain that predatory men are constantly hitting on them, the power dynamics are really the other way around. Tom Martin, a British former PhD student, channeled his inner Roy Den Hollander in 2011 and sued the London School of Economics because, he claimed, their women's and gender studies program "discriminated" against him as a man. Sex, he claims, is a women's domain: "Since the pill, women have been told they can and should be having orgasms. And because they haven't been, they categorise that as men's fault. . . . [I]t's women's job to make themselves sexually happy, it's not a man's burden."[33]

Well, okay. But isn't that idea—that women's pleasure was, and could be, women's responsibility—a *feminist* claim? Is it not, in fact, one of the basic tenets of that feminist classic *Our Bodies, Our Selves* (1971)? On the other side, a lot of MRAs complain that since feminism, women have gotten so good at pleasuring themselves they don't even really need men!

In a sense, this is the contradiction at the heart of the men's rights movement: women, especially feminist women, must be seen as to blame for every problem men seem to be having. If she wants a career, she's abandoning her traditionally feminine role and is probably overly sexually adventurous as well. If she doesn't, she's some gold-digger layabout who is too passive in bed. It's what I called earlier the "Goldilocks Dilemma"—like the porridge in the bears' house, contemporary American women are either "too hot" or "too cold" but never "just right." They're too sexually demanding, career driven (i.e., "masculinized"), or manipulative, money-hungry schemers who will rob a guy blind and take him to the cleaners.

WHAT DOES THE
MEN'S RIGHTS MOVEMENT WANT?

What else do the MRAs really want? Is there a method to this madness, some coherent set of policy issues, changes in relationships, shifts in gender roles that the men's rights movement wants?

The "Good Men Project"—a website that purports to be for such self-described "good men" but shows remarkable sympathy for anti-feminist diatribes (alongside some pro-equality content)—recently conducted a survey of its readers to find out the top-ten issues that incite MRA passion. The top issue was fathers' rights (with 20 percent of the total votes), which I will discuss in the next chapter. This was followed by

2. "Feminism," which has "harmed men."
3. "Anti-Male Double Standards" like this one: "An adult man has a relationship with a younger teenage girl? He's a disgusting pedophile. A teenage guy with an adult woman? She's lauded and called a cougar—it's considered hot."

4. "Removing the Notion That All Men Are Potential Rapists/Pedophiles"—reminding the public that rapists are few, and bad, and do not represent the entire male gender.

5. "Reproductive Rights"—complaints that there is no male pill or that men have no "right to choose." "There are countless options for women, and none for men."

6. "Better Treatment of Men Regarding False Accusations"—expanding anonymity for men accused of sexual assault and insistence that false accusations be prosecuted as a serious crime.

7. "Making Government Programs Gender Neutral"—since, MRAs claim, "tremendous amounts of government money goes to women's aid," men should have a right to equal amounts.

8. "Educating Boys"—helping boys improve their achievement and attendance in school.

9. "Negative Portrayal in the Media"—MRAs are tired of "seeing dumb and deadbeat dads," of "every man on TV being a sex-obsessed womanizer," as "incompetent, misogynistic, brutish slobs with few redeeming qualities."

10. "The Male Gender Role"—The complaint here is that the traditional male role, that is, honor, chivalry, and the like, "has got to go." "No longer should men be expected to be the providers and protectors of society." Men should be free to express their feelings. "Just because we have penises doesn't mean we should be forced to abide by additional societal expectations, especially when those lead to an early grave."

I have listed all of the top ten because I didn't want to cherry-pick only the more egregious reversals. Obviously, there are several issues with which feminists would agree—negative portrayals of men and women are harmful; sexual predation, especially toward children, is a bad thing no matter which sex is doing it; school reforms that pay attention to different learning styles, initially a feminist reform, are obviously good for both girls and boys.

And several rest on those tired and misplaced reversals—men's right to choose, the disparate public spending, the problem of false accusations that dissolve when contextualized. Men's right to choose, of course, needs to be coupled with men's increased responsibility for caring for children they father and for ensuring that women have access to safe and reliable birth control, for both their sakes.

It's interesting that discomfort with the "male gender role" came in last and that it expresses that same contradiction in the men's rights cosmology: men don't want to be saddled with those traditional expectations of robotic stoicism, but they also are tired of being nice to women, who should be pulling their own weight in the workplace.

It's also interesting that fathers' rights tops the list but that father-*hood* is utterly absent. Men's rights activists are furious about having burdensome responsibilities, like child support, but rarely, if ever, wax rhapsodic about the joys of fatherhood or the loving connections that fathers are capable of having with their children.

That right to be a dad, to be a devoted and loving parent, doesn't actually fall on the men's rights radar. That's probably because to be that kind of dad, you'd need to balance work and family responsibilities and work with your wife or partner to support their efforts to balance work and family, too. Involved fatherhood—a fatherhood based on shared family responsibilities as a foundation for the rights to experience the transcendent joys of parenthood—has actually always been a *feminist* issue. Feminist women have urged, pleaded, insisted, and demanded that men share housework and child care, because they know that women can't "have it all" as long as men do—that is, as long as women alone are responsible for the second shift, the housework, and the child care. It turns out that the only way women can have it all is if men and women halve it all. You want your rights to be a father? It's simple: take your share of the responsibility.

However, perhaps most revealing is what—or, rather, who—is missing from the men's rights top ten. There's not a word about the especially dismal plight of African American men, or Latino men, or working-class men—the types of racial and ethnic and class discrimination they experience, *as men*, the stereotypes of their masculinity they are forced to endure, all of which deprives them of the "rights" claimed by other men. Nor is there a word about gay men and the ways in which they suffer discrimination in employment, housing, or their ability to marry the person they love or the terrible violence that gay, bisexual, and transgender men suffer every day at the hands of *other men* (just who do we think commits virtually every single act of gay bashing?).

Where are the legions of men's rights guys when it comes to "other" men? Men's rights is almost entirely a movement of angry straight white men. Gay men, black men, Asian men, Latino men, and other racial and ethnic minority men feel no such sense of entitlement to power that these middle-class white men feel has been unceremoniously and illegitimately snatched from them. That's not to say that in their personal relationships they don't feel entitled to unfettered obedience from their children, subservience from women, and a drive to find their place in the hierarchical pecking order. Many do. They just don't make a federal case out of their sense of entitlement. They don't take it to court or demand legislation. It's personal, not political.

Are there some arenas in which men are disadvantaged—in which it's actually "better" to be a woman? Sure. It's here that the familiar litany of the MRAs makes some sense: men have to register for the draft; women don't. Men are more likely to be denied joint custody, no matter how much time and energy they spend with their children.

But there is a major difference between being disadvantaged and being discriminated against. The former suggests that there are areas of public policy that still rely on outdated stereotypes, paternalistic policies designed to "protect" helpless, fragile, vulnerable women from the predations of men and the privations of individual freedom. The latter, being the victim of discrimination, relies on policies implemented to single out certain groups for unequal treatment. For example, men are dramatically overrepresented in all those hazardous occupations— but every time women have sought entry into those occupations, men have vigorously opposed their entry. Once again, that contradiction: on the one hand, MRAs believe men shouldn't be "forced" to do all the dangerous jobs; on the other hand, they also believe that women shouldn't (and are probably ill qualified to) invade men's territory. Although it's true that there remain some areas in which being a man is a disadvantage, there is no evidence that white men are the victims of discrimination.

One more example should suffice. As Roy Den Hollander was suing Columbia for its discriminatory exclusion of men from its women's and gender studies curriculum and promoting the religion of feminism, a new academic "movement" was being created. This new group is notable, if only because it again captures the contradictions at the heart of the entire movement.

IN SEARCH OF MALE STUDIES

Academia has long been a bastion of untrammeled, if genteel, masculinity. So manly, in fact, was the college classroom, the chemistry lab, the frat house, the locker room that women were excluded from its hallowed halls for centuries. In the United States, women were excluded from higher education until the Civil War, but even after, for more than a century, women had to continue their campaign for admission to institutions of higher learning. Finally, in 1996, the Supreme Court ordered the Virginia Military Institute (and the Citadel), the last public universities to deny admission to women, to finally open their doors. And once there, they've had to fight these seemingly genteel institutions for institutional equality (equal access to hiring, tenure, promotion, and salary) and equal treatment in class (campaigning against sexual harassment and the use of pornographic slides to illustrate biological processes) as well as curricular visibility, in including women in the traditional liberal arts canon of great thinkers and writers. It's a struggle that continues to this day: although women outnumber men on campus as students, men are dramatically overrepresented the higher up the professorial and administrative ladders one looks.

Arguments justifying women's exclusion have nearly always rested on biological or biblical claims. Either biological or divinely created differences between women and men required the separation of spheres: "Man for the field, woman for the hearth," as Tennyson put it in 1849. "All else confusion."[34] Whenever women have sought to enter some public arena—whether the voting booth or the jury box, the corporate boardroom or the union hall, the foxhole or the firehouse—men have argued that women's physical inequality would prevent them from succeeding and that God had ordained women and men to separate spheres. (Actually, God never weighs in on this; only the interpreters do. The most we get is "Honor Thy Father and Thy Mother," which seems pretty egalitarian to me.)

Women's entry into higher education was met with derision and dismissal. In the late nineteenth century, Edward H. Clarke, a Harvard University professor (and the very first professor of education in the country), authored a book about women's education. *Sex in Education* (1873) was a runaway best seller; it went through seventeen editions and defined a field. In it, Clarke argued vigorously against women's access to higher education on biological and psychological grounds. First, he argued that if women went to college, their brains would grow heavier and their wombs would atrophy. Second, he argued that the intellectual demands of collegiate education would drive women mad.

What was the empirical evidence for these ridiculous claims? Clarke found that college-educated women had fewer children than noncollege women. See? After examining the records of Massachusetts mental hospitals, Clarke noticed that more college-educated women were institutionalized than non-college-educated women, but, on the other side, more non-college-educated men were institutionalized than college men. His conclusion was that college education so dramatically overtaxed the fragile and feeble female brain that the effort drove the women mad.

Today, of course, we'd recognize a correlation is not necessarily a cause, and we'd be more likely to attribute these statistical findings to expanding opportunities, not shrinking wombs, and to stymied and thwarted ambitions, rather than intellectual overtaxing. But women are still subject to that knee-jerk teleology, observing some empirical fact and reasoning backward to some putative cause. More than a century after Edward H. Clarke disgraced the Harvard brand, school president Lawrence Summers repeated the calumny. In January 2005, he offered some hypotheses about the dramatic underrepresentation of women as top-level professors in top-level science and math departments, and perhaps the most compelling one, in his view, was that women were biologically unsuited for the eighty-hour weeks that were required to become top scientists at top schools. (Given what an eighty-hour workweek entails, and what it means for one's family life, not to mention anything resembling a social life or relaxation, the only response was not to go out and find some women who were willing to do it, but to ask who in their right mind would put up with this requirement to succeed in their jobs. Moreover, what kind of insanity is it to think that such overidentification with the job is a marker of capacity to succeed? What gender thought this up? Obviously, not the one that cares for children.)

For most of our history, whatever the justification, campus life looked pretty much like this: men taught men about the great achievements of men. By the 1960s, women sought entry into the classroom and the curriculum and to be treated fairly once they got there. They sought equality in hiring and promotion in what had formerly been a man's world. And they campaigned not only for affirmative action hiring and promotion criteria, but also for integrating women into the curriculum. That was the original mission of women's studies: to remedy the historical exclusion of women from the traditional canon (a myopia that rendered the canon not politically incorrect, but *historically* inaccurate) and to provide a place where students could explore the centrality and significance of gender in their lives today.

Women's studies was remedial, designed to remedy previous inequality. So it's a bit ironic that today the men's rights groups are campaigning against *their* exclusion. "Where are *men's* studies?" they ask.

Seriously, though, pretty much every course that doesn't have the word *women* in the title is a course in "men's studies." It might even seem akin to former Louisiana state senator and imperial wizard of the Ku Klux Klan David Duke's calls for white studies on campuses— the cries of the formerly privileged railing against the loss of monopoly status. When you've commanded 100 percent of the oxygen, I guess having your share reduced to three-fourths must make you feel like you're suffocating.

Actually, the men's rights campaigners don't want anything to do with "men's studies." As far as they're concerned, men's studies already exists, and it's an outpost of the enemy.

There are several different headings under which men and masculinity are studied on campus today. For one thing, one of women's studies' more successful academic interventions was not only to make women visible, but also to make *gender* visible—both as one of the central elements by which one constructs one's identity and also as one of the axes along which society divides resources and power. Gender is central individually and socially. Before women's studies, we didn't really know that.

And as women's studies made gender visible, it meant that we could actually apply the insights of women's studies to men's lives: how is masculinity one of the constituent elements of men's identity? How do different groups of men understand the meanings of masculinity? And how do men experience the hierarchies and inequalities based on gender? Just as we might inquire how white people experience racial inequality, women's studies began to integrate men and masculinity into their courses and their analysis. That integration, in fact, has been so successful that about half of all women's studies programs have now changed their names to women's and gender studies, both to ensure that women's invisibility is not somehow magically restored but also to ensure that gender as both identity and inequality could be discussed and analyzed.

You'd think that men would be thrilled with this—finally, we could study men *as men*, understand how the dynamics of masculinity shape and distort our relationships with women, with other men, with our children, with our own sense of ourselves as men. (I know I was thrilled, anyway; my work has been within the women's studies framework because I've found that its analytic perspectives offer a compelling set of critical lenses through which to view men's lives.) Today, a dynamic subfield of gender studies, masculinity studies, is thriving on campuses—there are dozens of books series, scholarly journals, conferences, all the institutional trappings of the successful emergence of an academic subfield.

But Angry White Men are anything but happy about this state of affairs. As far as they're concerned, "men's studies"—or, as I like to call it, "masculinity studies"—is no friend to men, beholden as it is to feminist perspectives on gender inequality. In the past two years, a new group of disgruntled men has proposed a new field called "male studies," which is explicitly concerned with promoting the interests of men. "What are the ethical concerns of devoting 90 percent of resources to one gender?" asked Edward Stephens, chair of the On Step Institute for Mental Health Research and founder of the Institute for Male Studies and financial backer of the initiative. (No evidence is provided for the 90 percent figure.)

At their inaugural conference at a hotel in New York in 2010, attended by a few dozen scholars and activists, male studies activists made clear that they see, rightly in my view, women's studies and men's studies as allies in understanding gender dynamics. And they want nothing to do with it. (Like the rest of the men's rights movement, male studies exists almost entirely on the Internet; they have no meetings, and their single sparsely attended "conference" was beamed all over the world as a podcast that few, if any, actually watched.) According to Lionel Tiger, a retired professor of anthropology at Rutgers University, male studies was conceived as a riposte to feminism, which he characterized as "a well-meaning, highly successful, very colorful denigration of maleness as a force, as a phenomenon."[35]

Tiger is the author of the 1969 chestnut *Men in Groups*, which bemoaned the loss of all-male spaces in the public arena (because of women's invasion) and urged city planners to include ceremonial men's huts in their urban plans. His more recent works offer even more stunning formulations. In *The Decline of Males* (1999), Tiger argues that "the male and female sexes in industrial societies are slowly but inexorably moving apart"—this just at the moment of the greatest empirical convergence in men's and women's behaviors and attitudes in our history. This is due, he argues, to women's control over birth control, a force that gives them virtually all social power.[36]

In a new twist, Tiger "explains" the cause of the visibility of gay men in social life as—actually, it's more accurate to say he "blames" it on—you guessed it, women. Not the old "my mother made me a homosexual" slogan of 1950s psychoanalysis, this view contends that homosexuality is "caused" by overdominant mothers and absent fathers. After all, that formulation *might* be seen as blaming the fathers for their absence. Instead, Tiger has devised an explanation that leaves men entirely out of the equation and thus entirely off the hook. Women did this all by themselves. Here's how: by taking drugs.

I know it's startling, so hear him out: Tiger argues that women's use of barbiturates during pregnancy in the 1950s and 1960s caused the spike of male homosexuality in the 1960s and 1970s. "The sons of women using barbiturates are much more likely to be 'feminized,' to display bodies and behavior more typically female than male. Millions of American mothers of boys, an estimated eleven million in the 1950s and 60s, used barbiturates, and millions still do. A compelling thought is that this may have something to do with the evident increase in the number, or at least prominence, of male homosexuals," he writes. Now remember that there is not a scintilla of evidence that those same women who took barbiturates had gay sons, nor that there is even a correlation between barbiturate use and *having* a gay son. But Tiger goes even further than a simple "correlation implies causation" fallacy. He thinks barbiturates explain not only the cause but also the *prominence* of gay men. One can only imagine that causal reasoning: gay sons of barbiturate-using mothers support liberalized drug laws that bring them into public-policy arenas and make them more prominent.[37] It's hard to imagine male studies getting any loopier than these dicta from their éminence grise.

Perhaps the most prolific writers in the male studies canon are Paul Nathanson and Katherine Young, a researcher and a professor, respectively, in religious studies at McGill University, coauthors of a series of books on "misandry"—the hatred of men and boys. Misandry, they argue, is a most pernicious ideology that is "being generated by feminists," a pervasive cultural trope that has infected every aspect of cultural life in North America.

Misandry is, of course, intended as a parallel to misogyny, the widespread fear and loathing of women, the institutional denigration and discrimination of that hatred, and the recourse to violence to enforce it. Misogyny assumes a set of attitudes, yes, but also the political ability to institutionalize and legitimate it and the repressive apparatus to enforce it. Claiming some sort of equivalent parallel is, of course, utterly tendentious, but Nathanson and Young have made a cottage industry out of trying. Over a decade, they've coauthored four large tomes (made much larger by padding them with everything from reviews to e-mails about the books).

It is one thing—silly and untrue, to be sure—to argue that feminists hate men or that feminism presents a sustained and consistent ideological rant against men, the definition of that facile neologism. But it is truly ridiculous to argue that feminists have managed to infiltrate America's political and cultural capitals to such an extent that they now have the political capacity to institutionalize misandry.

But wait! Like a TV infomercial, there's more! In Nathanson's and Young's fevered imaginations, it's not feminist activists who have managed to pull off this coup without anyone noticing. It turns out that it was actually the handiwork of a few *academic feminist film critics*, who seem to have been both so well positioned and so powerful that they poisoned the cultural well and turned Hollywood against both men and masculinity. This tiny academic feminist cabal—I think it's probably only Pauline Kael—has so successfully infected popular media that it is *men* who are the object of contempt, scorn, and derision.

Based on astonishingly selective, simplistic, and shallow readings of several films from the 1990s, one of their books claims that we have witnessed, in the space of a decade, "gynocentrism's" complete triumph and the insinuation of misandrous ideas into mainstream

American culture, so that now all its products tell us that "there is nothing about men as such that is good or even acceptable."[38]

To Nathanson and Young, misandry has insinuated itself so insidiously that we've barely been aware of the how the process works. Misandry, they argue, proceeds from benign laughter to contemptuous sneering to bypassing men altogether in a far more pleasant "gurls club" (*Fried Green Tomatoes, The Color Purple, Thelma and Louise*). And the attitudes of the films proceed from blaming men (*Handmaid's Tale, Mr. and Mrs. Bridge*) to dehumanizing them (*Beauty and the Beast*) and ultimately demonizing men (*Wolf, Sleeping with the Enemy*), declaring men, themselves, to be devils incarnate.

This is, of course, appallingly bad history. Yet their analysis is instructive, I think, because it exposes the various misreadings that form the recipe of the male studies enterprise: a heaping dose of dramatic misreading of texts, with no foundational understanding of how texts are actually experienced by consumers, and more than a pinch of conspiratorial hysteria. These cultural products actually don't make fun of men at all; they make fun of *patriarchy*—and the inflated sense of entitlement, the arrogant bluster, and the silly prerogatives than any illegitimate form of power would confer on the powerful.

The word *misandry* itself is a neologism—my spell-check program consistently underlines it as unrecognizable. As anthropologist David Gilmore writes, in his masterful psychoanalytically informed treatise on misogyny, there is no parallel of misandry at all; it's a false equivalence. Misandry refers, Gilmore writes, "not to the hatred of men as men, but to the hatred of men's traditional male role, the obnoxious manly *pose*, a culture of machismo; that is, to an adopted sexual ideology," but not to some form of hatred of men or the establishment of the institutional apparatus by which to oppress them.[39]

Like medieval carnival—indeed, like most comedy in general—TV sitcoms turn reality upside down, providing momentary solace and a few laughs and ultimately reinforcing the powers that be. Indeed, among our greatest pleasures is the fantasy of turning the tables on those who make us miserable, encouraging illusions that the last shall be first. Any system that can provide such fantasies can't be half bad, can it? Imagine these erstwhile cultural guides in late-sixteenth-century Europe. After witnessing carnival, seeing Shakespeare's comedies, and hearing a spate of popular bawdy songs, Nathanson and Young would no doubt conclude that the nobility was under siege from "ideological serfs" who controlled all popular media and propounded "aristophobia." No doubt their colleagues would declare that quietly and deftly, feudalism had been utterly dismantled by a peasant rebellion that would usher in the bloodiest tyranny in history. Madame Defarge as feminist icon? In truth, of course, such cultural inversions are more compensations for power that some groups do not have, rather than literal expressions of power they do have.

Male studies reminds me of the right wing of the Republican Party, those who have been engaged in a long-standing class war against the 99 percent in favor of the 1 percent who write their checks, declaring that any form of "fair-share" taxation of the wealthy amounts to class warfare from below. The denizens of the male studies world howl because they feel ignored in the academic world, but they are ignored not because they are male, but because their scholarship is so shoddy and their theories so hysterical. Male studies has about as much chance of catching on in academia as would ruling-class studies. It's not because the powerful don't still maintain most of the world's power or the institutional apparatus to legitimate and enforce it. Frankly, I think it's more because they just don't want to draw any more attention to it.

WHY MEN'S RIGHTS IS WRONG (FOR THE RIGHT REASONS)

It might be easy, if facile, to simply demonstrate empirically that MRAs are "wrong" in their claims. I've indulged in a bit of that here. But I think it's important to acknowledge the authenticity of the pain and anguish that propel their misguided empirical analysis. That's real and important. Many men do not feel very good about their lives. They're casting about for someone to blame, some explanation for their anguish, confusion, malaise. In a sense, I think some of the original men's liberation rhetoric hit closer to the mark. Traditional masculinity can be a fool's errand, an effort to live up to standards set by others that leave you feeling empty, friendless, a Willy Loman surrounded by Mitt Romneys—shallow, happy cartoon characters. They feel themselves to be the "hollow men" in the T. S. Eliot poem. They're scared their lives are going to amount to little. That malaise is real and important—and able to be politically manipulated and mobilized. Failure to hear that pain means that rational assessments of these men's plights will never be heard.

As the country was being founded, Thomas Jefferson envisioned a democracy as a mix of rights and responsibilities—the rights to which we are endowed by our Creator are always set against the responsibilities to the community, to the other people's ability to pursue those same rights with the same freedoms. A focus on responsibilities alone dissolves the individual into simply a drone, a worker bee, part of the mass, indistinguishable from the rest. But a focus on rights only, as in men's rights rhetoric, aggrandizes into narcissistic solipsism, a competitive me-firstism that can only take without giving anything back.

In 1848, nearly a century after the nation embraced Jefferson's vision, American women realized they'd sort of been left out of the "life, liberty, and the pursuit of happiness" equation. They had few rights, and those they had still excluded them from having a public voice or presence. The motto of the woman suffrage movement, proclaimed by Susan B. Anthony in a slogan that formed the banner of the movement's newspaper, the *Revolution*, was simple: "Men, their rights and nothing more! Women, their rights and nothing less!" Still seems an apt framing.

4 | Angry White Dads

On August 20, 2007, two British guys, dressed up as Captain America and Batman, shimmied up Abraham Lincoln's trunk-like marble legs at the Lincoln Memorial in Washington, DC. No, this wasn't a stunt advertisement for some new superhero movie starring Robert Downey Jr. Jolly Stanesby and Mike Downes unfurled a banner that read simply "For the Fathers of the Nation."

They had been well prepared. Downes and Stanesby were members of Fathers 4 Justice (F4J), a British group of disgruntled divorced fathers who had resorted to dramatic tactics with the hopes of generating public attention for their plight. The organization was founded in 2002 by divorced dad Matt O'Connor, an advertising executive with a flair for the mediagenic.

F4J "quickly became the high-wire act of protest groups," according to its website, "whether powder-bombing the Prime Minister in the House of Commons, scaling the balcony at Buckingham Palace in a Batman Costume, invading the Pulpit at York Minster during a General Synod Service or taking the National Lottery Draw live off air on BBC1 in front of ten million viewers." Earlier in 2007, Stanesby had been arrested for climbing Stonehenge dressed as Fred Flintstone. In 2004 both men had forced the closure of Severn Bridge, a lovely span that links Wales and England, close to Bristol, while dressed as Father Christmas. In the United States, F4J members have tried similar, if less spectacular, stunts, such as unfurling banners at Ohio State football games, but with very little media attention and virtually no results.[1] (At least these guys have both a sense of humor and a knack for self-promotion.)

Fathers 4 Justice is just one of hundreds of organizations promoting what is generally known as fathers' rights. In large part, theirs is a campaign to help men retain the rights to *be* fathers in the first place following a divorce—maintaining visitation rights or sharing or gaining custody. These are laudable goals, to ensure that men can continue to be the active and engaged fathers after a divorce that they had been during their marriages. Sadly, the movement also contains activists who want nothing of the kind, but rather those who are virulently antifeminist and even those who seek to enable men who have been violent or abusive toward their ex-wives or even their children.

This is "a revolution where divorced, loving, and caring dads are now demanding equal access to their children," comments Joel Leyden, the head of Fathers 4 Justice in Israel. "We have drawn a line in the sand and have declared that we will no longer tolerate the breaking of the sacred bond between parents and child by the state," reads the F4J pledge. "We will finish what we have begun. For our children."[2] These statements express the tension at the heart of the movement. Just who are these guys? Are they devoted dads who are filled with love and abounding joy at being parents, or are they furious fathers, conflating their needs and their children's, "demanding" their rights, and pushing everyone else aside as they angrily pursue them?

The answer, as we'll see, is both. Some start as devoted dads and become furious fathers following divorce. Some stay devoted; they leave the movement almost as soon as they join. And that's the heart of their story. Most divorcing dads are not angry white men, efforts to turn them bitter and angry by the leaders of the fathers' rights movement (FRM) notwithstanding.

ANGRY DADS

Let's be clear from the outset: serious activist members of the FRM are decidedly *not* those legions of devoted daddies who are the media darlings heralding a new fatherhood—the ones who wax rhapsodic about the pleasures of potty training, the ecstasy of dirty-diaper changing at the drop of a Snuggly. These are not the "new" fathers whose faces positively glow with naive, sweet, starry-eyed glassiness when they describe their children falling asleep on their chests. Such wondrous new men do exist, of course, but they're unlikely to join fathers' rights groups or protest in courtrooms. And if they don a Batman costume, it's for their five-year-old's birthday party, not to stage a demonstration.

The fathers' rights activists (FRAs) aren't always "nice," nor are they particularly devoted. What they are is pissed off. The movement's leaders are the furious fathers, the ones who sneer about laws and custody battles and the "bitches" (their ex-wives) and their take-no-prisoner lawyers and the feminist edifice that keeps them from living the lives in their families to which they feel utterly entitled.

That sense of entitlement—that aggrieved entitlement—means, of course, that they're white, straight, and middle class. They tend to be youngish, late thirties to midforties, according to one survey, average age forty-six, according to another. Nearly nine of ten are white; four of five have white-collar jobs. Middle- and upper-middle-class, white, middle-aged men—what could they *possibly* have to complain about? Well, perhaps they're not facing midlife all that gracefully, confronting that stereotypic moment when they realize that "this"—wife, kids, late-model minivan, job with limited upward mobility—is what their lives are going to look like for the duration. Some will grow a ponytail, buy a red Lexus IS 250C convertible, and take up with a nubile twenty-six-year-old. Others will turn inward, toward their families. Some will get divorced, often initiated by their wives, seemingly out of nowhere. Some will recommit. Some get so mad that they want to get even. And some—as many as ten thousand or so, it would appear—join a movement.[3]

The transformation of devoted daddies into furious fathers is not inevitable. It has to be inculcated. In fact, many of the rank-and-file fathers' rights guys *are* the devoted daddies. Or at least they were, until they got divorced. Then, they felt blindsided, confused, bereft. It is the task of the movement's leaders to turn that confusion and pain into rage. Listen to Mickey, interviewed by Jocelyn Crowley for her book *Defiant Dads:* "Everyone that I know in the group right now is fighting with everything they have got to stay in their kids' lives. These aren't the . . . deadbeat dads coming to a fathers' group because they won't pay their child support. The guys in this group are just like me. They love their kids and their kids have been ripped out of their lives. These guys are hurting. It's not [about] having to coax a father back into their child's life."[4]

And here's what Jeff, a forty-four-year-old computer salesman, whom I met at a Long Island fathers' rights group meeting, said:

> *I did everything right, played by all the rules. I supported my family, put in countless hours with my kids. Jesus, I was like "Mr. Dad" around the neighborhood. My kids' friends all said they wished their dads were like me. But then my wife and I split up, and I just lost everything. I don't understand it. Just everything. I lost the house, the car, and money—oh Christ don't get me started on how much child support I have to pay. But I lost my kids, man. I barely get to see them one afternoon a week. I'd gladly give up all the rest if I could have more time with them. And they need me! What about their needs?[5]*

Fringe groups like the Coalition for Free Men, Men Achieving Liberation and Equality, the National Organization for Men, and Men's Rights, Inc., provide support for men in divorce proceedings and counseling and referrals to help them "fight dirty and win" to get custody of the kids. Recently divorced dads, bereft and confused, hear a ready-made antifeminist diatribe masquerading as an analysis of their situation; it both exonerates them of all responsibility for the situation in which they find themselves and focuses all their anger on their wives—and often on women in general. They hear how their wives, and their ex-wives' lawyers, manipulate a legal system into eviscerating men and rewarding women. They hear piles of anecdotes about guys who were blindsided by an unfair judicial system and ex-wives who fought dirty. (The movement has reams of anecdotes, but very little actual data.) They hear how men are increasingly the victims of discrimination: "Women are *privileged* because they are more frequently *allowed* to raise children, while men are being *oppressed* by denial of access to children."

There's rarely a divorce without some bitterness, of course. And some of these groups seem to give voice to that feminist axiom that "the personal is political." But sometimes one's soon-to-be ex-wife isn't a stand-in for the entire politically motivated, feminist-inspired female sex—just as each divorcing dad is hardly the feckless philanderer or absentee workaholic of soap-opera stereotypes. Real divorces are often messy and ugly and bring out the more petty complaints that leave bystanders wondering what the divorcing couple ever saw in each other in the first place. But they're personal tragedies. It's the task of many fathers' rights organizations to make them political treatises.

Other organizations offer healthier servings of support and advice, like the American Coalition for Fathers and Children, Fathers and Families, the Fatherhood Coalition, and Fathers Supporting Fathers. The National Fatherhood Initiative is among the most influential pro-marriage groups in the country. None of these, though, actually work with fathers to really improve their relationships with their children. That would fall more often to more feminist-friendly groups like Dads and Daughters (DADs), which works with men to be more supportive fathers to their daughters and help their daughters resist media stereotypes about body issues, girly-girl Barbie-doll femininity, and the hypersexualization of young girls. Or there's Grateful Dads, an obviously posthippie group that works with corporations as well as with fathers to facilitate more active fatherhood and promote work-family balance. To most of the fathers' rights groups, these last examples would be more the problem than the solution. They aren't really interested in changing the *content* of men's relationship with their children, just the form. And that's what makes them less than trustworthy as parents.

THE CHANGES IN FATHERS' LIVES

Fathers' rights groups may have turned nasty and negative, but they have their origins in a very positive historical trend—a sea change that has engulfed contemporary American family life. Stated most simply, men are more involved in their families than ever. Contemporary American men do more housework and more child care than any generation of American men has ever done. They are the most involved fathers in American history.

Just consider the enormous changes in fathering in the past half century. Fifty years ago, fathers who wanted to attend the birth were regarded as potentially deviant, and only 5 percent of fathers attended hospital births in the 1950s. (My dad tells me that he was physically barred from the door of the delivery room when I was born, as they thought he would be a distraction.) Today, attendance is pretty much de rigueur, with 97 percent of fathers attending hospital births (if they are married to the woman giving birth) since the 1990s. Indeed, being there to cut the umbilical cord is seen as a "badge of manhood."[6]

In those midcentury days, middle-class men were married as much to their jobs as to their wives. Home life was a luxury, something to be indulged after you'd arrived home on the 6:32 to Danbury, had that tall drink and dinner prepared from scratch by your wife, and had a few moments to sit down to read the newspaper. Kids were a head-ache, a responsibility, a drain—rarely a joy. Just watch TV's *Mad Men*'s Don Draper sometime with his children. He's stiff and formal and finds them tedious and distracting, particularly when he was married to his first wife, Betty. Now that he's remarried to a woman who actually enjoys them (but doesn't want any of her own, since she wants a career), he's actually a bit looser and more involved. Imagine what a downer they would be if he were still single and trying to get laid!

There's a marvelous *New Yorker* cartoon that captures this old pattern. A young corporate guy stands before his supervisor and says, "My wife is about to have a baby, so I wonder if you could make me work late for the next 18 years or so." So much for the good old days.

I vividly remember one incident just after my parents divorced in 1968, the year I graduated from high school and left home for college. My dad took me for lunch during his weekly visit, and we joined several other divorced dads, all friends of his. (Like a lot of dads, he was at somewhat of a loss about what, exactly, to do with his children for a whole weekend day.) At the round table in the cheesy cocktail lounge and restaurant, each of the men recited his postdivorce "arrangement"—did he pay alimony, how much, what sort of custody arrangements did he have, visitation rights, child-support payments, and the like. (I was the only "child" there, and I suppose my dad thought that, at seventeen, I was old enough to hear this manly conversation; all the rest of the guys had children who were still in middle or high school.)

Each guy told his sad story: one complained about paying for a lazy layabout wife, another about his massive child-support payments, and yet a third about the tedious and uncomfortable visitation time with his kids. (Perhaps bring them to lunch with other divorced dads?) No one seemed happy. No one, that is, except Paul. "No alimony, no child support, and, most of all, no custody or visitation," Paul announced. "Gents," he smiled, seemingly gloating, "I got away clean."

I scanned the table, watching the other men's faces. They were surprised, yes, but I was sure that every single one (except my dad) also had a sort of admiring, wistful look on his face as well. Envy, even. Paul "got away clean." He never had to see his children again. He was free!

I was somewhat taken aback by this, and my dad and I talked about it on the way home. He explained why the other guys might have been envious of Paul. For one thing, he could keep his entire income, which meant more money to spend on himself, and thus to have a leg up when he reentered the dating market. He didn't have to constantly be reminded, every single month, of how much he hated his ex-wife. But most of all, in the dating market, being saddled with children was a definite drawback for the younger women who wanted to have kids and families themselves. (My dad was barely forty, as were his friends; their second wives were, to a man, about twelve years younger than the men were.)

I doubt very many divorced dads these days use such a phrase like "got away clean"—especially when it comes to their children. More than likely, yesterday's divorced dad who got away clean is today's deadbeat dad—a reprehensible reprobate who ignores his family commitment. He's more of a cautionary tale than a role model.

Well, at least that's true in the popular imagination. Most deadbeat dads earn so little that they can't pay their own rents, let alone contribute to their kids' welfare. In a recent study in Ohio, for example, 23 percent of those divorced dads who were in arrears on child-support payment had no income at all for the six quarters preceding (and they owed 37 percent of the uncollected money); another 23 percent had income between one dollar and ten thousand dollars (and they owed 32 percent). Just 5 percent of the money was owed by men with annual earnings above forty thousand dollars. Deadbeat daddyism is often not a bunch of upper-middle-class guys skipping away free; it's a scathing indictment of our punitive family-assistance program that tries to foist financial responsibility on men who cannot stay afloat even without these ties that bind.[7]

Sure, plenty of men have acrimonious divorces, and many have strained relationships with their children. But most divorcing dads have also invested considerable time and energy in—not to mention feel a massive amount of love and devotion toward—their children. That today American men are spending far more time with their families may be the single biggest change in family life over the past half century. Those halcyon days of the 1950s looked more like *Mad Men* than *Leave It to Beaver*. For men of the 1950s and 1960s, real life lay elsewhere, outside the white picket fence of their suburban enclave.

Look at how far we've come. While many pundits lament the collapse of the family and high divorce rates and warn about the specter of fatherlessness—attempting to shore up an institution that feels like its crumbling like a sand castle in a hurricane of secularism and promiscuity—the other side of the story is equally important, especially when trying to understand why so many middle-aged, middle-class white guys are so furious. It's equally true that American men are more family focused than ever, and this is especially true for Gen X and Gen Y men, new fathers in their twenties and thirties.

You could measure this massive sea change by looking at the historical shift in men's attitudes. For all their liberated Woodstock going and tuning in and dropping out, baby-boomer men have been the most work-centric generation of American men ever, even more so than their fathers. Whereas only about 10 percent of Gen Y (under age twenty-three), Gen X (twenty-three to twenty-seven), and mature (sixty and older) male workers describe themselves as "work-centric," more than 23 percent of baby boomers do. Still, it's telling that younger men seek—and expect—to balance work and family at rates identical to their wives. Half of Gen Y and Gen X men describe themselves as "family-centric," ignoring the third option of "dual-centric."

Take another example. A recent poll in *Newsweek* found that 55 percent of fathers say that being a parent is more important to them than it was to their fathers, and 70 percent say they spend more time with their children than their fathers spent with them. A 1995 survey sponsored by the Families and Work Institute found that 21 percent of the 460 men surveyed said that they would prefer to be home caring for their families if they had enough money to live comfortably.[8]

You could even chart this historic shift by looking at the advice they're getting from experts. It's telling how Dr. Benjamin Spock's multidecade best-selling book *Babies and Child Care* (1946) noted (and perhaps even encouraged) the shift in thinking about fathers' involvement. In the first edition, Dr. Spock suggested that men could be somewhat involved in child care: "Some fathers have been brought up to think that the care of babies and children is the mother's job entirely. This is the wrong idea. You can be a warm father and a real man at the same time. . . . Of course I don't mean that the father has to give just as many bottles or change just as many diapers as the mother. But it's fine for him to do these things occasionally. He might make the formula on Sunday."

But a half century later, in the book's seventh edition, Spock records the shifts his work has helped to bring about: "Men, especially the husbands of women with outside jobs, have been participating increasingly in all aspects of home and child care. There is no reason why fathers shouldn't be able to do these jobs as well as mothers. . . . But the benefit may be lost if this work is done as a favor to the wife, since that implies that raising the child is not really the father's work but that he's merely being extraordinarily generous."[9]

Fathers listened, and they have done these jobs well. In 1924, 10 percent of working-class women said their husbands spent "no time" doing housework; today that percentage is less than 2 percent. Between the mid-1960s and the mid-1970s, men's housework increased from 104 to 130 minutes a day, while women's decreased from 7.4 to 6.8 hours a day. The median amount for men was about 5 hours a week; for women it was about 20 hours. Men reported that they did 10 percent of the housework in 1970 and 20 percent in 1990—which, depending upon how you look at it, represents double the percentage in only twenty years, or, still, only one-fifth the amount that needs to be done.[10]

Still, it remains pretty uneven. On an average day, 83 percent of women and 65 percent of men spent some time doing household activities such as housework, cooking, lawn care, or financial and other household management. On the days that they did household activities, women spent an average of 2.6 hours on such activities, whereas men spent 2.1 hours. About one in five men (19 percent) engaged in what you might call housework chores, such as cleaning and doing laundry, on an average day, compared with 48 percent of women. When it came to food preparation and cleanup, 40 percent of men did it versus 66 percent of women.[11]

One must, of course, always be circumspect with these figures. You can't just ask men how much housework they do; they systematically overestimate it. Actually, both women and men overreport the amount of housework they do—men overreport by about 150 percent, women by about 68 percent. (The overreporting by men was so significant that the original researchers doubted that "husbands have increased their supply of domestic labor to the household in the past 25 years.")[12]

Other survey methodologies have yielded results, however, suggesting that men's participation in housework and child care has increased somewhat over the past quarter century, though probably not as much as men themselves might claim. When couples were asked to keep accurate records of how much time they spent doing which household tasks, men still put in between one-fifth and one-fourth the time their wives put in. And not all men are doing more housework; rather, some men are doing more of it than others.

Men's changing experience of family life depends on age, race, class, and level of education. Younger men, for example, are doing far more around the house than their fathers did—though their wives still do a lot more. A poll of women younger than thirty in *Ladies' Home Journal* in May 1997 found that 76 percent said they did most of the laundry, 73 percent did most of the cooking, 70 percent did most of the housecleaning, 67 percent did most of the grocery shopping, and 56 percent paid most of the bills.[13] Black men, on average, do more housework than white men, and working-class white men do more than middle-class white men. (That black men do more seems to have more to do with class than race; middle-class black men do about the same amount as middle-class white men.) In one study, sociologists Carla Shows and Naomi Gerstel found that working-class emergency medical technicians did more housework and child care than higher-paid, better-educated physicians, though the physicians were far more "liberal" and "egalitarian" in their attitudes.[14]

Of course, this sea change in parenting is lumpy and uneven. When sociologists ask people about their participation in family life, we usually combine both housework and child care into one single measure. By that measure, men's "family participation" has increased moderately, as we saw above. But what really seems to be happening is that men are splitting housework and child care in their daily practices—they're doing virtually no more housework, but tons more child care. In general, men seem to maintain the contradictory ideas that they want to shield and protect their wives from life's unpleasantness, while they steadfastly refuse to perform a task as "degrading" as washing the toilet.

The truth is, men are changing as fathers a lot faster than they are changing as husbands. With men's child-care participation increasing so much faster than their housework activity, a dangerous disequilibrium is developing in which dad is becoming the "fun parent." *He* takes the kids to the park and plays soccer with them, while the mom stays home. "What a great time we had with Dad!" the kids announce as they burst through the kitchen door to a lunch that she prepared while also folding the laundry, making the beds, and vacuuming the living room. Of course, Dad pats himself on the back for being such an involved parent. (I generally refer to this as "premature self-congratulation.")

But as more men are doing more around the house, they're also catching up to women when it comes to struggling to achieve the work-and-life balance. Men report significantly higher levels of work-family conflict than they did thirty years ago; in fact, men's rates now sometimes surpass women's. Three of five fathers in dual-earner couples report significant work-family conflict, up from just over a third (35 percent) in 1977.[15]

These changes among American men are the real backdrop for the debate about fathers' rights. It's the good news. The pleasures of being an involved parent (married men are happier than unmarried men, and married fathers are the happiest of all) far outweigh the "equality of stress" that seems to be taking place (which points more to a workplace that still overvalues the unencumbered worker and makes few provisions for parents). Even though their workplaces are intransigent, men are still becoming more involved fathers—and families are becoming increasingly equal.

So ask yourself this: whom do men have to thank for the innumerable joys that come with this increase in their family commitments?

Why, feminist women, of course. If fathers today are spending more time and energy in family life than their predecessors did, feminist women should get a massive amount of the credit. Men didn't suddenly have a V-8 moment, slap themselves upside the head, and say, "Oh, my goodness, I could have been doing housework and child care!" Hardly. Feminism inspired women to get outside the home, to seek work and careers, and to try to balance work and family. Such balancing efforts were unsuccessful for one simple reason: women couldn't balance work and family unless men changed their behaviors around the home. Women couldn't, as that infelicitous phrase had it, "have it all" because, well, men did. And men had it all precisely because women did the "second shift," the housework and child care.

FROM ANGUISH TO ANGER

If men have increased their family time, it's not because they were marching to the beat of a male drum and bugle corps. Indeed, many men resisted for decades. It's been women, and especially those working mothers inspired by feminist ideals of workplace equality, who have been imploring, cajoling, insisting, yelling, and otherwise pleading with them to do their share. The dual-career, dual-caregiver family form—the family form that is becoming the norm in American society—is, let's be clear, a feminist invention. So it's a bit ironic, and a lot disingenuous, for these same men who have stepped up and become more active fathers to now declare they are doing so in opposition to feminism. Theirs is the other half of gender equality in the public sphere, and this massive cultural transformation, this blending of the public and the private, is partly the result of a relentless campaign by feminist women.

Instead of thanking women—and especially those feminist-inspired working mothers—for enabling and insisting that we spend more time in our families, the fathers' rights movement spends a lot of time attacking those same feminist women. They take their grief and confusion at the dissolution of their families and transform it into rage at their ex-wives, their ex-wives' lawyers, family-court judges—and, of course, the feminist women who seem to inspire them all.

They are often right to be angry at the system, which can hurt them, but their rage at women feels misplaced. Instead of pretending that feminists are the enemy, these involved and engaged fathers should be allying themselves with feminist women in supporting egalitarian parenting after divorce as during the marriage and an equal and equitable split of family assets. We should assume that *both* ex-husband and ex-wife are fully capable of supporting themselves in the workplace, so that alimony could be used only to supplement the ex-wives' income to compensate for the gender wage gap. We should also assume that both parents have been equally invested and equally responsible for their children's welfare and, with some demonstrable evidence that such is the case, all other things being equal, that both parents should share custody, which is, after all, not about possessing property, but raising human beings.

Let me go a step further. What are the forces that have prevented men from becoming the fathers that they say they want to be? They are a combination of an unyielding workplace and an ideology of masculinity that promotes robotic stoicism over nurturing, competition over patience, aggression over justice. That is, it's institutional inflexibility, giving guys the message that the "unencumbered worker" is really the best sort of worker (here they would find common cause with women who are also stymied by this). The set of attitudes and traits that is most closely associated with masculinity—robotic stoicism, competition, aggression—are those that contradict most with the qualities needed to be a good parent: patience, nurturing, emotional resilience. In that sense, men who seek to be really involved fathers have to choose between fatherhood and masculinity—at least in the traditional sense of masculinity. It's a false choice, of course, and the groups that have launched the most persuasive critique of traditional notions of masculinity have been black men, gay men, and feminist women.

Fathers' rights arguments actually do little to advance the cause of fathers; indeed, they detract from the movement's credibility—and lead the movement of involved and injured dads right into the waiting arms of the men's rights movement—rather than into a more credible alliance with those men of color who are promoting fathers' responsibility; gay men, who seek to become and are proving to be quite adept at fatherhood themselves; and feminist women.

I watched this process unfold when I attended some meetings of Fathers United (not its real name), a suburban support group for recently divorced guys. Arnie, the convener of the group, was hesitant at first, when I inquired about coming to some meetings. It wasn't my assurances of anonymity that he wanted; it was that he didn't trust me personally, since I'm known to be on the other side of this debate. I assured him that that was exactly *why* I wanted to come, because I wanted to get it right, didn't want to be too dismissive, and because I thought there was some value to what was happening among fathers.

At seven thirty, the men assembled in Arnie's apartment, a modest two-bedroom in a suburban low-rise building. *Apartment* may be the wrong word; it was his man cave. Divorced and left entirely to his own decorative devices, Arnie had paper sports posters of his favorite players hung with thumbtacks pressed into the walls, sports memorabilia scattered on the bookshelves where books might otherwise have gone, and a good-size flat-screen TV occupying one entire wall opposite the sofa and La-Z-Boy chair. A cliché? You bet. I suspect that is what he was actually going for, a deliberate stereotypical look, saying, "This is the narrative of a free man!" The second bedroom looked like a study—papers strewn on the desk, computer, office chair. There was a single bed against one wall, plain blanket and caseless pillow on it. (Arnie has two daughters; he does not have custody, but does have visitation rights.)

Back in the living room, a few bridge chairs were also assembled for the occasion, and chips and soft drinks were in red plastic beer cups. There was no alcohol. "We need guys to really focus," Arnie explains.

By eight o'clock, about six guys have gathered and are seated on the sofa and in a few of the chairs. Arnie's on the La-Z-Boy. Each guy describes his current status—whether he is dating, when his divorce came through, his custody arrangement, how often he sees his kids. Then we circle back, as each guy talks about how he's feeling about it.

Tom describes how upset and anguished he is over his current custody and child-support arrangements. He wants to have the kids more often (he has a boy and a girl, ages eight and five), but doesn't want to be paying so much in child support. "It's killing me," he says. "I get them once a week, for a day. We go do stuff, but they only get to *do* things. We don't really do what I think we all want, which is to just hang out together. I always feel like I have to *entertain* them. And then I have to pay two hundred dollars a week, and I just don't feel like I have enough at the end of the month, what with my rent and all. My wife doesn't kick in nearly as much for them."

Greg jumps in. "Hah! It's like 'pay to play' except all you do is pay, and you don't really get to play."

"It's like *she* gets to play, man," Hal adds.

"That's the problem, right?" Arnie now intercedes. "It's like *they* keep on winning. No matter what we do, it's not good enough. They made us miserable when we were married to them, but they're making us even more miserable now that we're divorced."

"No," Tom says, sadly now, his head hanging down and his shoulders sagging. "It's not my ex. She's a great mom; my kids are really happy with her. It's not her fault. It's that fucking judge, and the lawyers. They made it sound like I was some kind of monster or something, and then the judge never really listens to me, says 'Yeah, yeah, whatever' when I explain how much I'm involved with the kids, and then, like, slams me with this support shit."

"Yeah, but, you see, that's her fault too," says Arnie, refusing to let go of his line of reasoning. "Who the fuck do you think told the lawyers to say that? Who told the judge that, boo hoo, it's so hard to make ends meet, and how you have a good job and all? I guarantee if you follow the trail, it leads back to her—and probably some feminist support group she was part of, some crazed wife-abuse hag who told her to lie."

I could see Tom was uncomfortable with this argument. "No, man, that's not it. She and I, we were okay, and okay about everything. Like, it was an amicable divorce."

"No such fucking thing," muttered Greg.

"No, really, man. We were doing okay. She was going to have the kids during the week, I would have them on the weekends, and I'd help support them. But she has a job and doesn't really need me to support her at the same time I provide for them. But the judge was like from the Stone Age. It was like *her* job didn't even count and like mine counted double or something. He couldn't get it to work out fair."

"Well, why do you think the judge was so unfair?" Arnie asks. He will not relent. "It's because *they* got to him; they made his career depend on their liking him. I'm telling you . . ." His voice trails off, as Tom finally says, "It wasn't her. It was courts, the fucking system that screwed me. Not Alice. We're still trying to be friends. Really. And she is an awesome mom."

"Yeah, friends. That's likely," Arnie shrugs. "Friends. Okay, who's next?"

This miniature tableau is played out frequently at father support groups.[16] Some guys are confused, feeling somewhat or seriously bruised by the system. Others, in this case the group leader and convener (and the only guy in the room who was a member of any men's rights organization), tried to steer the conversation away from the institutions and toward women—in this case the ex-wife, Alice, in particular, and the feminist harridans who must have so poisoned her that she was willing to lie to get what they wanted her to have. Anguish is replaced by anger, confusion by caustic sarcasm, despair by a desire for vengeance. All misplaced, but convenient, and far more conducive to mobilization. Only when you feel entitled to have everything do you blame your former partner for having *anything*.

THE POLITICS OF FATHERS' RIGHTS

Rank-and-file divorced dads often feel blindsided by a system that takes no account of the actual involvement they have worked so hard to achieve. Most recently, divorced dads come to fatherhood groups not because they want to influence policy, but because they want support, legal and personal advice, some form of help. They grab at any straw that seems to offer them a shred of analysis of their situation, a justification for the rage they feel, and toward which they are trying to herd their followers.[17]

Some of those straws are pretty dubious. For example, some of them take a right-wing argument about fatherlessness as definitive proof that fathers must be present in the lives of their children. For example, David Blankenhorn claimed in his 1993 best seller, *Fatherless America*, that fatherlessness is the cause of myriad social problems, ranging from juvenile delinquency and crime and violence to unemployment. They recite a litany of social ills, like that 70 percent of all juveniles in state reform institutions come from fatherless homes. This bodes especially ill for young boys, because without a father, we are told, these young boys will grow up without a secure foundation in their manhood: "In families where the father is absent, the mother faces an impossible task: she cannot raise a boy into a man. He must bond with a man as he grows up," wrote one psychologist. It is a mistake to believe that "a mother is able to show a male child how to be a man."

"Boys raised by traditionally masculine fathers generally do not commit crimes," added Blankenhorn. "Fatherless boys commit crimes."[18]

It is true that more children of both sexes are being raised in single-parent homes and that the "single parent" doing that raising is more often than not a woman. Whereas just over one in ten (11 percent) children were being raised by unmarried mothers in 1970, more than one-fourth (25.8 percent) were being raised that way in 2007. More than one in four (26 percent) of all births are to single women. But the alarmists revel in a veritable orgy of correlations—and every introductory statistics student will tell you that correlation is not the same as causation. For example, even though fatherlessness may be correlated with high crime rates, that does not mean that fatherlessness *caused* the criminality. In fact, it might just be the other way around.

Yes, high crime rates and fatherlessness are correlated. But it turns out that they are *both* products of a larger and more overwhelming problem: poverty.[19] The National Academy of Sciences reports that the single best predictor of violent crime is not fatherlessness but "personal and neighborhood income." And, it turns out, fatherlessness also varies with income; the higher the income bracket, the more likely the father is home—which suggests that the crisis of fatherlessness is actually a crisis of poverty.

Unfortunately, the fathers' rights groups don't give a hoot about poverty in America—except, of course, their own. These middle-class guys are more concerned with how they've been "impoverished" by greedy ex-wives and punitive judges. It's not interesting to them that women fare worse financially after divorce than men do. And it's certainly not interesting to them that so many boys of color experience fatherlessness because of the very policies that these "profatherhood" guys vote for.

Fatherlessness may be a consequence of those larger, deeper, more structural forces that drive fathers from the home and keep them away—such as unemployment or increased workplace demands to maintain a standard of living. Pundits often attempt to transform the problem of fatherlessness into another excuse to blame women, and specifically women working outside the home, whom they then attack as feminists. They yearn for a traditional nuclear family, with traditional gender inequality. For example, David Popenoe writes nostalgically about the family form of the 1950s—"heterosexual, monogamous, life-long marriage in which there is a sharp division of labor, with the female as the full-time housewife and the male as primary provider and ultimate authority"—without pausing to underscore that such a family form was also dramatically unequal when viewed from a gender perspective. Such a vision substitutes form for content, apparently under the impression that if only the family conformed to a specific form, then the content of family life would dramatically improve.[20]

It also makes *men's* irresponsibility *women's* fault. If only those women didn't put career over family responsibilities, pining for an actual life outside the kitchen, they wouldn't have become dissatisfied with their familial arrangements and sought a divorce. They make it sound like divorce is an impulsive decision, made frivolously; most women who initiate divorce know very well that their lifestyles will actually suffer after divorce and their incomes will decline. The flip side of the "feminization of poverty" is not only "the masculinization of wealth," but just as likely the "masculinization of irresponsibility"—the refusal of fathers to provide emotionally or economically for their children.[21]

The purveyors of this cultural fear of fatherlessness emphasize form over content in another sense. Simply by virtue of being male, perhaps possessing that Y chromosome, fathers bring something irreplaceable to the family—something "inherently masculine" was how Wade Horn put it. (Horn was the former director of the National Fatherhood Initiative, once President Bush's assistant secretary in the US Department of Health and Human Services, Administration for Children and Families, who famously promoted the truly backward idea that marriage-based programs would alleviate poverty. All available evidence suggests that the causal arrows run more decidedly in the other direction, that alleviating poverty would actually lead to an increase in marriages.)[22]

Again and again, I heard this from fathers' rights activists. Only fathers can teach boys to become men; "women just cannot teach a boy to become a man," Roger, one activist in Washington, DC, told me. "When they try, it all goes wrong. Either he becomes some supermacho jerk who always had to prove he's not a mama's boy all the time, or he becomes the mama's boy." When I protest this vulgar psychological reductionism, he retorts, "Have you noticed how many, uh, gay guys [air quotes, letting me know that he'd like to be saying "fags" or some other less neutral term] come from fatherless homes?"

I'm sure I don't need to tell you that there is no empirical evidence whatsoever that suggests that overdominant or single mothers "produce" more gay sons than less dominant moms in husband-wife homes, nor that some fake correlation between two supposed "bad things"—absent fatherhood and homosexuality—is politically repugnant. But aren't you also wondering if the fathers of the fathers' rights movement ever have daughters? They almost never talk about them, so one has to simply assume that in their eyes, girls don't count politically.

But the fatherlessness crowd isn't really interested in promoting active, engaged fatherhood anyway; they just want to promote intact marriages and restrict the options for terminating a bad marriage. (They like no-divorce laws, covenant marriages, and other policies that restrict women's choices, not promote engaged fatherhood.) Most of the men who are attracted to the FRM position wouldn't recognize themselves in Blankenhorn et al.'s condemnation of the very changes about which they feel so proud. The absence of fatherlessness is not synonymous with the increased *presence* of fathers. Just listen to Blankenhorn discuss these sensitive New Age dads: "He is nurturing. He expresses his emotions. He is a healer, a companion, a colleague. He is a deeply involved parent. He changes diapers, gets up at 2:00 A.M. to feed the baby, goes beyond 'helping out' in order to share equally in the work, joys, and responsibilities of domestic life." How awful, Blankenhorn sneers. Obviously, this sensitive New Age father does all this because he "reflects the puerile desire for human omnipotentiality in the form of genderless parenthood, a direct repudiation of fatherhood as a gendered social role for men."[23]

Blankenhorn does claim that fathers have a role, of course. They are not to succumb to those efforts to "resocialize" and "domesticate" them, which take them away from all those "hard male values" like "toughness, competition, instrumentalism and aggression," though. Instead, the father, for example, "protects his family, provides for its material needs, devotes himself to the education of his children, and represents his family's interests in the larger world"—all valuable behaviors, to be sure. They are also all behaviors that do not require that he ever set foot in his child's room.[24]

Discussions of fatherlessness are a distraction for the fathers' rights movement, because they reassert traditional patriarchal arrangements for a group of men who have actually been living far more egalitarian lives. So, too, is their preoccupation with domestic violence. The fact that conversations about domestic violence crop up in conversations about fatherhood seems, at first, so out of joint, yet they keep circling around the fathers' rights conversation. Indeed, to visit a fathers' rights group or to read their literature, you'd think their primary concerns, after their shared sense of being discriminated against in the court system, were false allegations of men's violence and the hidden scourge of violence by mothers. In fact, the preoccupation with domestic violence—in which women are always the perpetrators—is one of the chief distractions of the movement and one that reveals that their political agenda is far less about promoting active, healthy, and engaged fatherhood and more about punishing women and restoring men's traditional position in the family. It's about rights, not about fatherhood. In other words, it's far more about the *entitlement* part of that phrase *aggrieved entitlement* and much less about the *grief*.[25]

BALANCING RIGHTS AND RESPONSIBILITIES

But just as revealing as what they *do* talk about is also what they don't talk about. Ironically, the fathers' rights movement spends virtually no time promoting fatherhood as a *relationship* between parents and children. A colleague told me that during his time as a custody evaluator in the Massachusetts family-court system, he often found divorcing fathers dramatically overstating their involvement in family life, especially child care. Several children, in fact, told him in interviews that their fathers spent virtually no time with them, "because he's always busy working on his fathers' organization."[26]

To many FRAs, then, fatherhood is a right fathers should have—the rights to see their children, share custody, or enjoy visitation as they desire. That is, the FRM sees fathers' rights as beginning at divorce, not at birth.

From what, then, does a father's "right" derive? Does it derive from his biological connection to some embryonic gamete? That is, is a father's right a property right? Or does it derive from what he *does*—that is, from the social relationship he develops with his child? Is parenthood a state of being or a social relationship?

As with the men's rights movement, a focus on rights without equally emphasizing responsibilities leaves the fathers' rights movement defending deadbeat dads, ignoring men's violence against women, explaining away child abuse and child sexual abuse (except, perhaps, when it's done by "fathers" as in priests but not fathers as in parents), and ignoring the real problems of gay dads or dads of color. That is to say, it privileges the *men's* rights and not the experiences of their children. That's why it's not really about fathers at all; it's about the entitlement of white men to have whatever it is that they decide they want.

Is there a fatherhood *responsibility* movement? In a word, yes. But it has virtually nothing in common with the fathers' rights movement. Indeed, looking at the fatherhood responsibility movement exposes the contradictions at the heart of the fathers' rights claims. There are, for example, all sorts of gay fathers' groups that celebrate fathers' rights quite differently; they're thrilled to be able to be fathers, legally, in the first place. For example, at groups like Center Kids in New York or Pop Luck in Los Angeles, there is little talk of "rights" and a lot of sharing of do-it-yourself fathering outside of conventional channels—everything from recipes to handling parent-teacher nights at school, but all in the context of doing what fathers *do,* not simply being what fathers *are.*

But for the most part, the father responsibility movement is largely a movement among minority men, most notably African American men. The crushing poverty and racism that define the lives of so many young African American men—dramatically high unemployment and high rates of incarceration—lead to what might appear as irresponsibility among African American men.[27] The father responsibility movement works at the policy and personal levels, developing programs to keep young black men in school and out of jail, working with local police and courts to present alternatives to incarceration, and getting black men into—and keep them in—America's colleges and universities. (Only 30 percent of all black college students in America are male.) Well-known community leaders such as Geoffrey Canada and Calvin Butts and scholars such as Ronald Mincy and Noel Cazenave—and, of course, President Obama himself—have been the spearheads of this movement. At the personal level, they implore young fathers to remain connected to their children because of the salutary effects that father involvement has for both daughters and sons. Structurally, they are concerned with "fragile families," not adversarial claims to rights; indeed, they are largely unconcerned with a rhetoric of rights, a discourse that doesn't really speak to their experience.[28]

The existence of the fatherhood responsibility movement running on a roughly parallel track to the fathers' rights movement exposes that when the fathers' rights movement says the word *father,* they mean *white* father. White fathers say they are concerned about the denial of their rights, but I think that what they're really objecting to is the thwarting of their sense of entitlement.

ABSTRACT RIGHTS, CONCRETE RELATIONSHIPS

Of course, parenthood is more than a set of rights and even more than a set of obligations. It's about the content of our relationships with our children, the actual day-to-day interactions, the emotional connections cemented through that contact. Here divorced dads are faring only slightly better than their fathers' generation.

Marriage-advocate David Popenoe notes that many divorced fathers "lose almost all contact with their children over time. They withdraw from their children's lives." More than half of all divorced fathers have no contact with their children. Nonresident mothers are more likely to visit their children and to see them more often than nonresident fathers. Sixteen percent of nonresident mothers had not visited their children in the past year, compared to one in three nonresident fathers.[29] This high percentage can be attributed to the fact that these fathers were living more than one hundred miles from their children within a year of the divorce, so there were fewer opportunities for face-to-face meetings from the initial stages of separation. Some of this is, no doubt, because the mothers move away and take the children. But when fathers have custody and move away and take the children, the mothers don't lose contact.

Geography, it turns out, is only one factor. Nearly two of five (38 percent) of noncustodial fathers have a lot of contact with their kids: they tend to be better educated and to have older children. Younger, less-well educated dads with younger children tend to be more likely to have no contact.[30] It matters too if the couple was married. In a large-scale survey, unwed mothers reported that roughly 40 percent of the men had no contact with their children during the previous year, but most divorced fathers had some contact.

Okay, you'll say, that's because they have been denied custody by their ex-wives, snarky lawyers, and a corrupt court system. Maybe. But then explain this: noncustodial mothers rarely lose contact with their children after divorce. Despite not having custody, they simply do not walk away, maintaining family connections over employment possibilities and new relationships.[31]

The differences between the men who do maintain contact and those who don't is also telling—if a bit ironic. It turns out that men who were more involved with their children prior to the divorce are most likely to disappear after it, whereas those who were relatively uninvolved prior to divorce tended to remain more active with their children afterward. In part, as Edward Kruk observes, this counterintuitive difference stems from the less involved fathers also being more "traditional" in their outlooks, which would increase their sense of commitment to family life even after divorce, whereas more "liberal" men were more likely to see themselves as "free" from family responsibilities. I think it might be that their sense of thwarted entitlement leads to a picking up of all of one's remaining marbles and walking away in a huff. Ultimately, what predicts continued paternal involvement in their children's lives after a divorce is the quality of the relationship between the ex-spouses prior to the divorce.[32] Being an involved dad means being a good husband—even after the divorce.

The major problem with the fathers' rights discourse has less to do with their relationships with their children and their commitments to their families and more to do with their feelings about women—their ex-wives being only the most perfect example of the machinations of the entire sex. Most of the divorced dads in the movement actually want to do right by their children, but they seem to want to punish their ex-wives. (To be fair, many ex-wives also want to punish their ex-husbands, and withholding access to their children is a well-worn strategy they may use.)[33] As long as they sustain these twin motives, their efforts will often conflict. (Really nurturing their children would require emotional as well as financial support to the other parent, and one would expect the same from that other parent as well. What children really need is not to be the arbiter, judge, or spoil of their parents' conflict.) For the fathers' rights movement, though, they seem to feel that nurturing their children means fighting their ex-wives. Their anger reaches its fevered pitch around custody and child-support claims.

Fathers' rights groups use a language of equality to exact their revenge against their ex-wives, their ex-wives' lawyers, and the entire legal system, demanding mandatory joint custody and an end to alimony and child-support payments. "Society cannot take away a father's right to his children and expect him to cheerfully pay child support," writes one activist. "Society cannot expect a father to make enough money to support two separate households. Society cannot afford to support mothers who choose not to work." Fathers must have equal rights—the right to custody and the right to financial freedom without burdensome alimony and child support.

To hear them tell it, men's responsibility toward their families after divorce is actually a form of involuntary servitude. White men are the new slaves of the family-court system. Here is one man:

> [Child support] reduces the other parent to slavery and starvation. My ex-wife lives in a palace and I live in a trailer house. What made me decide to go to the [state where my children live now] is I had one can of pork and beans left, I ate them, and then I had no food left. When my kids were here with me in the summer, we went to the day-old bread store. I turn my air conditioner off during the day. [I am] living like a Nicaraguan and she is living in a plush palace, which is fine. That is wonderful and my children are living there during the school year against my will and their will. They lose half of their family and I am languishing in this little trailer house. That is all I can do. It is slavery. I am in a slave cabin.[34]

It's a form of "theft," says another, "because I don't have a choice over whether I pay this or not."[35]

THE CUSTODY-VIOLENCE CONUNDRUM

Fathers' rights rhetoric often veers dramatically off-course toward the most vehemently vindictive of the men's rights positions by constantly linking discussions about child support and custody to discussions about domestic violence. Yes, it's true, many men feel vulnerable that domestic-violence issues are the vindictive ex-wives' trump card, and it's equally true that the courts sometimes see what they believe, not believe what they see. It happens, and we should try to find a path through this political thicket that does the least damage to the surrounding fragile ecosystem.

Claims about domestic violence get completely polarized. On the one hand, the domestic-violence advocates seem to believe that all cases of physical violence are equivalent—which would make the more than 90 percent of Americans who have ever spanked their toddlers and the three-fifths of mothers who spanked their three- to five-year-olds *in the past week* unindicted child abusers. On the other side are the fathers' rights activists who shout only about false accusations of domestic violence, with the wives and lawyers in cahoots with extremists in wresting children from the arms of loving fathers.

To hear the fathers' rights guys tell it, it's men who are more vulnerable around domestic violence, not women. They don't approach custody and divorce from a position of patriarchal proprietorship, confident of their stature and power. Instead, they feel terribly vulnerable, especially since accusations of domestic violence almost always result in instant and automatic awarding of sole custody to the mother. It matters not, they say, how great a dad he was, how devoted a husband he was—all could be undone in a heartbeat by the mother's simply accusing him of domestic violence. From their perspective, men who are terrific and loving dads are being falsely accused of domestic violence as a tactic by ex-wives to ensure themselves of full custody. The courts instantly believe the women, and these perfectly good parents are losing everything.

This has two negative consequences. In an acrimonious case, they argue, it gives the mother a trump card, to be played whenever she feels threatened or vulnerable that her desires might not be heard. It's like an Egyptian God Card in Yu-Gi-Oh—once Exodia is on the field, everything else dissolves and it wins automatically. And it seems to be so easily played, virtually without consequence for the mom. This can leave men feeling vulnerable and scared—even good guys—and it makes the playing field very uneven.

What's worse, they say, is that it makes those cases in which domestic violence *was* a part of the marriage far less likely to be believed.

When anyone can make such a claim, all such claims are rendered equal, and thus equally suspect. Those women who are victims of domestic violence are less likely to report it during their marriages or after if they feel that they won't be believed.

On the other side, though, some domestic-violence activists make pretty much the opposite case. According to an article by Stephanie Dallam posted on the website of the Leadership Council, a leading organization promoting the interests of battered women and abused children:

> Custody litigation can become a vehicle whereby batterers and child abusers attempt to extend or maintain their control and authority over their victims after separation. Although research has not found a higher incidence of false allegations of child abuse and domestic violence in the context of custody/visitation, officers of the court tend to be unreasonably suspicious of such claims and that too often custody decisions are based on bad science, misinterpretation of fact, and evaluator bias. As a result, many abused women and their children find themselves re-victimized by the justice system after separation.[36]

Dallam lists a large number of empirical studies that point to the ways that batterers are *more* likely to prevail in custody cases than the protective parents. These aren't studies by biased partisans, but many are by clear-eyed empiricists, who find, for example, that in three hundred contested court cases in which child sexual abuse was alleged, 10 percent of the custody awards were to the protective parent, and 20 percent went to the alleged abuser. (The remaining 70 percent were, shockingly, mandatory joint custody with no supervision of visitation.) Study after study provide solid evidence that judges still evince a strong "paternal preference" in contested custody cases; fathers are still more likely to prevail in getting what they ask for. In fact, courts rarely consider domestic violence as a negative reflection of his parenting. Raising a domestic-violence allegation actually leads to worse outcomes for divorcing mothers. It's easy to see why women—especially victims of domestic violence or mothers seeking to protect their children from fathers who physically or sexually abuse their children—might be wary of the courts. And it's also easy to see why divorce lawyers often counsel their female clients to avoid bringing up domestic-violence accusations, believing that it might actually hurt their cases.[37]

Of course, it's true that "if violence exists in relationships, and victims attempt to terminate a relationship, custody disputes may be employed by abusive partners to maintain control of victims,"[38] and it's also true that "the atmosphere of the courtroom and the demeanor of judges who are condescending, patronizing, and demeaning results in [divorcing dads] feeling frightened, degraded, humiliated and embarrassed." But it's also true that if relative equality exists in the relationship, one partner (often the mother) may allege a risk factor (alcohol or drug abuse, child abuse, domestic violence) to gain an upper hand in custody, leaving the other partner (often the father) tentative and vulnerable to false charges and judges and court personnel who are unable (for cultural or political reasons) to give full credit to the amount of care and time he has already invested.

It's crucial to remember that these are false equivalences—a man's fear of adjudication going against him is nothing compared to a woman's fear for her or her children's lives and safety. Both sides feel afraid, wary, and often angry. It's a broken system. And even though in most areas of life the table still tilts toward men, there are some where men are no longer the privileged ones. Yet their howls are not entirely delusional. Many white American middle-class men are, in fact, getting screwed. And, as Willy Loman put it, "attention must be paid."

In reality, the truth surely lies somewhere closer to the middle; hyperbole serves neither position well. The angry dads need to remember we are not talking about all custody cases here, only the contested ones that account for only a small percentage of divorces. To read many of the fathers' rights websites, magazines, and blogs, though, you'd think that 95 percent of custody cases are contested—that is, cases in which the husband and wife want different arrangements—and that the courts routinely side with the mother. The American courts are "engines of antifeminism," one activist told me, "turning mild-mannered gentlemen into raging warriors against the system."

Most of these claims feel inflated and hyperbolic and thus undermine the arguments that each side is making. The studies that do exist are from samples of battered women, not samples of custody cases, which would skew the findings. Actually, there are virtually no systematic data on these questions, no national surveys or federally collected information, so these sorts of percentages come from aggregating qualitative data, even when the data are not comparable. One state, Washington, has collected systematic data representative of the United States, and they found that 88 percent of cases are not adjudicated in court because the couple agrees on the custody arrangements. Another 10 percent of cases are decided by default (i.e., one party fails to appear to answer the divorce petition), leaving only 2 percent of all cases to be decided by a judge.[39]

That seems to be the case nationwide. Most of the time, the divorcing parents settle their custody issues without going to court. And when they do file the legal divorce papers, they agree on the custody arrangements. In one study of one thousand divorces in two California counties, Stanford psychologist Eleanor Maccoby and law professor Robert Mnookin found that a majority of mothers and fathers wanted joint legal custody, whereas those that didn't want joint custody preferred that they, and not their spouses, be given custody. Nearly 82 percent of mothers and 56 percent of fathers requested the custody arrangement they wanted, whereas 6.7 percent of women and 9.8 percent of men requested more than they wanted and 11.5 percent of women and 34.1 percent of men requested less than they wanted.

This suggests that "gender still matters" in what parents ask for and what they do to get it. That mothers were more likely to act on their desires by filing for a specific request also indicates that men need to ask for more up front to avoid feeling bitter later. But it also indicates that some men, possibly as many as one-third, wanted more than they asked for and perhaps asked for less out of fear that their wives would become vindictive and they would end up losing everything.[40]

Maccoby and Mnookin's research is notable for another finding: children living with mothers did as well as children living with fathers. "The welfare of kids following a divorce did not depend a lot on who got custody," Maccoby told a journalist, "but rather on how the household was managed and how the parents cooperated." But one consequence of current custody arrangements is paternal withdrawal. Whether this is because the father is bereft to be kept from regular contact with his children or because once the marital bond is severed, he experiences a euphoria of "freedom" and considers himself to have escaped from a conflict-ridden family situation, it appears that many men "see parenting and marriage as part of the same bargain—a package deal," write sociologists Frank Furstenberg and Andrew Cherlin. "It is as if they stop being fathers as soon as the marriage is over." In one nationally representative sample of eleven- to sixteen-year-old children living with their mothers, almost half had not seen their fathers in the previous twelve months. Nearly half of all divorced fathers in the United States pay no child support; in Europe the comparable number is about one-fourth.[41]

Paternal withdrawal, it turns out, actually affects the father-daughter relationship most significantly, even more than the much-touted father-son relationship, whereas the mother-daughter relationship seems to be the most resilient to divorce and custody disputes. This may surprise those who believe that the father-son bond is the most fragile and most hard-hit by postdivorce fatherlessness, but it illustrates how frequently daughters are ignored in that literature and how both boys and girls benefit from paternal responsibility and continued presence in their children's lives.[42]

The other side is that fathers are doing better when they contest custody. In 2008–2009, fathers got majority parenting time in only 15 percent of all cases, but only a year later it was nearly double—28 percent. (This suggests that when dads ask for custody, the courts are starting to listen.) On the other hand, moms get majority parenting time in about two-thirds of all cases, as well as those in which there are no parental risk factors. ("Risk factors" include admissions of domestic violence, drug or alcohol dependence, abandonment, or neglect of the child.) About one in ten dads and one in twenty moms have a risk factor. Fathers got full custody in about one in four (26 percent) cases in which the mother had one risk factor and the father had none, but when the sexes were reversed, mothers got full custody 44 percent of the time. When she had two risk factors and he had none, he got full custody 42 percent of the time. When the sexes were reversed, she got full custody 63 percent of the time.[43] (One has to ask what it takes to *not* get custody if you have two risk factors and your ex-spouse has none. Those percentages should be hovering around 100 percent, shouldn't they?)

Most fathers' rights advocates seem uninterested in discrediting those women who really have been victimized, but they do want to end what they often erroneously perceive is a divorcing woman's ability to casually drop in a domestic-violence charge in a case that doesn't seem to be going her way. I do understand this vulnerability that the men feel, even if I don't believe it's so firmly planted on solid evidence. Most of the evidence about domestic violence suggests that if a woman claims it's true, it probably is—especially given the hurdles women have to go through in order to be believed in the first place.

Not only are there shame, guilt, and embarrassment about reported intimate partner violence and child abuse, but judges don't often rule automatically in favor of the women in these cases. There is still a significant amount of underreporting of violence (the Bureau of Justice Statistics reports that only about 20–30 percent of all cases are known or reported); the women don't feel that they will be believed, or that the men will not be prosecuted, or that they are even more vulnerable if they report, or, worse, that their children will be put in danger. Many women have described how they would rather experience the violence themselves than have their spouses turn their rage on the children.[44]

If most women who come forward are telling the truth about their victimization, better that women report more often, rather than less. But perhaps the ideal case would require that either some physical evidence (a police or medical report) or some documentary record that precedes the acrimonious divorce proceedings substantiate such domestic-violence accusations.

WHAT'S RIGHT ABOUT FATHERS' RIGHTS?

The fathers' rights movement is not a movement of deadbeat dads—anything but. At least not the rank and file. It consists largely of distressed and unhappy divorcés who feel the divorce courts, and especially the current custody, visitation, and child-support arrangements, failed to take into account their significant investments in their families prior to the divorces and the significantly greater financial independence their ex-wives have following the divorces. That is, they're angry because they claim they have had good relationships with their families, especially their children, and that such involvement seems to count for nothing if the marriage dissolves.

In other words, the court system rests on antiquated notions of women's participation in the workforce and men's participation in the family. As those worlds increasingly converge (as men spend more time with their families and women spend time at work), those assumptions governing child support, custody, and visitation are looking increasingly—indeed, hopelessly—anachronistic. They're right: it's time for a rethinking—and an overhaul.

Just as there has been a sea change in men's parenting, the laws involving marital-dissolution and postdivorce family relationships are stuck on an anachronistic sandbar. American fathers live in early-twenty-first-century families, but when those families break up, they feel like they are being forced to play by mid-twentieth-century rules. Courts and couples both live in the present when it comes to alimony, rates of which have dropped significantly in recent decades. Court orders for permanent alimony have dropped far below 10 percent; three out of five alimony cases were for about five years (to get the kids grown up enough for the ex-wife to get a job).[45]

But custody is another matter altogether. Prior to the Industrial Revolution, when children were seen as an economic "good," capable of contributing to the family income, courts utilized an economic means test to determine who would receive custody. Under that criterion, custody was regularly and routinely given to fathers. In the early years of the twentieth century, though, children came to be seen as a luxury, and so a new test, based on care and nurture, was used to determine custody arrangements—a policy that favored mothers. Today, the "best interests of the child" is the criterion employed to provide the foundation for custody decisions, although in practice, the best interests of the child are presumed to be better served by staying with the mother, not the father, since the presumption is that mothers provide better child care—especially for young children—than do fathers.

That custody arrangements and support should be decided in the "best interests of the child" remains a pretty good standard. That's why it's the "golden rule" of adjudicating custody disputes. It certainly represents progress over the nineteenth-century "tender-years" doctrine, which automatically gave mothers custody of all children under the age of thirteen. But that tender-years doctrine had displaced only partially the early consistent idea that when a man wanted custody, he simply got it. As women fought, at the turn of the twentieth century, for the right to divorce, they also sought to shift the state's interest in a divorce from the man as head of household—and citizen, voter, and worker—to the ungendered "parent" whose caregiving was central to the welfare of the child. That is, the general presumption that women ought to get custody of children, especially when they are younger, is a relatively recent idea and one that women had to fight for.

It's not clear that all fathers' rights groups are campaigning for a return to the traditional patriarchal notion that men's rights trumped women's rights in all matters, legal and social. As with men's rights groups, it's probably true that there are some unrepentant (if un-crowned) patriarchs among their legions, but by and large, the ranks of the fathers' rights groups are somewhat less vociferous, and far less traditional, than the MRAs. It's their contention that, as "new" fathers—involved, engaged, and active with their children—the di-vorce and custody laws reflected an earlier time, when the father was more an absentee landlord at home whose only means of nurturing was his wallet.

Many family-court judges act as if they're adjudicating Don and Betty Draper's divorce in 1961. She's a full-time stay-at-home mom; he's a responsible breadwinner, but an unaffectionate and uninvolved parent. He should pay up for his infidelities and fecklessness, the courts say, when they divorce. Many men's rights and fathers' rights guys think the courts treat them as Don Drapers only in the negative sense—as irresponsible fathers who must now nurture only with their wallets. However, some want the courts to treat them like Don Drapers in the *positive* sense—as entitled patriarchs, who still run the show and command deference from those rightfully below them on the evolu-tionary totem pole, namely, women and children.

Neither of those Don Drapers—neither the open wallet nor the entitled patriarch—bears much resemblance to the world in which contemporary men are living. Fifty years after the show, Betty's mostly working full-time, and Don spends nearly as many hours in child care (but not housework) as Betty does. The law needs to reflect this. Sadly, it does not.

Sometimes, it appears that their rhetoric substitutes these ag-grieved fathers' vindictiveness against ex-wives, or their bewilderment at the entire divorce proceeding, for the "best interests" of children.

But most of the time, all things being equal, joint physical and legal custody ought to be the norm in custody decisions. Here, of course, "all things being equal" means that there is no discernible danger to the child of sexual or physical abuse, that the parents can manage to contain their own postdivorce conflict and prevent the children from becoming pawns in a parental power struggle, and that the parents agree to equally support the children financially and emotionally. Such arrangements may be more difficult for parents than for children, who often report "a sense of being loved by both parents," as well as "feeling strongly attached to two psychological parents, in contrast to feeling close to just one primary parent." Contrary to some popular opinion, joint custody "does not create uncertainty or confusion" and seems to benefit children, who say they are more satisfied with the arrangement than those in single-custody homes and consider having two homes advantageous.[46]

We know, too, that joint custody will benefit men, who will, by maintaining a legal connection to their children, be far more likely to continue to share financial responsibilities for their development. What's more, joint custody may relieve the deep sense of loss, disengagement, and depression often experienced by men who are cut loose from continued involvement with their families. On the other hand, mandated joint legal custody may not be so good for women. Feminist legal theorist Martha Fineman argues that mandated joint legal custody may appear to be gender neutral, but gender "neutrality" in one arena in an overall system of gender inequality may perpetuate gender discrimination, much the way the abandonment of affirmative action sounds race—or gender—neutral, but actually favors white males over others by withdrawal from an explicit challenge to historical discrimination. As Fineman writes, "What may have started out as a system which, focusing on the child's need for care, gave women a preference *solely* because they had usually been the child's primary caretaker, is evolving into a system which, by devaluing the content or necessity of such care, gives men more than an equal chance to gain the custody of their children after divorce if they choose to have it, because biologically equal parents are considered as equal in expressive regards. Nonnurturing factors assume importance which often favor men."[47]

Mandatory joint custody is hardly a panacea; I would be more comfortable with joint custody as the general guideline rather than universally mandated. Virtually no studies actually find any particularly compelling outcomes for children in joint custody arrangements—neither better nor worse for the kids. As Jocelyn Crowley puts it, "There simply is not an overwhelming case for joint custody." But that's only if we ask about the children. It may, indeed, be better for the parents—organized and structured, with clear boundaries and little room for slippage. When the parents both know the rules and buy into the arrangements they've agreed to, the resulting lack of conflict has to redound well for the children.

Perhaps the most judicious system of child custody would be one that recognizes the difference in "inputs" between fathers and mothers in the actual experiences of the children—time spent in child care, level of parental involvement in child development—while at the same time presuming that both parents are capable of and interested in (absent any evidence to the contrary) continued committed and involved relationships with their children. Men's increased involvement in predivorce child care ought to be reflected in custody arrangements, as should women's continuing to shoulder the overwhelming majority of such care, despite their commitments to work. Fathers' "rights" following divorce will come more readily if the fathers have recognized their responsibilities during the marriage.

Happy families may be all alike, as Tolstoy famously wrote, but not everyone has a happy marriage in any family, happy or not. And though each unhappy marriage may be unhappy in its own way, the way the divorce and custody courts are presently arranged, they pretty much end up being unhappy in the same way. Men's anger that the amounts of love, care, and support (financial and emotional) they put into the family are unrecognized if the family dissolves is both real and true. The deck is stacked—not because of some feminist-inspired judicial conspiracy (if that were true, no rape victim would ever be asked what she was wearing or why she was out so late at night by an incredulous male judge)—but because the courts have failed to take into account the enormous changes in men's lives as parents. These angry white men have some justified grievances—even though they often aim their arrows at the wrong targets.

5 | Targeting Women

On the evening of August 4, 2009, George Sodini, forty-eight, walked into the LA Fitness gym in Collier Township, Pennsylvania. No one paid much attention that he was dragging a large gym bag; after all, he worked out at the gym regularly and had just chatted with a number of regulars. At the door of the aerobics class, he put down his gym bag, took out an assault weapon, and opened fire. When he was done, five young women lay dead, another twelve injured. He then blew his brains out.

In his gym bag was a note, directing readers to a website where he had left an online diary for the months leading up to his carnage. The diary describes his failures with women, his constant rejections for dates (he claimed he had not had sex in twenty years), and his growing rage at women in general for such emasculation:

> *I dress good, am clean shaven, bathe, touch of cologne—yet 30 million women rejected me—over an 18 or 25 year period. Thirty*

million is my rough guesstimate of how many desirable single women there are. A man needs a woman for confidence. He gets a boost on the job, career, with other men, and everywhere else when he knows inside he has someone special to spend the night with and who is also a friend. This type of life I see is a closed world with me specifically and totally excluded. Every other guy does this successfully to a degree. Flying solo for many years is a destroyer.

For nearly a year after he had made his fateful decision, Sodini documented his growing sense of isolation, his despair that he could not find a woman to date, and his frustration that others were having so much more sex than he was. He wanted women; they rejected him. He wanted sex; they weren't attracted to him.

But more than that, he also felt *entitled* to them. It was his right, as a man, he felt, to have access to women. And when they turned him down, he didn't just get mad. He got even.

George Sodini is not alone. Less than twenty years earlier, on October 16, 1991, thirty-five-year-old George Hennard drove his light-blue pickup truck through the front window of Luby's Cafeteria in Killeen, Texas, and methodically shot and killed twenty-four people, fourteen of them women, before he turned the gun on himself. While police investigators and journalists combed through his troubled childhood, his isolation (he was described as a "loner"), and evidence of any possible psychiatric issues or a history of drug or alcohol abuse, Hennard himself had made his intentions clear to two young women who lived nearby (but to whom he had never spoken). Infatuated and obsessed with the sisters, his rambling letter contrasted them to the other "evil" women of small-town Texas, the "vipers" who apparently had rejected his advances over the previous couple of years. "I will prevail in the end," he wrote ominously. (The girls were so distressed by the letter that they actually brought it to the police, fearing that he was stalking them. The police apparently were not alarmed by what they saw as a slightly off-kilter declaration of romantic interest.)[1]

To be sure, Hennard was deranged, driven mad by circumstances over which he felt he had no control, gradually losing his grip on sanity, lashing out at the world that simply refused to provide what he wanted. As was Sodini. Within their worldview, they were completely sane and fully justified. It was the women's fault for rejecting them.

In Marc Lepine's case, it was women's fault for his having been rejected by his chosen college. A twenty-five-year-old Canadian, Lepine had applied for admission to study at the École Polytechnique at the University of Montreal in 1989. When he was rejected, he blamed it on Canadian-style affirmative action that had enabled women to be admitted. These women, he felt, had destroyed the educational opportunity to which he felt entitled. Enraged, Lepine walked into a chemical engineering lecture class on December 6, 1989, and, while holding an assault weapon, separated the male students from the female students. Arrayed along opposite walls, Lepine turned and opened fire randomly at the women, shouting, "You're all feminists! I hate feminists!" By the time he was finished and turned the gun on himself, Lepine had killed fourteen female students and wounded ten others.

Clearly, like George Sodini, Marc Lepine also likely had a serious mental disorder; most rampage killers do. But the disordered mind also had its own insane logic, a deliberateness. There was a madness to his method. In a suicide note found in his jacket, Lepine made clear that his actions were not for economic reasons, but for political reasons. And the politics was feminism:

> I have decided to send the feminists, who have always ruined my life, to their Maker. . . . I have decided to put an end to those viragos. . . . [T]he feminists have always enraged me. They want to keep the advantages of women (e.g. cheaper insurance, extended maternity leave preceded by a preventative leave, etc.) while seizing for themselves those of men. So the feminists are not fighting to remove that barrier. They are so opportunistic they do not neglect to profit from the knowledge accumulated by men through the ages. They always try to misrepresent them every time they can.

Clearly deranged, of course. Would it, therefore, surprise you to know that Lepine has some contemporary supporters—or at least some guys who claim to understand the legitimacy of his actions? Does Lepine, "perhaps, point to a possible future, one in which more and more men, shamed beyond endurance by a male-hating feminist establishment, strike out in desperation at those they judge responsible?" writes Dave Shakleton on a "men's rights" website.[2]

Sodini too, has legions of "fans" on men's rights blogs. Here are just a few comments:

George Sodini is an MRA hero. . . . Finally a mass murderer writes a relatively coherent manifesto. Could be better, but at least it is implied that feminism is to blame and he is taking a last stand. I had been waiting for this (almost thinking I had to do it myself) and I am impressed. Kudos.

Women have to accept this incident as a tax on their freeloading. Women get men to buy them drinks, dinners, and bridezilla weddings, all in return for virtually nothing. Once in a while, a few women get shot up. Given the $500 billion a year that women mooch off of men each year, that is a relatively small tax to pay. Women, particularly the feminazis, have a good deal of introspection to do.

. . . [H]e had every reason to lash out at the society that screwed him over and make its denizens feel some of the pain that they had inflicted on him. There are millions, tens of millions of men in this country who have been deceived in a similar fashion, and there are numerous Sodinis amongst their ranks who will react violently and murderously once they uncover the truth. What amuses me is how the women of this country and the West don't realize the role they have in creating men like Sodini.

I am calling him a hero for being a symbol for the consequences of denying men sex, not for killing those women. Obviously they didn't personally deserve it. But something like this has to happen, perhaps hundreds of times over again, before feminists get the message.

A decent looking man who earns a good living and does not abuse women DESERVES to get laid. Period. The fact that so many do not, is a crime. And in a just society, all crimes are eventually punished.

I first thought about those frigid harpies at the exercise studio who were too up-tight to give a guy a chance on a date. I bet when the lights went out and they felt those warm bullets entering their bodies they wished that they had been a little nicer to the guys out there who just needed a date.

As long as they can afford it, women will go for the best men, and they won't give up their equality, largely backed by affirmative action, without massive violence perpetrated by the minority of men who are left sexless under feminism. Therefore I applaud rape and purposeful violence against women where it is made clear that embittered men are

*hurting and killing them for not putting out. Only then will women
hopefully abandon their equality and be forced to settle monogamously
by sheer economic necessity.*[3]

Astonishing, really, but indicative of what aggrieved entitlement sounds
like. If women stop putting out for guys like Sodini, then don't say you
haven't been warned about what's coming your way.

And what about twenty-two-year-old George Huguely, the University
of Virginia lacrosse player who murdered his ex-girlfriend Yeardley Love, a
twenty-two-year-old lacrosse player on the UVA women's team? He'd sent
threatening e-mails and grabbed her violently at a party not long before
(he had to be restrained by several players from another team). Having
grown up in a world of country-club privilege—all Lexus, Lacoste, and
lacrosse—Huguely assumed he was entitled to be listened to. As a high-
prestige athlete at pretty UVA, the top-ranked lacrosse team in the nation,
Huguely was entitled to get what he wanted. And when it was withdrawn,
he went ballistic. Early in the morning of May 3, 2010, Huguely stormed
into Love's apartment, kicked his foot through her bedroom door, and
grabbed her, according to preliminary statements, shaking her against the
wall so violently, her head slamming repeatedly against the wall, that she
died. (Huguely was sentenced to twenty-three years in prison for man-
slaughter, though he is now appealing the sentence, not the verdict.)[4]

EVERYDAY SODINIS

Every single day in America there are similar mini rampages, as individual George Sodinis and George Huguelys beat and batter and murder
women. It's paradoxical that men could murder the women they say
they love. Yet every day in America, at least five women die at the hands
of their intimate partners; the United States has the highest rate of spousal homicide in the industrialized world. (Compare our rate of 1.07 female spousal homicide victims per 100,000 population to that of, say,
Canada [0.26] or Australia [0.40]. According to the United Nations, 35
percent of all female-victim homicides in Europe were by spouses or
ex-spouses, while only 5 percent of male-victim homicides were; in the
United States, 45 percent of female-victim homicides were by spouses
and ex-spouses, while 4.9 percent of male-victim homicides were.)[5]

The US Surgeon General has declared that attacks by male partners are the number one cause of injury to women between the ages of fifteen and forty-four. According to the standard nursing textbook, more than 1 million women seek medical care each year for injuries related to abuse; this makes up about 100,000 days of hospitalization and 30,000 emergency room visits.[6] One-third of all female murder victims are killed by an intimate partner (compared to about 3 percent of male murder victims). More than three-fourths of these victims were stalked by that partner first. Murder ranks second (after accidents) as the leading cause of death among young women—and it is *the* leading cause of death among pregnant women.[7]

Beyond spousal homicide, or what is known in the field as "femicide," nearly six hundred thousand women are beaten by an intimate partner (husband, ex-husband, or boyfriend) every year—that's a little more than one per minute. It's the single most common reason that women go to the hospital emergency room.[8]

The threat to women extends beyond actual murder or battery—to simply eliciting fear in the lives of women. More than a million women are stalked in the United States every year. In two-thirds of the cases where a woman asks for, and receives, an order of protection from the police, that order is violated.

It is true, of course, that there are a significant number of women who kill their intimate male partners. With movies like *The Burning Bed* (1984) and *Sleeping with the Enemy* (1991) etched indelibly into our consciousness, it makes sense to address these murders up front, especially since we will return to some of these questions of gender "symmetry" in domestic violence—or, in the current term of art, intimate partner violence—later in this chapter.

Data vary, but a significant number of men are killed by their female partners. In the United Kingdom, for example, for every one hundred men who kill their wives, twenty-three women kill their husbands. In Canada it's one hundred to thirty-one. In the United States, estimates range from forty up to nearly seventy-five men killed for every one hundred women killed. (Those top estimates exclude *ex*-partners from the data, however, which account for nearly one in five femicides in the United States and virtually no homicides. Including them would bring the numbers back in line with the other countries.) Nearly half of all women murdered in New York City were killed by their husbands or boyfriends, whereas about 3 percent of all male homicides are committed by wives, ex-wives, or girlfriends. (Including boyfriends and girlfriends really changes the story.)[9] Ex-wives rarely kill their ex-husbands; they're happy to have escaped and are eager to get on with their lives. Ex-boyfriends and ex-husbands seem to have a harder time letting go.

That difference actually speaks to the chief difference between women and men in spousal murder data. As in those famous films, women who kill their husbands typically do so after enduring years or even decades of violence, abuse, and marital rape. Some commit murder when they think that their children may be harmed. The motive for women to kill is very often *defensive,* either immediate defense in a violent confrontation or planned by a woman who sees no other way out. Husbands or boyfriends rarely kill their partners in self-defense; often they escalate the domestic violence beyond what they'd done previously, or they plan her murder quite deliberately.[10]

Sociologists R. Emerson and Russell Dobash and their colleagues enumerate some of these differences:

> *Men often kill wives after lengthy periods of prolonged physical violence accompanied by other forms of abuse and coercion; the roles in such cases are seldom if ever reversed. Men perpetrate familial massacres, killing spouse and children together; women do not. Men commonly hunt down and kill wives who have left them; women hardly ever behave similarly. Men kill wives as part of planned murder-suicides; analogous acts by women are almost unheard of. Men kill in response to revelations of wifely infidelity; women almost never respond similarly, though their mates are more often adulterous.*[11]

It is also worth noting that these disparate rates of spousal homicide in Western societies are relatively modest compared with the rates in developing societies, where the ratio is even greater. Where patriarchal control is relatively unchallenged, assault, rape, and even murder may be seen less as a crime and more of a prerogative.[12]

Take, for example, Timothy Hall, who killed his girlfriend when she changed her Facebook status to "single," or Woody Will Smith, who killed his wife after finding out she was having an affair with a coworker. (Smith based his defense on a caffeine overdose that made him crazy, since he was consuming caffeine-laced energy drinks and coffee to stay up all night so he could catch her.) In one 1999 high-profile case linking workplace rampages and violence against women, Mark Barton shot nine people in an office building in Atlanta—after bludgeoning to death his wife and children that morning. (Barton had earlier been a suspect in the beating death of his first wife and her mother.)

Put most simply, women kill their partners when they feel their lives, or the lives of their children, are in danger; men kill their partners when they feel their sense of entitlement and power is thwarted. That's quite a difference.

Interestingly, although rates of intimate partner homicide have decreased over the past thirty years, that decrease is almost entirely in the rates of *male* victims. According to the US Department of Justice, in 1976 1,596 women and 1,348 men were murdered by their spouse or partner; thirty years later, in 2006, the number had fallen to 1,159 women and only 385 men. (The reason is probably that the spread of shelters for battered women coupled with increased support for victims and greater public awareness has given women a greater sense that they have options other than murder, and many leave their abusive partners. So, ironically, shelters for battered women may be saving men's lives!)

The enormous number of physical injuries is only part of the story, as domestic violence also crushes the spirit and destroys the self-esteem of countless women in the United States. "About half of all battered women say that the psychological abuse is more devastating than the physical abuse," says Lundy Bancroft, an expert on violence and author of *Why Does He Do That?* (2003). These everyday Sodinis express the same rage and profess the same aggrieved entitlement as those who beat, rape, and murder the women they profess to love.[13]

VIOLENCE AS RESTORATIVE

Why would men hit the women they say they love? Why would they kill them? Little convincing evidence suggests that it is simply because they witnessed it in their homes as they were growing up (although many did, there are also many who break that cycle). Nor is it the untrammeled expression of men's power or the instrumental use of violence as a way to express that power. In fact, the evidence suggests something quite different.

This association between violence and love is so intimate, so central for men, that it practically screams out for answers. Freud wasn't the first to notice the association between love and anger, between sex and aggression. Perhaps it's because loving leaves us so exposed, so vulnerable, feelings that are antithetical to our sense of ourselves as masculine. Masculinity is about impermeability, independence. Perhaps feeling vulnerable and dependent is regressive, reminding us of our earliest dependence on our mothers.

Maybe. But the defense against vulnerability and exposure, however intimate its experience and how it recalls events early in our lives, seems to be activated only when something else breaks down. If masculinity is based on impermeable defenses and the feeling of being in control, then violence may be restorative, returning the situation to the moment before that sense of vulnerability and dependency was felt and one's sense of masculinity was so compromised.

But still, one needs an additional ingredient: the feeling of right, or entitlement. One must feel entitled to use violence as a means of restoring what was experienced as threatened, that part of the self that is suddenly made vulnerable. If you don't feel entitled to use violence, then all the vulnerability in the world won't lead you to hit somebody.

Linking one's masculinity to the maintenance of effective defenses against vulnerability and humiliation is, of course, a central argument of this book—that the surge in aggression from America's angry white men comes not only from the gradual dispossession of white men from virtually every single position of power and authority in the land, but also from the challenge to their sense that such positions are their birthright. It's the *my* in that talk show "A Black Woman Stole My Job" and the *our* in the Tea Party's motto "Let's take our country back" (as we've seen earlier). Violence is rarely justified when you initiate it. But it's always justified when you retaliate for an injury done to you.

This idea has a long history in America. In the aftermath of the Civil War, after the South had suffered a humiliating and emasculating defeat, young boys took to placing chips of wood on their shoulders, daring other boys to knock them off so they could legitimately fight with them. Only in America is "having a chip on one's shoulder" considered a badge of honor among boys. Violence was legitimate only as long as it was retaliatory. If someone else knocked that chip off, kicking his ass was a reasonable response. In his epic trilogy, acclaimed historian Richard Slotkin recounted the entire sweep of American westward expansion and the ever-receding frontier through a prism of "regenerative" violence—violence as creative, restorative, even healing.[14]

In her penetrating analysis of American violence, anthropologist Margaret Mead described the typically American refusal to initiate aggression but to retaliate far out of proportion to the original offense in "an aggression which can never be shown except when the other fellow starts it" and is "so unsure of itself that it had to be proved." Remember these words the next time you watch two young boys square off in a playground. "You wanna start something?" one of them yells. "No, but if you start it, I'll finish it!" replies the other. No one wants to take responsibility for the initial act of aggression, but everyone wants to finish the fight.[15]

Southern whites called it "honor"; by the turn of the century, it was called "reputation." By the 1950s, northern ghetto blacks spoke of "respect," which has now been transformed again into not showing "disrespect," or "dissing."

Another street hood gives a contemporary slant to the old "chip on the shoulder" when he describes what he calls the "accidental bump," when you're walking around Spanish Harlem "with your chest out, bumping into people and hoping they'll give you a bad time so you can pounce on them and beat 'em into the goddamn concrete."[16]

Of course, other cultures express particular constructions of violence and prescribe violence to prove manhood or group membership. The nexus among honor, masculinity, and violence is deep and profound in many cultures. The American version just happens to be so intimate as to feel primal, even natural. Violence has long been understood in America as the best way to ensure that others publicly recognize one's manhood. Fighting was once culturally prescribed for boys, who, the theory went, needed to demonstrate gender identity. In one of the best-selling advice manuals of the first part of the last century, parents learned:

> *There are times when every boy must defend his own rights if he is not to become a coward and lose the road to independence and true*

manhood. . . . The strong willed boy needs no inspiration to combat, but often a good deal of guidance and restraint. If he fights more than, let us say, a half dozen times a week, except, of course, during his first week at a new school, he is probably over-quarrelsome and needs to curb. The sensitive, retiring boy, on the other hand, needs encouragement to stand his ground and fight.

You did not misread: in this best seller, boys were encouraged to fight once a day, except during the first week at a new school, when, presumably, they would fight more often![17]

Lurking beneath such advice was the fear that boys who were not violent would not grow up to be real men. The specter of the "sissy"—encompassing the fears of emasculation, humiliation, and effeminacy that American men carry with them—is responsible for a significant amount of masculine violence. Violence is proof of masculinity; one is a "real" man because one is not afraid to be violent. Psychiatrist James Gilligan speaks of "the patriarchal code of honor and shame which generates and obligates male violence"—a code that sees violence as the chief demarcating line between women and men.[18]

This notion of violence as restorative is part of a gendered equation. Violence is but the means; the end is the restoration of honor and respect, the ability to rectify humiliation.

Rage is the way to displace the feelings of humiliation. "The emotion of shame is the primary or ultimate cause of all violence," writes Gilligan. "The purpose of violence is to diminish the intensity of shame and replace it as far as possible with its opposite, pride, thus preventing the individual from being overwhelmed by the feeling of shame."[19]

WHY WOMEN?

All this analysis of the origins of men's violence in fears of shame and humiliation begs the question: why target women? After all, our (male) bosses and colleagues humiliate us far more often than women do. But we don't often hit them or stab them with some office product. We don't shoot them with a staple gun or a nail gun. (Of course, there are many cases of such workplace violence. Furthermore, those cases of men "going postal," embarking on seemingly random workplace killing sprees, do stem from the same sense of humiliation as much of the violence that targets women. I'll discuss them in the next chapter.)

Part of the answer is because when our boss humiliates us, well, it's his right. He's above us on the social hierarchy. But those *below* do not have that right.

Thus, for example, it was not just black people who were targeted by white racists in the South for generations. It was "uppity" black people who had the temerity to believe they were equal to whites, who did not "know their place," who dared to think they could sit where they wanted, eat where they wanted, use the same toilets, or drink from the same water fountains. It was uppity black men and boys who dared to talk to a white girl, as if they were entitled. These symbolic moments of equality were seen as humiliating to whites, who were entitled to feel superior and whose honor was challenged. Racist violence expressed that aggrieved entitlement.

There's some fascinating research from the world of primates that might shed some light on this. It also, conveniently, will put to rest any sense that men's violence against women—or men's violence in general—is propelled biologically by the testosterone coursing through their systems. (If it were simply testosterone, then how can we explain our choice of targets?) Robert Sapolsky, a neuroprimatologist at Stanford University, did one of the classic experiments about male hierarchies, testosterone levels, and aggression. If you take a group of five male monkeys arranged in a dominance hierarchy from 1 to 5, then you can pretty much predict how everyone will behave toward everyone else. (The top monkey's testosterone level will be higher than the ones below him, and levels will decrease down the line.) Number 3, for example, will pick fights with numbers 4 and 5, but will avoid and run away from numbers 1 and 2. So the experiment removes monkey number 3 from the cage and gives him a massive injection of testosterone, so his level far exceeds that of monkeys 1 and 2. What do you think happens when you put him back in the cage with the other monkeys?

If you're like my students, your first thought was probably that monkey number 3 has now become the top monkey, the new number 1 monkey, and the hierarchy rearranges to show him deference. But that's not at all what happens. Monkey 3 still avoids numbers 1 and

2, but he beats the daylights out of monkeys 4 and 5. He makes their lives a living hell. "Testosterone isn't causing aggression; it's exaggerating the aggression that's already there."[20]

It turns out that testosterone has what scientists call a "permissive effect" on aggression: it doesn't cause it, but it does facilitate and enable the aggression that is already there. The target must already be seen as legitimate. In other words, you have to feel entitled to use violence.

This sense of entitlement is the key to understanding men's violence against women. Mountains of research suggest that men hit women not when everything is running smoothly, but when it breaks down, when things aren't going so well. It's when she doesn't have dinner ready, or when she doesn't want to have sex, or when she doesn't listen to him and his needs, or when she asserts a need or a preference or an interest entirely her own, or when she disagrees with him, or when she simply does something all by herself. He has a right; he's entitled. When that entitlement is compromised, he feels humiliated, aggrieved.

Listen to the voice of a young guy, only sixteen years old, describing to a researcher the way he uses violence in his dating life:

> She's pissed me off, and she won't stop. I've grabbed her arm, squeezed her, and slapped her. I've punched her after she put me down in front of my friends. My ex-girlfriend used to cry after we had fights. I had to punch her to get her to stop. . . . I mean, when she nags me for nothing, I'll tell her to "Shut up, bitch," or I'll call her a slut. . . . Almost every week I'll say to her "Stop it or I'll hit you." I punch her in the arm or the leg—not in her face. I'll never punch a girl in the face unless she punches me first. Sometimes she nags, and she won't stop. Once I punched this girl in the face and knocked her out. She grabbed my hair at a dance. When she pisses me off, sometimes, instead of hitting her, I'll push her or shove her down. I've busted pretty much all of her stuff: lamps, I kicked her radio, smashed her mirror, punched her walls—I've destroyed her things. I know it scares her, and I think that's why I keep doing it. She always does what I tell her to do. I don't like punching her in the face because it leaves bruises. Once I punched her in the leg and gave her a big purple mark. Once at a party she wouldn't leave. I grabbed my girlfriend and dragged her outside to give her shit. My friends saw it all and didn't say anything. . . . I don't know what to

do. It's like I know what I should be as a man, I mean—strong, lots of money, a good job, and a beautiful wife. But my life isn't like that. I'm not really much of a man without a good job and lots of money. She makes me so angry when she won't do what I want her to do. It's not supposed to be that way. A girl is supposed to get along with a man. She's supposed to respect him and listen to him. But that never happens to me. I feel like a piece of shit around my girlfriends. Sometimes it's them who has to pay for things because they've got the job. It's like they're more important than me and they think they can make the decisions because they've got the money. It's not right. It makes me feel like a wimp or a pussy. That's not the way things are supposed to be.[21]

Of course, you'll have noticed the language of *ought*—it's *supposed* to be this way; she's *supposed* to do this or that. When she doesn't do what she is supposed to do, when it's not the way it's supposed to be, he feels humiliated. He's saying, "I'm supposed to feel big, but when I don't get what I feel I'm entitled to, I feel small. A man must feel big, so I hit her to restore that, to retrieve something she's taken away from me, to compensate for what I don't have."

Listen now to the voice of a twenty-three-year-old guy named Jay who works as a stock boy in a San Francisco corporation. Jay was asked by writer Tim Beneke to think about under what circumstances he might commit rape. He has never committed rape, mind you. He's simply an average guy, considering the circumstances under which he would commit an act of violence against a woman. Here's what Jay says:

Let's say I see a woman and she looks really pretty and really clean and sexy and she's giving off very feminine, sexy vibes. I think, wow I would love to make love to her, but I know she's not interested. It's a tease. A lot of times a woman knows that she's looking really good and she'll use that and flaunt it and it makes me feel like she's laughing at me and I feel degraded. . . . If I were actually desperate enough to rape somebody it would be from wanting that person, but also it would be a very spiteful thing, just being able to say "I have power over you and I can do anything I want with you" because really I feel that they have power over me just by their presence. Just the fact that they can come up to me and just melt me makes me feel like a dummy, makes me want revenge. They have power over me so I want power over them.

Notice how Jay speaks not with the voice of someone in power, of someone in control over his life, but rather with the voice of powerlessness, of helplessness. For him, violence is a form of revenge, a form of retaliation, of getting even, a compensation for the power that he feels women have over him.

The researcher who interviewed Jay, Tim Beneke, placed these feelings of powerlessness in a different context. Think, for a moment, about the words we use to describe women's beauty, women's sexuality, women's attractiveness: they're words of violence and injury—to men. Women are *ravishing* or *stunning;* she's a *bombshell* or a *knockout;* she's *dressed to kill,* a real *femme fatale.* Women's beauty is perceived as violent to men: men use violence to even the playing field—or, more accurately, to return it to its previously uneven state that men thought was even.

Men who have been convicted of rape and domestic violence tell a similar story—about how they got even with women, how they got revenge. Men's violence toward women does not happen when men's power over women is intact and unthreatened; rather, it happens when men's power breaks down, when his entitlement to that power is threatened and insecure. Violence is restorative, retaliatory. It springs from that sense of entitlement, to women's domestic services to their sexual favors. When that sense of entitlement is aggrieved, they don't just get mad; they get even.

In a fascinating study of convicted rapists, sociologist Diana Scully develops these themes. Scully found that rapists have higher levels of consensual sexual activity than other men, are as likely to have significant relationships with women, and are as likely to be fathers as are other men. This should effectively demolish the evolutionary arguments that men who rape do so out of sexual frustration, out of desire for relationships with women, or because they are "losers" in the sexual marketplace. Rape was used by men "to put women in their place," she writes. "Rape is a man's right," one convicted rapist told her. "If a woman doesn't want to give it, a man should take it. Women have no right to say no. Women are made to have sex. It's all they are good for. Some women would rather take a beating, but they always give in; it's what they are for." Men rape, Scully concludes, "not because they are idiosyncratic or irrational, but because they have learned that in this culture sexual violence is rewarding" and because "they never thought they would be punished for what they did."[22] Indeed, they never thought they'd be punished not because they'd so cleverly concealed the evidence of their perceived crime, but because they considered their violent actions utterly justified. What jury could possibly convict them for *that*?

What men say about their use of violence against women is different from what analysts often say about that violence. We're often told that violence against women is the expression of men's power, of men's drive for power, for domination, for control. This makes a certain sense, because most of the theorizing about men's violence has been done by feminist women. Theorists from Andrea Dworkin to Robin Morgan understood the individual trauma, yes, but also the way that violence against women served as a social mechanism of domination, keeping an entire gender a submissive and subject population. Feminist women have understood men's propensity for violence from the perspective of those against whom that violence has so often been directed. Violence is an expression of masculinity in charge, and we are invited to think of masculinity as the drive for power, domination, and control.

This analysis led to certain political positions, a neat symmetry between individual and social levels of analysis. At the aggregate level, women were not "in power." This is easily measured by the levels of political representation, the gender differences in political, corporate, financial, or other leadership positions. It's an empirical observation and easily demonstrated as true. At the individual level, the argument goes, women do not feel powerful. They feel stymied, thwarted in their ability to live the lives they say they want.

Now apply that two-tiered analysis to men's lives. Men *are* "in power." Again, have a glance at all those corporations, legislatures, and other positions of power. So, logically, the symmetrical argument would be that men "feel powerful." And what seemed to be a sensible political position at the time claimed that men had to "give up the power."

The trouble came when one applied that tidy symmetry between social power and individual experience to men's lives. It completely fell apart. "What are you talking about?" men say. "I don't feel powerful! My wife bosses me around! My kids boss me around! My boss bosses me around! I'm completely powerless!"

That original analysis—that men have all the power and must give it up—may have resonated for some women, but it failed to resonate at all for men. It may be how some women experience masculinity. But it's not how men experience their masculinity. Men say they feel powerless.

Of course, it's true that a large number of men are not in power and don't feel especially powerful. Men who are racial, ethnic, religious, or sexual minorities are more likely to experience their marginalization than their being in the seat of power. Working-class men are certainly not in power. It's also the case that their marginalization is accomplished, in part, by questioning their masculinity, by suggesting that they aren't "real men" after all.

Such distinctions among men indicate that masculinity requires a double hierarchy: the power of men over women (as groups) and the power of some men over other men (by race, class, ethnicity, religion, sexuality, and so on). Women theorized from that first hierarchy—and they were right, of course. But men often theorize from that second hierarchy, more painfully aware of the power they don't have and that other men do.

Some of the groups I discuss in this book—from men's rights groups to the Tea Party, from Fathers 4 Justice to white supremacists—agree emphatically when men say they feel powerless. They each have a different bogeyman, a different villain that has thoroughly disempowered the men they address—liberal Democrats, feminists and their lackey lawyers, the International Jewish Banking Conspiracy. But they all agree that when men say they don't feel powerful, it is an accurate assessment of their situation. They don't feel powerful because they aren't.

I too think those men's voices tell us something important about how they feel. Again, I would say that their sense that they are powerless is *real*, as in that is how they experience it, even if it is not *true*—that is an accurate analysis of their situation.

But what that discussion of men's feelings leaves out is the normative, the "ought." They *should* feel powerful. As men experience it, masculinity may not be the experience of power. But it is the experience of *entitlement* to power.

This model of violence as the result of a breakdown of patriarchy, of entitlement thwarted, has become the bedrock of the therapeutic work with violent men. Again and again, what the research on rape and on domestic violence finds is that men initiate violence when they feel a loss of power to which they felt entitled. Listen, for example, to one guy, Emile, describing what caused him to beat his wife—and end up in a therapy group with a colleague of mine named Lundy Bancroft who worked at the Batterers Intervention Project in Boston. "One day Tanya went way overboard with her mouth, and I got so pissed off that I grabbed her by the neck and put her up against the wall," he tells Bancroft. Then, his voice filled with indignation, he continues, "Then she tried to knee me in the balls! How would you like it if a woman did that to you? Of course I lashed out. And when I swung my hand down, my fingernails make a long cut across her face. What the hell did she expect?"[23]

Emile's sense of entitlement leads him to invert cause and effect: she tries to defend herself from his violence, which he interprets as the *initiation* of violence and therefore something that *he* then has to defend himself against. Thus, his escalation is reimagined as self-defense, a defense against emasculation. Entitlement distorts our perceptions, reverses causation, and leads to an ability to justify a "right" that obtains neither in natural nor in civil law. (This was, Bancroft tells us, the moment when Emile confronted his violence and began to accept responsibility for his own actions.)

AN UNSENTIMENTAL EDUCATION

Some years ago, when I was a graduate student, I learned firsthand about men's violence against women. Having been a somewhat sheltered suburban boy, I had no idea, really, about the extent of violence against women, the terrible physical and emotional and even spiritual pain inflicted on women by the men who claim to love them. My girlfriend was working at a shelter at the time; it became the basis for her PhD dissertation. I wanted to do my part, so I offered to volunteer at the shelter where she worked. She informed me that the shelter was for women only and that if I really wanted to help, I should go talk to the men who beat women up. Made sense to me.

I was eventually trained in one of the country's first batterers' intervention programs. These programs were established by the courts as alternatives to incarceration for convicted batterers. During one of our early meetings, I listened as the men went around the room, describing the incidents that led to their arrests and subsequent convictions. To a man, they spoke about "losing control." This notion of losing control as a proximate cause of hitting one's wife was the default position, the most common and easily acknowledged nonpattern. Each guy began with a story about what he expected, what he deserved, what he was entitled to—dinner, sex, her being home, her listening to him. Then there was an argument, during which time he accused her of not providing whatever it was—again, food, sex, complete obedient attention—to which he felt entitled. "And then I just lost control," he would say, to nods of agreement all around the circle. Vague and unspecific, even at times offered in a somewhat lower tone, "I lost control" was almost a mantra—words they knew to say, but without much conviction.

If this sounds like college kids explaining why they hooked up last weekend—because they got so drunk that they just lost control—that is, using loss of control as an excuse to do what you may have wanted to do all along but needed social permission to do, well, there might be some truth to it. But with men who hit women, the logic is somewhat different. If you define masculinity as about always being in control, then losing control is a sign of damaged manhood, of a loss of manhood. Violence, as we've seen, is restorative, a way to set things right again, to return to the place where you are supposed to have been all along. But having to use violence to achieve what you should have been able to assume simply because you have a Y chromosome still doesn't fully repair—*can't* fully repair—that damaged sense of masculinity. So it'll happen again.

And that's why the "losing control" narrative also doesn't square with the data. Even the most cursory review of the data would tell you that domestic violence has a certain pattern and that it often keeps to this pattern despite the seemingly explosive spontaneity of any individual act. If, for example, he hits her in the kitchen around dinnertime, the odds are that will be the place where he will hit her every time he does. If he hits her for the first time in the bedroom, at night, then that's where the overwhelming majority of assaults will take place. Any individual act may feel spontaneous and impulsive—a loss of control—but it is a loss of control that has a definite shape.

At one point in the group, after each guy had described the crime for which he was convicted—although each professed his innocence and made clear that he had just lost it—I returned to one guy's story, to try to push back a bit on what felt too easy and pat an answer. I wanted to force the issue of this contradiction—the fact that the spontaneous loss of control had such a methodical pattern.

This guy—let's call him Al—had recounted that he had returned home from work one evening. It had been a particularly hard day; he was a contractor and several workers hadn't shown up, and he was already pissed that he had to pick up the slack for them. Deadlines were looming larger and larger, and he was starting to get anxious that they might not make it. When he arrived home, though, his wife, who did not have a job outside the home, was just starting dinner. "What could she have been doing all day?" Al asked.

As I'd been trained, I asked him to describe the room in as much detail as possible. (Therapists often argue that it's in these details, and especially in our recollections and narratives of these details, that the clues to successful interventions may lie.) Al described the kitchen. He was in the door frame between the dining room and kitchen, half in and half out of the room. His wife was by the stove, where there was a frying pan for the chicken she was cutting up on the cutting board next to the stove. Frozen french fries were in a bag on the counter, and some vegetables were lying, unwashed and uncut, on the counter.

"So that's when you lost control," I asked, "when she was standing there cooking, and you came in and she hadn't done what she was supposed to do?"

"Yeah," Al said. "I mean I do what *I'm* supposed to do, right? I work my ass off, and come home to that shit?"

"So what happened?" I asked.

"I start yelling, and so she starts yelling about all the stuff *she* has to do, like cleaning and cooking and shit, and we just start yelling, and it gets pretty intense in there. She's such a fucking bitch, man. I work, and she complains. I got really, really mad."

"And that's when you lost it?"

"Yeah, man, I just lost control. I just lost it."

"Hmm," I said, sort of buying time, wondering how to interrupt this self-justifying conversation. "Well, I'm trying to picture this. She's standing by the stove; there's food everywhere, some forks and knives and other cooking stuff around, right?"

"Yeah, so?"

"Well, why didn't you just pick up a knife and stab the bitch?" I asked.

Suddenly, the room grew silent. A couple of guys looked at me as if I finally "got it," finally understood things from their point of view, that I finally understood that sometimes the women just deserve it, you know?

But Al looked at me somewhat blankly. "What the fuck do you mean, man?" he said. "Stab her? Are you fucking crazy? I didn't even hit her with a closed fist! I didn't want to kill her!"

"Wait a minute, Al," I said. "You mean to tell me that you didn't even punch her, that you didn't close your fist when you hit her?"

"No, man! Open hand, open hand."

"Then how can you sit there and tell me that you lost control? I mean, if you and I got into it right here, and you lost control, do you think you'd say to yourself, 'Now, Al, don't close your fist. Hit him with an open hand'? Of course not. You *decided* to hit her. You *decided* not to pick up a knife. You *remembered* not to close your fist when you did. You were in control the whole time!"

Bear in mind that Al's wife had ended up in the hospital that night, with a black eye and a hairline fracture to her jaw. But what happened in that moment was that I had inadvertently interrupted the casual consensus that men hit women when they lose control. The loss of control is the pretext, the facilitator that enables him to do what he *intended* to do, which is to use violence to control her, as he feels entitled to do. Losing control provides plausible deniability, explains away the intentionality, the purposiveness, of the violence.

But if that violence is purposive—intentional, deliberate, and rational—it is also expressive of a feeling that the power and control that you assume, to which you feel entitled, have been eroded, compromised. Violence is the way to restore what should have been in the first place. It doesn't happen when everything is going smoothly, when "his" power is unchallenged. It's only when it breaks down. Violence is restorative. Afterward, everything is returned to its "rightful" state.[24]

THE GENDER ASYMMETRY OF DOMESTIC VIOLENCE

Domestic violence is such a "gendered" social problem because women don't ordinarily feel that sense of entitlement to being in control, being listened to, being in power. Women may feel entitled to be safe, but they don't feel entitled to be in charge.

In fact, the gender imbalance, or asymmetry, of intimate violence is staggering. Of those victims of violence who were injured by spouses or ex-spouses, women outnumber men by about nine to one. Eight times as many women were injured by their boyfriends than men injured by girlfriends. According to the Bureau of Justice Statistics, 85 percent of all victims of domestic violence are women. Domestic violence is the leading cause of injury to women in the nation, claiming nearly 2 million victims a year.[25]

There is a certain logic to this, after all: men disproportionately commit all acts of violence; gender and age are the two variables that predict about 95 percent of all violence in America. It's young men. Yet despite this, there is a chorus of men's rights activists who insist that "men are the victims of domestic violence at least as often as women" and that, therefore, domestic violence isn't a "gender" issue, but a "relationship" issue.

Claims of gender symmetry are bandied about with such frequency and fervor that it's become the mantra of America's angry white men. As I have already discussed, you might hear that women are "as likely"—or even more likely—to hit men as men are to hit women, and that women commit 50 percent of all spousal murders, and provide "facts" such as that 1.8 million women suffered one or more assaults by a husband or boyfriend, and more than 2 million men were assaulted by their wives or girlfriends; that 54 percent of all violence labeled as "severe" was committed by women; or that among teenage dating couples, girls were more violent than boys.

Such assertions are not supported at all by empirical research, and the inferences drawn from them are even more unwarranted. For example, in the original study of "the battered-husband syndrome," sociologist Susan Steinmetz surveyed fifty-seven couples. Four of the wives, but not one husband, reported having been seriously beaten. From this finding, Steinmetz concluded that men simply don't report abuse and that there must be a serious problem of husband abuse and that some 250,000 men were hit every year—this, remember, from a finding that no husbands were abused.[26]

An ongoing bibliographic project by a California psychologist, Martin Fiebert, currently cites 282 articles—218 empirical studies and 64 reviews or essays—that "demonstrate that women are as physically aggressive, or more aggressive, than men in their relationships with their spouses or male partners."[27]

The questions these studies raise are indeed troubling—but the questions they themselves *ask* are far from clear. For example, does gender symmetry mean that women hit women as *often* as men hit women? Or does it mean that an equal *number* of men and women hit each other? Or does symmetry refer to men's and women's *motivations* for such violence, or does it mean that the *consequences* of it are symmetrical? These questions are often lumped together in reviews of literature and "meta-analyses" that review existing data sets.

The two large-scale reviews of literature that demonstrate gender symmetry are useful indicators of the types of evidence offered and the arguments made by their proponents. (Obviously, the number of articles that suggest that there is no gender symmetry in domestic violence is significantly larger than 282 studies—it would probably be a safe bet to say that gender-asymmetry studies outnumber the gender-symmetry ones by about 1,000 to 1.)

Let's take a closer look at that much-heralded authoritative review. A few years ago, I read every single one of the articles that were cited in one of those reviews of the literature. I asked a few of the researchers on the list about their inclusion; they expressed dismay that their work had been so dramatically misunderstood for political ends. Indeed, they all sent me copies of the articles in question—along with several others they had done that showed that they had found dramatic gender differences in rates, severity, frequency, purpose, and initiation of the violence. In other words, this oft-cited review is anything but reliable.

Most of these studies involve the "Conflict Tactics Scale" (CTS) developed by University of New Hampshire sociologist Murray Straus. The scale asks people if they have used any of a set of "conflict tactics"— ranging from slapping and pushing and yelling to beating with various weapons and stabbing. And it's certainly true that if you were to ask women and men, "Have you ever . . . " kicked, pushed, punched, slapped, or scratched their partners, an equal number of women and men would say they had. Does this really tell us anything?

In the research based on the CTS, there was "gender symmetry" in the answer to the "Have you ever . . ." question. But the number changed dramatically when those same people were asked who initiated the violence (was it offensive or defensive?), how severe it was (did she push him before or after he'd broken her jaw?), and how often the violence occurred. When these three questions were posed, the results looked like what we knew all along: the amount, frequency, severity, and consistency of violence against women are far greater than anything done by women to men.[28]

An ever-closer look reveals more ambiguities. Of the actual empirical articles that Fiebert reviews, all but about twenty-five used the same empirical measure of "family conflict," using the CTS as the sole measure of domestic violence. In addition, twenty-eight of those studies noted by Fiebert discussed samples composed entirely of young people—college students, high school students, or dating couples under thirty—and not married couples. Of the remaining nine studies in Fiebert's 1997 survey that neither used the CTS nor sampled only young, dating, unmarried couples, two were based on people's perceptions of violence, but offered no data about violence itself, while another was based on reports of witnessing violence that contained no useful data at all. Another was a study of spousal homicide that did not include homicides by ex-spouses. One was a study of young people that had no comparisons by gender, and one more was based on violence in American comic strips—in 1950.[29]

Of the three remaining studies, two were based on clinical samples undertaken by my colleagues at the university where I teach. So I asked the authors about them. They reminded me that their data came not from a random sample of the population, but from a sample of people who sought marital therapy—and that those couples who see the problem as a relationship problem are far more likely to have high rates of "mutual aggression." Dan O'Leary, my colleague, also insisted that the age of the individuals dramatically changes the data and that clinical samples cannot necessarily be generalized to a national population. Furthermore, the study by Jean Malone and Andrea Tyree found that women's violence was a result of a "desire to improve contact with partners," by which they meant that the women tended to slap or push their partner in order to get him to pay attention to what she was saying—but not to hurt him.[30]

It would appear, therefore, that there is, after all is said and done, one study—an unpublished master's thesis that was written under Fiebert's supervision—that provides the only quantitative evidence of gender symmetry without relying on the CTS. But the author surveyed only women, which makes a comparison to men's use of violence impossible. It may be of interest that most of the women said their violence was a "spontaneous reaction to frustration," but without that comparison, one can make *no inferences whatsoever* about gender symmetry.

So the annotated bibliography turns out to be far more of an ideological polemic than a serious scholarly undertaking. But since it has become a touchstone for those who support a gender-symmetry analysis, it is important to consider the studies on which it is based.

Another problem stems from who was asked. The studies that found comparable rates of domestic violence asked only one partner about the incident. But studies in which both partners were interviewed separately found large discrepancies between reports from women and from men. It turns out that men dramatically underreport their use of violence—perhaps because they feel it's unmanly to beat up a woman, since "real men" never raise a hand against a woman.[31]

A third problem results from *when* the informants were asked about domestic violence. The studies that found comparability asked about incidents that occurred in a single year, thus equating a single slap with a reign of domestic terror that may have lasted decades. Moreover, although the research is clear and unequivocal that violence against women increases dramatically following divorce or separation, the CTS research excluded incidents that occurred after separation or divorce. About 76 percent of all assaults take place at that time, though—with a male perpetrator more than 93 percent of the time.[32]

Finally, the CTS does not take into account the physical differences between women and men, which lead to women being six times more likely to require medical care for injuries sustained in family violence. Nor does it include the nonphysical means by which women are compelled to remain in abusive relationships (income disparities, fears about their children, economic dependency). Nor does it include marital rape or sexual aggression. As one violence researcher asks, "Can you call two people equally aggressive when a woman punches her husband's chest with no physical harm resulting and a man punches his wife's face and her nose is bloodied and broken? These get the same scores on the CTS."[33]

So it's true that women are capable of using violence in intimate relationships—just at nowhere near the same rates or severity, which makes logical sense: violence is gendered, both the act and the sense of entitlement to act.

SOME VARIATIONS

Although my focus here is the aggrieved entitlement of angry white men, I do want to make clear that violence against women knows no class, racial, or ethnic bounds. "Educated, successful, sophisticated men—lawyers, doctors, politicians, business executives—beat their wives as regularly and viciously as dock workers." Yet there are some differences. For example, one of the best predictors of the onset of domestic violence is unemployment. A few studies have also found rates of domestic violence to be higher in African American families than in white families. Although subsequent studies have indicated a decrease in violence among black families, the rates are still somewhat higher than for white families.[34]

Among Latinos the evidence is even more contradictory: one study found significantly less violence in Latino families than in Anglo families, while another found a slightly higher rate. These contradictory findings were clarified by separating different groups of Latinos. Glenda Kaufman Kantor and colleagues found that Puerto Rican husbands were about twice as likely to hit their wives as Anglo husbands (20.4 percent to 9.9 percent) and about ten times more likely than Cuban husbands (2.5 percent). In many cases, however, these racial and ethnic differences disappear when social class is taken into account. Sociologist Noel Cazenave examined the same National Family Violence Survey and found that blacks had *lower* rates of wife abuse than whites in three of four income categories—the two highest and the lowest. Higher rates among blacks were reported only by those respondents in the $6,000–$11,999 income range (which included 40 percent of all blacks surveyed). Income and residence (urban) were also the variables that explained virtually all the ethnic differences between Latinos and Anglos. The same racial differences in spousal murder can be explained by class: two-thirds of all spousal murders in New York City took place in the poorest sections of the Bronx and Brooklyn.[35]

Of course, gay men and lesbians can engage in domestic violence as well. A recent informal survey of gay victims of violence in six major cities found that gay men and lesbians were more likely to be victims of domestic violence than of antigay hate crimes. One study presented to the Fourth International Family Violence Research conference found that abusive gay men had profiles similar to those of heterosexual batterers, including low self-esteem and an inability to sustain intimate relationships.[36]

TAKING RESPONSIBILITY FOR ANGER

My intention in this book is to document the various ways that America's angry white men are expressing their sense of aggrieved entitlement and to offer some more *social* remedies that will enable us both to preserve America's commitment to fairness and equality and to redress their sense that they have lost something palpable and real. But there has been so much attention to the more intimate expressions of men's anger and entitlement, so many initiatives to challenge its foundations and ameliorate its consequences, that it makes sense to address it briefly here. After all, countless men have recognized that they have a problem and have begun the road back, the road away from violence against those they say they love. Around the country, there are more than two hundred programs for violent men—in every state in the nation.

The truth is that men also have choices, and even angry white men can move beyond those feelings of impotent rage and aggrieved entitlement. If these men can choose different directions, then it's possible that some of the other angry men can find some ways to deal with their anger, too. Efforts to reduce the rage, turn down the volume, come in all shapes and sizes, and we ought never to ignore the poignant personal stories for the larger social policy initiatives. It's inspiring when men realize that those angry men aren't only "out there."

Take Dan, for example. One morning, he looked at himself in the mirror and said to himself, "I'm a wife batterer." Those weren't exactly the words he expected to hear himself say. He was a minister, after all, and wasn't an angry or violent guy—except with his wife. Sure, they'd argue, and, occasionally, it would get physical, "just pushing and shoving." But seven years ago, he hit her. Hard. The next morning, when he woke up and looked in the mirror, he prayed. Hard. When that didn't work, he realized he needed to get help.

Another guy, Steve, told me he'd been surrounded by violence all his life. He had been abused as a child and became psychologically and physically abusive in every relationship he had been in. One day, this affable fifty-four-year-old college professor realized "either I had to change the way I was acting, or I was going to be a miserable and lonely old man."

Dan and Steve, and thousands of men like them, stopped hitting their wives and partners. How? They did something truly revolutionary. They made a phone call. They got help. They stopped. "Men who are abusive can stop," says Steven Botkin, a founder of the Men's Resource Center of Western Massachusetts, which runs groups for batterers.

There are many programs springing up around the country and organizations emerging all around the world to engage men to end their violence against women. Domestically, some batterers' intervention programs have been around for a decade or more; others are new and experimental.

Dan needed to confront his sense that he was entitled to rule over his wife, even if he had to use violence to accomplish it. "It sounds so funny, coming from a minister," he said, "but I thought it was my 'God-given right.' I mean, it's right there in the Bible. Chapter and verse. So if I said something, it was right, and Beth had no right to disagree. Good grief, I'd developed such a distorted view of what God's love for man really meant."

Dan ended up in a group that enabled him to reconnect to his core spiritual values, not only to confront his sense that violence was "a reasonable response to an unreasonable situation" but also to remind him of the Christian values he had lost sight of. It's more than asking, "What would Jesus do?" he says now, a decade after the program. "It's about bearing witness to the destructive power of men's violence against women that tears apart families and terrorizes God's children."

Steve, also, had to confront that sense of entitlement. "When that's all you know growing up, you come to assume that's normal, rational.

How can you be a man and not stand up for yourself? I mean, especially if it's with the woman I love. I needed to come to terms with the deep sexism I felt, that somehow her thoughts and feelings were simply not equal in a sort of, I dunno, cosmic value to mine." Remarried for fourteen years, Steve also volunteers occasionally in a program for batterers. "It not only my way of giving back to that program that challenged me. It's also because I have credibility with those guys. I was them, and I know that sense of how men use violence."

Raising awareness of the men's violence toward women—especially toward the women they say they love—is a worldwide issue. It's one of the few places where there are men actively challenging other men, delegitimating that aggrieved entitlement, defusing that anger, and ensuring that it does not find expression on the bodies of women. One of the most visible is the White Ribbon Campaign, founded in Canada in 1991 to commemorate the Montreal massacre. "Most men are not violent. But we've been silent about it, and that silence allows it to continue," says Michael Kaufman, one of the campaign's founders. The White Ribbon Campaign has now spread to more than thirty-five countries, and now many college campuses in the United States are taking it up.

Globally, engaging men to speak out against men's violence against women has inspired men of many different walks of life. Here in the United States, some of our most revered celebrities—athletes—are among the leaders in the field. One of the most visible and galvanizing voices in that choir is Joe Torre, former manager of the New York Yankees and Los Angeles Dodgers.

Torre certainly knows the devastating impact of domestic violence. While he guided the New York Yankees to four World Series titles in his nine years as manager, he almost didn't make it out himself. "My brother and I stayed away from home as much as we could, because we were so afraid of my father," he told me. "We'd play ball all night if we could."

His mother, Margaret, didn't have that option. "My mother was a virtual prisoner in her own house," he recalled. "She never went out to dinner, never went to a movie." Sometimes, his father would come home late at night and demand dinner immediately. Then, he'd throw it against the wall if it wasn't perfect. His father, a police officer, threatened Margaret with a gun, more than once.

When his mother died in 2002, Torre founded the Safe at Home Foundation. Its mission is to raise awareness of how pervasive domestic violence really is and to give children a way to begin to talk about the way domestic violence affects them. "I'd like to believe that men who are abusing their spouses are not aware of the devastating impact it has on their partners and on their children."

Even Torre has been caught off guard by how pervasive it is—and how much people want to talk about it. "People come up to me all the time to tell me their stories of domestic violence. When I do an interview, maybe it's the cameraman, maybe the interviewer. When I went to speak at a school a few weeks ago," he said, "all the kids wanted to talk about was violence. No one asked me anything about baseball!"

The Safe at Home Foundation partners with schools and corporations to raise national awareness and help kids talk about violence at home. They've been broadcasting public service announcements on television and are developing corporate-sponsored "safe rooms" in schools, so that kids can find a safe place to begin to tell their secrets.

Last season the San Francisco Giants initiated a "Strike Out Domestic Violence Day" at PacBell Park. The Boston Red Sox have worked with the Mentors in Violence Prevention Program (known as MVP), which brings high-profile current and former athletes into schools and communities to engage with men to end domestic violence. This year, Safe at Home plans to bring it to every Major League Baseball park in America. They're also working to develop a program called "Coaching Boys into Men" to teach high school boys the danger of transferring violence from the field into the home.

"We send mixed messages to guys," Torre said. "We tell them to be aggressive, to get it done. But then they often feel they can get away with anything." When men feel dissed, it's easy to see how they might resort to the same aggression we try to instill on the playing field. "We have to draw a line and make it stick," Torre says. If women and children are going to be "safe at home," then men are going to have to step up to the plate.

Every day that we fail to understand the connections between men's idea of what it means to be a man and that sense of aggrieved entitlement—the entitlement to use violence to restore our manhood and the legitimacy of making others pay for our unhappinesses—is another day that the everyday Sodinis will embark on their murderous paths.

6 | Mad Men

The Rage(s) of the American Working Man

I've done my best to live the right way,
I get up every morning and go to work each day,
But your eyes go blind and your blood runs cold,
Sometimes I feel so weak I just want to explode.

—BRUCE SPRINGSTEEN, "THE PROMISED LAND" (1979)

Joe Stack had simply had enough. Every time this fifty-three-year-old independent engineer and software consultant from Austin, Texas, had set aside any money at all for retirement, the Internal Revenue Service (IRS) seemed to change the tax laws or whittled away at his earnings with new restrictions. A change in the income-tax regulations in 1986 had removed an exemption for software consultants and engineers, effectively consigning them, in his eyes, to low-income wage work. He just couldn't catch a break. He'd moved from Los Angeles to Austin, remarried, hoping to get better contract consulting work, but the wages in Texas were paltry compared with Southern California. Increasingly despairing that he would never get back on his feet, he began to see the IRS as an agent of discrimination against honest working people, while corporate fat cats got bailed out. Adding insult to injury, they'd recently initiated yet another audit against him.

On the morning of February 18, 2010, he snapped. Perhaps *snap* is the wrong word; it's too sudden, too precipitous. From Joe's perspective, he'd already bent far past the breaking point. He just couldn't bend anymore, couldn't accommodate all that weight. That Thursday morning, he set fire to his small house in North Austin. He then drove to a hangar that he rented at the Georgetown Municipal Airport and cleared his single-engine Piper airplane for takeoff. "Thanks for your help," he told the control tower as he left the airfield at 9:45. "Have a great day!"

Ten minutes later, he flew the plane directly into Echelon I, the building in a near-downtown Austin office complex that housed the IRS. The fully fueled plane exploded into a fireball, killing the pilot and also IRS manager Vernon Hunter, a sixty-three-year-old father of six. Thirteen others were injured, two seriously.

In the immediate media flurry, Stack was portrayed as a deranged individual, which, no doubt, he was. But he had hardly acted spontaneously. Indeed, as with so many of these deranged lone wolves who seem to explode one day out of the blue, Stack's explosion had been brewing for some time. Later that day, investigators found a lengthy suicide note, which Stack had written and revised over the previous three days. In this rambling diatribe against the forces that he believed had led him to this murderously suicidal rampage, Stack just couldn't get past the injustice of it all, the fact that there seemed to be two sets of rules—which further widened following the economic meltdown of 2008—one for the rich and powerful and one for the rest of us.

"Why is it," he asks rhetorically, "that a handful of thugs and plunderers can commit unthinkable atrocities (and in the case of the GM [General Motors] executives, for scores of years) and when it's time for their gravy train to crash under the weight of their gluttony and overwhelming stupidity, the force of the full federal government has no difficulty coming to their aid within days if not hours?"[1]

He described an eighty-year-old neighbor, a widow of a steelworker who worked in the mills in central Pennsylvania all his life, believing the promises from the mill owners and the unions that he would have a pension and medical care for a secure retirement. "Instead he was one of the thousands who got nothing because the incompetent mill management and corrupt union (not to mention the government) raided their pension funds and stole their retirement," Stack wrote. "All she had was Social Security to live on." She survives, he said, on cat food.

Like many other guys these days, Stack was mad as hell. Yes, he flipped out, and yes, he was probably clinically insane. But such armchair diagnoses miss the method in his madness, the logic of his psychotic break with reality. Stack considered himself a victim of the impersonal forces that wreak havoc with the lives and the futures of America's middle and working classes—the labyrinthine impersonal governmental bureaucracies and the impenetrable corporations whose CEOs and shareholders were lavishly compensated. Joe Stack was Joe Sixpack, Joe Lunchbucket, Joe the Plumber. He was a New Economy Everyman. Everything piled up on him, and he just lost it.

So Joe Stack "went postal," as that new phrase coined during the Reagan era put it, named after that spate of rampage murders in which US Postal Service (USPS) workers shot and killed managers, supervisors, and fellow workers. Between 1986 and 1997, forty people were murdered in at least twenty incidents involving postal workers. Before 1986—nary a one. What happened?

Reaganomics happened. Under a Reagan-era policy, the USPS stopped receiving federal tax moneys starting in the early 1980s and was pushed to streamline its operations to maximize efficiency, including cutting wages, firing staff, and slashing benefits. The workers who went postal were all post-office workers who had been laid off or downsized or had their benefits slashed.

One such worker was Patrick Sherrill, the postal worker who started the "trend" and launched that tragic neologism. On August 20, 1986, Sherrill walked through the post office in Edmond, Oklahoma, where he worked, targeting his supervisors and several coworkers. By the time he was done, fifteen postal employees lay dead, and another six were injured—at the time, the third-largest massacre in American history. The last bullet he reserved for himself. As the police arrived on the scene, they heard only one shot.

Yes, Stack and Sherrill were insane, but they were also familiar. They didn't start out mad. No, they were driven crazy by the sense that the world had spun so far off its axis that there was no hope of righting it. Underneath that sense of victimhood, that sense that the corporations and the government were coconspirators in perpetrating the great fleecing of the American common man, lay a defining despair in making things right. And under that despair lay their tragic flaw, a deep and abiding faith in America, in its institutions and its ideals. Like Willy Loman, perhaps the quintessential true believer in the ideology of self-made American masculinity, they believed that if they worked hard and lived right, they, too, could share in the American Dream. When it is revealed that no matter what you do, no matter how hard you work, that dreams are for Disneyland, then they morph into a tragic American Everymen, defeated by circumstances instead of rising above them.

Stack and Sherrill believed in that America. They believed that there was a contract between themselves, and guys like them, and the government "of the people" that is supposed to represent us. They believed in the corporations that they worked for, confident in the knowledge that they could support a family, enjoy a secure retirement, and provide for their families. That contract was the stable foundation for several generations of America's working men—an implied but inviolable understanding between businesses and workers, between government and employers. They had kept the faith, fulfilled their part of the bargain. And somehow their share had been snatched away by faceless, feckless hands. They had played by all the rules, only to find the game was rigged from the start.

It feels like even the unions have betrayed them. At their origin, the union movement established the baseline that enabled working- and middle-class American men to plant a stake in the American Dream. The relentless recent attacks on unions, both in the public sector and in private companies, and the self-serving corruption in many unions that legitimized those attacks have hit lower-middle-class and working-class men the hardest—the same group that is now most ardently antiunion. It's a tragic irony of the American worker—they've been persuaded to put their trust in the very companies that betray them and shun the organizations that once protected them.

Generations of men had staked their claim for manhood on being good family providers, reliable breadwinners. It has been the defining feature of American manhood since the early nineteenth century. With neither a feudal aristocracy nor clerical indulgence, American manhood was defined in opposition to the European version, where rank and birth and blood determined your fate. Here, in the American

Eden, all was new and naked, and a man could rise as high as his talents and aspirations and hard work could take him.

He could do that because he assumed the playing field was level. But all that has changed in America. The playing field is no longer level. Of course, it never was; it had always tilted decidedly in favor of middle-class white men. But what *has* changed is the angle of that tilt. On the one hand, it's not quite so lopsided, as more of "them" seem to be catching up with "us." On the other hand, it's more dramatically lopsided than it has been since the Gilded Age—and perhaps even more than that. The gap between the middle class and the rich has never been as large as it now is in the United States. Today, the United States is coming to resemble prerevolutionary France, with teeming masses who have less and less and a noble few who tweet about twenty-five-dollar cupcakes. Although a higher percentage of white people now believe that they are the victims of discrimination than do black people, they fail to see the very rich white people who are doing massively better.

But these middle-class white men are right in one sense: the social contract that enabled self-made men to feel that they *could* make it, even if they somehow failed to realize their dreams, has, indeed, been shredded, abandoned for lavish profiteering by the rich, enabled by a government composed of foxes who have long ago abandoned their posts at the henhouse. That safety net, always thin, has been undone by decades of neglect since the establishment of the Great Society in 1960s. There's a painful sense of betrayal from their government, from the companies to whom we give our lives, from the unions. There was a *moral* contract, that if we fulfill our duty to society, society will fulfill its duty to us in our retirement, taking care of those who served so loyally.

Although the contract may have been shredded by greedy companies driven by greedier financiers, the sense of entitlement on the part of white men remains intact. Many white men feel they have played by the rules and expected to reap the rewards of that obedient responsibility. It's pretty infuriating not to get what you feel you deserve. That's the aggrieved entitlement that lies underneath the anger of American white men.

They had played the game like real men—honorably, honestly. And if they were going to go down, they were going to go down like real men—making somebody pay. Even if they had to die trying.

MAD MEN

For decades, every single morning, guys like Joe Stack—middle-class corporate guys, office workers, salesmen, and independent professionals—have lined up to take the 7:23 from Anywhere, USA, to the big city. Every night they've returned, briefcase and hat in hand, to their suburban castles. Like characters on *Mad Men*, they assumed their place in the long line of American breadwinners, of family men. They worked in the city, but were successful enough to escape to the suburbs, where life was greener and safer, where the schools were better for their children. They and their families shopped in malls, mowed their grass, and watched their children ride their bikes.

On the other side of the tracks, working-class guys like Patrick Sherrill have driven their pickup trucks to work in America's factories, producing the cars we crave, the clothes we wear, the stuff we use. They have delivered America's packages, paved America's roads and built her bridges, and erected the skyscrapers in which corporate moguls reap their fortunes.

But all is not well. There's a mounting anger underneath those perfectly manicured lawns, and it erupts like small volcanoes in our homes, in our corporate offices, and on those peaceful suburban streets themselves. Jim Anderson (of *Father Knows Best*) has been supplanted by Homer Simpson, the bumptious blowhard who's neither a stable family man nor a reliable employee. In the near–ghost towns of America's factory cities, white workers seethe into their beers, wondering where it all went wrong—and how it all went to hell so fast. Perhaps more menacingly, some of these obedient men have now been replaced by violent men, who lash out at their spouses, while their sons learn their lessons well, as they drive through suburban neighborhoods looking for immigrants to beat up, and even to kill.

Despite these enormous class differences, these different groups of white men are angry—angry at a system that has so let them down. The most passionate believers in the American Dream, "the Promised Land" Bruce Springsteen sings about, they've seen it gradually erode into a postindustrial nightmare, a world of corroding Rust Belt infrastructure and faceless cubicles that dull the senses and numb the soul. The white working class and the white middle class have rarely been so close *emotionally* as they are today; together they have drifted away from unions, from big government, from the Democratic Party, into the further reaches of the right wing. Together they listen to Glenn Beck and Rush Limbaugh. And together they watched Brad Pitt initiate Ed Norton into "Fight Club," searching for something— anything—that would feel authentic, that would feel real. Middle- and working-class white men—well, they just are beginning to actually *understand* each other.

Some non-post-office rampage murders were regular working guys who simply snapped. Take, for example, Joseph Wesbecker, who worked at the Standard Gravure plant in Louisville, Kentucky, a printing plant that exclusively printed the local newspaper, the *Louisville Courier-Journal*. For months, even years, managers had refused to listen to Wesbecker's complaints that operating the folder press was too hard for him, that his workplace-induced stress made it hard for him to perform all the operations of heavy equipment. On September 14, 1989, Wesbecker roamed through the factory floor, purposefully toward the supervisors' office, opening fire at anyone who had ever crossed him. By the time he put the gun to his own head, seven coworkers lay dead, and another twenty had been wounded.

Others were more corporate, like Gian Luigi Ferri, a chubby fifty-five-year-old businessman who, in 1993, slaughtered seven people and injured six others at the tony, white-shoe downtown San Francisco law firm that had represented him. As the police entered the building, he killed himself.

Some were more in between the have-mores and the have-nots. Matthew Beck was a socially awkward yet conscientious accountant at the Connecticut State Lottery, who had worked diligently for eight years, until, in the summer of 1997, he was unceremoniously passed over for promotion (despite flawless work). He became bitter, angry, and withdrawn, and he began to fall apart. After Beck returned from a two-month medical leave, one of his supervisors added to his workload a particularly demeaning task for a trained accountant, monitoring the use of state cars given to those who had been promoted—that is, those who received perks to which Beck thought he was entitled. He snapped. On March 6, 1998, Beck came to work on a "casual Friday" and stabbed his former supervisor (who was the first to deny his grievance over his nonpromotion), then walked to a staff meeting of several senior staff, and shot the company chief financial officer, his senior supervisor who had also turned down his promotion. He lowered his gun and walked out of the meeting room and through the executive suite where the vice president of operations poked his head out of his office and asked, "Is everything okay?" This VP had also rejected Beck's promotion, and Beck shot and killed him.

Finally, he confronted the lottery president himself, Otho Brown, in the parking lot of the building. Brown had been the final top authority who had signed off on the rejection of Beck's promotion. While most of the lottery employees huddled at the edge of the parking lot, in the apparent safety of a grove of trees, Brown stood alone in the lot. Beck's fellow employees begged him to stop. He calmly shot Brown three times. As the police pulled up, Beck put the pistol to his own head and shot himself. "They were the people who had the power in the Lottery," said one of the supervisors who was in that meeting room but was spared by Beck. "They were the ones who had turned down his promotion."[2]

It's not just white guys, either. On August 2, 2010, Omar Thornton, a thirty-four-year-old black truck driver for a major Connecticut beer distributor, walked into the main office in Hartford and opened fire, killing eight people before turning the gun on himself. According to his girlfriend's mother, Thornton was a "mellow" guy who had complained for a long time about racial harassment. He claimed to have pictures on his cell phone that he had taken at the distributor—pictures of the N word and hangman's nooses graffitied on the bathroom walls. No one listened. So he began to take his revenge against a company that he felt was indifferent to his plight; he started stealing cases of beer. Caught on a company video, he was brought in for a disciplinary hearing with his union on that fateful day and offered the choice of being fired or quitting. He chose a horrifying, fatal, third path.

"It's got nothing to do with race," commented Teamster official Christopher Roos to a television journalist. "This is a disgruntled employee who shot a bunch of people." He almost made it sound tame. But in one sense, Roos is right. Thornton may have complained about racial harassment and may have thought there was some racial bias at the distributor. But his actions that fateful day were those of a working man who had snapped. Not a black working man, but a working man.

He was *not* a working woman. In my research, I could find no cases of working women coming into their workplaces, packing assault weapons, and opening fire, seemingly indiscriminately. It's not that they don't get depressed and enraged when they get downsized, laid off, or mistreated, their wages cut, their pensions slashed, or their benefits reduced. Some had brought a handgun and often carried over a domestic-violence dispute into the workplace. They just don't go postal.[3]

Let's be clear: just as we cannot understand rampage school shootings by focusing on the fact that they are always committed by boys, neither can we understand these cases simply by recognizing that they're all men. Surely, too, recognizing that they're all men doesn't mean that all men are likely to become deranged mass murderers. Neither, however, can we explain it simply by the easy American access to guns or chalk it up to yet another deranged killer, the standard fare on *CSI*-like television.

But we can't ignore it, either. There is no one single explanation. What is required is that we look inside the economic and social shifts inside America's workplaces and the broader patterns of class in America. Just as we needed to profile the school shooters and their schools, we also need to profile these guys gone postal and the places where they made their living. We need to ask some questions about the changing conditions of work in America, the political economy in which these men became deranged enough to go postal.

THE RATIONALITY OF THE MAD GUNMAN

Most disgruntled male workers don't go postal, of course. Indeed, it's pretty obvious that well over 99 percent of us don't bring assault weapons to work, ready to open fire on our coworkers or supervisors. It is telling, though, to listen to how regular folks respond when someone does embark on such a murderous spree. How different are the comments from those of neighbors of, say, serial killers or other mass murderers. When the media or police interview neighbors of serial killers, like Jeffrey Dahmer, the typical response is a surprised version of "He was very quiet," "He kept to himself," or "We had no idea we were living next door to a monster."

Not so with the guys who go postal. "You could sorta see it coming" is by far the more likely response. Coworkers and workers in other companies mention the erosion of benefits, the capricious cuts in staff, the constant fears of layoffs and downsizing, the seething resentment at the bonuses the managers pay themselves. They *can* see it coming. Says one survivor, "There are a lot of people who are sort of on your side. There are people . . . who claim 'I'm not going to say that he did the right thing, but I can understand where he came from, and maybe if I had been in his spot, I'd have done it too.'"

Over and over, this is what you hear: "I could see it coming," "If it wasn't him, it would have been someone else," "What did you expect?" "They've been treating us so bad for so long, someone was going to snap." (That the "someone" is always a man seems to escape everyone's notice, as if it's simply the most normal thing in the world for men—and not women—to react this way.)

When the story of Matthew Beck was posted recently to a website, comments were guarded but compassionate. "I can sorta understand why he did it," wrote one. "I don't agree with his actions either," wrote another. "But on some level I understand him." "You can't put people down and expect them to take it with a smile," wrote a third. "I can't help but feel some sympathy for the shooter. His life must have been hell and I can't blame him for hating them."[4]

But let's be clear: these guys committed murder. Joe Stack flew his plane into the IRS building. This wasn't just a minor case of road rage. This was an act of domestic terrorism. He attacked a government office, just as Timothy McVeigh had done. But in the aftermath, there was far more sympathy for him among ordinary Americans than there was for McVeigh in 1995. There are entire websites devoted to calling him "an American hero." Why? For one thing, it wasn't "political"—that is, Joe Stack wasn't trying to start a revolution. He was just at the end of his rope, having been jerked around callously by those in charge.

"Oh, c'mon," says Bill, a patron at a local coffee shop, on the afternoon after Stack's death, as the news feeds come in over the Internet. He's sitting at the table next to me. Bill has his laptop open; his cell phone sits next to it on the table. Both are plugged into the only electric outlets nearby, monopolizing them. "Fuck, no," he says, loud enough for me to hear. I look at him, curious. I hadn't been anticipating an interview just then. He says it again.

"Did you hear about this guy in Texas? Flew his plane into the IRS office. That's not terrorism. Not like 9/11. I mean, the guy'd just had it. He was fed up, fucked. Probably thought he had no way out."

"But why do you think he just snapped that way?" I ask.

"Look at what's happening," Bill says. "Everywhere you look, it's downsizing, outsourcing, laying off. No more pension funds, no more health benefits, no more retirement. He was cornered, and he came out swinging."

"But he flew his airplane into a building, killing an innocent man and injuring many others. He killed a guy who was probably as trapped as he was. How can you justify that?"

Bill sits for a moment. "I'm not justifying it. I'm not excusing it. But I'm trying to understand it. I think there are a lot of people who sorta feel like they're at the end of their rope and don't know what to do. They're panicking, freaking out, you know? Back in the day, if you got screwed by your company, you could go to the government, get unemployment, get food stamps, whatever, get some help. Now there's nowhere to go. The government does nothing; the corporations—well, they're the problem. Nowhere to go."

"You know," I say, "you sound like a socialist. The government is in the pockets of the big corporations that are ruled by greed and intent on screwing the workers."

"Hah!" says Bill. "A socialist! I'm as far from that as you could imagine. I'm an American. Heck, I'd even support the Tea Party if they could get the government out of my wallet. I don't want to pay *more* taxes! And I don't want a bigger government. I want a responsive one. I mean, just look at me, for Christ's sake."

Bill, I soon learn, is looking for work, a euphemism for the newly unemployed in the current "he-cession"—the economic recession that has hit men so hard. More than 80 percent of all the jobs lost between November 2008 and December 2010 had been jobs that had been held by men. Sure, most of those have been in manufacturing and especially construction, as the housing boom went south. But the ripples have been felt in midsize local businesses across the country. (Just as surely, there's been a "he-covery," as the overwhelming number of new jobs created since 2011 have been jobs that have gone to men, while public-sector jobs, like administrators and teachers and public-sector employees, mostly women, have been laid off by the thousands.)

Bill had been in sales. "But who the fuck is buying anything that anyone is selling?" He doesn't wait for an answer. "I'll tell you who. Nobody. That's who. It feels like such a scam, the whole thing, a big Madoff Ponzi scheme where the rich get everything. And this . . . ," he says, pointing to his technological arsenal on the small table, "well, it's not helping. We're all networked up the wazoo, we have every networking device known to man, and yet we can't find a job. And when you do find one, it's never as good as the one you had before. Working conditions, benefits, you name it. Always worse, always worse."

He drifts back to the laptop. If we'd been in a bar, drowning our sorrows, instead of in a coffee shop, trying to stay pumped and focused, this would be the signal to look at his beer and mutter something over and over, under his breath.

Bill expressed so many of the concerns of today's middle-class and working-class men—the constant downward pressure, a sense that they are no longer climbing the ladder of success but rather just trying to fight off being pushed down the ladder. They feel lucky if they are just holding on.

The deteriorating working conditions, the crap people have to put up with in their jobs, lead to some unlikely heroes. Enter Steven Slater, the Jet Blue flight attendant who became an instant celebrity after he exploded in a workplace tirade in early August 2010. Working a routine flight from Pittsburgh to New York City, Slater had, witnesses said, already been yelled at by abusive passengers when he had tried to intervene when two passengers were fighting over the overhead space. One of the passengers' suitcase hit him in the head as it tumbled from the overstuffed overhead bin. As the plane landed and was taxiing to the gate, that same woman stood up and was furious that the gate-checked bag was not immediately available, and she began to curse at him. Slater snapped. He grabbed the intercom, cursed her out right back, grabbed a beer from the stowed service cart, and opened the door of the plane. "That's it, I'm done," he said. He inflated the emergency evacuation slide, slid down to the tarmac, and ran off. He was arrested a few hours later.

Immediately, people rallied to his defense. Although his workplace explosion was utterly unprofessional and was gradually revised by other passengers on the plane in a way that made him look a little less heroic, it was Slater's version of the story that has stuck. He was hailed by Stephen Colbert as the "Alpha Dog of the Week" for his testicular fortitude—he slid down the evacuation slide "using his balls as a sled," Colbert reported. Late-night hosts scrambled to book him, and his newly enlisted agent is fending off offers for books and television rights.

Whether Slater was "justified" is hardly the point. The public reaction to his antics reveals something important about how many people feel about their jobs. Slater's classic "take this job and shove it" attitude expressed what millions of Americans seem to feel about their working conditions. People cheer him as a hero.

In that sense, Slater's actions are understandable, if not justifiable, rational, if not reasonable—not as the flipping out of a madman, but as a desperate effort to draw attention to the miserable conditions that working people endure. More, it's that conditions have become so much worse, that the social contract has been torn apart by corporate greed and government inaction. Instead of armchair psychologizing by a public tut-tutting their way to self-satisfied judgment, commentators reached for the business sections of the newspapers, reporting the gradual erosion of the friendly skies in today's cut-throat business climate. Yes, it's true that passengers have been nickeled and dimed by baggage fees, convenience fees, talk-to-a-real-agent fees, paying for food and beverages and entertainment, and every conceivable additional fee. But the working conditions of the airplane as a workplace have also steadily eroded—and not just because passengers are more irate and more entitled.

Over the past decade, airline passengers have increased from 629 million to 770 million, an 8 percent increase. In 2010 domestic airlines employed about 463,000 full-time workers, compared with 607,307 a decade earlier—a decrease of roughly 8 percent. At the same time, fuel costs have doubled, operating costs have soared, and gate fees and landing fees charged by municipalities to airlines have all risen significantly. That means that profits have to come from the labor side of the economic equation, not the materials side. Sure enough, airline workers have been hit hard by cuts: their salaries have been cut, pensions slashed, health benefits reduced or even eliminated, and various unions abandoned by new airlines and undermined at the old ones.

Airline workers, like their passengers, are being required to do more and more for less and less. And no one, neither the passengers nor those who serve them their drinks, seems to be able to do anything about it. This isn't just about little bags of pretzels. It's about daily erosions of those feelings of pride in your work, the compromising of archaic feelings like honor and integrity, self-respect for a job well done. In that sense, Steven Slater did not show what balls he had, as Colbert reported, but rather illustrated just how impotent American workers really feel.

TURNING RAGE INWARD

Workplace rampages, real or symbolic, are only part of the story. Anger doesn't explode only outward at external targets. It can explode inward as well. You don't have to take out your imagined enemy or lash out blindly. You can take your own life.

Actually, going postal and committing suicide are often intimately related. In most recent cases, the mad gunman who goes postal actually saves the last bullet for himself. As with the post-Columbine rampage school shooters, this is also a case of "suicide by mass murder."

But what of suicide itself—that is, regular, "ordinary" suicide, without the mass-murderous trimmings? Ever since the days of Emile Durkheim, sociologists have documented how suicide rates fluctuate with economic trends. Actually, Durkheim showed that suicide rates tend to increase not only when times get bad, but also when they turn suddenly very good. During those moments of dramatic personal or social prosperity, the rules seem to shift, and the expectation begins to manifest that your positive change of fortune will solve all of life's problems. But when that transformation inevitably fails to materialize, the depression can be more profound.

On the other side, of course, economic hard times are typically accompanied by a spike in suicides. Images of white-collars bankers and financiers jumping out of buildings during the Great Depression have passed into part of our great national narrative.[5] During the farm crisis of the mid-1980s, when punitive financial policies implemented by the Reagan administration suppressed prices and ignored increased energy and feed costs, which led to massive foreclosures—between eighty to ninety thousand between 1985 and 1986 alone—suicides of small farmers, many of whose families had worked their now-foreclosed family farms for several generations, spiked to an all-time high for rural suicide. (Suicide rates, as well as rates of alcoholism, are generally higher in rural than in urban areas; somehow loneliness is more suicidally depressing than overcrowding.)

It became so dire back then that Willie Nelson organized a series of concerts in what became known as Farm Aid across the Midwest and South. Asked to comment on the rash of suicides that led to Farm Aid, civil rights leader Reverend Jesse Jackson commented caustically about the Reagan administration's indifference to the plight of the family farmer. "If a flood occurred affecting 80,000 to 90,000 people," Jackson observed, "the president would be in a helicopter and emergency funds would be made available to the victims immediately."[6] Bear in mind that Jackson made this comment in 1986, fifteen years before Hurricane Katrina created the flood that demolished much of New Orleans and left ten times that number in the direst of straits. Even then, it was unimaginable that such a catastrophe could have been met with such administrative indifference at the top.

Researchers noticed a strong correlation between the farm crisis and suicide rates among male farmers in the first half of the 1980s—significantly higher than for truck drivers (another manual occupation with a notably high rate of suicide).[7] In the upper Midwest states of North and South Dakotas, Montana, Minnesota, and Wisconsin alone, more than nine hundred male farmers committed suicide in the 1980s, more than double the national average.[8]

Since the beginning of the recession of 2008, suicide rates among farmers began increasing again. Calls to seven Sowing the Seeds of Hope crisis hotlines for farmers and ranchers in the Midwest rose 40 percent—just in the first half of 2009 alone. In early 2009, one farmer in Maine hanged himself in his barn; a year later, two more killed themselves. In one particularly poignant case, in January 2010, an upstate New York dairy farmer, Dean Pierson, killed the fifty-one dairy cows he milked twice a day, before turning the gun on himself.[9]

Why farmers, and why again, why now? To understand the despair of the small farmer in America is to enter a world of labyrinthine economics—of not only prices set by domestic or even global markets, but also government subsidies, tax breaks, and massive social inequality that squeeze the small farmer at every turn. Costs escalate, especially for fuel and equipment, and environmental regulations often require the use of more expensive, but less despoiling, fertilizers and chemicals.

So take Dean Pierson, dairy farmer. The United States produces 21 billion gallons of milk a year—far more than we consume. (Indeed, milk consumption has steadily declined in the United States since the middle of the twentieth century and is down 20 percent since the 1980s.) This pushes prices down. On average, it costs about seventeen dollars to produce one hundred pounds of milk. But by March 2009, the price of milk had dropped to twelve dollars for one hundred pounds. Government subsidies brought the price up to sixteen dollars. Rising costs and declining prices—this is the recipe for economic crisis.

In rural areas and small towns across the country, a feeling of impending doom often leads to dire outcomes. One town, Elkhart, Indiana, has tried to react collectively—after 22 local residents killed themselves in this one rural northern Indiana county in less than a year, between 2008 and 2009. In Elkhart County's population of 830,000, 81 people on average commit suicide every year—which is somewhat lower than the national average of 11 per 100,000. But the number jumped to 104 in 2008 and topped 200 for 2009—more than two and a half times its former rate. More than one-quarter had "left notes specifically stating that the reason they did this was because of the economy," noted the coroner. "We've had many situations where people lost their jobs and that was the reason for why they do what they do," commented Sheriff Mark Hackel, whose office now fields about one suicide-attempt phone call every single day.

Across the border, Kent County, Michigan, averages about 47 suicides a year out of a population of 605,000. That number jumped to 66 in 2008 and about the same in 2009—an increase of 40 percent. Once again, the county's chief medical examiner notes that many of the deaths were related to unemployment and financial trouble. This included a fifty-two-year-old man who hanged himself because he was "despondent over financial stress," a thirty-one-year-old who hanged himself in the wake of home foreclosure and looming bills, and a forty-five-year-old man who shot himself after telling family members that he was overwhelmed with credit-card debt.[10]

It's not just on our nation's farms. Men have long been "the suicide gender"; currently in the United States, suicides among males outnumber those among females by a factor of four.[11] But what is also interesting is the distribution of suicides among males. The old have historically been the category with the highest rate of suicide, followed by the young. Rates continue to climb for divorced middle-aged men—their rates are nearly 40 percent higher than among married men, higher even than among single men. (Among women, differences in suicide rates among single, married, and divorced women are statistically insignificant.) Marriage keeps men connected, and connected men do not commit suicide. Unmarried middle-aged men are nearly four times more likely to commit suicide than are married men. And recent data suggest that the biggest jump has been among men in their fifties.[12]

Which is why the most recent data on suicide among men are troubling. In the past decade, the largest increases in suicides have been among middle-aged men—the group that is most tethered to their families and their communities. Sociologists Julie Philips and Ellen Idler have documented significant increases of suicide among middle-aged men, from 21.8 per 100,000 in 1979 to more than 25 today. Suicide rates fluctuate with rates of unemployment for both white- and blue-collar workers, as well as with rates of personal bankruptcy. Unemployed people are two to three times more likely to commit suicide—and the risk rises the longer one is jobless.[13]

The current economic recession has ushered in a growing sense of despair. Calls to the National Suicide Prevention Lifeline have jumped dramatically—from 13,423 in January 2007 to a high of 57,625 in August 2009.[14]

Rates have also spiked among white working-class men (men without a college degree)—that is, the group of workers most likely to have been hit with unemployment. It's gone up among construction and manufacturing workers, as well as among finance—three of the more gender-skewed occupations, and the ones hardest hit by the recession. (The unemployment rate among construction workers is 20 percent, and 95 percent of those seeking work are men; manufacturing jobs decline at a rate of almost 5 percent a year, and 80 percent of those jobs are held by men.) Calls to suicide hotlines have increased dramatically, "tied, largely, to lost jobs, housing problems and loss of status," commented Sarah Trondone, the director of outpatient and emergency services at Advocates, Inc., a Boston-area organization that serves diverse groups of troubled and disabled people. "When people lose their jobs, they feel they've lost their status in society and their roles as breadwinners," she continued. "Hopelessness often sets in."[15]

DESPAIR AND DEPRESSION

The spike in suicides is a molehill compared to the mountainous increases in depression among men, especially middle-aged men. What is depression, psychologists tell us, but anger turned inward, against the self? Depression is the implosion, swallowing the rage. Some guys "feel so weak," they "just want to explode," as Bruce Springsteen sings in the chapter's epigraph. Some explode outward, taking everything in their path. Most of us swallow it and try to keep going.

Several psychiatrists have begun to pick up on this trend. For decades, therapists understood depression as a "feminine" psychological problem. Depression is anger without voice, anger that has no way to express itself in public, so it turns inward, shuts down. Real men, by contrast, don't swallow their pain or hurt; they explode. Thus, therapists saw anxiety disorders as more "masculine" on the mental-illness continuum.

In the past decade, however, a veritable epidemic of depression among men has been seeping into the public consciousness. Psychologist Terrence Real, whose pathbreaking book *I Don't Want to Talk About It* both diagnosed the epidemic and linked depression to masculinity, explained it this way:

> One of the ironies about men's depression is that the very forces that help create it keep us from seeing it. Men are not supposed to be vulnerable. Pain is something we are to rise above. He who has been brought down by it will most likely see himself as shameful, and so, too, may his family and friends, even the mental health profession. [Depression] is this secret pain that lies at the heart of many of the difficulties in men's lives. Hidden depression drives several of the problems we think of as typically male: physical illness, alcohol and drug abuse, domestic violence, failures in intimacy, self-sabotage in careers.[16]

Real explains social problems—such as workplace failure, violence, substance abuse—as the outcome of male depression. But those social issues are just as much the cause of that depression in the first place. Although depression has a physiological basis, and each of us has a different level of genetic predisposition toward it, depression is also socially distributed—that is, different groups of people in different social circumstances (the newly divorced or the recently downsized or laid off) are far more likely to experience depression than those who are married or employed or both.

A recent team of medical researchers in Philadelphia recruited a sample of 250 people through a mortgage counseling agency—that is, a sample of people who were in some sort of financial trouble, ranging from falling behind on payments, being "under water" (paying a mortgage that was for more than the house was worth), or facing foreclosure. They found that 37 percent of the sample met the clinical criteria for major depression. What's more, having serious mental health problems and foreclosure seemed to be correlated: having a medical problem caused people to fall behind on mortgage payments, while for others falling behind led to serious medical problems. Having neither adequate health care coverage nor any other financial safety net when facing mortgage problems makes for a mutually reinforcing cycle.[17]

Feeling so weak you just want to explode—"and tear this whole town apart," Springsteen sings, "take a knife and cut their pain from my heart." Take them all out. Take them with me. Just do myself in. Or spiral downward into a cellar of gloom and despair. Or self-medicate with alcohol or drugs. Just how many men are in such pain? Maybe there are 20 cases of men going postal—but the zeroes keep adding up when you add in suicides, depression, alcoholism, drugs. Just swallow your pain. Keep on going. Is this not the mantra of American masculinity?

This is a notion of masculinity that seems to be about endurance—not only "How long can you last?" but also "How much can you stand?" You go on, suppressing doubt, feigning fearlessness, unwilling to yield. At its best, it's a template for feats of such wrenching heroism that every generation wells up with tears at the mention of those brave men who sacrificed so much in the name of proving themselves—on battlefields and ball fields, in boardrooms and laboratories. At its worst, it's a recipe for depression, suicidal rage, and a simmering numbness that some psychologists have even labeled a mental illness called *alexithymia*—the socially conditioned "inability to feel or express feelings."[18]

But such diagnoses locate the problem within and among men, not in the social conditions in which men live and in which they attempt to prove themselves as men. A more accurate reading, I think, would bring that personal focus into a dialogue with the social context in which men struggle to prove themselves, against odds so stacked against them they are doomed to fail. American men are, in my view, less emotionally stunted sociopaths and more like Willy Loman—desperate to prove themselves.

"As soon as you're born, they make you feel small," sang John Lennon in "Working Class Hero," his dirge-like fanfare for the common man. "'Til the pain is so great you feel nothing at all."

FANTASY ISLAND

It's not like being numb is encoded on the Y chromosome. It's a response to what happens to us, the tragic mismatch between who we think we're supposed to be and what our society allows us to become. No wonder so many guys find media escape so gratifying—you get to be king of the hill, blow everyone else up, score the winning touchdown, or just get even with all the bureaucratic impersonal forces arrayed against you. There's an old axiom in psychoanalysis: what we lose in reality, we re-create in fantasy. If you feel yourself to always be taking it on the chin, media fantasy is the place where you get to pump your fist in defiance. If you feel emasculated in real life, you can feel like a man in "reel life."

When I was researching my book *Guyland*, I was somewhat surprised to hear some of this anger so ready to explode among so many younger guys, especially white guys in their twenties. I understood it among their dads—that mismatch between means and ends, between what they believe it means to be a man and the ability to achieve it in today's world, the tragic sense of thwarted entitlement to power, status, wealth, or other goods. Their dads, I reasoned, had begun their adult lives with that ideology of manhood, that sense of entitlement, and the means to achieve it.

But their sons? Hadn't things changed so much that their sons would have let go of some of that sense of entitlement, perhaps modified their ideals of masculinity in light of the shrinking means to achieve it? It turns out that the ideology remains relatively firmly in place, judging by the relentless policing of guys' behavior by other guys, that scrutiny about doing anything that's "so gay" that ranges from playful adolescent banter to serious homophobic bullying and assault. Young men define manhood in ways similar to their fathers. They are no less entitled, though the means to achieve that vision have shrunk precipitously. Funny thing about democracy: it dramatically levels the playing field, so that you have to compete now with women, immigrants, men of color, and even gay men. One can no longer presume that the positions once reserved for "people like us" are still yours for the taking.

Often, beneath the casual affability of "Guyland" lies an uneasiness born of economic insecurity and a sense of impending doom about how this generation of young men will find their way in the world. Most of the time, it's harmless fun, a way to blow off steam and feel like a winner. "Where else can you get the chance to storm the beach at Normandy or duel with light sabers or even fight the system and go out for a pizza when you're done?" asks David, an avid video gamer for more than two decades.

A few years ago, *New York Times* journalist Anna Quindlen happened on a young man who expressed this sense of thwarted entitlement to her. "It seems like if you're a white male you don't have a chance," he explained—this from a guy who attended a college where 5 percent of his classmates were black. Quindlen explains this strange comment to her readers: "What the kid really means is that he no longer has the edge, that the rules of a system that may have served his father will have changed. It is one of those good-old-days constructs to believe it was a system based purely on merit, but we know that's not true. It is a system that once favored him, and others like him. Now sometimes—just sometimes—it favors someone different."[19]

I was also constantly struck by how strongly so many young men identified with Tyler Durden, the antihero and doppelgänger of the unnamed narrator and protagonist in *Fight Club*. While the 1999 film (and Chuck Palahniuk's 1996 novel) initially fared modestly at the box office, the movie quickly became a cult classic among young men, who saw in it a touchstone text of Gen Y gendered ennui.

Here's how the director, David Fincher, understood the film: "We're designed to be hunters and we're in a society of shopping. There's nothing to kill anymore, there's nothing to fight, nothing to overcome, nothing to explore. In that societal emasculation this every-man [the narrator] is created."[20]

And here are the words of Tyler Durden, the protagonist in the film:

> *I see in fight club the strongest and smartest men who've ever lived. I see all this potential, and I see squandering. God damn it, an entire generation pumping gas, waiting tables; slaves with white collars. Advertising has us chasing cars and clothes, working jobs we hate so we can buy shit we don't need. We're the middle children of history, man. No purpose or place. . . . We've all been raised on television to believe that one day we'd all be millionaires, and movie gods, and rock stars. But we won't. And we're slowly learning that fact. And we're very, very pissed off.*

While the film resolves in an over-the-top orgy of mayhem and self-inflicted violence, viewers saw it as purgative, even healing. "There's something so, I don't know, *healing* about that movie, you know," says Jeff, a thirty-two-year-old Wall Street wannabe I met through a woman he is dating. (He's working off the trading floor, at an entry-level position in a large financial firm.) "I mean, you know, they say it right out front: we live in cubicles, work in cubicles, ride in cubicles, our whole lives are just one big fucking box. Everything is so insulated, so antiseptic. I completely identify with Ed Norton at all those self-help groups, you know. At least those people think they can change their lives."

The movie resonated powerfully with young men who faced such an uncertain future. Immediately after the film was released, real-life fight clubs sprang up all over America. In suburban garages and urban abandoned buildings, real guys, mostly drawn from white-collar sales and marketing sides of business, would gather to enact their own critique of white-collar middle-class masculinity.

When I interviewed some of the participants in these real-life fight clubs—guys who were willing to violate the First Rule of Fight Club:

not to talk about Fight Club—I was startled to hear them describe their motivations and their experiences. I had expected them to say that since they lived such cushioned lives, they wanted to lash out, express their anger, explode in rage. Hit somebody. Hard. (The guys in the fight club in Silicon Valley use computer keyboards, wrapped in pillows, and they swing them around by their cords and try to whack the other guy in the head.)

I was wrong. I was interviewed for a short documentary on these real-life fight clubs on *ESPN 360* and got to talk with a few of the participants. To hear them tell it, the thrill of fight clubs is not hitting some guy, bare-knuckled, in the face and knocking him unconscious, or watching a guy who just came after you, snarling ferociously, now spitting blood and perhaps a tooth.

Sure, several of them talked about the thrill of hitting someone. But far more spoke as did Jonas, a thirty-one-year-old originally from Salinas, California, now working in Silicon Valley in marketing:

> *Yeah, it's a great feeling and all to hit somebody and knock them down. You know, my whole life I'd never been in a fight. I never knew I could take a punch and get back up. I built my whole life around avoiding it, avoiding getting hit, avoiding confrontations, avoiding pain. My life was a life of running away, not really, but in my head. I wanted to see how it felt to get hit, stand there and take it, get back up. Once you know you can take a punch, you don't spend your whole life covering up.*

Jonas made me think of a line in Bruce Springsteen's anthemic "Born in the U.S.A."—"you spend half your life just covering up."

"It's not about hitting that guy," says Alan, a thirty-one-year-old enthusiast who works in corporate finance at a large and quite groovy Silicon Valley dot-com start-up. "It's really about being hit. Can I take it? Can I feel it? Can I fucking feel *anything* in this world?"

Alan echoes what fight-club participants all across the country say: it's not about hitting, it's about being hit. It's about feeling pain as a way to feel something, anything at all. By day they work in faceless cubicles, like Tyler Durden, but at night they feel pain. And that is how they know they're alive. It's like that Nine Inch Nails song "Hurt," released five years before *Fight Club:*

I hurt myself today
to see if I still feel
I focus on the pain
the only thing that's real.

Matt, a twenty-seven-year-old computer software engineer with a PhD, said it more simply: "You live in this world, and you feel nothing, man. Everything's a joke, like Colbert. Everything's, you know, [air quotes] constructed. Fight club is real. The blood is real. The cracked ribs are real. The pain is real. The pain is fucking real. You actually *felt* something. I don't know. That just matters. To feel pain is to feel something. Maybe the only feeling left is pain."

It's perhaps ironic to hear guys who are relatively privileged—white-collar workers in the computer industry, many with PhD's in computer science and electrical engineering, some with master's degrees in business administration—talk about needing to feel pain to feel authentic. Many of the guys who are drifting into angry-white-male politics are coming from such privileged positions, thinking that the world they had come to assume was theirs is theirs no longer. Their pain is no less real, if less immediately physical.

From mosh pits to real-life fight clubs—they are all the province of young white men, searching for something that feels real, that feels authentic, that actually enables them to feel, well, anything at all. There's a lot of anger out there, just under the surface. Sometimes, it gets pushed down into depression and efforts to get numb. Others try to surface, to feel something. Others lash out—some at themselves, some at others.

To a sociologist, the specific choices men may make to express or suppress these feelings of rage are of less interest than the social origins of those feelings in the first place. Why are so many men feeling—or trying not to feel—so much pain?

Only a very few and very disturbed guys actually go postal. Although the numbers are alarming, not that many men actually turn to suicide, either. Perhaps the most common way to express one's frustration and rage at increasingly impossible workplaces is to direct your anger elsewhere. Like Bill, my coffee-shop conversationalist, they don't turn to the political Left, working to organize the bottom against the top, to vote in large blocs against the corporate-funded, lobbyist-sustained politicians who line their friends' pockets with the tax money of average Americans. They don't make common cause with others who have been so marginalized by the class war that has been the unspoken secret of American domestic policies for the past three decades, a stealth war by the wealthy against the remaining 90 percent of Americans. None of that European Union–style social democracy in the face of economic tough times—strengthening the safety nets during tough times to ensure that unemployment insurance remains intact, the health care system remains adequate, schools remain funded.

No, they turn to the Right—harangued by a volatile group of ultra-right-wing extremists who dominate America's airwaves. There, they are seduced into blaming other people who are in the same situation that they are in—other groups who are equally hurting because of the rapacious greed of the bankers and their pals in politics. They lash out at immigrants or minorities, whom they accuse of stealing "their" jobs. They lash out at women, whose inroads into the workplace have coincided with the collapse of a living wage among white men.

Others politicize their anger less electorally and more interpersonally. They pick up cues from the political right wing and make their politics personal, more immediate, more corporate. They fight the growing movement for inclusiveness, diversity, multiculturalism, and equality in the workplace.

Listen to Dustin (not his real name), a twenty-two-year-old senior at Vanderbilt, who had just been accepted to law school—but not the one he most wanted to go to:

> I was raised to believe in the whole enchilada, you know, like truth, justice and the American way. Fairness and equality. And I busted my ass to get in here, and to get good enough grades to go to a good law school. And did I get into Duke or Virginia? No. And are there guys in my classes who had lower grades than me and lower LSATs [Law School Administration Tests], and did they get in—just because they were minorities? Uh, yeah. And girls?! Unbelievable. More of them than guys applied, and yet they get in because they're girls? They're richer than shit, and their daddies paid for everything. I'm fed up with it. It's not fair. My family didn't own slaves. We're from Pennsylvania, for Chrissakes. I'm not racist; I don't care what color you are. But I shouldn't be penalized because of my race, my color, right? I mean, that's just not fair.

But I think the answers lie deeper than simply the presence of "them" meaning the demise of "us." Remember the snarling contempt expressed by William (Hootie) Johnson in his intransigent refusal to allow women to become members of Augusta National Golf Club? When their male-only policy was exposed by Martha Burk, a Washington, DC–based feminist activist, Hootie's resistance seemed accompanied by genuine confusion: why would women want to join in the first place?

Every time men resist women's entry, they claim that the presence of women would somehow "dilute" the all-male purity of the organization and thus make more tenuous those mythic sacred bonds that men, and men alone, can forge with one another as a band of brothers.

Such arguments about the changes in our workplaces actually mistake the form for the content. It's not women's *presence* that's so scary. It never has been. It's their *equality*. There are plenty of women already at Augusta National. Just who do you think serves all those cocktails at the nineteenth hole? Who serves the meals, prepares the food, make the beds in the guest rooms? Women are all over the place— except they are not allowed to wear the heralded green blazer. (Well, not until they recently decided to finally admit two women, Condoleezza Rice and Darla Moore.) Doctors are rarely threatened by female nurses; it's female doctors they resent. Corporate executives feel just fine about female secretaries serving their coffee and taking dictation; it's just that they don't feel comfortable when they're sitting across the table from them in the corporate boardroom.

A journalist recently offered this description of this "not your father's workplace," using a media image familiar to most readers:

> If Ward Cleaver were alive today, he'd rarely be home to see his wife and children; and when home, he'd be an impossible crank, always getting called on the cellphone or buzzed on the Blackberry. The stress from seeing his health insurance get slashed would only be overshadowed by the fear caused by another round of white-collar downsizing and vicious memos from the senior executives implying that more fat was yet to be cut from the company payrolls. Mr. Cleaver would work weekends and forego vacations, and likely vote Republican, forced to choose between the hypertension medication and the blood-thinner pills since he can't afford both, not under the

new corporate HMO [health maintenance organization] plan. . . .
His anger and stress would push him into cursing Canada for being
a hotbed of anti-American liberalism while at the same time he'd
agonize over whether or not to order his medicines from their cheap
online pharmacies. He'd have no time for imparting little moral
lessons. "Not now, leave me alone," he'd grumble, washing down
the last of the Coumadins with a low-carb non-alcoholic beer while
watching The O'Reilly Factor *through clenched teeth. His wife June*
would be stuck at a three-day merchandising conference at a Holiday
Inn in Tempe—if they weren't divorced by now—while the Beaver
would be standing in front of his bedroom dresser mirror in his long
black trenchcoat, clutching his homemade pipebombs, and plotting
revenge on Eddie Haskell and all the other kids who call him "gay"
and "bitch" and make his life a living hell. [21]

If this is the suburban nuclear family of the twenty-first century, it gives
a whole new meaning to the word *nuclear.*

And so the unprecedented entry of women and minorities—and
the demands for workplace equality—becomes the place onto which
American men project their anxieties. The traditional "other" becomes
a target, a convenient screen against which to project this gnawing
anxiety that what made a man a man in the old days has been super-
seded, but nothing new has come along to take its place. It's women—
the ones we want or the ones to whom we are or were married—who
become targets. And it's minorities and immigrants, who want their
share of the pie, but, say the Angry White Men, are unwilling to work
for it and expect it as a matter of course.

No, this is no longer our father's or our grandfather's workplace—
any more than it is our father's or grandfather's political electorate or
any other institution. The men who turn their rage outward at work,
or at home in their relationships with their wives and partners, are
isolated, sporadic, individual cases that are often misdiagnosed simply
as individual psychotics who explode or "bad" men who beat up their
wives or loved ones. But treating them as a set of isolated individuals is like looking at a pointillist painting up close, to see the individual dots of paint. We must also stand back, see the patterns, discern
the outlines of the larger context for each of these seemingly random,
tragic, awful acts.

Some angry white men save us the trouble. They organize themselves politically, not into a bunch of starstruck dittoheads or isolated guys lashing out wildly, but into what they believe is a social movement that will reverse America's slide into the multicultural mud and restore the country's Aryan greatness—and, coincidentally, restore them to the patriarchal positions of familial, economic, and political authority to which they feel most entitled. They are America's White Wing.

7 | The White Wing

August 5, 2012, seemed like a typical summer Sunday in Oak Creek, Wisconsin. Unseasonably warm, perhaps, as members of the local Sikh community filed into the local Gurdwara for their Sunday service. Without warning, Wade Michael Page, a forty-year-old ex-soldier, burst in and opened fire on the families that had come to meditate together. When he was done, he had murdered six and wounded three others before he was shot dead by the police.

Just two weeks earlier, James Holmes, a seemingly mentally unstable young man, burst into a movie theater in Aurora, Colorado, at a midnight showing of *The Dark Knight Rises,* the final installment of the Batman series, and opened fire in the middle of a particularly kinetic action scene in the movie. After murdering twelve people and injuring fifty-eight others, the single worst mass shooting by a single gunman in American history at the time, Holmes walked to his car, where he was arrested. Now awaiting trial, he looks like he has experienced a terrible psychotic break from the young, eager PhD student in neuro-science that he was known as earlier.

Linked only by the coincidence of timing—and the incomprehensible and irresponsible easy access that anyone has to assault weapons in the United States—Page and Holmes dominated the headlines in the waning days of the Olympics coverage and the beginning of the presidential election campaign. Were such events by lone psychotic gunmen becoming such a commonplace that our collective horror wears off after only a few days? Do we become weary of the missed opportunities for serious discussion about the relationships among guns, masculinity—especially, let's face it, *white* masculinity—mental illness, and the increasingly violent way that white men vent their rage in America?

By treating them similarly—as individual, psychotic mass murderers—we missed a startling difference. Holmes's murderous rampage was an isolated attack by a lone, mentally unstable gunman. But not Page's. He may have acted alone, but he believed he was acting in the name of a nation, striking a blow against the creeping multiculturalism that was destroying America. A self-proclaimed white supremacist, Page was a member of a white supremacist band, End Apathy, who played "hate rock" at various concerts and festivals around the country, and a well-known local neo-Nazi. He was part of Hammerskin Nation, a racist skinhead group that organizes through the Internet but has outposts all over the country. His tattoos were all insignia of the movement, including "88"—the numerical sign for "Heil Hitler," since *H* is the eighth letter of the alphabet—and "14," signifying the motto of the white supremacists, the fourteen words that make up their sacred oath: "*We must secure the existence of our people and a future for White Children.*"

This was not simply murder, not even mass murder; it was not a crime spree. It was an act of domestic terrorism. It was intentional and political. Embracing the new "lone-wolf" strategy of the white supremacist movement—in which individuals take it upon themselves to strike blows against the supposed enemies, with no links to any central or coordinated efforts that could be traced back to some organizations and movement leaders—Page hoped to inspire others to strike their blow for RaHoWa, the Racial Holy War in which they believe they are engaged. (The lone-wolf strategy was adopted after the FBI, working

228   **ANGRY WHITE MEN**

with local law enforcement agencies, began to use lawsuits and other methods to break the banks and disturb the funding of these white supremacist groups.) Though the members of these extreme right-wing groups can recognize each other by their ink and their ideologies, they belong to fewer national organizations and often act alone. Their connections are cultural, political, ideological—but not organizational.

While journalists scrambled for a tidy sound bite about Page's motivation for his hateful rampage, sifting through the hateful lyrics of his band's songs, and parsing every interview for some key to his murderous spree, I kept remembering Timothy McVeigh's letter to the editor of his hometown paper, about how the American Dream "has all but disappeared." McVeigh and Page are connected; together, they represent the growing bands of America's domestic terrorists, a group that runs the spectrum from older, established right-wing fringe groups, like the John Birch Society, Ku Klux Klan, and American Nazi Party, to more contemporary, younger neo-Nazi groups, White Power groups like Posse Comitatus and the White Aryan Resistance (WAR), the radical militias that have sprung up in the northern Midwest and mountain states since the 1990s, cryptoreligious groups like the Church of the Creator, and the thousands of racist skinheads. Here, one finds some of the nation's angriest of angry white men. But who are they? And what are they angry about?

They are filled with rage at the disappearance of the America into which they believe they were born and to which they feel entitled. One fellow traveler once put it so succinctly to a friend when she was interviewing him: "Is this a white country, or what?" The answer, they believe, is "what." America is no longer a white country, no longer the country of their forebears. And boy are they pissed off about it.

THE RISE OF THE EXTREME RIGHT

The racist Right has been around as long as there has been an America. What eminent historian Richard Hofstadter called "paranoid politics" seeks political mobilization against the subversive forces from within that are secretly doing the bidding of even more satanic and evil forces outside. In his essay, written in 1964, as Barry Goldwater grabbed the mantle of a recharged paranoid Republican Party (and handed that party its worst defeat ever), Hofstadter observed the ways that paranoia has driven various social movements, usually on the Right, but occasionally on the Left. What characterizes paranoid politics, Hofstadter writes, is its emotions, not its ideological vision; it's a politics based on equal measures of rage and fear:

> American politics has often been an arena for angry minds. In recent years, we have seen angry minds at work, mainly among extreme right wingers who have now demonstrated, in the Goldwater movement, how much political leverage can be got out of the animosities and passions of a small minority. But, behind this, I believe, there is a style of mind that is far from new, and that is not necessarily right-wing. I call it the paranoid style, simply because no other word adequately evokes the sense of heated exaggeration, suspiciousness, and conspiratorial fantasy that I have in mind.[1]

Ranging from anti-Illuminati and anti-Masonic fearmongering in the eighteenth century, through anti-Catholic crazes in the nineteenth, all the way through to McCarthyism, the John Birch Society, and Goldwater Republicans, Hofstadter shows how the political psychology of paranoid politics works: (1) posit, as Senator Joseph McCarthy did, "a great conspiracy on a scale so immense as to dwarf any previous such venture in the history of man"; (2) declare its infiltration of the government to be massive and pernicious; and (3) insist that time is running out, and without immediate action their takeover will be complete.

Paranoid politics is thus a psychological disposition—projecting one's problem onto the fiendish machinations of others, so as both to uphold one's own purity and goodness and simultaneously to identify the source of the problem. As with many projects that rely on psychological displacement, the groups often produce the very thing they most fear; they become the enemy they are seeking to destroy:

> It is hard to resist the conclusion that this enemy is, on many counts, the projection of the self; both the ideal and the unacceptable aspects of the self are attributed to him. The enemy may be the cosmopolitan intellectual, but the paranoid will outdo him in the apparatus of scholarship, even of pedantry. Secret organizations, set up to com-

bat secret organizations, give the same flattery. The Ku Klux Klan imitated Catholicism to the point of donning priestly vestments, developing an elaborate ritual and an equally elaborate hierarchy. The John Birch Society emulates Communist cells and quasi-secret operation through "front" groups, and preaches a ruthless prosecution of the ideological war along lines very similar to those it finds in the Communist enemy. Spokesmen of the various fundamentalist anti-Communist "crusades" openly express their admiration for the dedication and discipline the Communist cause calls forth.[2]

Historically, Hofstadter tells us, members of those paranoid movements believed they still were in possession of the country, that they were "fending off threats to a still established way of life." But he notes that Daniel Bell's 1955 essay in his book *The Radical Right* suggests that the postwar radical Right already feels dispossessed. "America has been largely taken away from them and their kind," he writes, "though they are determined to try and repossess it and to prevent the final destructive act of subversion."[3] (Hofstadter died in 1970, Bell not until 2011, but it is difficult, even today, to read this essay without writing names like Glenn Beck and Rush Limbaugh in the margins. The angry white men of hate radio are today's Elmer Gantrys of paranoid politics, sounding the alarm for subversive enemies who threaten to undermine our way of life, while becoming the very antidemocratic, antiegalitarian—indeed, anti-American—zealots about whom they believe themselves to be warning.)

The collapse of McCarthyism left few organizations capable of sustaining the paranoid politics of the Far Right. Every group, from the John Birch Society and the Ku Klux Klan to the American Nazi Party, was increasingly marginalized as kooks and cranks, looking under beds for nefarious communists. But the movements of the 1960s, notably the civil rights movement, the women's movement, the student movement, the peace movement, and later the gay and lesbian movement—coupled with increased immigration from Mexico and Latin America—galvanized the opposition, ignited their passions again, and created a new opportunity.

Some movements recharged in the face of these new threats, such as the idea that the Jewish-controlled media are the cause of the sexual revolution, which is distracting healthy Aryans away from white marriage and family life and toward decadent, interracial mongrelization and sexual depravity. New groups proliferated in the 1970s fueled by fears of black political power in the South, women's entry into the public sphere, and the gender blending embodied by the hippies. The New Right was born.

The New Right brought together old conservative elites and nouveau riche businessmen into an uneasy alliance, characterized by the Reagan-Bush 1980 presidential ticket. Reagan represented the new financial elites, entitled and bellicose, and the ressentiment of the nouveaux riches, while his vice president represented the older bluer-blooded, aristocratic noblesse oblige, preppy arrogance mixed with a sense of service that was foreign to Reagan's politics of resentment.

On their Far Right flank were those who were convinced that even these right-wingers were on the verge of selling them out to the big corporations and a politics of statism, that is, increased government control over personal life. As if Reaganism wasn't extreme enough, denizens of the Far Right demimonde claimed that the income tax was illegitimate and that free men had the right to mint their own money, form armed militias, and live as sovereign, free citizens. Others saw increased tolerance for religious diversity as a sign that America had lost its way (or been steered away from God), and they sought to establish Christian cults and sects that would return America to God and Christ.

Through the 1980s and 1990s, their numbers increased and their organizations proliferated. The farm crisis of the 1980s, periodic economic shocks, increased globalization, and the gradual corporatization of the American economy added fuel to the sense that the very people who had built America were the ones who were being pushed aside. All around them, they heard the shrill sounds of the formerly marginalized—blacks and women, immigrants and gays—all clamoring for a share of the power that they, native-born white American men, actually deserved.

"I don't get it at all," says Alex, when I ask about this notion that white men are the ones who have power in America. Alex trained for a while with a militia unit in Michigan, and he still lives in Grand Rapids. His father and his grandfather worked for Ford in Dearborn, but Alex never could latch on there. Now there's little to latch on to.

He drives his 1988 Chevy pickup truck for various contractors around town, doing errands, scraping together a job.

> We have nothing. Nothing. It's all going to them. I mean, seriously, they get all the breaks—the fucking welfare, the health care, the jobs. I mean, a white guy has no chance for the job these days—the government says you have to give it to them! It's like completely upside down now. My grandfather and my father both fought to keep this country free, and for what? So their kid could get laid off, and some [he looks around the diner, sheepishly], well, you know, the N word, can get the damned job? This isn't right, man. It isn't right. We got nothing.

Doesn't exactly sound like a guy in power, does it? Powerless, yes, but he still feels entitled to power—as a white American man—by a combination of historical legacy, religious fiat, biological destiny, and moral legitimacy. Once they had it, perhaps once, even, they "had it all," but it's now been surrendered or stolen from them by a federal government controlled and staffed by legions of the newly enfranchised minorities, women, and immigrants, all in service to the omnipotent Jews who control international economic and political life.

WHITE SUPREMACISTS IN OBAMA'S AMERICA

The dawn of the twenty-first century witnessed a major shift in the organizing strategies of the extreme Right. The Clinton years had accelerated their economic dispossession—the North American Free Trade Agreement (NAFTA), globalization, outsourcing, and downsizing—but it was couched in an economic boom that left the country giddy, feeling rich, with a massive surplus. For the extreme Right, though, the Clinton years served to make their situation only more desperate. What the extreme right wing learned when agents of the Bureau of Alcohol, Tobacco, and Firearms stormed Branch Davidian cult figure David Koresh's compound in Waco, Texas, in 1993, and when the FBI opened fire on Randy Weaver's homestead in Ruby Ridge, Idaho, the year before, killing his wife and son, was that the federal government—*their* government—would declare war on its own citizens in its quest to establish total domination over white Aryan men.

To the White Wing, the inauguration of George W. Bush heralded a new era, in which, for the first time since Reagan, they believed they had a friend in the White House. Many threw their lot in with Bush and Cheney, thinking that their energy and extractive form of capitalist expansion would finally relieve them of burdensome taxes, debilitating government regulation, and excessive federal interference, as well as supporting their positions on a wealth of social policies from abortion to homosexuality. Unfortunately, they were blindsided by Bush, too, with the Republican strategy of couching corporatist economic policies in conservative social agenda (leading to the "what's the matter with Kansas?" debate, as working- and middle-class people voted against their own economic interests and in favor of politicians who stripped their cupboards bare).

Later, they also felt cheated by Bush on immigration—they wanted him to build an impenetrable wall and send all the illegal immigrants back, but instead he chose a policy far more amenable to large corporations who needed the cheap labor—and on the Middle East, where he sent white American boys to die in a war for Israel and for the oil companies, neither of which was exactly a friend of regular white Americans. Declaring two wars without allocating a single penny for them through legislative fiat wiped out the Clinton surplus and ran up the American deficit to a dizzying, vertiginous level. By the end of the Bush presidency, the extreme Right felt as cheated by Bush as they had by any other president.

"I voted for Bush—I mean, it's like crazy that I actually voted at all!" said Jeff (not his real name), a thirty-eight-year-old former housing construction worker who now works on the sales floor at a Target superstore in Ohio. (He wore long sleeves to cover up his tattoos.) We're speaking in the parking lot outside the store, where he has gone for a smoke.

Can you believe that fucker? I voted for him twice even. I thought, okay, here's a guy who gets the border thing, who is gonna just seal it up, you know, and get rid of all those illegals finally. And after 9/11, I said nuke those towel heads and kick them the fuck outta here. And what does Bush do? He sends in ground troops to get killed, protects fucking Israel, and then lets the illegals stay because the corporations [here he jerks his thumb back over his shoulder at the store] need 'em, want to pay 'em less, which means, well, you know, that I get less, that we, real Americans, get less. Completely sold us out. Fucker. Cheney mighta been better, though.

September 11 did change everything. Both the scale of the terrorist attack and its audacity captured the imaginations of the extreme Right. To some it was the clarion signal of Armageddon, the first salvo of the apocalyptic global race war. There were calls for the expulsion of all immigrants to create a purely white country. "ALL NON CITIZENS OUT OF U.S.," urged Glenn Spencer, a leader of American Patrol. "Contact your Congressman, Senators and the President. Demand that all non-citizens leave the United States IMMEDIATELY!!" Paul Mullet, Minnesota leader of the Aryan Nations was prepared: "The current events in Jew York City have caused me to activate my unit. We are preparing a strike here in Minnesota and other surrounding areas. Please be advised that the time for ALL ARYANS TO ATTACK IS NOW NOT LATER. Our opportunity may never be the same. The call to arms goes out to all true Aryans around the world. We will be ready next week for our revolution."

"The Twin Towers are our Bunker Hill," Randall told me, calmly, over lunch at a diner near Aliquippa, Pennsylvania. "I said to my wife, 'Honey, it's time. Time to start shooting niggers. Time to start shooting the spics. And time to start shooting the Islamists. Let's load up, honey, it's time for the race war.' I really thought it was the signal. A lot of guys I knew thought it should be open season—at least on those fucking Arabians. We got fucking attacked! This means war!"

Even political candidates dropped any pretense at decorum and prudence. "If I see someone [who] comes in that's got a diaper on his head and a fan belt wrapped around the diaper on his head, that guy needs to be pulled over," said John Cooksey, a Republican congressman from Louisiana who was running for the US Senate. When a reporter suggested that this was racial profiling, Cooksey seemed pleased the reporter understood his meaning. Right-wing commentator Ann Coulter summed it up by saying, "We should invade their countries, kill their leaders and convert them to Christianity." (I thought the forced conversion a particularly loving Christian touch.)[4]

But wait, said others. Not so fast! Let's look again before we reach for our AK-47s and head off into the woods. These guys just flew suicide missions into the Twin Towers of the World Trade Center in New York City, the global capital of ZOG (Zionist Occupied Government), and the Pentagon, the fortress of ZOG's enablers. Those guys aren't our enemies! They hate Israel as much as we do! (They even deny the Holocaust, like we do!) "Anyone who is willing to drive a plane into a building to kill Jews is alright by me," wrote Bill Roper of the National Alliance. "I wish our members had half as much testicular fortitude."[5]

Maybe they aren't the enemy; rather, they remind us who the real enemy is. Those terrorists didn't just get mad. They got even. "It's a disgrace that in a population of at least 150 million White/Aryan Americans, we provide so few that are willing to do the same [as the terrorists]," bemoaned Rocky Suhayda, Nazi Party chairman from Eastpointe, Michigan. "A bunch of towel head/sand niggers put our great White Movement to shame."[6]

The views split down the middle between the racist Right, who saw al-Qaeda as the enemy, and the more anti-Semitic Right, who saw them as a potential ally. As a consequence, the extreme Right spent most of the next several years bickering among themselves for leadership. Sounding more like the socialist Left in the 1930s—Trotskyite! Schachtmanite! Stalinist!—they tore into the commitment of each other's memberships, vied for leadership, and fought for table scraps of ideology and organization. Occasionally, some leader, like David Duke, the former Klan leader who actually got elected to the Louisiana State Senate as a Republican (and ran unsuccessfully for the Republican nomination for US Senate), would try to go mainstream, or some would go rogue and start a new group, or some "lone wolf" would do something stupid or audacious, depending on your point of view, like murder a doctor who provided abortions. But mostly they cannibalized their own.

The election of Barack Obama sent the pendulum swinging wildly back in the other direction. It broke the stalemate, bringing those previously warring sides back together, if not in unity, at least in a political détente in which they stopped attacking each other and started focusing on what Obama represented. Electing a black president was the symbolic last straw. Now there was no going back; America had delivered itself, in the voting booth no less, to the forces that had long sought to completely control the government: a conspiracy of blacks, Jews, women, gays, and immigrants. All over the country, the extreme Right was apoplectic—we'd elected a black president. This was all the evidence they needed that we had turned a corner and that only a desperate and courageous group of true patriots could save America from itself. It would be bloody, but it was now necessary.[7]

Two days after the election, David Duke attempted to convene the European American Unity and Rights Conference, inviting representatives from every racist and extremist group in the nation and from around the world to Memphis for two days of strategic planning. It was bad enough that Obama had been elected, but he was utterly in thrall to the Jews, Duke claimed on his website (his biggest contributor was Goldman Sachs!), and he had "prostrated himself" before AIPAC, the American-Israel Public Affairs Committee, one of many pro-Israel lobbying groups.[8] (This is interesting because the Republicans try to paint Obama as weak on Israel, while the extreme Right sees him as overly strong. The extreme Right is the only consistent group in the bunch: they hate Israel, *and* they hate Jews.) In the end, the conference was canceled because, Duke's allies said, the hotel annulled the contract, fearing reprisals from antiracist organizations. In the topsy-turvy world of paranoid politics, the antiracist organizations have all the power, and the white power groups—or "white civil rights," as Duke likes to call his mission—have none.

So virulent was the increased threat of the extreme Right that President Obama's Secret Service detail is double the strength of those details that protected former presidents. A year after Obama took office, in April 2009, the Department of Homeland Security released an assessment of "Rightwing Extremism" and concluded that "rightwing extremists may be gaining new recruits by playing on their fears about several emergent issues," including the election of the nation's first African American president and the economic downturn. (The report was withdrawn after a firestorm of protest by Republican congressmen.)[9]

Today, the Southern Poverty Law Center (SPLC), which tracks all active hate groups, has documented 1,108 active hate groups in the United States alone—more than a 50 percent increase since 2000; "nativist extremist" groups have increased by 80 percent just since

2008. Perhaps as many as a half-million people visit their websites and read their materials every year. These groups range from the neo-Nazis and the Ku Klux Klan to militias, Aryan survivalists, white supremacist youth groups, violent religious cults, and even men's rights groups.[10]

Increasingly agitated, yes, more and more young men are streaming to their websites and organizations. At the same time, the groups are increasingly dispersed, organizationally weakened, as an organized campaign by the SPLC has brought crippling lawsuits against some of their organizations. Successful lawsuits against National Alliance leader William Pierce, Aryan Nations' Richard Butler, and WAR's Tom Metzger decimated their financial reserves and sent the membership into some disarray. As a result, the movement has adopted a decentralized organizational structure, relying less on organization and identifiable leaders and more on individual acts of violent resistance and organizing and maintaining websites on the Internet. Indeed, the Web is now the prime organizing arena for White Power groups: organizational membership in all organizations probably totals around two hundred thousand, but website traffic at the movement's largest portals generates ten times that traffic virtually every month.

The extreme Right has all the hallmarks of a counterculture existing right alongside the mainstream culture. They have alternative institutions that parallel mainstream institutions. If you do it right—buy white recipe books to cook white food, homeschool your children, buy them Aryan comic books and White Power coloring books, purchase neo-Nazi video games, buy her a blue-eyed Barbie and transform a GI Joe into a "GI Nazi" doll (instructions available online), dress them in racist clothing with racist symbols, listen to White Power music, read White Power newspapers and magazines—you probably don't have to interact very much with the mainstream culture at all.[11]

Here's Trey, a Southern California skinhead: "It's really cool how you can get all this shit off the Net now. Ten years ago there really wasn't that much, but now you've got all the music, the clothes. I bought my daughter a toy figure of Hitler from a website. I mean you're not going to find that at WalMart."[12]

The increased visibility and heightened virulence of America's White Wing has been so pronounced that there seemed to be only one thing to do. I decided to talk to them.

AMONG THE NEO-NAZIS

Chatting up white supremacists and neo-Nazis was not exactly the travel itinerary that this nice Jewish boy from Brooklyn had originally planned. I thought I could learn what I needed in their chat rooms on the Internet and through their published materials, both archived at various libraries and by ordering it through the mail. I did go to the one repository of archival material about the extreme right wing, the Spencer Collection at the University of Kansas. I spent a large amount of time lurking about chat rooms entered through Internet portals like Stormfront.

But then one day in one chat room on another site, I realized I needed more. There were eight people writing at that moment, saying vile stuff about the Jew-controlled media, especially Hollywood, which, one guy said, completely corrupts white people's minds with multiculturalism and images of strong black men and weak white men. Another chimed in about how the media always make white guys look so weak. And then a third started talking about how the movement needed more Aryan heroes, like Bruce Willis, Arnold Schwarzenegger—one asserted that he knew "for a fact" that Schwarzenegger was a neo-Nazi sympathizer way back in his Austrian childhood—and Mel Gibson. Someone pointed out that those guys *were* action heroes in movies, so maybe the media weren't so dismissive of strong white Aryan men.

Then the conversation took a more "academic" turn, as a couple of people were describing Hollywood movies in a language that sounded more like a media studies seminar than a white supremacist chat room. That's when I got nervous. Maybe of these eight people, three are graduate students doing their "field work." Maybe two are high school students who are just sort of goofing around. And maybe one or two were actual white supremacists. The trouble was, I couldn't tell which ones they were; I needed to go meet them.

When I have told colleagues and friends that I've been interviewing neo-Nazis and white supremacists in the United States (as well as ex-neo-Nazis in both Germany and Sweden), they have asked, reasonably, where I met them. Had I gone to Metarie, Louisiana, home of David Duke and the modernized Klan? Or rural Mississippi or Alabama?

Perhaps windswept eastern Oregon and Idaho? Well, yes, I did travel through some of those places and did meet people there. But I did the lion's share of my interviews in areas like the soulless suburban sprawl north of San Diego, in towns like Temecula, or Fallbrook, or Poway, or around Long Beach and San Pedro, a bit farther north, closer to Los Angeles. I ventured around Tennessee, close to Nashville and Murfreesboro.

But mostly, I stayed pretty close to home. It turns out, it's not so hard to find white supremacists in the Northeast. As I wrote in the author's note, I went to gun shows in Pennsylvania, along the original Mason-Dixon Line, not that far from Penn State, or along the western border between New Jersey and Pennsylvania. Many of the men I encountered wouldn't talk to me. The second I open my mouth, I'm pretty identifiably a New Yorker and Jewish, unless you think that all middle Americans sound like Woody Allen or Jerry Seinfeld. I wasn't going to "pass," so I didn't even try. "I'm your worst nightmare," I said to three guys staffing a leaflet table outside a gun show in a suburban high school in East Stroudsberg. "I'm a liberal New York Jewish sociologist, and I live in the bluest city in the bluest state in the country." At least they laughed.

I explained I was interested in talking about how they see the world and how it's so different from how I see it. I tried to explain that I wasn't at all interested in arguing with them; it was unlikely that anyone would change anyone else's mind. Rather, I wanted to know, as a researcher, how they see things. "It's all so foreign to me," I explained. "I need help in understanding it."

At this stage, my analysis of their situation steered me toward giving them the floor. Most of the guys I did talk to feel so unheard, so ignored by the powers that be. "It's like we're nothing," said Jeff, one of the guys who did agree to meet me. "No one listens to the little guy. You know who I liked? Fuckin' Joe the Plumber. I thought he was listening to us. I'd have voted for that sucker—even though, I gotta say, he didn't know shit."

Eventually, I talked with about forty guys, some just for a few minutes outside the school, others for full-scale interviews. I had ground rules. I never went to their homes, meetings, concerts, or festivals; I never met them after dark and never more than one on one. I met them at diners off highways near the towns with the gun shows; usually, I took them to lunch. I never tape-recorded them. I learned that lesson because Ron, my first interview subject, got up from the table and started to leave the second I took the tape recorder out of my briefcase during the first interview. "You're FBI, aren't you?" he said (believing the myth that if asked, police and FBI must identify themselves). I showed up an hour before the meeting, parked my car a few blocks away, and waited. Afterward, I waited again, frantically scribbling notes from the interview and then walked to my car.

Of the guys I spoke with, about a dozen were active in specific organizations, and another dozen were occasional members, who didn't really go to meetings but did follow the scene and have connections to specific groups. The rest were fellow travelers, the sort that, had this been 1953 and they been leftists, the FBI would have been questioning about their known ties to actual members of the Communist Party. Like those fellow travelers, these guys wouldn't have named names either.

WHO ARE THEY?

Who are the white supremacists? There has been no formal survey, for obvious reasons, but there are several noticeable patterns. Geographically, they come from America's heartland—small towns, rural cities, swelling suburban sprawl outside larger Sunbelt cities. These aren't the prosperous towns, but the single-story working-class exurbs that stretch for what feels like forever in the corridor between Long Beach and San Diego (not the San Fernando Valley), or along the southern tier of Pennsylvania, or spread all through the Upper Peninsula of Michigan, across the vast high plains of eastern Washington and Oregon, through Idaho and Montana. There are plenty in the declining cities of the Rust Belt, in Dearborn and Flint, Buffalo and Milwaukee, in the bars that remain in the shadows of the hulking deserted factories that once were America's manufacturing centers. And that doesn't even touch the former states of the Confederacy, where flying the Confederate flag is a culturally approved symbol of "southern pride"—in the same way that wearing a swastika would be a symbol of German "heritage" (except it's illegal in Germany to wear a swastika).

There's a large rural component. Although "the spread of far-right groups over the last decade has not been limited to rural areas alone," writes Osha Gray Davidson, "the social and economic unraveling of rural communities—especially in the midwest—has provided far-right groups with new audiences for their messages of hate. Some of these groups have enjoyed considerable success in their rural campaign." For many farmers facing foreclosures, the Far Right promises to help them save their land have been appealing, offering farmers various schemes and legal maneuvers to help prevent foreclosures, blaming the farmers' troubles on Jewish bankers and the one-world government. "As rural communities started to collapse," Davidson writes, the Far Right "could be seen at farm auctions comforting families . . . confirming what rural people knew to be true: that their livelihoods, their families, their communities—their very lives—were falling apart." In stark contrast to the government indifference encountered by rural Americans, a range of Far Right groups, most recently the militias, have seemingly provided support, community, and answers.[13]

In that sense, the contemporary militias and other white supremacist groups are following in the footsteps of the Ku Klux Klan, the Posse Comitatus, and other Far Right patriot groups who recruited members in rural America throughout the 1980s. They tap into a long history of racial and ethnic paranoia in rural America, as well as an equally long tradition of collective local action and vigilante justice. There remains a widespread notion that "Jews, African-Americans, and other minority-group members 'do not entirely belong,'" which may, in part, "be responsible for rural people's easy acceptance of the far right's agenda of hate," writes Matthew Snipp. "The far right didn't create bigotry in the Midwest; it didn't need to," Davidson concludes. "It merely had to tap into the existing undercurrent of prejudice once this had been inflamed by widespread economic failure and social discontent."[14]

And many have moved from their deindustrializing cities, foreclosed suburban tracts, and wasted farmlands to smaller rural areas because they seek the companionship of like-minded fellows, in relatively remote areas far from large numbers of nonwhites and Jews and where they can organize, train, and build protective fortresses. Many groups have established refuge in rural communities, where they can practice military tactics, stockpile food and weapons, hone their survivalist skills, and become self-sufficient in preparation for Armageddon, the final race war, or whatever cataclysm they envision. Think of it as the twenty-first-century version of postwar suburban "white flight"—but on steroids.

They're certainly Christian, but not just any Christian—they're evangelical Protestant, Pentacostalist, and members of radical sects that preach racial purity as the Word of Jesus. (Catholicism is certainly stocked with conservatives on social issues, but white supremacists tap into such a long and ignoble tradition of anti-Catholicism that they tend to have their own right-wing organizations, mostly fighting against women's rights and gay rights.) Some belong to churches like the Christian Identity Church, which gained a foothold on the Far Right in the early 1980s. Christian Identity's focus on racism and anti-Semitism provides the theological underpinnings to the shift from a more "traditional agrarian protest" to paramilitarism. It is from the Christian Identity movement that the Far Right gets its theological claims that Adam is the ancestor of the Caucasian race, whereas non-whites are pre-Adamic "mud people," without souls, and Jews are the children of Satan. According to this doctrine, Jesus was not Jewish and not from the Middle East; actually, he was northern European, his Second Coming is close at hand, and followers can hasten the apocalypse. It is the birthright of Anglo-Saxons to establish God's kingdom on earth; America's and Britain's "birthright is to be the wealthiest, most powerful nations on earth . . . able, by divine right, to dominate and colonize the world."[15]

A large proportion of the extreme right wing are military veterans. Several leaders served in Vietnam and were shocked at the national disgust that greeted them as they returned home after that debacle. "America's failure to win that war was a truly profound blow," writes William J. Gibson. "If Americans were no longer winners, then who were they?"[16] Some veterans believed they were sold out by the government, caving in to effeminate cowardly protesters; they can no longer trust the government to fight for what is right. Bo Gritz, a former Green Beret in Vietnam, returned to Southeast Asia several times in clandestine missions to search for prisoners of war and was the real-life basis for the film *Rambo*. He uses his military heroism to increase his credibility among potential recruits; one brochure describes him as "this country's most decorated Vietnam veteran" who "killed some 400 Communists in his illustrious military career." In 1993 Gritz began a traveling SPIKE (Specially Prepared Individuals for Key Events) training program, a rigorous survival course in paramilitary techniques.[17]

Many of the younger guys are veterans of the first Gulf War, a war that they came to believe was fought for no moral principles at all, but simply to make America's oil supply safer and to protect Israel from possible Arab attack. They feel they've been used, pawns in a larger political game, serving their country honorably only to be spit out and stepped on when they returned home to slashed veteran benefits, bureaucratic indifference to post-traumatic stress disorder, and general social contempt for having fought in the war in the first place. They believed they were entitled to be hailed as heroes, as had earlier generations of American veterans, not to be scorned as outcasts. Now a guy like Bo Gritz symbolizes "true" warrior-style masculinity, and reclaiming their manhood is the reward for signing up with the Far Right.[18]

THE CLASS ORIGINS OF RACIAL POLITICS

Perhaps what binds them all together, though, is class. Rural or small town, urban or suburban, the extreme Right is populated by downwardly mobile, lower-middle-class white men. All of the men I interviewed—all—fitted this class profile. When I compared with other ethnographies and other surveys, they all had the same profile as well.

In the United States, class is often a proxy for race. When politicians speak of the "urban poor," we know it's a code for black people. When they talk about "welfare queens," we know the race of that woman driving the late-model Cadillac. In polite society, racism remains hidden behind a screen spelled CLASS.

On the extreme Right, by contrast, race is a proxy for class. Among the white supremacists, when they speak of race consciousness, defending white people, protesting for equal rights for white people, they actually don't mean *all* white people. They don't mean Wall Street bankers and lawyers, though they are pretty much entirely white and male. They don't mean white male doctors, or lawyers, or architects, or even engineers. They don't mean the legions of young white hipster guys, or computer geeks flocking to the Silicon Valley, or the legions of white preppies in their boat shoes and seersucker jackets "interning" at white-shoe law firms in major cities. Not at all. They mean middle- and working-class white people. Race consciousness is actually class consciousness without actually having to "see" class. "Race blindness" leads working-class people to turn right; if they did see class, they'd turn left and make common cause with different races in the same economic class.

That's certainly what I found among them. Most are in their midthirties to early forties, educated at least through high school and often beyond. (The average age of the guys I talked with was thirty-six.) They are the sons of skilled workers in industries like textiles and tobacco, the sons of the owners of small farms, shops, and grocery stores. Buffeted by global political and economic forces, the sons have inherited little of their fathers' legacies. The family farms have been lost to foreclosure, the small shops squeezed out by Walmarts and malls. These young men face a spiral of downward mobility and economic uncertainty. They complain that they are squeezed between the omnivorous jaws of global capital concentration and a federal bureaucracy that is at best indifferent to their plight and at worst complicit in their demise.

And they're right. It is the lower middle class—that strata of independent farmers, small shopkeepers, craft and highly skilled workers, and small-scale entrepreneurs—that has been hit hardest by globalization. "Western industry has displaced traditional crafts—female as well as male—and large-scale multinational-controlled agriculture has downgraded the independent farmer to the status of hired hand," writes journalist Barbara Ehrenreich. This has resulted in massive male displacement—migration, downward mobility. It has been felt the most not by the adult men who were the tradesmen, shopkeepers, and skilled workers, but by their sons, by the young men whose inheritance has been seemingly stolen from them. They feel entitled and deprived—and furious. These angry young men are the foot soldiers of the armies of rage that have sprung up around the world.[19]

What's important to note is that they are literally the sons. It was their fathers who closed the family store, who lost the family farm. Some are men who have worked all their adult lives, hoping to pass on the family farm to their sons and retire comfortably. They believed that if they worked hard, their legacy would be ensured, but they leave their sons little but a legacy of foreclosures, economic insecurity, and debt.

It was their status next to their father's and grandfather's names on the cabinetmaking storefront that said "Jones and Sons." These were businesses that came not only with the ability to make a living, but came with dignity, with a sense of craft pride, a sense that you owned your own store or farm, owned and controlled your own labor—even employed some other people—and that this economic autonomy had been a source of great pride in the family for generations. In a near-throwaway footnote in his classic study of identity development, *Childhood and Society* (1950), Erik Erikson locates the origins of young men's anger in a multigenerational story:

> *In psychoanalytic patients the overwhelming importance of the grandfather is often apparent. He may have been a blacksmith of the old world or a railroad builder of the new, and as yet proud Jew or an unreconstructed Southerner. What these grandfathers have in common is that fact that they were the last representatives of a more homogeneous world, masterly and cruel with good conscience, disciplined and pious without loss of self-esteem. Their world invented bigger and better machinery like gigantic playthings which were not expected to challenge the social values of the men who made them. Their mastery persists in their grandsons as a stubborn, an angry sense of superiority. Overtly inhibited, they yet can accept others only on terms of prearranged privilege.* [20]

"It wasn't my daddy's farm," said Andy, "it was my granddaddy's, and his daddy's, and his daddy's. Five generations of Hoosier farmers."

Generations of Hoosier *men*, who worked the farm, supported a family, made a living with dignity. They proved their masculinity in that most time-honored way in America: as family providers. And it was their fathers who lost it all, squandered their birthright. Instead of getting angry at their fathers, Andy and his comrades claim the mantle of the grandfathers, displace their rage outward, onto an impermeable and unfeeling government bureaucracy that didn't offer help, onto soulless corporations that squeezed them mercilessly. By displacing their anger onto those enormous faceless entities, the sons justify their political rage and rescue their own fathers from their anger.

Some can't do it. Some of the sons—and the fathers—turn their rage inward. We have already discussed the wave of suicides that rippled across the American heartland in the 1980s and 1990s—spawning widespread concern and a series of Farm Aid concerts to raise awareness. The number of suicides in America's Midwest was higher in the 1990s than during the Great Depression; suicide was the leading cause of agricultural fatalities for two decades—by far. Men were five times more likely to kill themselves than die by accident. "To fail several generations of relatives (both backwards and forwards into those unborn descendants who will now not be able to farm), to see yourself as the one weak link in a strong chain that spans more than a century, is a terrible, and for some, an unbearable burden," writes Osha Gray Davidson. "When a fellow in a steel mill loses his job, he has basically lost his paycheck," a physician at the University of Iowa explained. "When an Iowa farmer loses his farm, he's lost the guts of his life."[21]

One woman, speaking at a town meeting in Tonkawa, Oklahoma, in 1991, provided an eloquent narrative of this process:

I am a 46-year-old mother of three children. We have lost two farms since 1980, my mother in law's farm as well as our own. We were forced to sell 160 acres of land that was very special to us. It was homesteaded by my husband's great grandfather and for years had served as home to our cow and calf operation which we were forced to sell just a few months before we sold the land.

My husband became completely consumed by our circumstances caused by the farm crisis. He left me. Our family continued to deteriorate and our marriage ended in divorce. We had been through natural crises before—drought, flood, crop failure—these we accepted and went on.

But when the threat of losing everything comes to your doorstep because of the bad economy, low commodity prices and high interest on your base notes has left you hopelessly in debt, your faith is sometimes shaken. No one likes to consider that their life has been pointless.[22]

Others direct this seething rage outward. "Many debt ridden farm families will become more suspicious of government, as their self-worth, their sense of belonging, their hope for the future deteriorates," predicted Oklahoma psychologist Glen Wallace presciently in 1989. "The farms are gone," writes Dyer, "yet the farmers remain. They've been transformed into a wildfire of rage, fueled by the grief of their loss and blown by the winds of conspiracy and hate-filled rhetoric."[23] "It is hardly surprising, then, that American men—lacking confidence in the government and the economy, troubled by the changing relations between the sexes, uncertain of their identity or their future—began to *dream*, to fantasize about the powers and features of another kind of man who could retake and reorder the world. And the hero of all these dreams was the paramilitary warrior." The contemporary white supremacist movement is the embodiment of these warrior dreams.[24]

Their plan is to get even. Unlike Joe Wesbecker, some guys don't just get even by rampaging through their factory floor or their corporate offices, shooting at their former colleagues and coworkers. They get mad, and they get organized. They cobble together a theory that explains their plight—grafting together fringe elements of evangelical Christianity, traditional anti-Semitism and racism, and general right-wing paranoia into an amalgam that is loosely held together by a nostalgic vision of hardy, independent frontier manhood. Like the guys who go postal, they externalize their rage—their anguish is clearly the fault of someone else—but they don't externalize it to their immediate surroundings, their boss, supervisor, or coworkers. Instead, it's larger, more powerful, and pernicious social forces—Jews, Muslims, minorities generally, women.

These are the sons of small-town America, the Jeffersonian yeoman of the nineteenth century, disfigured by global restructuring and economic downturns. They come from the "large and growing number of US citizens disaffected from and alienated by a government that seems indifferent, if not hostile, to their interests. This predominantly white, male, and middle- and working-class sector has been buffeted by global economic restructuring with its attendant job losses, declining real wages, and social dislocations. While under economic stress, this sector has also seen its traditional privileges and status challenged by 1960s-style social movements, such as feminism, minority rights, and environmentalism."[25]

The sons of these farmers and shopkeepers expected to—and felt entitled to—inherit their fathers' legacy. And when it became evident it was not going to happen, they became murderously angry—at a system that emasculated their fathers and threatens their manhood. They live in what they call a "Walmart economy" and are governed by a "nanny state" that doles out their birthright to ungrateful and undeserving immigrants. What they want, says one guy, is to "take back what is rightfully ours."[26]

Here's a graphic illustration of who they think they are. It's a cartoon from a 1987 issue of *WAR*, the magazine of the White Aryan Resistance. Here, a working-class white man, in hard hat and flak jacket, stands proudly before a suspension bridge while a jet plane soars overhead. "White Men *Built* This nation!!" reads the text. "White Men *Are* This nation!!!"

Timothy McVeigh's story is typical. A young man from Lockport, New York, an industrial city outside Buffalo—part of what used to be called the "Burned-Over District" because of the fiery intensity of the religious revivalism that enthralled the northwestern corner of New York (the home of apocalyptic Millerism, which spun off Seventh-Day Adventists and Jehovah's Witnesses, as well as the birthplace of Mormonism). McVeigh's father, William, who raised Tim after his parents' divorce, worked for more than thirty-five years as a machine operator at Harrison Radiator, a factory that makes cooling systems for General Motors cars. It was a high-wage, high-skill job, and William belonged to a union—a union that protected him when Harrison began laying off workers in the 1970s as the region began a long downward spiral.[27]

In high school, McVeigh tested reasonably well but was an indifferent student, and after a brief attempt at college, he enlisted in the army. He served in the Gulf War, earned a bronze star, and believed he had found his calling in the military. He signed up for training in the special forces, but the psychological test found him unsuitable. Discharged in 1991, he returned home to a different Lockport, less industrial, with fewer jobs. (Harrison Radiator struggled and declared bankruptcy in 2005; the company was saved by the economic bailout of the auto industry and was acquired by General Motors in 2009— another irony that the bailout opposed by the Republicans saved the jobs of the voters who supported the Republicans.)

He got a job as a security guard, earning about six dollars an hour, which isn't enough to live on even if you live in your parents' home. Frustrated, bitter, McVeigh drifted through friends and postwar veterans, stumbling into some neo-Nazis who had a ready explanation for his personal problems. Alone and lonely (he had a difficult time meeting women and never had a real relationship), aimless and angry, McVeigh began to blame the government for his problems.

Waco sealed the deal: the government was willing to gun down its own sovereign citizens. It was time to strike a blow against that government. At nine o'clock on April 19, 1995, the second anniversary of the government assault on the Branch Davidian compound in Waco, McVeigh parked his rented truck laden with homemade explosives by the Murrah Federal Building in downtown Oklahoma City. Two minutes later, it exploded, destroying the building and killing 168 people. "I am sorry these people had to lose their lives," he wrote in a letter to the editor of the *Buffalo News* on the eve of his execution. "But that's the nature of the beast. It's understood going in what the human toll will be."[28]

What makes McVeigh's story so compelling is that it could have been so different. Imagine if he'd returned from the war with sufficient veterans' benefits that he could have enrolled in community college, learned some practical skills, and found a meaningful job. Or had he returned to a less-desolate industrial landscape, the Lockport of his father, where union-protected jobs enabled working-class men to support a family and feel some sense of dignity in their work. Or had his working-class mates been more aware of their denigrated class position than of their fictive racial superiority and shifted to the Left instead of to the Far Right. There is nothing inevitable about the drift to the Right among so many dispossessed and downwardly mobile young white men. It has to be massaged, maneuvered, even manipulated by ideologues who see them as the shock troops of their effort to reclaim the country from what they perceive as the cancerous forces within.

Prior to his execution in June 2001—three months before the attack on the World Trade Center—McVeigh chose William Ernest Henley's poem "Invictus" as his final statement, the same Victorian poem that gave Nelson Mandela such comfort during his imprisonment at Robben Island in Cape Town. A poem of manly defiance in the face of seemingly insurmountable odds, it gave comfort to a black leftist who was imprisoned in one of the world's most unequal systems and a young white man who had failed to hold a job and seemed to have lost his way. But he felt oppressed—and, of course, oppressed as a man:

> It matters not how strait the gate,
> How charged with punishments the scroll,

I am the master of my fate,
I am the captain of my soul.

Timothy McVeigh or Nelson Mandela? How about McVeigh or Tom Joad? You can almost imagine McVeigh hunkering down by the campfires by the side of the road, where good, decent American families were forced to live, the detritus of American progress:

> *I been thinking about us, too, about our people living like pigs and good rich land layin' fallow. Or maybe one guy with a million acres and a hundred thousand farmers starvin'. And I been wonderin' if all our folks got together and yelled. . . .*
>
> *I'll be all around in the dark—I'll be everywhere. Wherever you can look—wherever there's a fight, so hungry people can eat, I'll be there. Wherever there's a cop beatin' up a guy, I'll be there. I'll be in the way guys yell when they're mad. I'll be in the way kids laugh when they're hungry and they know supper's ready, and when the people are eatin' the stuff they raise and livin' in the houses they build—I'll be there, too.*

So, who are they really, these hundred thousand white supremacists? They're every white guy who believed that this land was his land, was made for you and me. They're every down-on-his-luck guy who just wanted to live a decent life but got stepped on, every character in a Bruce Springsteen or Merle Haggard song, every cop, soldier, auto mechanic, steelworker, and construction worker in America's small towns who can't make ends meet and wonders why everyone else is getting a break except him. But instead of becoming Tom Joad, a left-leaning populist, they take a hard right turn, ultimately supporting the very people who have dispossessed them.

They're America's Everymen, whose pain at downward mobility and whose anger at what they see as an indifferent government have become twisted by a hate that tells them they are better than others, disfigured by a resentment so deep that there are no more bridges to be built, no more ladders of upward mobility to be climbed, a howl of pain mangled into the scream of a warrior. Their rage is as sad as it is frightening, as impotent as it is shrill.

WALKING THE
PATRIOTIC CAPITALIST TIGHTROPE

You might think that the political ideology of the white supremacist movement is as simple as their list of enemies: put down minorities, expel immigrants, push the women out of the workplace, and round up and execute the gays and the Jews. But it's not nearly so simple. Actually, they have to navigate some treacherous ideological waters and reconcile seemingly contradictory ideological visions with their emotions.

There are three parts to their ideological vision. For one thing, they are ferociously procapitalist. They are firm believers in the free market and free enterprise. They just don't like what it's brought. They like capitalism; they just hate corporations. They identify, often, as the vast middle class of office workers and white-collar employees, even though that is hardly their class background. (They've a fungible understanding of class warfare.) "For generations, white middle class men defined themselves by their careers, believing that loyalty to employers would be rewarded by job security and, therefore, the ability to provide for their families" is the way one issue of *Racial Loyalty* (a racist skinhead magazine) puts it. "But the past decade—marked by an epidemic of takeovers, mergers, downsizings and consolidations—has shattered that illusion."

Aryans support capitalist enterprise and entrepreneurship, even those who make it rich, but especially the virtues of the small proprietor, but are vehemently antiurban, anticosmopolitan, and anticorporate. In their eyes, Wall Street is ruled by Jewish-influenced corporate plutocrats who hate "real" Americans. Theirs is the Jeffersonian vision of a nation of *producers*—not financiers, not bankers, and not those other "masters of the universe" whose entire careers consist of cutting the cake ever more finely and living on the crumbs. It's Andrew Jackson's producerist attack on the "parasitic" bankers. It is "the desire to own small property, to produce crops and foodstuffs, to control local affairs, to be served but never coerced by a representative government, and to have traditional ways of life and labor respected," writes historian Catherine Stock.[29]

White supremacists see themselves as squeezed between global capital and an emasculated state that supports voracious global profiteering. In the song "No Crime Being White," Day of the Sword, a popular racist skinhead band, confronts the greedy class:

> The birthplace is the death of our race.
> Our brothers being laid off is a truth we have to face.
> Take my job, it's equal opportunity
> The least I can do, you were so oppressed by me
> I've only put in twenty years now.
> Suddenly my country favors gooks and spicks and queers.
> Fuck you, then, boy I hope you're happy when your new employees are
> the reason why your business ends.[30]

Second, the extreme Right is extremely patriotic. They love their country, their flag, and everything it stands for. These are the guys who get teary at the playing of the national anthem, who choke up when they hear the word *America*. They have bumper stickers on their pickups that show the flag with the slogan "These colors don't run."

The problem is that the America they love doesn't happen to be the America in which they live. They love America—but they hate its government. They believe that the government has become so un-American that it has joined in global institutions that undermine and threaten the American way of life. Many fuse critiques of international organizations such as the United Nations with protectionism and neoisolationism, arguing that all internationalisms are part of a larger Zionist conspiracy. Some embrace a grand imperial vision of American (and other Aryan) domination and the final subjugation of "inferior races."

As he traveled through the rural West, journalist Joel Dyer constantly heard these refrains: "Environmentalists wouldn't let me run my cows cause some damn little sparrow they said was endangered lived on my place," "They took my farm," "The IRS took everything I owned." "These people believe the government is responsible for where they are, because they are finding themselves ignored, basically, by the economic system. People are losing their homes, their farms, their jobs, their sources of income. Corporations have been allowed to move wherever they want, and to take away jobs by the truckload. People are becoming economically dispossessed."[31]

NAFTA took away American jobs; what they see as the "Burger King" economy leaves no room at the top, so "many youngsters see themselves as being forced to compete with nonwhites for the available minimum wage, service economy jobs that have replaced their parents' unionized industry opportunities."[32]

That such ardent patriots are so passionately antigovernment might strike the observer as contradictory. After all, are these not the same men who served their country in Vietnam or in the Gulf War? Are these not the same men who believe so passionately in the American Dream? Are they not the backbone of the Reagan Revolution? Indeed, they are. The extreme Right faces the difficult cognitive task of maintaining their faith in America and in capitalism and simultaneously providing an analysis of an indifferent state, at best, or an actively interventionist one, at worst, and a way to embrace capitalism, despite a cynical corporate logic that leaves them, often literally, out in the cold—homeless, jobless, hopeless.

Finally, they believe themselves to be the true heirs of the real America. They are the ones who are entitled to inherit the bounty of the American system. It's their birthright—as native-born, white American men. As sociologist Lillian Rubin puts it, "It's this confluence of forces—the racial and cultural diversity of our new immigrant population; the claims on the resources of the nation now being made by those minorities who, for generations, have called America their home; the failure of some of our basic institutions to serve the needs of our people; the contracting economy, which threatens the mobility aspirations of working class families—all these have come together to leave white workers feeling as if everyone else is getting a piece of the action while they get nothing."[33]

This persistent reversal—white men as victim, the "other" as undeservedly privileged—resounds through the rhetoric of the extreme Right. Take, for example, Pat Buchanan's "A Brief for Whitey," a response to candidate Barack Obama's call for a national conversation about race in America: "It is the same old con, the same old shakedown. America has been the best country on earth for black folks. It was here that 600,000 black people, brought from Africa in slave ships, grew into a community of 40 million, were introduced to Christian salvation, and reached the greatest levels of freedom and prosperity blacks have ever known."[34]

And now, I suppose, Buchanan would say, *we're* supposed to apologize to *them*? Pay *them* reparations? They should be kissing our feet with gratitude! But no. We live in a fun-house version of America, Buchanan argues, where minorities rule and white folks are the new oppressed minority. It was ours, but it's not anymore. It has been taken—because we let it! And the fact that it has been stolen from us leaves white American men feeling emasculated—and furious.

It is through a decidedly gendered and sexualized rhetoric of masculinity that this contradiction between loving America and hating its government, loving capitalism and hating its corporate iterations, is resolved. Racism, nativism, anti-Semitism, antifeminism—these discourses of hate provide an explanation for the feelings of entitlement thwarted, fixing the blame squarely on "others" whom the state must now serve at the expense of white men. The unifying theme is *gender*.

These men feel emasculated by big money and big government. In their eyes, most white American men collude in their emasculation. They've grown soft, feminized, weak. White supremacist websites abound with complaints about the "whimpering collapse of the blond male," the "legions of sissies and weaklings, of flabby, limp-wristed, non-aggressive, non-physical, indecisive, slack-jawed, fearful males who, while still heterosexual in theory and practice, have not even a vestige of the old macho spirit."

THE EMASCULATION OF THE AMERICAN WHITE MAN

"Nationalism," writes feminist political scientist Cynthia Enloe, "typically springs from masculinized memory, masculinized humiliation and masculinized hope."[35] We've seen how historical memory has been masculinized in white-wing rhetoric: once we were hardy yeomen in a Jeffersonian village; we controlled our own labor, owned our own homes, shops, and farms, and supported our families. We served our country, and it repaid us with the fruits of freedom.

But somewhere along the way, America lost its center. In the process, the world has been turned upside down: the government has abandoned the very men who have fought and died to protect it, the corporations have abandoned the very guys who have worked tirelessly to create the wealth the owners and shareholders enjoy, and our doors have been flung open to allow all sorts of unworthy types to come and take our jobs, our homes, even our women. Feminism is just one more straw, the symbolic straw that signals a compete reversal: women are the new men, and men are the new women.

The chief complaint of the White Wing is that white men have been emasculated in modern America. This is the "masculinized humiliation" of which Enloe writes. In some cases, it's been stolen from them, deliberately and methodically, by nefarious forces, using governmental policies. In other cases, the "live and let live" liberalism of the "Me Decade" self-actualizers has left white men complacent with their modest consumer goods, conspiring in their own demise, whistling on the *Titanic* of natural white rule.

Among the hallmarks of paranoid politics—whether men's rights activists or Tea Partiers or white supremacists—is the sense of righteous victimization. You were raised to be a real man, countless pamphlets and cartoons suggest, but you've given that away or had it stolen from you. Of course, this is the first stage of the classic heroic narrative. The arc begins with the eventual hero's abjection, the symbolic fall from grace. He loses everything and must wander through the land, fighting all enemies, and emerge the hero, reclaiming his manhood (winning the hand of the beautiful damsel optional). This political emasculation is a dominant theme in white-wing websites, blogs, magazines, and newsletters.

Article after article decry how white men have surrendered to the plot. According to *The Turner Diaries*, the highly popular white supremacist novel that provided the blueprint for Timothy McVeigh, American men have lost the right to be free; slavery "is the just and proper state for a people who have gown soft."[36] It is there that the movement simultaneously offers white men an analysis of their present situation and a political strategy for retrieving their manhood. As the neo-Nazi publication *National Vanguard* puts it:

> As Northern males have continued to become more wimpish, the result of the media-created image of the "new male"—more pacifist, less authoritarian, more "sensitive," less competitive, more androgynous, less possessive—the controlled media, the homosexual lobby and the feminist movement have cheered. . . . [T]he number of effeminate males has increased greatly . . . legions of sissies and

weaklings, of flabby, limp-wristed, non-aggressive, non-physical, indecisive, slack-jawed, fearful males who, while still heterosexual in theory and practice, have not even a vestige of the old macho spirit, so deprecated today, left in them.

And here's Aryan Nations: "What has become of your men? Are these powder puffs in their sky-blue, three-piece suits the descendents of George Washington, Thomas Jefferson, Andrew Jackson? What would your fathers say if they watched you give your country away?"[37] (Notice the generational reversal here. The fathers—the actual fathers who lost the farms and closed the stores—are now standing in mute masculine judgment of the sons for not stopping it.)

THE FRAUDULENT MASCULINITY OF THE "OTHER"

If the first "gendered strategy" of the White Wing is to trumpet the emasculation of the American white man, the second gendered strategy is to criticize the masculinity of the other—Jews, gays, blacks, Latinos, women, basically everyone who is not an American white man. They are illegitimate pretenders to the throne of masculinity; it is *their* masculinity that is the problem, not ours. They reap rewards they have not earned and do not deserve, doled out by a government in the thrall of Jewish bankers, feminist women, and African American guiltmongers.

And this effort to emasculate the other has a long and sour history in America. In the nineteenth century, arguments against emancipation of the slaves, immigration, and woman suffrage drew on any available pseudoscientific shred to make the "other" appear unmanly. The "other"—whether racial, sexual, religious, or any other identity—was either "too masculine" or "not masculine enough," that is, *hypermasculine* or *hypomasculine*.

It was another example of what I've earlier called the Goldilocks Dilemma: like the porridge that was either too hot or too cold, the chair that was either too big or too little, the masculinity of the other is either too much or too little. Never just right. *Our* masculinity is just right, of course; theirs is too hot or too cold. They're either wild, out-of-control animals, violent and rapacious (too masculine, unciv-ilized), or they are weak, dependent, irresponsible (not masculine enough).

In the middle of the nineteenth century, these were the sorts of arguments used by the racist and nativist Know-Nothings to justify their opposition to immigration. Irish and German immigrants were depicted as weaker, dependent, and less self-reliant than native-born men, since they took their orders not from nature but from the pope in Rome. Late-nineteenth-century racists and anti-immigrants har-nessed social Darwinism to their gendered critique of the other.[38] Francis Parkman believed that white Anglo-Saxons were "peculiarly masculine"; they were "frugal and productive," whereas black men represented "laziness and license." Even Georges Clemenceau, the fu-ture French prime minister, commented, during a visit to the United States in 1869, that the black man "must gird up their loins and strug-gle for their existence," that is, "they must become men."[39]

By the turn of the twentieth century, the gender of racism and na-tivism had been joined to the grand sweep of European anti-Semitism. As I noted earlier, Lothrop Stoddard's *The Rising Tide of Color* (1920), Homer Lea's *The Day of the Saxon* (1912), and Madison Grant's *The Passing of the Great Race* (1916) provided ample ammunition for the nativist hysteria. Blacks and immigrants were "teeming hordes," ir-responsible breeding machines, with no social conventions to keep them from raping white women, leading to "disintegration and disso-lution," an "apocalypse of the white man's ignorance."[40]

The "other" was rendered hypermasculine by linking him to prim-itive, animalistic urges; he was rendered hypomasculine by linking him to women. As women were a step below men on the Darwinian evolutionary ladder, linking them to immigrant or black men exposed the other as not real men. In the 1880s, an anatomist argued that the adult Negro male was the intellectual equal of "the child, the female, and the senile white." Negros' brains weighed as much as white wom-en's brains, another biologist observed, about a quarter less than white men's brains. A study of crime attributed the frequency of rape in the South to the "primitive impulses of the black race." His solution? "To-tal ablation of the sexual organs." If the problem was hypermasculin-ity, the solution could be surgical emasculation.[41]

To the fears of the hypermasculine hordes of freed black men and the swarthy, unwashed, and uncivilized throngs of southern European immigrants, Madison Grant added the specter of the Jew as hypomasculine conniver—bookish and effete. Yet he was hypermasculine in his greed for money and craving for power. Too much, too little.

So too were Asian immigrants; in his 1890 best seller, *Caesar's Column*, Ignatius Donnelly railed against those "wretched yellow, under-fed coolies, with women's garments over their effeminate limbs, who will not have the courage or the desire or the capacity to make soldiers and defend their oppressors." Samuel Gompers contrasted hardy American workers to the Chinese who "allow themselves to be barbarously tyrannized over in their own country." On the other hand, the Chinese were "invariably degenerate," "savage, vicious." One writer wanted it both ways; he labeled the Chinese "a barbarous race, devoid of energy."[42]

Harvard zoologist Louis Agassiz was alarmed that "the manly populations" that descended from Nordic stock would be replaced by the "effeminate progeny of mixed races." And many agreed with the editor of a New York newspaper that US domination of Mexico could be attributed to Mexicans' lack of "all the manlier virtues," which made them "perfectly accustomed to being conquered."[43]

Native Americans were singled out as infantilized children—hypomasculine, dependent—and barbarian hypermasculine savages. When we wanted to decimate them, they were hypermasculine; when we wanted to pacify them, they were hypomasculine. One particularly effective strategy was to declare the Native Americans once fierce warriors, a noble race, but now but "a degraded relic of a decayed race." This temporizing strategy—once hypermasculine, now hypomasculine—was particularly noticeable for erasing the cause of that degradation: the decimation of the Native population through their contact with the white man. First eviscerate them, then blame them for their own destruction and help them, patronizingly, by infantilizing them.

The revival of racism in the postwar South also rested on claims about gender. The Knights of the Ku Klux Klan's principles included the reclamation of southern manhood, whose virtues included "all that is chivalric in conduct, noble in sentiment, generous in manhood," whose purpose it is to "protect the weak, the innocent, and the defenseless, from the indignities, wrongs, and outrages of the lawless, the violent, and the brutal; to relieve the injured and oppressed; to succor the suffering and unfortunate, and especially the widows and orphans of Confederate soldiers."

Klan rhetoric was filled with evocations of this noble Christian white southern manhood, contrasted with violent and rapacious black masculinity. "God give us Men!" was a shout that punctuated every initiation ritual.[44] As it is today. Contemporary white supremacists thus draw on a long history of using gender—specifically masculinity—as a way to delegitimate and discredit the other.

Take the portrayal of gay men, for example. To contemporary white supremacists, gay men are effete fops who have men do to them what real men should only do to women. Here's Tom, a thirty-two-year-old welder from Riverside, California: "Oh, c'mon, man, just look at 'em, for Christ's sake. There's not a masculine bone in their body. They walk like girls, talk like girls, Jesus, they *are* girls as far as I can tell, especially since they take it up the ass. It's like they are a girl in a guy's body or something. It's not natural. They're like women. Just makes me . . . uh . . . [he pauses, searching for the right word] . . . it's just so fucking disgusting . . . [another pause] . . . so wrong, so, so wrong."

On the other hand, gay men are so sexually voracious and promiscuously carnal that straight men can only stand back in awe. Jeff, a twenty-seven-year-old auto mechanic in Buffalo, New York, said: "I read this article that said that, like, faggots have like a thousand different sex partners a year. Fuck! Unbelievable. It's like all they do is have sex. Christ, I can't even imagine. I'm lucky if I get laid by like two or three girls in a whole year! Damn, I wish girls were more like gay men. Ah [he sighs], that would be a miracle."

Websites are flooded with lurid descriptions of "gay public orgies" in San Francisco, including claims that these orgies are public and sponsored by the city's municipal government. Effete femininity of the failed man, the savage hypersexuality of the carnal Superman: hypermasculine/hypomasculine.

Women are *supposed* to be hypomasculine—that is their natural femininity. But women in the military? Women in politics? Women working in factories, driving trucks? Feminist women? They're freaks of nature, inversions, masculine women. "When I was an ironworker,"

William Miller, a member of the Republic of Texas militia, told journalist Susan Faludi, "there were some women up there, thirty feet in the air. Women shouldn't be up that high. They're gonna get you killed. They need to stay where they're placed."[45]

Feminist women are more masculine than many American men. The Clinton years represented the complete capture of the American government by gender inverts, feminist women. A constant barrage of jokes described how "President Clinton, and her husband Bill," have done something or other. One book sold by the Militia of Montana illustrates these themes. In *Big Sister Is Watching You: Hillary Clinton and the White House Feminists Who Now Control America—and Tell the President What to Do* (1993), Texe Marrs argues that Hillary Clinton and her feminist coconspirators control the country and are threatening American's rights and our national sovereignty. Marrs describes "Hillary's Hellcats" and "Gore's Whores"—a "motley collection [including] lesbians, sex perverts, child molester advocates, Christian haters, and the most doctrinaire of communists." These women—such as Jocelyn Elders, Janet Reno, Maya Angelou, Donna Shalala, Laura D'Andrea Tyson, Roberta Actenberg, and Ruth Bader Ginsburg—are said to be members of the "conspiratorial Council on Foreign Relations and the elitist Trilateral Commission, [they] attend the annual conclave of the notorious Bilderbergers [and are] hirelings of the left-wing, radical foundations designed to promote the New World Order." Today, he warns, "feminist vultures . . . the most militant of the militant . . . femiNazis . . . control a heartless police establishment more efficient than Stalin's."[46]

Of course, black men are imagined as both violent hypersexual beasts, possessed of an "irresponsible sexuality," seeking white women to rape, and less than fully manly, "weak, stupid, lazy." In *The Turner Diaries,* author William Pierce depicts a nightmarish world where white women and girls are constantly threatened and raped by "gangs of Black thugs." Blacks are primal, nature itself—untamed, cannibalistic, uncontrolled, but also stupid and lazy—and whites are the driving force of civilization. "America and all civilized society are the exclusive products of White man's mind and muscle" is how the *Thunderbolt* put it. Whites are the "instruments of God," proclaims *The Turner Diaries.* "The White race is the Master race of the earth . . . the Master Builders, the Master Minds, and the Master warriors of civilization." What can a black man do but "clumsily shuffle off, scratching his wooley head, to search for shoebrush and mop"?[47]

Most interesting is the portrait of the Jew. On the one hand, the Jew is a greedy, cunning, conniving, omnivorous predator; on the other, the Jew is small, beady-eyed, and incapable of masculine virtue. By asserting the hypermasculine power of the Jew, the Far Right can support capitalism as a system while decrying the actions of capitalists and their corporations. According to that logic, it's not the capitalist corporations that have turned the government against them, but the international cartel of Jewish bankers and financiers, media moguls, and intellectuals who have already taken over the US state and turned it into ZOG. The United States is called the "Jewnited States," and Jews are blamed for orchestrating the demise of the once-proud Aryan man.

In white supremacist ideology, the Jew is the archetypal villain, both hypermasculine (greedy, omnivorous, sexually predatory, capable of the destruction of the Aryan way of life) and hypomasculine (small, effete, homosexual, pernicious, weaselly). In their anti-Semitism, the White Wing joins a long lineage of American paranoia. Recall that in *The International Jew* (1920–1922), Henry Ford accused Jews of promoting a decay of morality, loss of family values, intrusive central government, monopolies, and corrupt banks. A 1986 Harris poll found that 27 percent of Nebraska and Iowa residents believed that "farmers have always been exploited by international Jewish bankers who are behind those who overcharge them for farm equipment or jack up the interest on their loans." Wisconsin Militia's pamphlet *American Farmer: 20th Century Slave* explains how banks were foreclosing on farms because Jews, incapable of farming themselves, had to control the world's monetary system in order to control the global food supply.[48]

In the White Wing's cosmology, Jews are both hypermasculine and effeminate. Hypermasculinity is expressed in the Jewish domination of the world's media and financial institutions and especially Hollywood. They're sexually omnivorous, but calling them "rabid, sexperverted" is not a compliment. The *Thunderbolt* claims that 90 percent of pornographers are Jewish. At the same time, Jewish men are seen as wimpish, small, nerdy, and utterly unmasculine—likely, in fact, to be homosexual. It's Jewish *women* who are seen as "real men"—strong, large, and hairy.

In lieu of their brawn power, Jewish men have harnessed their brain power in their quest for world domination. Jews are seen as the masterminds behind the other social groups who are seen as dispossessing rural American men of their birthright. And toward that end, they have co-opted blacks, women, and gays and brainwashed cowardly white men to do their bidding. In a revealing passage, white supremacists cast the economic plight of white workers as being squeezed between nonwhite workers and Jewish owners: "It is our RACE we must preserve, not just one class. . . . White Power means a permanent end to unemployment because with the non-Whites gone, the labor market will no longer be over-crowded with unproductive niggers, spics and other racial low-life. It means an end to inflation eating up a man's paycheck faster than he can raise it because OUR economy will not be run by a criminal pack of international Jewish bankers, bent on using the White worker's tax money in selfish and even destructive schemes."[49]

Since Jews are incapable of acting like real men—strong, hardy, virtuous manual workers and farmers—a central axiom of the international Jewish conspiracy for world domination is their plan to "feminize White men and to masculinize White women," observes *Racial Loyalty*, the white supremacist magazine. William Pierce echoes this theme: "One of the characteristics of nations which are controlled by the Jews is the gradual eradication of masculine influence and power and the transfer of influence into feminine forms."[50]

RECLAIMING MASCULINITY, RESTORING WHITENESS, RESCUING AMERICA

We've seen how the White Wing imagines the humiliation of the American white man, how they've been emasculated, sometimes even with their own permission. We've seen how they depict the doubly humiliating appropriation of manhood by all the undeserving others, the ones who pretend to be real men, but have no chance to be so. There remains only one thing for any self-respecting white man to do: join the movement—and get his manhood back.

Emasculation, appropriation, restoration: such a common dynamic of social movements, especially on the Right. Right-wing movements are almost always nostalgic, seeking to restore something that has been lost rather than create something new. Words like *restoration, reclamation, retrieval,* and *revival* saturate white supremacist discourse. Among the men's rights activists, these words refer to that recent time when men both ruled domestic life unchallenged and when they were not threatened by women's equality in the public sphere. Among the white supremacists, it harks back to ancient times—some Viking or primitive communal family, some "natural" hierarchy that has been perverted, or, at least, to the antebellum days when everyone knew their place. Contemporary American white supremacists tap into a general malaise among American men who seek some explanations for the contemporary "crisis" of masculinity. Like the Sons of Liberty who threw off the British yoke of tyranny in 1776, these contemporary Sons of Liberty see "R-2," the Second American Revolution, as restorative, to retrieve and refound traditional masculinity on the exclusion of others. The entire rhetorical apparatus that serves this purpose is saturated with gendered readings—of the problematized masculinity of the "others," of the emasculating policies of the state, and of the rightful masculine entitlement of white men. They hark back now to some mythic era, before feminism, before civil rights, before gay liberation. The Jews may have been assembling the tools of their internationalist power grab, but they were held in check by governments not yet entirely in the thrall of multiculturalism.

White supremacist organizations thus offer themselves as the antidote to America's current social problems by promising to empower men who feel they no longer have any power. The movement seemingly offers white men the chance to prove their masculinity. The fate of the white race hinges upon the need for real white men to act. White men are repeatedly attacked by the movement for becoming feminized (and unsettling the natural order) and are encouraged to become real men by standing up and protecting white women, reasserting their place in the natural hierarchy, and taking over the world. Their websites are saturated with images of warrior-like men, donning weaponry, shields, and armor.

Reclaiming the country, though, is a bit abstract; white men also seek to reclaim their manhood. This provides an enormously successful recruiting strategy. Join us, and we will see to it that your manhood is restored. And you'll probably get a girl. The political is really personal.

Reclaiming masculinity is more than a process; it's a statement—to yourself, to other men, to the world. Manhood is nothing if it is not validated by others; it is a "homosocial" performance. Of course, getting a girl is a sure sign that you're successful as a man. But one wants more than that—to be a "man among men." Contemporary white supremacists need constant validation that they are among the chosen, even if they are self-nominated. Their outfits often mimic a racist amalgam, like Nazi storm trooper meets British racist skinhead—a lot of Nazi tattoos, swastika armbands, black insignia T-shirts, and combat boots. Some of these guys would feel appropriately dressed in a gay S&M leather bar. That's not quite the look they're going for—they seek to be menacing, not pretenders, the signified, not the signifier. Blood and Glory can come to mean Ink and Attitude.

This desperate need to prove masculinity and to have one's masculinity validated by other guys is what fuels the social life of today's Aryan American. There are dozens of outings and social events. If you are feeling lonely, isolated, or emasculated, the White Wing is your new family, your new set of best friends, your new community, your new home. The ritualistic salutes, the impression-management techniques of wearing just the right uniform, having the right tattoos, ensure your validation as a man.

And the festivals. Small, unannounced rock festivals, mini-Hatestocks featuring lineups of White Power music. Hatecore—the particularly virulent form of angry hard-core punk with explicitly racist lyrics—is a major recruiting tool of the Far Right and also the basis for the traveling festival road shows that serve the movement as moments of expression of the community. Guys who otherwise spend their days in boring dead-end jobs, if that, and their evenings surfing the Web in search of new conspiracy theories and right-wing takes on the news find these festivals energizing, validating, community building. It's ceremonial, a near-religious experience. They experience the intense solidarity of the mosh pit, where they flail around, violently crashing into each other, bare-chested, pushing and shoving in a sweaty, homoerotic (and therefore vehemently homophobic) mass, fists pumping: the mosh pit looks like Turkish oil wrestling, without the same kind of lubrication.

Wade Page, the Oak Creek, Wisconsin, terrorist who murdered Sikh worshippers, was the leader in a band called End Apathy and had played also with bands like Definite Hate. "The violence begins with the music," says George Burdi, once the lead singer with RaHoWa, who has now left the movement. "They're always fighting with each other. Friends would beat each other up and then laugh about it afterwards, with their eyes swollen shut and their noses broken and picking their teeth up off the ground."

"If I can't dance—I don't want to be part of your revolution," the great anarchist agitator Emma Goldman famously said. Although I'm not sure the mosh pit at a Hammerskin festival was exactly what she had in mind, festivalgoers release their pent-up frustration, give voice to their rage, and validate each other's manhood—all to a thunderous three-chord anthem.

Joining the White Wing restores you to your rightful place, at the top of the hierarchy, where you belong. It's an act of reclamation. Perhaps this is best illustrated with another cartoon from *WAR*, the magazine of the White Aryan Resistance. In this deliberate parody of countless Charles Atlas advertisements, the timid white ninety-seven-pound weakling finds his power, his strength as a man, through racial hatred. In the ideology of the white supremacist movement, and their organized militia allies, it is racism that will again enable white men to reclaim their manhood.

On the recorded message of the Militia of Michigan, one could hear the following telling narrative:

Once they were praised. Once they were toasted. But that was over 200 years ago. Today the Militia Men are a threat. Our new King has told us so. "Begone with your pride and away with your honor! Who cares about what has been? Down with the old! It's a new world order—there's no place for you Militia Men. Give up your guns, you have no right. Just who do you think you are? Your God is dead and so is your dream." Stand firm, stand strong, Militia Men! America has much need of you today. Be vigilant now, as never before. Evil is trying to steal our country away. Perhaps tomorrow or in a thousand years you will receive the rewards you are due. Our flag will fly, our spirit will soar, and it will happen because of you. History will record many of your names, stories will tell of where you've been.[51]

On the farthest margins of the political spectrum, outside the boundaries of polite political discourse, American's white supremacists see themselves as reclaiming their manhood and restoring their country to those who are entitled to run it and reap its benefits: themselves. They are the unsung heroes of contemporary history, unknown, unloved, and unwanted. But they know, in their hearts, that their names will be etched into the historical record as the great martyrs who gave all for the cause. Like the suicide bombers and al-Qaeda terrorists who know that scores of gorgeous virgins await them in paradise, America's extremists would be happy with just one, right here and right now. She doesn't even have to be a virgin.

WOMEN OF THE RIGHT

Of course, these movements on the extreme Right are not populated entirely by men. Lori Linzer, a researcher at the Anti-Defamation League, found that although there are small numbers of women involved in the movement, they are likely to become involved with Internet discussions and websites and less likely to be active in paramilitary training and other militia activities. Women are a crucial part of the white supremacist movement, both corporeally and symbolically. Indeed, one could even say that they're pivotal; they're what these guys are fighting for. Yet there are contradictions, fissures among white supremacists on the role of women.

On the one hand, some of the older, established organizations have historically been for men only; women are venerated for their work in the home, but excluded from actual membership. The KKK, for example, is male only, with clearly delineated roles and auxiliary organizations for women. "We believe in the protection of pure womanhood," a 1960s United Klans of America pamphlet, *The Fiery Cross*, put it. "This is a stand for the purity of the home, for morality, for the protection of our mothers, our sisters, our wives, our daughters." More recently, a Klan writer put it this way, using the American flag as a gendered symbol: "The white of our flag's folds cries out for unstained purity and virtue in manhood and womanhood, and bears silent testimony that the men of the nation would rise as one to protect and keep spotless the honor and chastity of our home-builders—our women."[52]

This traditionalism is equally true of some of the newer skinhead organizations like Hammerskin Nation, which is male only. Obviously, the Christian Identity groups have very clearly prescribed and proscribed roles for women as helpmeets and servants of men. One leader, John Trochman, argues that women must relinquish the right to vote and to own property. On the other hand, in newer groups that cater to younger men, women skinheads are equally eager to engage in violence. But virtually all groups venerate a traditional family in which the breadwinner father returns to his "castle" in which housewife and children await the benevolent patriarch.[53]

Most white supremacist men tend to see women through rose-colored traditionalist lenses, simultaneously venerated as "the single greatest treasure of the White Race, the heart of our people, the center of our homes, of our lives" and excluded from most of the activities of the groups. Like many antifeminists before them, including, we're told, Hitler himself, white supremacists wouldn't "exclude" women so much as "exempt" them from working, from fighting, from any public activities, in part because their frail constitution couldn't withstand the exertion and because gender integration violates the laws of nature. (Hitler called gender equality a "deprivation of rights" because it would draw women "into an arena in which she will necessarily be inferior. . . . [N]either sex should try to do that which belongs to the other sphere.") "It doesn't matter what to the contrary you read in the jew-controlled newspapers or what you are told and shown on the jew-controlled TV, women are not inventors or mechanics," explains Jack Rader of the Aryan Nations: "They are not land developers, farmers, ranchers, miners, construction workers, or lumberjacks tetc [sic]. Women have been put in the armed forces and they have been made so-called cops, but the truth is that they just don't have what it takes to do these things."[54]

What's more, though, women must remain in their prescribed sphere—or exempted from entering men's sphere—because gender equality emasculates men, giving men no firm foundation of difference on which to rest their manhood. "Can you think of anything more demeaning to masculinity," asks Jack Rader, of the Aryan Nations, "than a woman as the so-called commander-in-chief over the armed forces?"[55]

On the other side, though, is Tom Metzger, founder and leader of the White Aryan Resistance. While extolling the tonic virtue of racism and anti-Semitism as restorative of American manhood, Metzger also thinks that sex segregation is a tool of the Jewish conspiracy to keep white men and women from forming a united front. He sneers at the Judeo-Christian heritage, claiming that it perpetuates the "worst" stereotypes, massive oppression, and that both Christians and Jews promote "ridiculous attitudes" about women's innate inferiority.

By contrast, Metzger proposes letting the women decide what they want to do. "If they are capable and are able to show that ability, then forget all of the artificial barriers," he writes. On the other hand, he has little patience for arguments that sex segregation would enable the restoration of manhood. "Just because a man is white and male, this should carry no special ticket to our struggle." You know that famous feminist bumper sticker that says, "A man of quality isn't threatened by women's equality"? Metzger would only add the word *white* to modify the word *man*. WAR welcomes women—as equals, says Metzger.[56] (On the other hand, WAR also maintained a ladies' auxiliary, the Aryan Women's League, a "support group" that offers everything from tips to new mothers to inspirational history. Maybe not so equal after all.)

Women compose about a quarter of the white supremacist movement. Their motives for joining are similar to those of the men, or at least run a parallel course. Sociologist Kathleen Blee interviewed nearly three dozen women on the extreme Right, and their narratives provide a fascinating parallel to the narratives of the men I interviewed. Of the neo-Nazis, Klanswomen, White Power skinheads, and Christian Identity or other cult members she interviewed, Blee found that virtually all were of the same class background as the men I interviewed, indeed, as the men profiled in virtually every study of the extreme Right. They were all lower-middle- and middle-class, and the overwhelming majority were educated (more than a third had some sort of postsecondary degree or were currently in college). None had been subject to abuse as girls.[57]

What brings the women in? The same mundane reasons that bring most people to all sorts of intense identity-oriented politics—a need to belong to something larger than themselves, the collapse of traditional familial or communal forms or identity. Maybe the trickle down of loneliness and suburban isolation chronicled by Robert Putnam in *Bowling Alone* (2000). Only a handful of the women followed a man into the racist world; many were not especially racist when they entered and developed their ideology after they joined. Others simply drifted into the deviant subculture. One's friend liked skinhead fashion, another thought it would be fun to hang out with the fringe groups.

Ideologically, many embrace the same traditionalist gender ideals as the men, suggesting that their greatest contribution to the cause is bearing and raising white babies. "We were put on this earth to bare [*sic*] the pure white children and if we don't do something to help fight for our White Race, then there won't be a future for our Pure White Children" is how the Ladies of the Invisible Empire (a ladies' auxiliary of the KKK) puts it. Women "should nurture the family as well as keep the household in order," chimes the Aryan Confederations.[58]

Unsurprisingly, the dominant image among white supremacist women is that of Aryan mother. "The life of a race is in the wombs of its women," says Aryan Nations. Websites depict her gazing lovingly at her blond children, standing with her arms around them in a nature setting, or hugging and playing with them. The Aryan Women's League sells Aryan coloring books, cookbooks, and "Aryan Baby on Board" stickers for your car.[59] On the other hand, some organizations, like WAR and WAU (Women for Aryan Unity), promote a stronger, sexier Aryan babe, a skinhead fantasy (though she invariably has long, flowing hair). WAU wants it both ways; their magazines feature homemakers and helpmeets alongside skinhead fashion tips. They have even produced a cookbook, *Food—Folk—Family*, which they sell to benefit Aryan families around the world.

The women's levels of involvement vary enormously. For some, white supremacy is a life commitment; for others, it's a series of festivals and parties; still others are like hobbyists, drawing occasional communal feelings, but mostly shopping for fun things like racist coloring books for their children and cooking the recipes from those Aryan cookbooks, participating in camping trips and barbecues with fellow Aryans.

Many of the women see embracing the traditional patriarchal bargain—he works to provide for the family while she stays home to cook and clean and raise the children—as an enormous improvement over the lives they had been living, lives in which they had to work to barely stay afloat or where the men in their lives spent a lot of time and money carousing, hanging with their buddies, getting drunk or stoned, or sleeping around. A dedicated and committed neo-Nazi swears off such excess; a true revolutionary, he commits to his family and to his race.

Of course, this pattern is far more likely in the older established organizations like the Klan. A visit to their website, and linked sites, can provide age-appropriate curricula for homeschooling your children (since the public school curriculum is so corrupted by multiculturalism and diversity that it's hard to teach the story of the triumphant white race) or even "white" recipes, untainted by the foods of immigrants. Al, one of the Klansmen I interviewed, let me know, twice, in fact, that salsa is the most popular condiment in America, passing ketchup in 2010—which prompted Jay Leno to quip that "you know it's bad when even our vegetables are starting to lose their jobs to Mexico."

They're wrong, of course: sales of mayonnaise dwarf both ketchup and salsa, and there is no whiter food than mayonnaise. However, Al didn't seem to know that mac 'n' cheese, pizza, and peanut butter all have immigrant origins.

For many women, racism becomes almost a form of recovery, a way to move from victim to vanguard. Like many in the recovery movement, their statements often have a certain robotic recitation, a loose stringing together of rote racist homilies. "Only rarely," writes Blee, "could an interviewee say what she objected to about African Americans, Jews, or other enemy groups without lapsing into the pat phrases of racist groups or describing some personal affront." Far more common were lines like these, from a Christian Identity member: "I'm proud that I'm a white female who realizes what is happening to my people. I'm proud that I completed my education and will continue to educate myself. I'm proud of the way I live my life and will continue to do so because it gives me strength and self-pride."[60]

To the men of the White Wing, women serve several vital purposes. Most important, they are the idealized mother of the traditional family—the marital helpmeet, the contented mother raising the next generation of white children, a symbol of racial purity, Christian goodness. She is, symbolically, the one the men are sworn to protect, so that the race can be preserved. She is the symbolic nation itself.

More pragmatically, women are cast as the "prize" to which men will be entitled when they join the movement. White men who feel thoroughly emasculated by the multicultural society restore their manhood through joining the movement—and then they suddenly expect to be instant blue-eyed babe magnets. Surely, reclaiming their manhood will restore the interest of the opposite sex.

The women know this; here's one woman on a white supremacist dating site: "There are PLENTY of us proud white women out here looking for just that—a strong white man that adores us for our values and the way we believe in raising our children. . . . All I see here is a bunch of sniveling teenage boys. . . . Call me when the real white men arrive someone please!!!!"[61]

Several websites offer dating services to match Aryan men and women. Organizations like Aryanist Assignations (which sounds like a Nazi escort service) and websites like allwhitedating.com as well as dating and relationship sections on portals like stormfront.org (white singles) have literally thousands of members looking to hook up. (The photos they post look indistinguishable from the photos on Match.com, except the white supremacists generally pose in front of Confederate flags.) Man up, white guys, and get a date with a real white woman!

In the subordinate role of housewife and mother, women restore manhood in another way, as traditional patriarchs. The women of the extreme Right are not the sort of career-climbing, sexually adventurous, single gal pals of *Sex and the City*; these are good Christian women who channel Tammy Wynette when the chips are down.

They probably also provide a little cover, a small speck of insurance. After all, the men in the movement spend a lot of time with each other—that is, with other men—drinking and carousing, moshing in the mud, and wrestling with each other. One might be tempted to get the wrong idea, mightn't one? The presence of women and the explicit interest in women "sanitize" the homosocial (male-male camaraderie) and the homoerotic (the obvious sensuality of all that physicality) and ensure that they never spill over into the homosexual. The presence of women has always "lubricated" and thus legitimated male-male interactions—in the workplace, in bars, and at social events.

Politically, the women's positions run in tandem with those of the men. Although they're not proving their gender identity, they *are* demonstrating their racial identity every minute. Yet their ideology is no less contradictory than the men's. For example, on the one hand, they vehemently deny the Holocaust, but heap praise on Hitler for trying so hard to rid the world of pernicious Jews. Hitler had the right idea, but he didn't pull it off. "A belief in Jewish extermination can be empowering to anti-Semitic activists even as claims about Jewish manipulation of history require that the extermination be denied," Blee writes. Some of them support abortion for Jewish women, women of color, and women in the third world, while they also claim that abortion is a Jewish-inspired plot to "deplete the white race." Several women told Blee they had abortions despite their group's adamant opposition to it. And several have close Jewish, black, or gay friends, even when their political ideology demands that they shun "mud people" and deviants. At least one-third of the women had mixed-race or homosexual family members, and one Aryan supremacist in New England confessed she was in a lesbian-dominated goddess-worship group, while another embeds her white supremacy in a sort of neo-hippie back-to-the-land mentality of "natural family planning, ecological breastfeeding and home schooling."[62]

Lucy, a young Klanswoman, resolved these contradictions in a typical American fashion. "In school my best friend was black. . . . I've got a family member that's bisexual, and the Klan's supposed to be against that. So you know it's just the person, not the race, not the religion. If I'm gonna like you, I like you for *who* you are, not *what* you are."[63] Were she not a member of the KKK, she might be a liberal Democrat! (It's an interesting gender question that so many of the women of the extreme Right who have been interviewed by journalists and scholars seem to resolve this contradiction so much more easily than the men do—if they ever do. It's as if the men retain their commitment to ideology over the concreteness of their relationships, and the women are more willing to compromise their ideological rigidity when faced with disconfirming relational evidence.)

But the central contradiction is the image of women itself. Are they kick-ass activists, "courageous young women warriors," as the Aryan Women's League puts it, fighting the scions of the New World Order? Or are they happy, contented breeding machines who toil as backstage helpmeets to their men and "find their greatest fulfillment as mothers of our children," as the Klan has it? Several want it both ways—participating in violent attacks by day and racing home to pick up the kids and cook their husbands' dinner.[64]

Take, for example, the case of Molly Gill, a middle-aged woman from St. Petersburg, Florida. Starting in the mid-1980s, Molly has written a series of newsletters, under the names *Independent Woman* and the *Radical Feminist* and eventually deciding on the *Rational Feminist* for like-minded Aryan women. Unaffiliated with any organization, she tried desperately to balance traditional notions of femininity and an obvious impulse for equality and power. On the one hand, she instructs young white women to have sex with their men in prison, lest they get tempted toward homosexuality or pornography (though sending sexy photos of yourself is not a good idea because those pictures can too easily find their way into the wrong hands). At the same time, she bristles against male leaders of the movement who want to keep women down. "What makes them think that one submissive partner bred with a dominant one results in warrior offspring?" she asks. Don't they realize that "the most ignorant and poorest" peoples are the ones with the "most downtrodden women"?[65]

In response to a questionnaire by two sociologists, Gill shifts her position squarely in the middle of her narrative. After being asked if the White Power movement is sexist, she writes, "The Movement is dominated by men and should be. . . . Women do whatever needs to be done at any given time: support & nurturing, activism; fighting; running defense funds; family asst. projects; publishing. Cooking, serving, childcare, teaching; leading; writing. . . . Women are assuming more exec. positions and being asked to. Aryan women are scarce and not answering men's pen friend ads because the men are abusive and too macho. In this world macho doesn't cut it, not to the extent they got away with it previously."[66] Notice how she starts, asserting the legitimacy of male dominance and listing all the roles that women take. But suddenly, midlist, her narrative shifts, in between "childcare [and] teaching" and "leading." Suddenly, she spins full circle and criticizes the men and promotes women's equality. Perhaps unwittingly, Gill expresses the contradiction for women at the heart of their participation in the White Power movement: they remain committed to a second-class status that feels increasingly awful and leaves men's entitlement unchecked.

Or take the case of Misty Cook, the thirty-one-year-old former girl-friend of Wade Page, an active white supremacist herself. When Wade joined the Hammerskin Nation, one of the country's largest racist skinhead organizations (active mostly on the Internet), Misty joined Crew 38, which was sort of the Hammerskin's ladies' auxiliary. She posted to their Internet site constantly, averaging nearly one a day for the two-plus years she had been a member. She sounds perfectly suited as Wade Page's partner, except she broke up with him, and he moved out of their shared apartment just about five weeks before Page's terrorist attack.[67]

No doubt pop psychologists will claim that the breakup was so traumatic that Page descended into a madness that only violent and suicidal extirpation could possible resolve. But that misses the point. Page and Cook were part of a movement, and they trained for the day that a spark would ignite RaHoWa. That Page became despondent enough to become messianically deranged may have been precipitated by an immediate relationship crisis. But the causes lay much deeper than such armchair psychiatric diagnoses. Their relationship was sensible only in the context of their political commitments; they were equally committed to the cause, but unequally able to express it. More, her ability to hold a decent job as a waitress must have irked the inconsistent and often-fired Page—how could the woman be the breadwinner? Perhaps she was tired of waiting for him to step up and be a man, a real white man, able to support a wife and family.

We'll never know; Page took his complex motives to the grave. But the difficulty in negotiating gender roles, where both he and she expect and want a more traditional family structure of provider husband and homemaker/mother-wife, is increasingly difficult in all but the top 1 percent of the economic ladder. Economic realities clash with gendered expectations; this is the source of conflict in large numbers of couples all across America. Wade Page's political commitments gave him a convenient target for his anguish (the Sikh temple was a short walk from the restaurant where Cook worked); easy access to assault weapons gave him the means. Throw in unrealizable gender expectations and the refusal of his girlfriend to utterly subordinate her life to his. His racial hatred and gendered grief provided both the motivation to load those weapons and an ideological justification to open fire.

In the face of those real threats, the racist Right wants to restore those birthrights with policies that would refeminize women, by returning them to their ordained place as marital helpmeets and contented mothers, and remasculinize men, who, through glorious violence, become the heroic real men their Confederate grandfathers were. Gendered rhetoric becomes a currency by which these groups explain their pain and seek to recover. As the pace of global economic restructuring only continues to heat up, we will only see their ranks grow.

WHAT'S RIGHT ABOUT BEING WHITE

It's ironic that of all the groups I've discussed in this book, it's the white supremacists who are probably more right than any of the others. It's pretty hard to sympathize with the dizzying reversals of the MRAs, or the scions of male studies, casting middle-class white men— middle-class *college professors,* no less—as the victims of some pervasive feminist conspiracy.

But the white supremacists are at least half right—they *have* been forgotten in the rush to the global marketplace. They may have some legitimate gripes, though they are delivering their mail to the wrong address. (The right address is, of course, neoliberal economic policy.) It hasn't been black people who have foreclosed on their farms, or feminist women who have outsourced their jobs and closed the factories, or gay people who have sunk their mortgages underwater, or immigrants who opened the big-box store with massive tax breaks and spectacular local governmental incentives that forced them to close the small hardware store their family had been operating for generations. The combination of aggrieved entitlement and their misdirected rage has led to their sporadic outbursts, clandestine terrorist conspiracies, and paranoid political thinking.

That such coherence is composed of loosely connected and ultimately incoherent ideological strands provides the dynamic of prejudice since Gordon Allport's classic studies. Today, also, racist movements are "about" many things at once—antiglobalization, anti-immigrant, anti-Semitic, racist, sexist, and homophobic, all at one go. And underneath it all is the seething resentment of a lower middle class that finds itself utterly disenfranchised, dispossessed of their entitlement, threatened by new competition. Like the other terrorist groups chronicled by Benjamin Barber in his brilliant book *Jihad vs. McWorld* (1995), they are trapped between two worlds, unheeded by either. So they, like their closest "allies"—al-Qaeda—choose terrorism, fueled by vague anti-Semitism, messianic zeal for racial purity, and the fantasy belief that diaphanous virgins await their heroic reclamation of manhood.

It's that aggrieved entitlement that fuels their rage: once they were in power, they believe, but now they've been emasculated, their birthright transferred to others who don't deserve it. And now they march, and fight, and bomb innocent civilians to reclaim their manhood, to ignite the conflagration that will restore America to its rightful heirs. Entirely unaware of the privileges that they already had accrued, just by virtue of being white and male, they focus instead—again, partly correctly in my view—at their dispossession as members of the formerly autonomous, independent lower middle class of independent farmers, small shopkeepers, and skilled workers. Movements composed of such groups can be either of the Far Left or the Far Right, Neo-Nazis or sansculottes, Aryans or anarchists, real populists seeking to bring together farmers and workers in the late nineteenth century or faux populists in the Tea Party enriching the Koch brothers' industrial fortunes in the twenty-first.

The American White Power movement is filled with guys over whom history is rolling. It's a steamroller, and it is unstoppable. Theirs is an anguished wail, the scream of a hatecore lyric, the venomous hatred of others who are in the same boat, scratching and clawing their way for their stake in the American Dream

The American white supremacists are also, as Bruce Springsteen sang in "The Promised Land," "itching for something to start"—and when they're done, they promise American men the restoration of their masculinity, a manhood in which individual white men control the fruits of their own labor and are not subject to the emasculation of Jewish-owned finance capital, a black- and feminist-controlled welfare state. Theirs is the militarized manhood of the heroic John Rambo—a manhood that celebrates their God-sanctioned right to band together in armed militias if anyone, or any governmental agency, tries to take it away from them. If the state and capital emasculate them, and if the masculinity of the "others" is problematic, then only "real" white men can rescue this American Eden from a feminized, multicultural androgynous melting pot.

In the song's refrain of "The Promised Land," Springsteen sings, "Mister, I ain't a boy, no I'm a man / And I believe in the Promised Land." The song captures these guys' stories. They tried to live the right way. They're not boys: the sons have grown up; they're men, they tell the man they're singing to. And they are true believers in the promise of America. Maybe the last of the True Believers. And, as America has tuned its back on them, they, too, feel so weak they want to explode. And so they do. America, they believe, has declared war on its own white men. It's time to accept the gauntlet, take to the streets, build the bunkers.

As these first brave white men reclaimed their nation, "millions of soft, city-bred, brainwashed Whites" gradually began to regain their manhood, recalls the narrator of *The Turner Diaries*. "Once he is united, inspired by a great ideal and led by real men, his world will again become livable, safe, and happy." The men of the extreme Right seek to reclaim their manhood also—gloriously, violently.

And the rest of us? "The rest died."

Epilogue

Can we turn down the volume? Is there any way to reduce the rage? To some of these groups, one wants to simply say get over it. It's a done deal. For example, the men's rights activists may want to turn back the clock on women's progress, and male-female relationships more generally, but that ship has long sailed. Women are unlikely to have some cosmic revelatory moment and say, "Oh, wow, all these 'rights' we've claimed—like voting, serving on a jury, going to college or professional school, joining a union, working outside the home, becoming a doctor, a lawyer, an architect, or any other professional, serving in the military, having an orgasm—what a big headache. Let's go back to the way it was."

Or to the scions of outrage radio, or the anti-immigrant border patrols who want to restore that past sense of entitlement, who insist on their right to "take our country back," you might want to echo *New York Times* columnist Charles Blow, who sagely says, "You may want 'your country back,' you can't have it. That sound you hear is the relentless, irrepressible march of change."[1]

It's true, the future is now. It's America 2.0. America the Multi-cultural. Angry white men are on the losing side of history, which is poised to roll over them like a demographic steamroller. Theirs is a rearguard action, the circling of wagons, Custer's last stand. In fact, they've already lost.

All is not, however, over—not even for them. For the truth is that Angry White Men may make a lot of noise, but they are a fast-disappearing minority. Despite the anger I've discussed, this is not the new normal. The rage is actually declining, and we are, individually and culturally, accommodating ourselves to greater equality. The overwhelming majority of America's white men are quietly accommodating themselves to the new world of greater gender equality—doing more housework and a lot more child care than American men have ever done before.

We're developing cross-sex friendships. Virtually every young person with whom I spoke has a good friend of the opposite sex. And, given that we make friends with those we consider our peers, our equals—neither boss nor servant—we can say with some confidence that this new generation of Americans has more day-to-day experience with gender equality in their friendships and relationships than any generation of Americans in our history.

It's equally true that we have never been more equal racially. Though far from equal, African Americans have made greater strides in education, employment, voting, and housing than at any time in our history. We are led by a black president. Electoral shenanigans designed to suppress the black vote are immediately unmasked, and judges issue injunctions. We are less segregated in education or housing than ever—though we are far from integrated. Furthermore, if, by race, we include Asians and Latinos, we have a larger percentage of nonwhites in the middle class than at any point in our history.

Of course, it's incontestable that gays and lesbians are more equal today than ever. Barriers to sexual equality seem to be falling every day, as the shameful "Don't Ask/Don't Tell" policies have been lifted that prevented gays and lesbians from serving openly in the military. Same-sex marriage is now legal in twelve states and will soon become legal throughout the country as the Defense of Marriage Act is officially declared the unconstitutional travesty it is. Even as I write, the Boy Scouts of America have just rescinded their long-standing policy of excluding gay and lesbian Scouts (though they are clinging to an equally outdated and unjustified exclusion of gay or lesbian Scoutmasters). That isn't to say that women or gay people or people of color *are* being treated equally; of course, significant obstacles remain in their path. But I think it is unmistakable that we have never been *more* equal than we are today.

It's ironic, isn't it, that this dramatic and irreversible increase in social equality is happening at the same time that economically we are more *unequal* than we have been in about a century. The dramatic skewing of the economic pyramid, pushing all the increases in income and wealth upward—the very opposite of the much-trumpeted and utterly discredited notion of trickle-down economics. We're becoming a more socially equal and class-unequal society at the same time. Indeed, we are more unequal economically than at any time since the Gilded Age—the age that brought with it the most colossal economic collapse in our history.

So it's easy to think these phenomena are related—that the greater class inequality is somehow attendant upon, even caused by, greater social equality. Perhaps we can be convinced that the reason for the dramatic skewing of our country's riches is somehow that these newly arrived groups are siphoning off the very benefits that were supposed to be trickling down to middle- and lower-middle-class white men. And that really pisses us off—because it seems so utterly unfair.

Of course, it's untrue: greater social equality can accompany, or parallel, shifts in economic distribution. In our case, they run at cross-purposes; in other countries, notably in the European Union, greater economic equality has actually accompanied greater social equality. There is no necessary and inevitable relationship between them. To believe that greater social equality is the cause of your economic misery requires a significant amount of manipulation, perhaps the single greatest bait and switch that has ever been perpetuated against middle- and lower-middle-class white Americans.

This has been the cultural mission of the ruling elites—to deny their own existence (at least the robber barons and other plutocrats were up-front about their economic standing) and pretend that they are on the side of the very people they are disenfranchising, even at the very moment they are disenfranchising them. (Occasionally, such sleights of hand are easily seen, as when the corporate elites and their minions in state government in the Midwest waged an all-out assault against public-sector unions, until they realized that police departments and fire departments were also members of those unions.)

The anger of middle-class white Americans is real; its aim, however, is misdirected not toward those who are the cause of their misery but against those who are just below them on the economic ladder.

Yes, it's true that their sense of entitlement may be illegitimate—if that entitlement has to do with superiority over others who are in the same position that they are. But it's quite another thing to believe yourself entitled to a decent job and a social safety net that enables you to wake up in the morning and go to work and feel you are making a contribution to the greater good—and for which you are granted not only a decent wage, capable (with your spouse) of supporting a family, with something put aide for your retirement, but also granted the respect of your coworkers and a secure place in your community.

Middle-class white men and women may not be entitled to "more," nor even "more than" those who may look different, come from a different place, or love differently than we do. But we *are* entitled to a feeling of dignity about our work; respect in our families and communities; security as we face decline, illness, and mortality; and a sense of honor about how we have conducted our lives. To that we are most certainly entitled. That is our birthright as Americans.

If we're looking for reasons we don't have that, we can look not to our past but to our future and toward those countries that are providing those values to their citizens. Despite all the austerity measures demanded by the current economic recession, the countries of the European Union have protected the policies that provide that safety net. When you have that safety net underneath, you can both take greater risks, knowing you'll be cushioned if you make a mistake, and exhale, relax, and enjoy the life you are actually living. In the United States, this current rage, fueled by aggrieved entitlement, is a decidedly gendered rage. It is middle-class white *men* who are expressing their anguish, confusion, and fear through this politicized rage. If there were a real social safety net, perhaps men (and women) would be less fearful of failure. So alleviating that fear of falling is part of a redefinition of masculinity that is a central component of addressing that anger.

Focusing only on the few individuals at the extremes who go postal in their workplaces, who seek to foment violent revolution or racial purification here at home, or who track down and murder immigrants as a "lesson" to the others can take us inside the psychology of aggrieved entitlement. Yes, we need to enable men to grieve for that lost entitlement so they can then let those feelings go and instead embrace a new, more honest, meritocracy.

But I think we need more than anger-management programs—either for individual men or for men in general. We need to begin to decouple masculinity from that sense of unexamined and unearned entitlement. And, more, it is not by fighting against those newcomers to the public arena—immigrants, women, minorities, gays—that white men will find their way to a new definition of masculinity. Rather, it is only by joining together across race, and gender, and other identities that we think divide us—both personally and politically—that we can begin to alleviate white men's anger.

In our families, we are finding that abandoning that sense of masculine entitlement actually enables us to live happier lives. Men who are more egalitarian in their marriages, who share housework and child care, report significantly happier marriages—as well as lower levels of depression (which is, after all, anger turned inward against the self). Equality, it turns out, is not a "loss" for men, in some zero-sum calculus; it is a win-win. As women—and minorities and other "others"—win, so too will angry white men. Ironically, increasingly equality will actually make us *less* angry.

In our workplaces also, we find that those companies that have implemented the best diversity training programs are also those where the workers say they are happiest—and are therefore most productive, with the lowest turnover. This is even true for white men, ostensibly the "losers" in this new workplace calculus. But, it turns out, the white men also feel valued in those companies. Diversity, when done right, means *everybody can get the opportunities and rewards they deserve.* Listening to the voices of *everyone* means just that.

Finally, that means we have to do more to change those workplaces, from places where workers feel expendable, devalued, and scorned to places where they feel valued for their contributions. It means confronting the fact that so many observers of workplace violence say they could see it coming, that it was only a matter of time before someone cracked and went postal. Addressing only the individual men will not defuse the seething rage that propels so many in America today, will not prevent their hurt or humiliation from being so readily manipulated into anger.

Much of the anger of America's angry white men comes from feeling entitled, but also feeling disempowered. Addressing this anger requires that we "empower" men to embrace a new definition of masculinity, decoupled from that false sense of entitlement, so that white men may move confidently into the more egalitarian future that is inevitable. At the same time, we must work to restrain those whose policies and programs disenfranchise wide swaths of American men, leaving them lost, itching for something to start.

Addressing the anger of America's angry white men is a national political issue, not a therapeutic one. In some cases, as I've mentioned, their anger is atavistic, nostalgic, reactionary, and ultimately historically irrelevant. (That's true of the men's rights activists, or the fulminators on outrage radio.) But in many cases—especially the working-class and middle-class guys who feel unable to support their families any longer, the younger dads who put in long hours being devoted dads, only to feel screwed by a system that ignores all their "inputs," or the dedicated workers who suddenly lose their health benefits or are outsourced or downsized by a company that cares far more about its CEO's offshore accounts than it does the lives of its own workers— these guys have a legitimate complaint. We need concerted political action to address their anger. We need a new New Deal.

In April 1932, on the eve of announcing the New Deal, Franklin Roosevelt gave a radio address to the nation. The topic was "the forgotten man." Roosevelt spoke with great compassion about the plight of the little guy and argued that our national compassion requires us to harness the entire government to alleviate his suffering. It's time, he argued, "to build from the bottom up and not from the top down" and time that we put our "faith once more in the forgotten man at the bottom of the economic pyramid."

FDR vowed to reverse Hoover's trickle-down supply-side policies of offering "temporary relief from the top down rather than permanent relief from the bottom up." Instead, he advocated massive Keynesian government intervention, to put money in the hands of the people, not the corporations, and thus "restore the purchasing power to the farming half of the country" and keep "the farmer and the homeowner where he is, without being dispossessed through the foreclosure of his mortgage." Government must, he insisted, "provide at least as much assistance to the little fellow as it is now giving to the large banks and corporations."[2]

That's the sort of political engagement that we should expect from our government, the sort of compassion we should expect from those politicians who claim to care so much about the little guy. To really care about them, we need to put the resources of the government at their disposal—making sure they have a safety net that will support and catch them, making sure they have adequate incomes to provide for their families in both sickness and health, making sure their children can go to decent schools, and making sure, at the end of the day, they can look back at their lives and smile with pride that their hard work, dedication, and sacrifice will have earned them the dignity and respect to which they are, indeed, entitled.

NOTES

Preface

1. Arlie Russell Hochschild, *Strangers in Their Own Land: Anger and Mourning on the American Right* (New York: New Press, 2016).

Introduction

1. Check it out: www.youtube.com/watch?v=xqbw4nHrHc0 (not safe for work!).

2. www.census.gov/prod/2012pubs/p60-243.pdf; www2.census.gov/prod2/popscan/p60-085 .pdf.

3. Susan Faludi, *Stiffed: The Betrayal of the American Man* (New York: Crown, 1999), 40.

4. I wish I could say that my comment provided a pivot and that these men were able to see beyond their own myopic anger, but, alas, it did not. However, just after I spoke, an elegantly dressed African American man rose to comment. He said that as a corporate attorney for a very prominent downtown law firm, he often found it difficult to find a taxi that would stop for him going south on Michigan Avenue. He looked at the angry white panelists, steeled his eyes, and said, as I recall, "You think the system is fair and equal because you go to the curb, stick out your hand, and a taxi stops. See, equality. But you never get to see the people for whom the taxis do not stop. You don't see the inequality, so you think the playing field is even—hand out, taxi stops. And that's why you don't see how privileged you are." The largely African American audience burst into applause, and the panelists suddenly appeared quite a bit more sheepish than they had when I had spoken.

5. www.sfgate.com/news/article/Economists-back-tech-industry-s-overseas-hiring-2831699.php.

6. See, for example, Eric Wolf, *Peasant Wars of the Twentieth Century* (New York: Harper and Row, 1979) and *Europe and the People Without History* (Berkeley: University of California Press, 1980).

7. Barrington Moore, *The Social Origins of Democracy and Dictatorship: Lord and Peasant in the Making of the Modern World* (Boston: Beacon, 1966), 505.

8. Carol Gilligan, *Joining the Resistance* (London: Polity), 128–129.

9. Susan Tolchin, *The Angry American: How Voter Rage Is Changing the Nation* (Boulder, CO: Westview Press, 1996), 27.

10. Ibid., 105–106.

11. Willard Gaylin, *The Rage Within: Anger in Modern Life* (New York: Simon and Schuster, 1984), 37.

Chapter 1 Manufacturing Rage

1. Jackson Katz, "Rush Limbaugh and the Mobilization of White Male Anger in the Health Care Debate," *Huffington Post*, September 8, 2009, www.huffingtonpost.com/jackson-katz /rush-limbaugh-and-the-mob_b_279696.html.

2. Jeffrey Berry and Sarah Sobieraj, "Understanding the Rise of Talk Radio," *PS: Political Science and Politics* 44, no. 4 (2011): 762.

3. Pew Research Center for the People and the Press, "In Changing News Landscape, Even Television Is Vulnerable," September 27, 2012, www.people-press.org/2012/09/27.

4. www.quantcast.com/rushlimbaugh.com#!demo.

‌

5. Sarah Sobieraj and Jeffrey Berry, "From Incivility to Outrage: Political Discourse in Blogs, Talk Radio, and Cable News," *Political Communication* 28 (2011): 19.

6. S. Derek Tucker, "Off the Dial: Female and Minority Radio Station Ownership in the United States," www.stopbigmedia.com/files/off_the_dial.pdf.

7. http://nation.foxnews.com/2012-elections/2012/11/07/o-reilly-what-heck-happened-last-night; www.realclearpolitics.com/video/2012/11/07/dennis_miller_reacts_to_romney_losing_election _america_under_obama.html.

8. Sam Donaldson, the venerable TV newsman, replied, "Guys, it's not your country anymore—it's our country and you're part of it, but that thinking is going to defeat Republicans nationally if they don't get rid of it." www.realclearpolitics.com/video/2012/12/26/sam_donaldson_to _tea_partiers_its_not_your_country_anymore_its_our_country.html.

9. Thomas Frank, *What's the Matter with Kansas?* (New York: Henry Holt, 2005), 8.

10. www.washingtonpost.com/wp-dyn/content/article/2009/03/06/AR2009030603435.html.

11. http://mediamatters.org/mmtv/200909150017.

12. www.rushlimbaugh.com/home/daily/site_052909/content/01125106.guest.html.

13. Sharri Paris, "In Bed with Rush Limbaugh," *Tikkun* 10, no. 2 (1995): 33.

14. Only Jackson Katz's columns in the *Huffington Post*, cited above, offer any sort of gender analysis of Limbaugh's politics.

15. Both quoted in Stephen J. Ducat, *The Wimp Factor* (Boston: Beacon Press, 2004), 45, 159.

16. *The Savage Nation*, August 4, 2009; my transcription from the recording.

17. *The Savage Nation*, August 20, 2009, http://mediamatters.org/mmtv/200908210049.

18. Paris, "In Bed with Rush Limbaugh," 35.

19. Joe Klein, "Stalking the Radical Middle," *Newsweek*, September 25, 1995, 32–36.

20. Citizens Project, 1998–1999, 3.

21. Much of this section is condensed from a far-fuller discussion in my *Manhood in America: A Cultural History* (New York: Free Press, 1996).

22. Henry James, *The Bostonians* (1885; reprint, New York: Bantam, 1984), 293.

23. Zane Grey, "Inside Baseball," *Baseball Magazine* 3, no. 4 (1909).

24. G. Stanley Hall, cited in Michael C. C. Adams, *The Great Adventure: Male Desire and the Coming of World War I* (Bloomington: Indiana University Press, 1990), 38.

25. George Evans, "The Wilderness," *Overland Monthly* 43 (January 1904): 33.

26. Billy Sunday quoted in William McLaughlin, *Billy Sunday Was His Real Name* (Chicago: University of Chicago Press, 1955), 141, 179. See also Roger Bruns, *Preacher: Billy Sunday and Big Time American Evangelism* (New York: W. W. Norton, 1992), 15.

27. Samuel Sullivan Cox, *Eight Years in Congress, from 1857 to 1865: Memoir and Speeches* (New York: W. Appleton, 1865), 250.

28. Cited in Alexander Saxton, *The Indispensable Enemy: Labor and the Anti-Chinese Movement in California* (Berkeley: University of California Press, 1971), 59.

29. Lothrop Stoddard, *The Rising Tide of Color* (New York: Scribner's, 1920), 297–298; Madison Grant, *The Passing of the Great Race* (New York: Scribner's, 1916), 68–81; Homer Lea, *The Day of the Saxon* (New York: Harper Brothers, 1912), 71, 234. All these texts are discussed far more fully in my book *Manhood in America*, especially Chapter 3.

30. Southern Poverty Law Center, "American Border Patrol/American Patrol" file, www .splcenter.org/get-informed/intelligence-files/groups/american-border-patrol/american -patrol.

31. Joe Arpaio, GQ, October 9, 2009, www.gq.com/news-politics/big-issues/200911/joe-arpaio -sheriff-phoenix-mexico-border-immigration#ixzz28f5fc0jd.

32. Cited in Len Sherman and Sheriff Joe Arpaio, *Joe's Law: America's Toughest Sheriff Takes on Illegal Immigration, Drugs, and Everything Else That Threatens America* (Saranac Lake, NY: AMACOM Books, 2008), 48.

33. www.minutemanproject.com.

34. Stephen Webster, "Elegy for the White Man," *American Renaissance* (September 2009): n.p., www.amren.com/ar/2009/09/index.html#article2.

35. Peter Roff, "The Tea Party Movement Is a Women's Movement," *U.S. News*, September 23, 2010, www.usnews.com/opnion/blogs/peter-roff/2010/09/23/the-tea-party-movement-is -a-womens-movement.

36. Hanna Rosin, "Is the Tea Party a Feminist Movement?," *Slate*, May 12, 2010, www.slate.com/toolbar.aspx?action=print&id=2253645.

37. Kate Zernike and Megan Thee-Brenan, "Discontent's Demography: Who Backs the Tea Party," *New York Times*, April 15, 2010, 1.

38. Ruth Rosen, "The Tea Party and Angry White Women," *Dissent* 59, no. 1 (2012): 61–65.

39. Arianna Huffington, "Sarah Palin, 'Mama Grizzlies,' Carl Jung, and the Power of Archetypes," *Huffington Post*, October 7, 2012, www.huffingtonpost.com/arianna-huffington/sarah-palin-mama-grizzlie_b_666642.html; Rosin, "Is the Tea Party a Feminist Movement?"

40. See, for example, Melissa Deckman, "Women and the Tea Party: Motherhood, Families, and the Role of Government in America," paper presented at the American Political Science Association's annual meeting, August 30–September 2, 2012.

41. Tammy Bruce, "Why Tea Party Women Lead the Charge," *Guardian*, October 19, 2010, www.guardian.co.uk/commentisfree/cifamerica/2010/oct/19/tea-party-movement-sarah-palin.

Chapter 2 Angry White Boys

1. Ralph Larkin, "The Columbine Legacy: Rampage Shootings as Political Acts," *American Behavioral Scientist* 52, no. 9 (2009): 1311.

2. Thomas Sowell, "Are Today's Mass Shootings a Consequence of '60s Collective Guilt?," *Baltimore Sun*, April 26, 2007, A19; "News of the Weak in Review," *Nation*, November 15, 1999, 5.

3. Michael Gurian, quoted in Richard Lacayo, "Toward the Root of the Evil," *Time*, April 6, 1998, 39; Sissela Bok, *Mayhem: Violence as Public Entertainment* (Cambridge, MA: Perseus, 1999), 78.

4. Michael D. Kelleher, *When Good Kids Kill* (New York: Praeger, 1998), 10.

5. Richard Lacayo, "Toward the Root of the Evil," *Time*, April 6, 1998, 38–39.

6. T. Nansel et al., "Bullying Behaviors Among U.S. Youth: Prevalence and Association with Psychosocial Adjustment," *Journal of the American Medical Association* 285, no. 16 (2001): 2094–2100.

7. David Cullen, *Columbine* (New York: Twelve, 2009).

8. In an article, Peter Langman argues that it was Klebold who was psychotic and Harris merely "psychopathic." Langman, "Rampage School Shooters: A Typology," *Aggression and Violent Behavior* 14 (2009): 79–86.

9. Ibid.

10. Karen Tonso, "Violent Masculinities as Tropes for School Shooters: The Montreal Massacre, the Columbine Attack, and Rethinking Schools," *American Behavioral Scientist* 52, no. 9 (2009): 1278.

11. www.schoolsecurity.org/trends/school_violence.html. (The organization's founder refused to give us permission to reprint his chart.)

12. J. A. Daniels et al., "Content Analysis of News Reports of Averted School Rampages," *Journal of School Violence* 6, no. 1 (2007): 83–99. See also Larkin, "Columbine Legacy."

13. James Gilligan, *Violence* (New York: Vintage, 1998), 77.

14. Katherine Newman et al., *Rampage: The Social Roots of School Shootings* (New York: Basic Books, 2004), 230 and passim. See also Katherine Newman and Cybelle Fox, "Repeat Tragedy: Rampage Shootings in American High School and College Settings, 2002–2008," *American Behavioral Scientist* 52, no. 9 (2009).

15. Adam Lankford and Nayab Hakim, "From Columbine to Palestine: A Comparative Analysis of Rampage Shooters in the United States and Volunteer Suicide Bombers in the Middle East," *Aggression and Violent Behavior* 16, no. 2 (2011): 98–107.

16. Jonah Blank, "The Kid No One Noticed," *U.S. News and World Report*, October 4, 1998, 27.

17. Richard Lacayo, "Toward the Root of the Evil," *Time*, April 6, 1998, 38–39.

18. Mark Ames, "Virginia Tech: Is the Scene of the Crime the Cause of the Crime?," April 20, 2007, www.alternet.org/story/50758/?page=entire.

19. J. Buckley, "The Tragedy in Room 108," *U.S. News and World Report*, November 8, 1993, 41; "Did Taunts Lead to Killing?," *Minneapolis Star-Tribune*, February 4, 1996, 14; S. Fainaru, "Alaska Teen's Path to Murder," *Dallas Morning News*, December 4, 1998, A48.

20. *Time*, December 20, 1999, 50–51.

21. Ralph Larkin, *Comprehending Columbine* (Philadelphia: Temple University Press, 2007), 91.

22. Eric Pooley, "Portrait of a Deadly Bond," *Time*, May 10, 1999, 26–27.

23. Mark Ames, *Going Postal: Rage, Murder, and Rebellion, from Reagan's Workplaces to Clinton's Columbine and Beyond* (Brooklyn, NY: Soft Skull Press, 2005), 187–191.

24. K. Green and B. Lieberman, "Bullying, Ridicule of Williams Were Routine, Friends Say," *San Diego Union-Tribune*, March 10, 2001, A1.

25. This section on Seung-Hui Cho is based on my earlier essay "Profiling School Shooters and Shooters' Schools: The Cultural Context of Aggrieved Entitlement and Restorative Masculinity," in *There's a Gunman on Campus: Tragedy and Terror at Virginia Tech*, edited by Ben Agger and Timothy Luke (Lanham, MD: Rowman and Littlefield, 2008).

26. ABC News, "Last Words of a Killer: Seung-Hui Cho's Shocking Diatribe," http://abcnews-go.com/US/popup?id=3054668.

27. Ames, "Virginia Tech."

28. Larkin, *Comprehending Columbine*, 107, 121.

29. Ibid., 17, 119, 53, 61, 60.

30. Lorraine Adams and Dale Russakoff, "Dissecting Columbine's Cult of the Athlete," *Washington Post*, December 9, 1998, A1.

31. A. Chase, "Violent Reaction: What Do Teen Killers Have in Common?," *In These Times*, July 9, 2001.

32. Bob Herbert, "A Volatile Young Man, Humiliation, and a Gun," *New York Times*, April 19, 2007.

33. The case against the State of Virginia was eventually settled out of court, and the Supreme Court eventually ruled that Congress had overreached its authority by basing the Violence Against Women Act (VAWA) on the Commerce Clause of the US Constitution, thus rendering moot Brzonkala's federal case against the university.

34. *Christy Brzonkala v. Virginia Polytechnic Institute and State University*, 132 F.3d 949 (4th Cir. 1997).

35. See Timothy Luke, "April 16, 2007, at Virginia Tech—To: Multiple Recipients: A Gunman Is Loose on Campus . . . ," in *There Is a Gunman on Campus*, edited by Agger and Luke.

Chapter 3 White Men as Victims

1. Lauren Collins, "Hey, La-a-a-dies!," *New Yorker*, August 8, 2007.

2. www.colbertnation.com/the-colbert-report-videos/379605/march-31-2011/difference-makers-roy-den.-hollander.

3. www.roydenhollander.com.

4. Ibid.

5. *Seidenberg v. McSorley's Old Ale House*, 317 F. Supp. 593 (S.D.N.Y. 1970), was a landmark sex-discrimination case that enabled women to finally enter all places of public accommodation.

6. www.roydenhollander.com.

7. Corey Kilgannon, "Court Rejects Men's Studies Lawsuit," *New York Times*, City Room, April 27, 2009.

8. www.roydenhollander.com.

9. Alan Alda, "What Every Woman Should Know," *Ms.*, October 1975.

10. W. F. Price, "The White Elephant," *The Spearhead*, November 27, 2009, www.the-spearhead.com/2009/11/27/the-white-elephant/.

11. Alan Baron cited in Michael Flood, "Backlash: Angry Men's Movements," in *The Battle and Backlash Rage On*, edited by Stacey Elin Rossi (Bloomington, IN: Xlibris, 2004), 263.

12. "Southern Poverty Law Center Names Men's Rights Activists (MRAs) as Hate Group," http://radfemworldnews.wordpress.com/2012/03/09. See also Southern Poverty Law Center, "Misogyny: The Sites," *Intelligence Report*, no. 145 (Spring 2012).

13. http://manboobz.blogspot.com/search/label/misandry.

14. Asa Baber, *Naked at Gender Gap* (New York: Birch Lane Press, 1992), 27, 50, 112.

15. Ilene Barth, "Now It's the Men Who Want Liberation!," *Parade*, April 2, 1972, 6.

16. Warren Farrell, workshop at the First International Men's Conference, San Antonio, Texas, 1991, author's notes.

17. Richard Doyle, *The Rape of the Male* (St. Paul: Poor Richard's Press, 1986); Mary Sheiner, "What Do Men Really Want—and Why We Should Care," *East Bay Express*, July 10, 1992, 11.

18. Robert Menzies, "Virtual Backlash: Representations of Men's 'Rights' and Feminist 'Wrongs' in Cyberspace," in *Reaction and Resistance: Feminism, Law, and Social Change*, edited by D. E. Chunn, S. B. Boyd, and H. Hessard (Vancouver: University of British Columbia Press, 2007), 65.

19. Amanda Marcotte, personal communication, May 5, 2013.

20. J. Suler, "The Online Disinhibition Effect," *Cyberpsychological Behavior* 7, no. 3 (2004): 321–326.

21. http://mensnewsdaily.com/2010/05/12/how-to-build-a-man-bomb/comment-page-1.

22. Paul Elam, "When Is It OK to Punch Your Wife?," www.avoiceformen.com/feminism/government-tyranny/when-is-ot-ok-to-punch-your-wife.htm.

23. Ian Ironwood, personal correspondence, January 11, 2012.

24. "The Chaplain's Lament," letter to the editor, *New York Times*, June 12, 1992; Warren Farrell, *The Myth of Male Power* (New York: Simon and Schuster, 1993), 298.

25. Farrell, *Myth of Male Power*, 298.

26. Ibid., 310.

27. I have reviewed all the empirical studies that claim to show this "gender symmetry" in my article "'Gender Symmetry' in Domestic Violence," *Violence Against Women* 8, no. 11 (2002). There is a lot less there than meets the eye.

28. Richard J. Gelles, "Domestic Violence: Not an Even Playing Field," Safety Zone, 1999, www.serve.com/zone/everyone/gelles.html.

29. The National Coalition for Free Men, Minnesota chapter, has this on their website: www.ncfm.org/chapters/tc.

30. Actually, that's not true. There is a whole legion of male-bashing academics who argue that males are biologically hardwired for rape and pillage. They're called evolutionary psychologists, and they consider themselves antifeminist. See my chapter "Who Are the Real Male Bashers?," in *Misframing Men* (New Brunswick, NJ: Rutgers University Press, 2011).

31. Molly Dragiewicz, *Equality with a Vengeance: Men's Rights Groups, Battered Women, and Antifeminist Backlash* (Boston: Northeastern University Press, 2011), 1, 3.

32. Farrell, workshop at the First International Men's Conference, notes by the author.

33. Cited in Tom de Castella, "Just Who Are the Men's Rights Activists?," *BBC News Magazine*, May 2, 2012, www.bbc.co.uk/news/magazine-17907534.

34. Alfred Lord Tennyson, "The Princess" (1849).

35. www.insidehighered.com/news/2010/04/08/males#ixzz1ywU2x9pf.

36. See Lionel Tiger, *Men in Groups* (New York: Vintage, 1969) and *The Decline of Males* (New York: Golden Books, 1999).

37. Tiger, *The Decline of Males*, 95.

38. Paul Nathanson and Katherine Young, *Spreading Misandry* (Montreal: McGill University Press, 2001), 8. Much of my analysis of their books is adapted from my essay "Man Trouble," *Common Review* 9, no. 3 (2002).

39. David Gilmore, *Misogyny* (Philadelphia: University of Pennsylvania Press, 1999), 12.

Chapter 4 Angry White Dads

1. See, for example, www.fathers-4-justice.org/f4j/ and www.fathers-4-justice.us/. The protest at the Lincoln Memorial drew only a handful of superhero dads.

2. www.fathers-4-justice.org/our_pledge/index.htm.

3. Jocelyn Crowley, *Defiant Dads: Fathers' Rights Activists in America* (Ithaca, NY: Cornell University Press, 2008), 45. Crowley provides the estimate of ten thousand.

4. Ibid., 243.

5. For this chapter, I interviewed several leaders of the movement by e-mail and telephone and attended meetings of two different fathers' rights groups, one in Long Island and one in the Los Angeles area. I've changed the attendees' names to preserve anonymity, but I've identified the leaders by name.

6. Tim Blackshaw, "Fathers and Childbirth," in *The Social Context of Birth*, edited by C. Squire (Oxford: Radcliffe, 2009), 215–235.

7. Elaine Sorenson, Simone Shaner, and Liliana Sousa, "Assessing Child Support Arrears in Nine Large States and the Nation," paper prepared for the US Department of Health and Human Services, 2007, http://aspe.hhs.gov/hsp/07/assessing-cs-debt/.

8. Jerry Adler, "Building a Better Dad," *Newsweek*, June 17, 1996; Tamar Lewin, "Workers of Both Sexes Make Trade-Offs for Family, Study Shows," *New York Times*, October 29, 1995, 25.

9. Benjamin Spock and Steven J. Parker, *Dr. Spock's Baby and Child Care*, 7th ed. (New York: Pocket Books, 1998), 10.

10. On men's involvement in family work, see Joseph Pleck, "Men's Family Work: Three Perspectives and Some New Data," *Family Coordinator* 28 (1979); "American Fathering in Historical Perspective," in *Changing Men: New Directions in Research on Men and Masculinity*, edited by M. S. Kimmel (Beverly Hills, CA: Sage, 1987); *Working Wives/Working Husbands* (Newbury Park, CA: Sage, 1985); "Families and Work: Small Changes with Big Implications," *Qualitative Sociology* 15 (1992); and "Father Involvement: Levels, Origins, and Consequences," in *The Father's Role*, edited by M. Lamb, 3rd ed. (New York: John Wiley, 1997).

11. www.bls.gov/news.release/atus.nr0.htm/.

12. Julie Press and Eleanor Townsley, "Wives' and Husbands' Housework Reporting: Gender, Class, and Social Desirability," *Gender & Society* 12, no. 2 (1998): 214.

13. *Ladies' Home Journal*, September 1997; John Gray, "Domesticity, Diapers, and Dad," *Toronto Globe and Mail*, June 15, 1996.

14. Carla Shows and Naomi Gerstel, "Fathering, Class, and Gender: A Comparison of Physicians and EMTs," *Gender and Society* 23, no. 2 (2009).

15. Ellen Galinsky, Kerstin Aumann, and James T. Bond, *Times Are Changing: Gender and Generation at Work and at Home* (New York: Families and Work Institute, 2009), 18.

16. See, for example, Anna Gavanas, *Fatherhood Politics in the United States: Masculinity, Sexuality, Race, and Marriage* (Urbana: University of Illinois Press, 2004); and Crowley, *Defiant Dads*.

17. See, for example, Jocelyn Crowley, "Organizational Responses to the Fatherhood Crisis: The Case of Fathers' Rights Groups in the United States," *Marriage and Family Review* 39, nos. 1–2 (2006): 109. Crowley finds that half come only for the support and advice.

18. Cited in Olga Silverstein, "Is a Bad Dad Better than No Dad?," *On the Issues* (Winter 1997): 15; David Blankenhorn, *Fatherless America: Confronting Our Most Urgent Social Problem* (New York: Basic Books, 1993), 30; Robert Bly, *Iron John* (Reading, MA: Addison-Wesley, 1990), 96; David Popenoe, *Life Without Father* (New York: Free Press, 1996), 12.

19. Kristin Luker, "Dubious Conceptions: The Controversy over Teen Pregnancy," *American Prospect* 5 (1991); Paul Amato and Alan Booth, *A Generation at Risk: Growing Up in an Era of Family Upheaval* (Cambridge, MA: Harvard University Press, 1997), 229.

20. David Popenoe, "Evolution of Marriage and Stepfamily Problems," in *Stepfamilies: Who Benefits? Who Does Not?*, edited by A. Booth and J. Dunn (Hillsdale, NJ: Lawrence Erlbaum, 1994), 528.

21. This is, of course, only one cause and surely not the most important. In his book *Divorced Dads*, Sanford Braver found that it ranked tenth on the list of why women initiated divorce, mentioned by about three in ten women, although several of the more common factors, like "gradually growing apart" and "serious differences in lifestyles and/or values," might certainly capture the resentment so often expressed by women who initiate divorces in dramatically unequal families. See Braver, *Divorced Dads* (Los Angeles: Tarcher, 1998).

22. Susan Chira, "War over Role of American Fathers," *New York Times*, June 19, 1994.

23. Blankenhorn, *Fatherless America*, 96, 102.

24. Ibid., 225, 122.

25. Leora Rosen, Molly Dragiewicz, and Jennifer Gibbbs, "Fathers' Rights Groups: Demographic Correlates and Impact on Custody Policy," *Violence Against Women* 15, no. 5 (2009): 513–531.

26. Lundy Bancroft, personal communication, August 21, 2012.

27. www.bls.gov/news.release/empsit.t02.htm.

28. See, for example, Gavanas, *Fatherhood Politics in the United States*; and Ronald Mincy and Hillard Pouncy, "Paternalism, Child Support Enforcement, and Fragile Families," in *The New Paternalism: Supervisory Approaches to Poverty*, edited by L. Mead (Washington, DC: Brookings Institution Press, 1997), 130–160.

29. http://fatherhood.hhs.gov/sipp/PT2.HTM.

30. www.mensrights.com/index.php/Articles/Post-Divorce-Contact-Between-Children-Non-Custodial-Fathers.html.

31. Popenoe, *Life Without Father*, 27; Frank Furstenberg and Andrew Cherlin, *Divided Families: What Happens to Children When Parents Part?* (Cambridge, MA: Harvard University Press, 1991); Debra Umberson and Christine Williams, "Divorced Fathers: Parental Role Strain and Psychological Distress," *Journal of Family Issues* 14, no. 3 (1993).

32. Valerie King, "Nonresident Father Involvement and Child Well-Being," *Journal of Family Issues* 15, no. 1 (1994); Edward Kruk, "The Disengaged Noncustodial Father: Implications for Social Work Practice with the Divorced Family," *Social Work* 39, no. 1 (1994).

33. In his survey, Sanford Braver found that 40 percent of the ex-wives admitted having done that. See Braver, *Divorced Dads*.

34. Crowley, *Defiant Dads*, 119.

35. Ibid., 120.

36. Stephanie Dallam, "Are 'Good Enough' Parents Losing Custody to Abusive Ex-Partners?" (2008), www.leadershipcouncil.org/1/pas/dv.html.

37. See, generally, www.leadershipcouncil.org/1/pas/dv.html. See, specifically, Amy Neustein and Ann Goetting, "Judicial Responses to Protective Parents," *Journal of Child Sexual Abuse* 4 (1999): 103–122; and Nancy Polikoff, "Why Are Mothers Losing? A Brief Analysis of Criteria Used in Child Custody Determinations," *Women's Rights Law Reporter* 14 (1992): 175–184. See also Lundy Bancroft and Jay G. Silverman, *The Batterer as Parent* (Thousand Oaks, CA: Sage, 2002), chap. 5, citing L. Horvath, T. Logan, and R. Walker, "Child Custody Cases: A Content Analysis of Evaluations in Practice," *Professional Psychology Research and Practice* 33, no. 6 (2002): 557–565.

38. Sharon Araji and Rebecca Bosek, "Domestic Violence, Contested Child Custody, and the Courts: Findings from Five Studies," in *Domestic Violence, Abuse, and Child Custody: Legal Strategies and Policy Issues*, edited by M. Hannah and B. Goldstein (New York: Civic Research Institute, 2009).

39. www.courts.wa.gov/wsccr/docs/ResidentialTimeSummaryReport2010.pdf.

40. Robert Griswold, *Fatherhood in America* (New York: Basic Books, 1995), 263; Nancy Polikoff, "Gender and Child Custody Determinations: Exploding the Myths," in *Families, Politics, and Public Policy: A Feminist Dialogue on Women and the State*, edited by I. Diamond (New York: Longman, 1983), 184–185; Robert H. Mnookin et al., "Private Ordering Revisited: What Custodial Arrangements Are Parents Negotiating?," in *Divorce Reform at the Crossroads*, edited by S. Sugarman and H. Kaye (New Haven, CT: Yale University Press, 1990), esp. 55; Eleanor Maccoby and Robert Mnookin, *Dividing the Child: Social and Legal Dilemmas of Custody* (Cambridge, MA: Harvard University Press, 1992), esp. 101.

41. Maccoby quoted in Dirk Johnson, "More and More, the Single Parent Is Dad," *New York Times*, August 31, 1993, A15; Furstenberg and Cherlin, *Divided Families*; Frank Furstenberg, "Good Dads–Bad Dads: Two Faces of Fatherhood," in *The Changing American Family and Public Policy*, edited by A. Cherlin (Lanham, MD: Urban Institute Press, 1988); William J. Goode, "Why Men Resist," in *Rethinking the Family: Some Feminist Questions*, edited by B. Thorne and M. Yalom (New York: Longman, 1982). The European comparison is modified by the fact that the US amounts are significantly higher, and most of the "obligors" do not pay because they simply don't have enough money.

42. Amato and Booth, *Generation at Risk*, 74.

43. www.courts.wa.gov/wsccr/docs/ResidentialTimeSummaryReport2010.pdf.

44. R. Bachman and L. Saltzman, *Bureau of Justice Statistics Special Report: Violence Against Women; Estimates from the Redesigned Survey (NCJ-1543)*.

45. Judith McMullen and Debra Oswald, "Why Do We Need a Lawyer? An Empirical Study of Divorce Cases," *Journal of Law and Family Studies* 57 (2010): 75.

46. See, for example, Joan Kelly and Robert Emery, "Children's Adjustments Following Divorce: Risk and Resiliency Perspectives," *Family Relations* 52, no. 4 (2003): 131; D. Leupnitz, *Child Custody: A Study of Families After Divorce* (Lexington, MA: Lexington Books, 1982); D. Leupnitz, "A Comparison of Maternal, Paternal, and Joint Custody: Understanding the Varieties of Post-Divorce Family Life," *Journal of Divorce* 9 (1986); and V. Shiller, "Loyalty Conflicts and Family Relationships in Latency Age Boys: A Comparison of Joint and Maternal Custody," *Journal of Divorce* 9 (1986).

47. Joan Kelly, "Longer-Term Adjustment in Children of Divorce: Converging Findings and Implications for Practice," *Journal of Family Psychology* 2, no. 2 (1988): 136; Nancy Crowell

and Ethel Leeper, eds., *America's Fathers and Public Policy,* Report of a Workshop, National Research Council, Institute of Medicine (Washington, DC: National Academy Press, 1994), 27.

Chapter 5 Targeting Women

1. "Shooting Rampage at Killeen Luby's Left 24 Dead," *Houston Chronicle,* August 11, 2001, www .chron.com/life/article/Shooting-rampage-at-Killeen-Luby-s-left-24-dead-2037092.php.

2. www.menweb.org/waragain.htm.

3. www.amptoons.com/blog/2009/08/06/mens-rights-activists-anti-feminists-and-other-mis ogynists-comment-on-george-sodini/.

4. http://msmagazine.com/blog/blog/2010/05/17/lexus-lacoste-and-lacrosse-the-entitled-elite -male-athlete.

5. www.statcan.gc.ca/daily-quotidien/121204/dq121204a-eng.htm; www.aic.gov.au/publications /current%20series/cfi/181-200/cfi182.html;   www.unodc.org/documents/data-and-analysis /statistics/Homicide/Globa_study_on_homicide_2011_web.pdf.

6. Lundy Bancroft, *Why Does He Do That? Inside the Minds of Angry and Controlling Men* (New York: Putnam, 2002), 7; Janet Weber and Jane Kelley, *Health Assessment in Nursing,* 4th ed. (New York: Lippincott, 2010).

7. E. G. Krug et al., *World Report on Violence and Health* (Geneva: World Health Organization, 2002); James Ridgeway, "Mass Murderers and Women," *Mother Jones,* April 20, 2007.

8. Jenny Lewis and Terry Allen, "Dimensions of Spousal Homicide," *Social Dialogue* 1, no. 2 (2008). See also R. E. Dobash et al., "Not an Ordinary Killer—Just an Ordinary Guy: When Men Murder an Intimate Woman Partner," *Violence Against Women* 10 (2004): 577–605.

9. R. Bachman and L. E. Saltzman, *Violence Against Women: A National Crime Victimization Survey Report* (NCJ 154348) (Washington, DC: US Department of Justice, 1994); Murray Straus and Richard Gelles, eds., *Physical Violence in American Families* (New Brunswick, NJ: Transaction, 1990); A. L. Kellerman and J. A. Marcy, "Men, Women, and Murder: Gender Specific Differences in Rates of Fatal Violence and Victimization," *Journal of Trauma* 33, no. 1 (1992). See also Evan Stark and Anne Flitcraft, "Violence Among Intimates: An Epidemiological Review," in *Handbook of Family Violence,* edited by V. van Hasselt et al. (New York: Plenum, 1988).

10. M. Wilson and M. Daly, "Spousal Homicide Risk and Estrangement," *Violence and Victims* 8, no. 1 (1993): 3–15. See also T. K. Shakleford, "Partner Killing by Women in Cohabiting Relationships," *Homicide Studies* 5 (2001): 253–266.

11. R. Emerson Dobash et al., "The Myth of Sexual Symmetry in Marital Violence," *Social Problems* 39 (1992): 81. See also R. Emerson Dobash and Russell Dobash, *Violence Against Wives* (New York: Free Press, 1979) and "The Case of Wife Beating," *Journal of Family Issues* 2 (1981).

12. Walter DeKeserdy and Martin Schwartz, *Contemporary Criminology* (Mountain View, CA: Wadsworth, 1996).

13. Lundy Bancroft, personal interview, June 10, 2011.

14. Richard Slotkin, *Regeneration Through Violence: The Mythology of the Frontier, 1600–1860* (New York: Atheneum, 1973) and *Gunfighter Nation: The Myth of the Frontier in Twentieth Century America* (New York: Atheneum, 1992).

15. Margaret Mead, *And Keep Your Powder Dry* (New York: William Morrow, 1965), 151, 157.

16. Fox Butterfield, *All God's Children* (New York: Alfred A. Knopf, 1995), 206–207; Kit Roane, "New York Gangs Mimic California Original," *New York Times,* September 14, 1997, A37. Others cited in Jack Katz, *Seductions of Crime* (New York: Basic Books, 1988), 88, 107; Vic Seidler, "Raging Bull," *Achilles Heel* 5 (1980): 9; and Hans Toch, "Hypermasculinity and Prison Violence," in *Masculinities and Violence,* edited by L. Bowker (Newbury Park, CA: Sage, 1998), 170.

17. J. Adams Puffer, *The Boy and His Gang* (Boston: Houghton Mifflin, 1912), 91.

18. James Gilligan, *Violence* (New York: Putnam, 1996).

19. Ibid., 67, 110, cited in E. Anthony Rotundo, *American Manhood* (New York: Basic Books, 1993), 264; Darcia Harris Bowman, "Male Adolescent Identity and the Roots of Aggression: A Conversation with James Garbarino," in *Adolescents at School,* edited by Michael Sadowski (Cambridge, MA: Harvard Education Press, 2004), 79.

20. Robert Sapolsky, *The Trouble with Testosterone* (New York: Simon and Schuster, 1997), 155.

21. Cited in Mark Totten, *Guys, Gangs, and Girlfriend Abuse* (Toronto: University of Toronto Press, 2002), 11–12.

22. Diana Scully, *Understanding Sexual Violence* (New York: Routledge, 1990), 74, 140, 166, 159.

23. Bancroft, *Why Does He Do That?*, 61.

24. Because these were all court-mandated batterers, I have no information about whether this powerful moment actually produced any sort of epiphany for any of the men, especially Al. I've wondered about this in the ensuing years. One of the difficulties of this sort of work is that you can never really measure its effectiveness. How do you measure the number of women who have *not* been hit?

25. Data from the *New York Times*, August 25, 1997; Reva Siegel, "The 'Rule of Love': Wife Beating as Prerogative and Privacy," *Yale Law Journal* 105, no. 8 (1996); Deborah Rhode, *Speaking of Sex: The Denial of Gender Inequality* (Cambridge, MA: Harvard University Press, 1997), 108; June Stephenson, *Men Are Not Cost Effective* (Fullerton, CA: Diemer Smith, 1991), 285. See also Neil Websdale and Meda Chesney-Lind, "Doing Violence to Women: Research Synthesis on the Victimization of Women," in *Masculinities and Violence*, edited by Bowker.

26. Susan Steinmetz, "The Battered Husband Syndrome," *Victimology* 2 (1978); M. D. Pagelow, "The 'Battered Husband Syndrome': Social Problem or Much Ado About Little?," in *Marital Violence*, edited by N. Johnson (London: Routledge and Kegan Paul, 1985); Elizabeth Pleck et al., "The Battered Data Syndrome: A Comment on Steinmetz's Article," *Victimology* 2 (1978); G. Storch, "Claim of 12 Million Battered Husbands Takes a Beating," *Miami Herald*, August 7, 1978; Jack C. Straton, "The Myth of the 'Battered Husband Syndrome,'" *Masculinities* 2, no. 4 (1994); Kerrie James, "Truth or Fiction: Men as Victims of Domestic Violence?," *Australian and New Zealand Journal of Family Therapy* 17, no. 3 (1996); Betsy Lucal, "The Problem with 'Battered Husbands,'" *Deviant Behavior* 16 (1995): 95–112. Since the first edition of this book was published, I became increasingly distressed that social science research was being so badly misused for political ends. So I undertook an attempt to thoroughly investigate the case of "gender symmetry." See Michael Kimmel, "'Gender Symmetry' in Domestic Violence: A Substantive and Methodological Research Review," *Violence Against Women* 8, no. 11 (2002): 1332–1363. Useful current data can be found in Callie Marie Rennison, *Intimate Partner Violence and Age of Victim, 1993–1999* (Washington, DC: US Department of Justice, Bureau of Justice Statistics, October 2001).

27. www.csulb.edu/~mfiebert/assault.htm.

28. See James, "Truth or Fiction," who found the same results in a sample of Australian and New Zealand couples.

29. The results of my inquiry into this annotated bibliography are contained in my essay "'Gender Symmetry' in Domestic Violence."

30. Daniel O'Leary, "Are Women Really More Aggressive Than Men in Intimate Relationships?," *Psychological Bulletin* 126 (2000): 685–689; Daniel O'Leary et al., "Prevalence and Stability of Physical Aggression Between Spouses: A Longitudinal Analysis," *Journal of Consulting and Clinical Psychology* 57 (1989): 263–268; Andrea Tyree and Jean Malone, "How Can It Be That Wives Hit Husbands as Much as Husbands Hit Wives and None of Us Knew It?," paper presented at the annual meeting of the American Sociological Association, 1989.

31. J. E. Stets and Murray Straus, "The Marriage License as a Hitting License: A Comparison of Assaults in Dating, Cohabiting, and Married Couples," *Journal of Family Violence* 4, no. 2 (1989) and "Gender Differences in Reporting Marital Violence and Its Medical and Psychological Consequences," in *Physical Violence in American Families*, edited by Straus and Gelles.

32. US Department of Justice, Bureau of Justice Statistics, *Family Violence*, 1984.

33. Glenda Kaufman Kantor, Jana Janinski, and E. Aldorondo, "Sociocultural Status and Incidence of Marital Violence in Hispanic Families," *Violence and Victims* 9, no. 3 (1994); Jana Janinski, "Dynamics of Partner Violence and Types of Abuse and Abusers," www.nnfr.org/nnfr/research/pv_ch1.html; Kersti Yllo, personal communication, March 2002.

34. C. Saline, "Bleeding in the Suburbs," *Philadelphia Magazine*, March 1984, 82; Murray Straus, Richard J. Gelles, and Suzanne K. Steinmetz, *Behind Closed Doors: Violence in the American Family* (New Brunswick, NJ: Transaction, 2006); R. L. Hampton, "Family Violence and Homicides in the Black Community: Are They Linked?," in *Violence in the Black Family: Correlates and Consequences* (Lexington, MA: Lexington Books, 1987); R. L. Hampton and Richard Gelles, "Violence Towards Black Women in a Nationally Representative Sample of Black Families," *Journal of Comparative Family Studies* 25, no. 1 (1994).

35. Noel Cazenave and Murray Straus, "Race, Class, Network Embeddedness, and Family Violence: A Search for Potent Support Systems," in *Physical Violence in American Families*, edited by Straus and Gelles; Pam Belluck, "Women's Killers and Very Often Their Partners," *New York Times*, March 31, 1997, B1.

36. Vicki Haddock, "Survey Tracks Gay Domestic Violence," *San Francisco Examiner*, October 22, 1996.

Chapter 6 Mad Men

1. www.nydailynews.com/news/national/2010/02/18/2010-02-18_austin_plane_crash_full_text _joe_stack_manifesto_posted_on_website_embeddedartco.html#ixzz0wyfdX8Op.

2. Mark Ames, *Going Postal: Rage, Murder, and Rebellion, from Reagan's Workplaces to Clinton's Columbine and Beyond* (Brooklyn, NY: Soft Skull Press, 2005). Ames's book is perhaps the most thorough accounting of these murderous sprees out there, and his analysis points decidedly toward an understanding of the interplay between the deranged killers and the insane circumstances that contributed to their growing feverishness.

3. A report from Handgun-Free America notes that more than 90 percent of all workplace shooters were male and that more than 13 percent involved some type of domestic violence. Handgun-Free America, *Terror Nine to Five: Guns in the American Workplace, 1994–2003* (Arlington, VA: Handgun-Free America, 2004).

4. These comments are at www.ex-christian.net/5085-if-ward-cleaver-were-alive-today/.

5. D. S. Hamermesh and N. M. Soss, "An Economic Theory of Suicide," *Journal of Political Economy* 82 (1974): 83–98; I. M. Wasserman, "Influence of Economic Business Cycles on U.S. Suicide Rates," *Suicide and Life-Threatening Behavior* 14 (1984): 143–156.

6. Cited in "Farm Foreclosures," *Progressive Populist*, January 18, 2011, www.progressivepopulist .blogspot.com/2011/01/farm-foreclosures.html.

7. John D. Ragland and Alan L. Berman, "Farm Crisis and Suicide: Dying on the Vine?," *Omega: Journal of Death and Dying* 22, no. 1 (1990–1991): 173–185.

8. "Farmer Suicide Rate Swells in 1980s, Study Says," *New York Times*, October 14, 1991.

9. See "Daily Focus: Suicides a Tragic Result of Farm Economy," www.extension.org/pages /Dairy_Focus/; and "Farmer Suicides Increase in Poor Economy," www.foodsafetynews.com /2010/01.

10. See "Suicides Raise Worries About Recession's Real Cost," www.msnbc.com/id/33738656/.

11. Alice Walton, "The Gender Inequality of Suicide: Why Men Are at Such High Risk," *Forbes*, September 24, 2012, www.forbes.com/sites/alicegwalton/2012/09/24/the-gender-inequality -of-suicide-why-are-men-at-such-high-risk/.

12. Maggie Fox, "Middle-Aged Suicides on Rise in U.S., Study Finds," www.reuters.com/article /idUSTRE68Q5OK20100927; Tara Parker-Pope, "Suicide Rates Rise Sharply in the U.S.," *New York Times*, May 2, 2013.

13. See Guoqing Hu et al., "Mid-life Suicide: An Increasing Problem in U.S. Whites, 1999–2005," *American Journal of Preventive Medicine* (2008); and Julie Phillips et al., "Understanding Recent Changes in Suicide Rates Among the Middle-Aged: Period or Cohort Effects," *Public Health Reports* 125 (September 2010): 680–688.

14. See http://theweek.com/article/index/206180/is-the-recession-fueling-a-suicide-epidemic.

15. See, for example, Justin Denney, "Family and Household Formations and Suicide in the United States," *Journal of Marriage and Family* 72 (February 2010): 202–213; Justin Denney et al., "Adult Suicide Mortality in the United States: Marital Status, Family Size, Socioeconomic Status, and Differences by Sex," *Social Science Quarterly* 90, no. 5 (2009): 1167–1185.

16. Terrence Real, *I Don't Want to Talk About It: Overcoming the Secret Legacy of Male Depression* (New York: Simon and Schuster, 1997), 22.

17. Craig Evan Pollack and Julia Lynch, "Health Status of People Undergoing Foreclosure in the Philadelphia Region," *American Journal of Public Health* 99, no. 10 (2009).

18. Ronald Levant, "Nonrelational Sexuality," in *Men and Sex: New Psychological Perspectives*, edited by G. Brooks and R. Levant (New York: John Wiley, 1997).

19. Anna Quindlen, "The Great White Myth," *New York Times*, January 15, 1992.

20. David Fincher, interview in *Film Comment*, October–November 1999.

21. Ames, *Going Postal*, 114–115.

Chapter 7 The White Wing

1. Richard Hofstadter, "The Paranoid Style in American Politics," *Harper's Magazine*, November 1964, 77.

2. Ibid., 85.

3. Ibid., 81. See also Daniel Bell, ed., *The Radical Right* (New York: Criterion Books, 1955).

4. All quotes from Southern Poverty Law Center, "Reaping the Whirlwind," *Intelligence Report* (Winter 2001).

5. Ibid.

6. Jim Ridgeway, "Osama's New Recruits," *Village Voice*, November 6, 2001, 41.

7. Listen to David Duke on the "morning after" the election: www.stormfront.org/audio /stormfront_radio-dr_david_duke-11-04-08-obama_response.mp3.

8. www.davidduke.com/?p=5524.

9. Daily Kos, "Remember the DHS Right Wing Extremist Report?," August 6, 2012, www.dailykos .com/story/2012/08/06/1117242/-Remember-the-DHS-Right-Wing-Extremist-Report.

10. Charles M. Blow, "Whose Country Is It?," *New York Times*, March 26, 2010.

11. See Pete Simi and Robert Futrell, *American Swastika: Inside the White Power Movement's Hidden Spaces of Hate* (Lanham, MD: Rowman and Littlefield, 2010), 25.

12. Ibid., 85.

13. Osha Gray Davidson, *Broken Heartland: The Rise of America's Rural Ghetto* (Iowa City: University of Iowa Press, 1986), 109, 118.

14. Matthew Snipp, "Understanding Race and Ethnicity in Rural America," *Rural Sociology* 61, no. 1 (1996): 127, 122; Davidson, *Broken Heartland*, 120.

15. See Michael Barkun, *Religion and the Racist Right: The Origins of the Christian Identity Movement* (Chapel Hill: University of North Carolina Press, 1997); Chip Berlet, "Christian Identity: The Apocalyptic Style, Political Religion, Palingenesis, and Neo-Fascism," in *Fascism, Totalitarianism, and Political Religion*, edited by Roger Griffin (London: Routledge, 2005).

16. William J. Gibson, *Warrior Dreams: Violence and Manhood in Post-Vietnam America* (New York: Hill and Wang, 1994), 10.

17. Jonathan Mozzachi and L. Events Rhinegard, *Rambo, Gnomes, and the New World Order: The Emerging Politics of "Populism"* (Portland, OR: Coalition for Human Dignity, 1991), 4.

18. Although there is no research documenting the number of militia and Patriot group members with military experience, a quick perusal of militia websites reveals anecdotal evidence. For example, in the "Meet the Commander" section of the Michigan Militia Corps' homepage, readers are told that "during the Viet Nam War, Lynn had a farmer's deferment, but he decided to give it up when he was 20 to be drafted. . . . Lynn spent 1 1/2 years in Viet Nam between 1967–69 and was given an Honorable Discharge with a Purple Heart. After his discharge, he came back to Michigan and worked on a farm until September of 1978 when he developed 'Stiff Man's Syndrome,' a rare neuro-muscular disease that incapacitates the effected individual. He was confined to a wheelchair until 1991 . . . [when] he started his gun store" (July 11, 1999). Other sites, like the webpage of the Ohio Unorganized Militia, fly a "POW/MIA" flag, with the words "We will never forget" beneath it.

19. Barbara Ehrenreich, "Veiled Threat," *Los Angeles Times*, November 4, 2001.

20. Erik Erikson, *Childhood and Society* (New York: W. W. Norton, 1950), 314–315.

21. Eric Ramirez-Flores, *Troubled Fields: Men, Emotions, and the Crisis of American Farming* (New York: Columbia University Press, 2005); Davidson, *Broken Heartland*, 75.

22. Cited in Dyer, *Harvest of Rage*, 64.

23. Ibid.

24. William Gibson, *Warrior Dreams*, 97. See also more generally on gender and anger Jerry Lembke, *Hanoi Jane: War, Sex, and Fantasies of Betrayal* (Amherst: University of Massachusetts Press, 2010); and Chip Berlet, "Mapping the Political Right: Gender and Race Oppression in Right-Wing Movements," in *Home Grown Hate: Gender and Organized Racism*, edited by Abby Ferber (New York: Routledge, 2004).

25. Daniel Junas, "Rise of Citizen Militias: Angry White Guys with Guns," *Covertaction Quarterly*, April 24, 1995, www.publiceye.org/rightist/dj_mili.html. See also Evelyn Schlatter, *Aryan Cowboys: White Supremacists and the Search for a New Frontier, 1970–2000* (Austin: University of Texas Press, 2006).

26. Betty Dobratz and Stephanie L. Shanks-Meile, *The White Separatist Movement in the United States* (Baltimore: Johns Hopkins University Press, 2001), 115, 10.

27. See Brandon Stickney, *"All-American Monster": The Unauthorized Biography of Timothy McVeigh* (Amherst, NY: Prometheus Books, 1996), 59.

28. http://abcnews.go.com/US/story?id=93140&page=1#.UZfdEWjD_cs.

29. Catherine McNichol Stock, *Rural Radicals: Righteous Rage in the American Grain* (Ithaca, NY: Cornell University Press), 16.

30. Cited in Betty A. Dobratz and Stephanie L. Shanks-Meile, "The White Separatist Movement: Worldviews on Gender, Nature, and Change," in *Home Grown Hate*, edited by Ferber, 131.

31. Cited in Deborah Kaplan, "Republic of Rage: A Look Inside the Patriot Movement," paper presented at the annual meeting of the American Sociological Association, August 21–25, 1998, 34.

32. Jeff Coplon, "The Roots of Skinhead Violence: Dim Economic Prospects for Young Men," *Utne Reader*, May–June 1989, 84.

33. Lillian Rubin, *Families on the Fault Line* (New York: HarperCollins, 1994), 186.

34. Pat Buchanan, "A Brief for Whitey," March 21, 2008, http://buchanan.org./blog/pjb-a-brief -for-whitey-969.

35. Cynthia Enloe, *Bananas, Beaches, and Bases* (Berkeley: University of California Press, 1989), 44.

36. William Pierce, *The Turner Diaries* (Hillsboro, WV: National Vanguard Books, 1978), 33.

37. Randy Duey, "Yahweh, Give Us Men!," *Aryan Nations*, no. 36 (1979): 18.

38. Samuel S. Cox, "Emancipation and Its Results—Is Ohio to Be Africanized?," June 3, 1862, http://teachingamericanhistory.org/library/document/emancipation-and-its-results-is-ohio -to-be-africanized/.

39. Cited in Richard Hofstadter, *Social Darwinism in America* (Boston: Beacon Press, 1955), 51; George Frederickson, *The Inner Civil War: Northern Intellectuals and the Crisis of the Union* (Urbana: University of Illinois Press, 1993), 192–193.

40. Lothrop Stoddard, *The Rising Tide of Color* (New York: Scribner's, 1920), 297–298; Madison Grant, *The Passing of the Great Race* (New York: Scribner's, 1916), 68, 81; Homer Lea, *The Day of the Saxon* (New York: Harper Brothers, 1912), 234, 71.

41. George Lydston, *Diseases of Society and Degeneracy* (Philadelphia: Lippincott, 1904), 424. If they were executed, they'd be "forgotten," he continued, but "unsexed and free they would be a constant warning and ever-present admonition to others of their race."

42. Donnelley is cited in Ronald Takaki, *Strangers from a Different Shore* (Boston: Little, Brown, 1989), 249; Gompers is cited in Alexander Saxton, *The Indispensible Enemy* (Berkeley: University of California Press, 1971), 276, 59.

43. Agassiz is cited in Stephen Jay Gould, *The Mismeasure of Man* (New York: W. W. Norton, 1981), 49; the editor is cited in Richard Slotkin, *The Fatal Environment* (New York: Atheneum, 1985), 185.

44. See John C. Lester and David Wilson, *The Ku Klux Klan* (1884; reprint, New York: Neale, 1905), 155.

45. Susan Faludi, *Stiffed: The Betrayal of the American Man* (New York: Crown, 1991), 415.

46. Texe Marrs, *Big Sister Is Watching You: Hillary Clinton and the White House Feminists Who Now Control America—and Tell the President What to Do* (Austin, TX: Living Truth, 1993), 11, 14–15.

47. *WAR* 8, no. 2 (1989): 11; N. S. Mobilizer cited in Ferber, *Home Grown Hate*, 81; Pierce, *The Turner Diaries*, 1978, 58; *Thunderbolt* cited in Ferber, *Home Grown Hate*, 76; *New Order* cited in Ferber, *Home Grown Hate*, 91.

48. Cited in Ferber, *Home Grown Hate*, 149. See also Jessica Stern, *Terror in the Name of God* (New York: Harper, 2004).

49. Cited in Ferber, *Home Grown Hate*, 140.

50. Pierce, *The Turner Diaries*, 1978, 42, cited in Ferber, *Home Grown Hate*, 125–126.

51. Cited in *Detroit Metrotimes*, 1995, 46.

52. Evelyn Rich, "Ku Klux Klan Ideology, 1954–1988" (PhD diss., Boston University, 1988); Rory McVeigh, *The Rise of the Ku Klux Klan: Right Wing Movements and National Politics* (Minneapolis: University of Minnesota Press, 2009), 74.

53. Stern, *Terror in the Name of God*, 69.

54. Eugene Kinerk, "The Aryan Woman in Perspective," *Aryan Nations*, no. 43 (1979): 7; Hitler cited in Jack Rader, "The Plot Against Aryan Masculinity," *Aryan Nations*, no. 37 (1985): 17, 18.

55. Rader, "Plot Against Aryan Masculinity," 17.

56. Tom Metzger, "What We Believe as White Racists," in *Extreme Deviance*, edited by Erich Goode and D. Angus Vail (Thousand Oaks, CA: Pine Forge Press, 2008), 131.

57. Kathleen Blee, *Inside Organized Racism: Women in the Hate Movement* (Berkeley: University of California Press, 2006).

58. Ladies of the Invisible Empire, http://swkloties2.homestead.com/MAIN~ns4.html; Aryan Confederations, www.geocities.com.arcon_wp/policies.htm.

59. See *White Sisters* (newsletter of the Aryan Women's League) (Winter 1991), available at Kenneth Spencer Research Library, University of Kansas.

60. Blee, *Inside Organized Racism*, 71, 77.

61. Memo from Randi Fishman, July 24, 2008.

62. Blee, *Inside Organized Racism*, 93, 114, 143.

63. Ibid., 105.

64. Ibid., 140, 139.

65. *Rational Feminist*, Winter 1991, Spring 1995, Summer 1998, Spring 1998, Yuletide 1997, Yuletide 2000, all available at Kenneth Spencer Research Library, University of Kansas.

66. Betty A. Dobratz and Stephanie L. Shanks-Meile, "White Separatist Movement," in *Home-Grown Hate*, edited by Ferber, 118.

67. John Elgion, "Investigators Seek Clues in Gunman's Last Weeks Before Temple Murders," *New York Times*, August 9, 2012, A17.

Epilogue

1. Charles M. Blow, "Whose Country Is It?," *New York Times*, March 27, 2010.

2. Franklin Delano Roosevelt, "The Forgotten Man," radio address, April 7, 1932, http://newdeal.feri.org/speeches/1932c.htm.

INDEX

ABC's Wide World of Sports, 20, 48
Affirmative action
    blamed for Lepine's rejection from
        school, 171
    as reverse discrimination, 17
    for women in higher education, 128
    as world history, 8–9
African American men
    changing involvement in family lives,
        144–145
    domestic violence rates, 194
    promote fathers' responsibility, 29, 147,
        155–156
    rights claimed by white men, 124
    unemployment rates, 155
    white supremacists' racist portrayals,
        258–262
African American women, 8
Agassiz, Louis, 259
Aggression
    perceived as legitimate when retaliatory,
        177–178
    and testosterone, 120, 180–181
Aggrieved entitlement
    introduced, 18–21
    combined with misdirected rage, 276
    felt by poor people, people of color vs.
        angry white men, 62–63
    fuels rage of white middle- and lower-
        class men, 277
    of men perceiving women's rejection,
        170–173
    mobilizes politically, 21–25
    of nativists, 53
    transformed into mass murders by boys,
        75, 93
    needs decoupling from masculinity, 283
    See also Language of aggrieved
        entitlement

Airlines, 210–212
Alan Harper (*Two and a Half Men* character),
        105, 106
Alda, Alan, 106
Alexithymia, 218
Alger, Horatio, 19, 48
Alimony, 140–141, 158, 165
Allport, Gordon, 276
Al-Qaeda as allies to white supremacists,
        236, 277
American Dream
    believing in, 11–14
    disappears, according to white
        supremacists, 229
    of endless upward mobility, 19–20
    in *Falling Down*, 60–61
    of men's rights activists, 112
    for middle-class white men, 15, 202
American Farmer: 20th Century Slave
        (Wisconsin Militia), 262
American Nazi Party, 229, 231
American Revolution. *See* Second American
        Revolution (R-2)
American White Power movement. *See*
        White supremacists
Ames, Mark, 84
Angry American white boys
    Farmingville attacks, murder, 57
    needing to escape feminizing women,
        49
    as rampage shooters, 69–82
    as sons of angry men, 5, 26
    transform aggrieved entitlement into
        mass murders, 75, 93
Angry American women, 6, 63–67
Angry white men radio. *See* Talk radio
Anthony, Susan B., 134
Anti-Communist paranoid movements,
        230–231

301

Anti-immigrant nativism
    exclusion strategy, 51–53
    extremists, 237–238
    Know-Nothings of 1840s, 51, 64–65, 258
    language used, 53
    linked by racism, sexism, 40, 43, 54–55,
        258–259
Anti-male double standards, 125
Anti-Semitic extreme Right, 236–237, 243,
    262
Anti-Semitism
    with Aryans viewing al-Qaeda as
        potential ally, 236, 277
    denial of Holocaust but praise of Hitler,
        273
    as exclusion strategy to protect white
        race, masculinity, 51–52
    and Jewish conspiracies, 44–45, 185,
        242, 257, 263
    Jews portrayed as hypermasculine-
        hypomasculine, 259, 262–263
    media-control stereotype, 239
Are Men Necessary? (Dowd), 111
Arpaio, Joe, 12, 54–55
Aryan Nations, 235, 238, 257, 268–270
Aryan Women's League, 269, 270, 273–274
Asian American men
    gendered as hypomasculine, 51, 85–86
    immigrants, 47, 61, 259
Athletes against men's violence against
    women, 197–198
Augusta National Golf Club male-only
    policy, 224
Aurora, Colorado theater shooting, 227
Austin, Texas IRS-airplane rampage,
    199–202
Auvinen, Pekka-Eric, 96

Baber, Asa, 110
Babies and Child Care (Spock), 143
Bachman, Michele, 63
Bancroft, Lundy, 186
Barber, Benjamin, 277
Baron, Alan, 108
Barton, Mark, 176
Battered men. See Violence by women
    against men
Battered-husband syndrome, 190–191
Batterers' intervention programs, 187, 195,
    196–198
Beck, Glenn, 1, 205, 231
Beck, Matthew, 205–206, 208
Bell, Daniel, 231
Beneke, Tim, 182–183
Berry, Jeffrey, 33
Bethel, Alaska school shooting, 79

Big Sister Is Watching You (Marrs), 261
BIRGing, 91
Birth control. See Reproductive rights
"A Black Woman Stole My Job" talk show
    program, 17, 177
Blankenhorn, David, 150–151
Blee, Kathleen, 269–270, 271
Blow, Charles, 279
Bly, Robert, 16, 105–106
Bok, Sissela, 70
Boone and Crockett Club, 50
Booth v. Hvass, 120–121
Border closings, 51
Border patrols, 12, 53–58, 279
"Born in the U.S.A." song (Springsteen), 221
Boston Tea Party, 55
The Bostonians (James), 47
Botkin, Steven, 196
Bowling Alone (Putnam), 270
Boy Scouts of America, 49–50, 280–281
Boyle, T. Coraghessan, 49
Boys
    culturally prescribed fighting, 178–179
    educating, 123
    fight for conflict resolution, 75
    See also Angry American white boys
Bradley effect, 6
Brady Bill, 24
"A Brief for Whitey" (Buchanan), 254–255
Brown, Brooks, 93
Brown, Harley, 55
Brown, Otho, 206
Brown supremacists, 42
Brzonkala, Christy, 94–95
Buchanan, Pat, 254–255
Bullying and torture
    as factor contributing to rampage
        shootings, 77–79
    homophobic (see Gay baiting)
    ignored by school administrators, 84, 95
    as pattern in shootings, 77–80, 82–85
    by sons of angry white men, 26
Burk, Martha, 224
The Burning Bed movie, 174
Bush, George H. W., 232
Bush, George W., 10, 84, 234
Butler, Richard, 238
Butts, Calvin, 155

Caesar's Column (Donnelly), 259
Canada
    female spousal homicide victims rates,
        173, 174
    Montreal rampage shooting, 171, 197
    rifles per capita, 70
Canada, Geoffrey, 155

Capitalism
  creative destruction of, 19
  of white supremacists, 252, 254, 262
    (*see also* Corporations and capitalist
    elites)
Carender, Keli, 64
Carneal, Michael, 74–75, 78, 93
Catholicism, 230, 231, 243
Cazenave, Noel, 155, 194–195
Charles Atlas ads, 48–49, 266
Charlie Harper (*Two and a Half Men*
  character), 105, 107
Cheney, Dick, 6, 234, 235
Cheney, Liz, 6
Cherlin, Andrew, 162–163
Child abuse
  not a focus of father's rights activists,
    155, 159–160
  not present in school shooters' lives, 71
  as underreported, 164
Childhood and Society (Erikson), 246
Chinese men, 51
Cho, Seung-Hui, 73, 74–75, 84–87, 92
Christian Identity Church, 243, 268, 269,
  271
Christianity
  forced conversion to, 235
  and Klan rhetoric, 259
  values for batterers, 196
  white supremacists preach racial purity,
    243
  women's roles, 271–272
  See also Evangelical Protestants
City Slickers movie, 20
Civil rights of white middle-class men,
  99–101
Clarke, Edward H., 126–127
Class inequality
  as central to white men's anger, 25
  economic gap widens, 203, 281
Clay, Henry, 18–19
Clemenceau, Georges, 258
Clinton, Bill, 70, 261
Clinton, Hillary, 117, 261
Clinton administration, 233, 234, 261
Coalition for Free Men, 111, 138
Colbert, Stephen, 32–33, 100, 210–211, 212
Collier Township, Pennsylvania gym
  rampage, 169
Columbia University women's and gender
  studies (WGS), 101–102
Columbine (Cullen), 71–72
Columbine High School shootings
  background, 69–70, 93
  administrators, teachers, collude with
    bullying, 90–92

bullying as factor, 79–81
  religious intolerance as factor, 91
  used as model by other shooters, 76
  See also Harris, Eric; Klebold, Dylan
Compositional fallacy, 121
Conflict Tactics Scale (CTS), 191–194
Connecticut beer distributor shootings, 206
Connecticut State Lottery shootings,
  205–206
Conservative feminism, 66
Conspiratorial Council on Foreign
  Relations, 261
Consumerist femininity, 108
Cook, Misty, 275
Cooksey, John, 235
Corporations and capitalist elites
  betray American men, 13–14
  and economic dispossession of middle
    class, 253–254, 276, 281
  fund faux populism, 12
  not blamed for problems by radio ragers,
    37–38
  perceived as downsizing, outsourcing,
    American men out of jobs, 16, 209
Correlation implies causation fallacy, 130
Coulter, Ann, 235
Counseling in schools, 90
Court system. *See* Family-court systems
Cox, Samuel Sullivan, 51, 258
Crowley, Jocelyn, 138, 168
Crystal, Billy, 20
Cullen, Dave, 71–74
Cultural marginalization, 81–82, 86, 91
Custody and child support
  based on outdated laws, 165
  data, 161–163
  fathers' rights arguments, 147–149
  increased joint custody, 158, 160, 162,
    167–168
  with more family-focused men, 140–141
  paternal withdrawal effects, 162–163
  polarized claims linked to domestic
    violence, 157–161
  reflect fathers' predivorce childcare, 168

Dads and Daughters (DADs), 139
Dallam, Stephanie, 160
The Dark Knight Rises movie, 227
Daughter-father relationships, 139, 153,
  155–156, 163
Davids, Chris, 85
Davidson, Osha Gray, 241–242, 247
The Day of the Saxon (Lea), 52, 258
Deadbeat dads, 123, 138, 141–142, 155,
  164
The Decline of Males (Tiger), 130

Defiant Dads (Crowley), 138
DeLay, Tom, 70
Depression
    epidemic among men, 216–218
    lowered with gender equality, 283
    and masculinity, 216–218, 222
Die Hard movies, 59
Discrimination. *See* Gender discrimination; Workplace discrimination
Dittoheads, 44, 45, 226
Divorce
    court system discriminates against fathers, 147–149, 150, 154, 158
    father support groups, 147–149
    fathers who refuse to provide for children, 152
    with outdated custody, child support, laws, 165
    paternal involvement relates to predivorce spousal relationships, 156–158
    as source of rage, 17, 26, 137–139
    See also Fathers' rights movement
Dobash, Russell, 175
Domestic terrorism, 208, 228–229
Domestic violence
    with custody disputes, 158–161
    gender symmetry/asymmetry, 119–121, 190–194
    perceived as a justified right, 183, 186
    under pretext of losing control, 187–189
    racial, class, differences, 194–195
    rates for gay men, lesbians, 195
    rates of intimate partner homicides and attacks, 173–176
    reduced through batterers programs, 195–198
    as underreported, 164, 193
Don Draper (*Mad Men* character), 140, 166
Donnelly, Ignatius, 259
Douglas, Michael, 60
Dowd, Maureen, 111
Downes, Mike, 135
Downward mobility
    of extreme Right, 244–245, 251
    of middle- and lower-middle classes, 22–23
    of talk radio audiences, 33
Doyle, Richard, 111
Dr. Phil (Phil McGraw), 70
Duke, David, 1–2, 128, 236, 237, 239
Durkheim, Emile, 212
Dyer, Joel, 247, 253

Eastwood, Clint, 61–62
Economic dispossession of white middle-class men, 9, 253–254, 276–277, 281
Economic gap between middle class and ruling elites, 10, 203, 281–282
Economic recession
    effects on Angry Class, MRAs, 8–10, 112–113
    as gendered crisis, 14–15, 121
    impacts on white middle-class men, 209–210
    suicides spike, 212–214
Edmond, Oklahoma postal rampage, 201
Education. *See* Higher education of men and women; Women's and gender studies (WGS) programs
Elam, Paul, 114, 116–118
Eliot, T. S., 133
Elites. *See* Corporations and capitalist elites
Elkhart, Indiana suicides, 214
Emasculation
    masculinized humiliation, 75, 256–257, 263–264
    as source of rage, 169
    See also Feminization of men
Emerson, R., 175
Emotions
    change from productive anxiety to reactive anger, 21
    as gendered, 75
    manipulated into rage, 32
The End of Men (Rosin), 111
Enloe, Cynthia, 255–256
Entitlement of men
    to dignity about work, security, honor, 17, 282
    grievance linked to privilege, 23–24
    as key to understanding violence against women, 180–183
    perceived as thwarted by others, 218–220, 255
    to power, 46
    with sense of proprietorship of America, 35–36
    See also Aggrieved entitlement
Equality. *See* Gender equality; Racial equality
Erikson, Erik, 246
ESPN 360 television program, 221
European American Unity and Rights Conference, 237
European Union countries, 223, 281, 282
Evangelical Protestants, 46, 91, 243, 248
Evans, George, 50

Exclusion strategies to protect masculinity, 10, 50–52, 112, 126, 128, 264
Extreme Right
  background pre- and post-September 11, 233–238
  connected to skinheads, Aryan youth, 26
  as lower-middle-class, working-class, white men, 244–245
  nostalgic for traditional masculinity, 264
  politics of, 41
  profiled, 241–244
  women (*see* Angry American women; Women of the extreme Right)
  See also Neo-Nazis; White supremacists

F4J. *See* Fathers 4 Justice
Falling Down movie, 60–61
False accusations of sexual assault and domestic violence, 123, 159–161, 164
Faludi, Susan, 10, 12, 13–14, 261
Family-court systems
  based on outdated notions needing overhaul, 112, 165
  complexities in contested custody cases, 160–161
  data on custody cases, 161–163
  vs. fathers' rights groups, 146–150, 158–159
Farm Aid, 213, 246–247
Farm crises of 1980s and 1990s, 13, 22, 212–213, 232, 242, 247
Farmers
  believing in international Jewish bankers' exploitation, 242, 262
  restored through FDR's programs, 284–285
  suicides spike, 212–214, 246–248
Farmingville, New York hate crimes, 57
Farrell, Warren, 110–111, 118–119, 121
Fatherhood
  absent from MRAs' concerns, 124
  increasing participation in child care, 139–145, 280
  and outdated custody laws, 113
  quality relates to predivorce spousal relationships, 156–158
Fatherhood responsibility movement
  among black men, 29, 155–156
  benefits boys and girls, 163
  promoted by men of color, gay men, feminists, 147
Fatherless America (Blankenhorn), 150
Fatherlessness, 142, 150–154, 163
Fathers 4 Justice (F4J), 135–136

Fathers' rights movement (FRM)
  introduced, 28–29, 113, 124, 135–136
  campaign against outmoded custody laws, 166–168
  detracts from fathers' causes, responsibilities, 147–149, 155
  and increased family involvement, 145–147
  men's personal tragedies changed to political treatises, 137–139
  nurturing children means fighting ex-wives, 157–158
  reassert traditional patriarchal arrangements, 152–154
Faux populism, 12, 64
Felson, Richard, 92
Femicides, 174. *See also* Women-victim homicides
Feminazis, 5, 42–43, 99–100, 172, 261
The Feminine Mystique (Friedan), 103, 104
Feminism
  blamed for white men's problems, 42–43, 122
  conservative vs. liberal, 66–67
  as hateful ideology to men's rights activists, 107–108
  perceived as discriminatory to men, 101–102
  viewed as attack on masculinity, 110
  in White Power movement, 274–275
Feminists
  blamed by rampage shooters, 171–173
  blamed for fatherlessness, 151–152
  blamed for white boys' problems, 110
  film critics blamed for misandry, 131
  as gender inverts in politics, 260–261
  oppress white men, 99–100
Feminization of men, 46–47, 48–53. *See also* Emasculation
Feminization of poverty, 152
Ferri, Gian Luigi, 205
Fiebert, Martin, 191–193
The Fiery Cross (KKK), 267–268
Fight Club (Palahniuk) book and movie, 60, 205
Fight clubs (real-life), 219–221, 222
Finch, Peter, 34, 46
Fincher, David, 220
Fiorina, Carly, 18
Fluke, Sandra, 40, 41
Ford, Henry, 262
Frank, Thomas, 14, 38
Fraternal orders and lodges, 50, 52
Freud, Sigmund, 177
Friedan, Betty, 103, 104, 106
Furstenberg, Frank, 162–163

Gay baiting, 72, 77–78, 81, 92
Gay men
  blamed for white men's problems, 12
  discrimination against, 124
  domestic violence rates, 195
  portrayed by white supremacists,
    260–261
  promote fathers' responsibility
    movement, 147
  visibility blamed on feminists, 130
  as more equal today, 280–281
Gaylin, Willard, 25
Gelles, Richard, 120
Gender discrimination
  vs. disadvantaged, 125
  experienced by men (gay, black, Latino,
    working-class), 124–125
  reverse discrimination, 17, 40
  white men perceived as victims of
    feminists, 99–103
Gender equality
  and bias in the media, 44
  in friendships and relationships, 280
  in higher education, 128
  linked to greater happiness, lower
    depression, 283
  and men's increased family time, 146
  viewed as threatening, invasion of
    all-male turf, 115, 224–225
Gender gap, 6, 112
Gender symmetry/asymmetry, 119–120,
  190–194
Gendered rhetoric, 133, 254–255, 264, 276
Gerstel, Naomi, 144
GI Jane movie, 58
Gibson, Mel, 239
Gibson, William J., 243
Gill, Molly, 274
Gilligan, Carol, 23, 24
Gilligan, James, 77, 179
Gilmore, David, 132
Gingrich, Newt, 70
Giovanni, Nikki, 87
Globalization displaces lower-middle-class
  white men, 232, 233, 245–246
God-given right, 18, 196
Going postal. See Postal rampages
Golden, Andrew, 74–75
Goldilocks Dilemma, 51, 122, 257
Goldman, Emma, 266
Government
  antigovernment stance of extreme Right,
    253–254
  blamed for family farm losses, 246–248
  bureaucrats perceived as ignoring men's
    cries for help, 16–17

and dreams crushed, 11–12
  exacerbates problems through policies,
    17
  as feminist, 58, 117
  needs to provide safety net to middle-
    and lower-class men, 284–285
  programs to aid men, 123
  takeover, 55–56
  turns against white supremacists by Jews,
    262
Gran Torino movie, 61–62
Grant, Madison, 40, 52, 53, 258
Grateful Dads, 139
Grayson, Kentucky school shooting, 79
Grey, Zane, 48
Gritz, Bo, 243–244
Gulf War veterans, 244
Gun shows, 1, 240
Guns
  accessed by mentally ill, 85, 228,
    275–276
  availability to school shooters, 77–78,
    93
  gun culture, 89–90
  as one explanation for rampage
    shootings, 70, 207
Gurian, Michael, 70
Gurr, Ted Robert, 22
Guyland (Kimmel), 11, 59, 115, 218

Hackel, Mark, 214
Hakim, Nayab, 78
Hale, Tabitha, 63–64
Hall, G. Stanley, 48
Hall, Timothy, 175
Hammerskin Nation, 228, 266, 268, 275
Hannity, Sean, 32, 37, 38
Harris, Eric, 69–75, 79–81, 85, 90–93, 95
Hate crimes, 57, 195. See also Rampage
  shooters
Hate groups, 29, 109, 237–238, 242
Hatecore, 265, 277
Hayward, Fred, 111
Henley, William Ernest, 250
Hennard, George, 170
Herbert, Bob, 92
Heston, Charlton, 46, 70–71
Higher education of men and women,
  126–133, 155
Hispanic women, 8
History of American angry white men,
  46–53
Hitler, Adolf
  on gender integration, gender equality,
    268
  Germany of, 45

on Internet, 238
praised for efforts to exterminate Jews, 273
symbol 88 for Heil Hitler, 228
Hockey moms, 63, 65
Hofstadter, Richard, 229–231
Hollander, Roy Den, 99–103, 121, 125
Holmes, James, 227–228
Horn, Wade, 152
Horrible Bosses movie, 59–60
Housework, 143–144
Hugo, Victor, 21
Huguely, George, 173
Humiliation as emasculation, 75–76, 77, 85, 92, 256–257, 263–264
Hunter, Vernon, 200
"Hurt" song (Nine Inch Nails), 221–222
Hypermasculinity-hypomasculinity of the "other," 51, 58, 257, 259–263

I Don't Want to Talk About It (Real), 216–217
Idler, Ellen, 215
Immigrants
G.W. Bush's policies, 234
perceived as alien invaders, 53, 56
perceived as displacing American men in workplace, 16
targeted by enraged white men, 4, 7
See also Anti-immigrant nativism
Incest, 119
Income of white middle-class men, 10, 14, 32–33
Independent Woman newsletter, 274
Information Age disorder, 45
The International Jew (Ford), 262
International Jewish conspiracy for world domination, 43–44, 263, 269
Internet
active hate groups, 237–238
as base for male studies, 129
as manosphere, locker room, 113–118
with narratives of aggrieved entitlement, 96
violence as explanation for rampage shootings, 70
Intimate partner violence. *See* Domestic violence; Spousal homicides; Women-victim homicides
"Invictus" poem (Henley), 250–251
Iraq, invasion of, 36
IRS-airplane rampage, 199–202, 208
Islamic community center in Lower Manhattan, 56–57
Israel, 44, 234–237, 244

Jackson, Jesse, 213

Jake Harper (*Two and a Half Men* character), 105
James, Henry, 47
Jefferson, Thomas, 23, 134, 252, 255, 257
Jet Blue flight attendant meltdown, 210–212
Jewish banking conspiracy, 185, 242, 257, 262–263
Jews, hatred of. *See* Anti-Semitism
Jihad vs. McWorld (Barber), 277
Jock culture
with administrators complicit with rape, 94–95
and school shootings, 77, 79–80, 91–92, 95, 183
Joe the Plumber, 2, 5, 18, 201, 240
John Birch Society, 229, 230–231
John Wayne model, 105, 108–109
Johnson, William (Hootie), 224

Kantor, Glenda Kaufman, 194
Katz, Jackson, 32
Kaufman, Michael, 197
Keen, Sam, 104, 105–106
Kent County, Michigan suicides, 214
Kinkel, Kip, 74
Klebold, Dylan, 69–74, 79–81, 85, 90–93, 95, 97
Klein, Joe, 45
Know-Nothings, 51, 64–65, 258
Koch brothers, 64, 277
Koresh, David, 233
Kremer, Amy, 63–64
Krisberg, Barry, 70–71
Kristofferson, Kris, 21–22
Kruk, Edward, 157
Ku Klux Klan (KKK)
background, 230–231
expunges aliens, resists racial equality, 52
in rural America, 242
uses gender to discredit others, 259–260
women's role, 267, 271, 273, 274

Ladies of the Invisible Empire of KKK, 270
Langman, Peter, 74–75
Language of aggrieved entitlement
of batterers, 181
compared to Nazis, Hutus, promoting genocide, 53
English-only, 58
of fathers' rights groups, 158
nativists reminiscent of King George III, 56
Lankford, Adam, 78
LaPierre, Wayne, 71
Larkin, Ralph, 76, 90–91

Latino/Hispanic men, 8, 52, 57, 60–61, 124, 194–195
Lea, Homer, 52, 258
Leave It to Beaver television program, 142, 224–225
Lennon, John, 218
Leno, Jay, 271
Lepine, Marc, 171
Les Miserables (Hugo), 65
Lesbians, 12, 195, 280–281
Lethal Weapon movies, 58
Leyden, Joel, 136
Limbaugh, Rush
    dominates angry white male radio, 5, 37–38
    politics of victimization, 37–41
    radio persona, 31–33
    on 2012 election results, 35
    typical listeners, 64
Lincoln Memorial protest, Washington, DC, 135–136
Linzer, Lori, 267
Lone-wolf strategy of white supremacists, 228–229, 236
Losing control narrative for batterers, 187–189
Louis, C. K., 9
Loukaitis, Barry, 74, 79
Love, Yeardley, 173
Lower middle class
    betrayed by corporations, unions, 202–203
    as downwardly mobile, declining, 9, 13, 22–23
    hit by globalization, 245

Maccoby, Eleanor, 162–163
Mad Men television program, 140, 142, 204
Mahler, Matt, 77
Maine farmer suicides, 214
Male studies in academic institutions, 126–133
Malone, Jean, 192–193
Mandela, Nelson, 250, 251
Manhood in America (Kimmel), 14, 18
Manipulation of expression of emotions, 32, 36
Manliness, 9–10, 15, 48
Mansfield, Harvey, 9–10
Marcotte, Amanda, 114
Marcuse, Herbert, 45
Marginalization
    by class war, 223
    of Far Right after McCarthyism, 231
    from masculinity being questioned, 185
    of school shooters, 77, 80–81, 85–87, 91, 96

Marketing strategies using anger, 34
Marrs, Texe, 261
Martin, Jenny Beth, 63–64
Martin, Tom, 121
Marx, Karl, 22, 43
Masculinity
    compromised/damaged/restored through violence, 177–179, 187–189, 277–278
    history in America, 18–21
    linked to depression, 216–218
    needs decoupling from entitlement, 283
    new definitions searched for, 16
    and powerlessness/entitlement to power, 184–186
    of school shooters attacked by classmates, 77
    traditional, contradicts good parenting, 146–147
    white-collar, critiqued in fight clubs, 220–221
    See also Hypermasculinity-hypomasculinity of the "other"
Masculinity bonus, 8
Masculinity crisis, 46–53
Masculinity ideology
    defined by self-made man, 14
    excludes others from competitive marketplace, 10
    heroic, 62
    includes entitlement and blame, 9, 15
    key to understanding anger, 13
    mythopoetic men's movement, 105–106
    of Savage, 41–43
    See also Men's rights activists
McCarthyism, 230, 231
McVeigh, Timothy, 15, 208, 229, 249–251, 256
McVeigh, William, 249
Mead, Margaret, 178
Meade, Michael, 105–106
Media
    culture, 218–220
    as explanation for rampage shootings, 70–71
    films blamed for misandry, 132
    globalized, 96–97
    with men portrayed negatively, 123
    perceived by white supremacists as controlled by Jews, 239
    stunts of F4J, 135–136
    See also Movies and angry white men
Men Achieving Liberation and Equality (Male), 111, 138
Men Confront Pornography (Kimmel), 39
Men in Groups (Tiger), 130

Men killed or attacked by female partners, 174–176, 190–194
Men-only religious revivals, 50
Men's liberation
    history, 103–109
    rhetoric, 133–134
    and traditional sex roles, 103–107, 110, 133
"Men's Manifesto" (Baron), 108
Men's News Daily website, 116
Men's rights activists (MRAs)
    origins, background, 103–108
    affected by economics, upward shift of wealth, 113
    as fans of Sodini, Lepine, 171–173
    as movement of angry straight white men, 109–110, 124–125
    policy issues, 122–125
    propelled by pain, anguish, 133–134
    seek to restore traditional masculinity, 264
    on women's studies, 128–129
    See also Fathers' rights movement
Men's Rights Association, 111
Men's Rights, Inc. (MR, Inc.), 111, 138
Men's rights movement. See Men's rights activists
Mental illness
    claimed for college-educated women (late 1800s), 126–127
    and depression in men, 216–218
    dynamics of Wade Page and Misty Cook, 275
    of men who go postal, 201–202
    psychosis of James Holmes, 227–228
    resulting from bullying, gay bashing, 92, 96
    resulting in suicide attempts, 92
    of school shooters, 85–86, 87
    of Sodini, Hennard, Lepine, 170–171
Mentors in Violence Prevention Program (MVP), 198
Merit-based society
    as the American Dream for white men, 18, 112
    and lost entitlement for men, 219, 283
    with men as victims, 10
Meritocracy. See Merit-based society
Metzger, Tom, 238, 269
Middle class
    betrayed by corporations, unions, government, 202–203
    close to working-class men, 204–205
    as downwardly mobile, 23
    gap widens with the rich, 203
    See also Lower middle class

Military veterans, 243–244, 249, 250
Militia of Michigan, 266
Militia of Montana, 261
Militias
    anti-Semitism of, 262
    of right-wing extremists, 232, 238, 266
    in rural areas, 26, 55, 261–262
    support failing farmers, 242
Miller, Dennis, 35
Mincy, Ronald, 155
Mini rampages, 173–176
Minnesota suit against funding battered women's shelters, 120–121
Minutemen and Patriot organizations, 5, 7, 18, 55–56, 253–254
Misandry, 116, 131–132
Misogyny, 109, 131–132
Mnookin, Robert, 162–163
Montreal rampage shooting, 171, 197
Moore, Barrington, 22
Moore, Demi, 58
Moore, Michael, 70
Moses Lake, Washington school shooting, 79, 89
Mosh pit dancing, 265
Movies and angry white men, 58–62
MRAs. See Men's rights activists
Ms. magazine, 106
Muehl, William, 118
Mullet, Paul, 235
Muscular Christianity, 50
The Myth of Male Power (Farrell), 110
Mythopoetic men's movement, 105–106

NAFTA, 233, 253
Naked at Gender Gap (Baber), 110
Nathanson, Paul, 131–133
National Fatherhood Initiative, 139
National Organization for Women (NOW), 110
National Rifle Association (NRA), 24, 46, 70–71, 89–90
National Vanguard, 256
Native Americans, 259
Nativism. See Anti-immigrant nativism
Nazi tattoos, 228, 265
Nelson, Willie, 213
Neo-Nazis
    committed to race and family, 271
    as domestic terrorists, 229
    of downwardly mobile lower middle class, 23
    interviewing process, 239–241
    Sikh temple shooter Page, 228
    See also White supremacists
New Right, 232

New Yorker magazine, 140
Newman, Katherine, 77–78
Newsweek magazine, 41
Newtown, Connecticut school shooting, 71
Nine Inch Nails, 221–222
9/11 attacks. *See* September 11 attacks
No Child Left Behind Act, 8, 90
"No Crime Being White" song (Day of the Sword), 253
No Easy Answers (Brown), 93
Norton, Ed, 205, 220
NRA. *See* National Rifle Association

Oak Creek, Wisconsin Sikh temple shooting, 227, 228, 266, 275–276
Obama, Barack
    elections elicit racist public discourse, 6–7, 237–238
    and Limbaugh's racism, 40
    on rise of rage, 24
    spearheads fathers' responsibility, 155
    2012 victory generates aggrieved entitlement, 34–35
Obamacare, 55–56
O'Connor, Matt, 135
Office Space movie, 59–60
Oklahoma City bombing (1995), 15
Olbermann, Keith, 6
O'Leary, Dan, 192
Oprah Winfrey Show television program, 39
O'Reilly, Bill, 35, 225
Our Bodies, Our Selves (1971), 128–129
Outrage media, 33–34, 43–45. *See also* Talk radio
Outsourcing American jobs, 16, 22–23, 209, 284

Paducah, Kentucky school shooting, 78, 93, 97–98
Page, Wade Michael, 227–229, 266, 275–276
Palahniuk, Chuck, 60, 219–220
Palin, Sarah, 6, 63, 65, 112
Paranoid politics of right-wing extremists, 229–231, 237, 248, 256, 262–263
Parkman, Francis, 258
The Passing of the Great Race (Grant), 52, 258
Paternal withdrawal effects on children, 162–163
Patriarchal control, traditional, 154, 159, 166, 175, 179, 271
Pearl, Mississippi school shooting, 69, 73, 78–79, 93
Pennington, Gary Scott, 74, 79
Philips, Julie, 215
Pierce, William, 238, 256, 261–262, 263

Pierson, Dean, 213–214
Pitt, Brad, 205
Pleck, Joseph, 106
Political anger
    as expression of sadness, anguish, 32, 282–283
    lack of civility in discourse, 4
    manipulated for Iraq involvement, 36
    as pattern of victimization, 37
    scapegoating to explain defeats, 24–25
Political cultures and school violence, 89–90
Political incorrectness, 5–6
Popenoe, David, 151–152, 156
Populism, 7, 64–65, 66–67
Pornography, 39, 115–116, 126, 262, 274
Posse Comitatus, 229, 242
Postal rampages, 5, 201–202, 207, 208, 212
Poverty
    correlated to crime, fatherlessness, 151–152
    linked to domestic violence across ethnicities, 194–195
Power
    compensated for as cultural inversions, 133
    and MRAs' perceived entitlement to power, 110–112
    and rape, 182–186
    and traditional sex roles of men, women, 104
    white men displaced from, 33–34, 46, 232
    white middle class men's powerlessness, 182–186, 232–233, 284
Privilege as rightful, entitled, 7, 16, 24, 45–46
Profeminist men, 106–107
"The Promised Land" song (Springsteen), 11, 199, 204, 277–278
Protestant Christians. *See* Evangelical Protestants
Putnam, Robert, 270

Queen for a Day television program, 39
Quindlen, Anna, 219

Rachel Maddow, 32–33
Racial equality, 44
Racial Loyalty magazine, 263
Racism
    elicited by Obama's election/reelection, 2–3, 6–7
    exclusion strategies, 51
    interracial sex and miscegenation, 52
    of Limbaugh, 40

to reclaim manhood for white
supremacists, 266–267
resting on hypermasculinity-
hypomasculinity arguments, 257–263
violence of, 180
of women of extreme Right, 271–272
Racists. *See* Extreme Right; White
supremacists
Rader, Jack, 268
Radical Feminist newsletter, 274
The Radical Right (Bell), 231
Radio. *See* Talk radio
Rage
introduced, 3–6
associated with love, sex, 177–179
displaced outward onto government,
246–248
of fathers' rights movement leaders,
137–138
fueled by aggrieved entitlement,
170–173, 276–277, 282
linked to aspiration for advertising
strategies, 34
over courts' custody failures, 168
passing for political discourse, 44–46, 223
taking responsibility for, 195–198
turned inward as depression, 216–218, 222
begins to decline among America's white
men, 280–281
Rambo movie, 58, 243
Rampage (Newman), 77–78
Rampage shooters
compared to Middle East suicide
bombers, 78
factors contributing to shootings, 71–75,
77–79
marginalized by jockocracy, 77, 79–80,
91–92, 95
as nonconformists, overconformists,
81–82
pre-Columbine, 72–73, 76
profiled, 71–74, 76–87, 207–212
shootings shown on political map,
89–90
use Columbine as model, 76
white supremacists, 227–229
of women, 169–173
working-class, middle-class, men, 201,
205–207
See also Mini rampages; School shootings;
Workplace violence; *specific incidences
and persons*
Ramsey, Evan, 74–75, 79
Rape
false accusations of, 123
as form of power, 182–186

and jockocracy, 94–95
as a justified right, 183–184
MRAs' positions, 126
and perceived hypermasculinity, 258
sexual component of, 119
The Rape of the Male (Doyle), 111
Rational Feminist newsletter, 274
Reagan, Ronald, 212, 213, 232, 254
Reaganomics, 201
Real, Terrence, 216–217
Recession. *See* Economic recession
Relative depravation, 22
Religion
cryptoreligious groups, 229
Far Right influences, 232
feminism as, according to MRAs,
101–102
feminization of, 47
intolerance as factor in school shootings,
91
muscular Christianity, 50
Repressive desublimation, 45
Reproductive rights, 123, 130
Republic of Texas militia, 261
Republican Party, 40, 89, 133
Ressentiment as creative hatred, 38
Restlessness of American masculinity, 16,
18–20
Retaliation with violence, 81, 92, 176–179,
183
Revenge
for bullying, humiliation, 75–77
justified by aggrieved entitlement, 82,
87, 93
through violence, rape, 183
Right-wing extremists. *See* Extreme Right
Right-wing racists. *See* Racism; White
supremacists
The Rising Tide of Color (Stoddard), 52, 258
"The River" song (Springsteen), 18
The Road to Wellville (Boyle), 49
Romney, Mitt, 34
Roos, Christopher, 206
Roosevelt, Franklin D., 284–285
Roosevelt, Theodore, 48
Roper, Bill, 236
Rosen, Ruth, 65
Rosin, Hanna, 64, 111
Rubin, Lillian, 254
Ruby Ridge, Idaho raid by FBI, 233–234
Rural component of far-right groups, 26, 67,
73, 88–89, 241–242, 266
Rush Hour movies, 59

Saddam Hussein, 36
Safe at Home Foundation, 198

Sandy Hook Elementary School rampage shooting, 71
Santana High School shooting, Santee, California, 82–84
Santelli, Rick, 64
Sapolsky, Robert, 180
Sasser, Jim, 24–25
Savage, Mike, 37, 38, 41–43
The Savage Nation radio program, 38
Scapegoating, 24
School shootings
    with bullying, madness, ignored by administrators, 84, 87, 90, 95
    contexts: cultural, sociological, psychological, 74, 90–91, 93
    history in America, 72–73, 76
    shooters profiled, 71–74, 76–87
    See also specific incidences and persons
Schools of shootings profiled
    geography and political map, 88–89
    identification of violent students needed, 96–97
    institutional complicity with bullying, gay baiting, rape, 90–91, 95, 96
Schwarzenegger, Arnold, 239
Scully, Diana, 183–184
Second American Revolution (R-2), 5, 7, 56, 264
Self-control as strategy for restoring masculinity, 48–49
Self-made man ideology, 14, 15, 18–19
September 11 attacks, 26, 57, 234–236
Seton, Ernest Thompson, 49–50
Sex in Education (Clarke), 126–127
Sex roles (traditional), 103–107, 123, 124, 133
Sexual harassment, 104, 118–119
Sexual predation, 107, 121, 123
Shakleton, Dave, 171
Shelters for battered women, 120–121, 176, 186
Sherrill, Patrick, 201–202, 204
Shootings. *See* Rampage shooters
Shows, Carla, 144
Sikh temple shooting, Oak Creek, Wisconsin, 227, 228, 266, 275–276
Slater, Steven, 210–212
Sleeping with the Enemy movie, 132, 174
Slotkin, Richard, 178
Smith, Woody Will, 175–176
Snipp, Matthew, 242
Sobieraj, Sarah, 33
Social Darwinism, 51, 258
Social marginalization. *See* Bullying and torture; Gay baiting
Social patterns of school shootings, 74–75, 77

Sodini, George, 29, 169–173, 176, 198
Solutions to white men's anger, 10–11, 280–285
Sons of angry white men. *See* Angry American white boys
Sorel, Georges, 38
Southern Poverty Law Center (SPLC), 109, 237–238
Sowell, Thomas, 70
Spencer, Glenn, 235
Spock, Benjamin, 143
Sports prescribed to promote manhood, 20, 48
Spousal homicides, 173–176, 190, 195
Springsteen, Bruce, 11, 18, 199, 204, 216, 218, 277–278
Stack, Joe, 199–202, 208
Stalking, 174
Stallone, Sylvester, 58
Standard Gravure plant, Louisville, Kentucky rampage murders, 205
Stanesby, Jolly, 135–136
Steinmetz, Susan, 190–191
Stephens, Edward, 129
Stiffed (Faludi), 10, 13
Stock, Catherine, 252
Stoddard, Lothrop, 40, 52, 53, 258
Straus, Murray, 191–192
Student athletes' harassment. *See* Jock culture
Suhayda, Rocky, 236
Suicide among men
    as inwardly exploding anger, 212–216
    Joe Stack, 200–201
    leading cause of death in agricultural fatalities, 246–247
Suicide bombers, 78
Suicides by mass murders
    of school shooters, 5, 28–29, 73, 82, 87, 171, 212
    of workplace rampages, 200, 201, 205–206, 212
Summers, Lawrence, 127
Sunday, Billy, 50
Survivalist groups, 5, 238, 242

Talk radio
    with audiences of angry white men, 32–33, 38
    faux populism of, 12
    grounded in victimhood, 37–38
    as outrage media, 33–35, 37–43, 279
    sounds alarm for subversive enemies, 231
    translates listeners' distress into rage, 4, 5, 11
Tavris, Carol, 23

Tea Party
    as fake populism, 12, 64
    formed by downwardly mobile middle
        classes, 23
    members described, 64
    motivated by desire to restore manhood,
        6
    racist public discourse of, 7
    revises history, 11
    slogans, aphorisms, 55–56, 66, 177
    on 2012 presidential campaign, 35
    as White People's Party, 6–7
    women's roles in, 63–67
Tea Party Express, 63–64
Tea Party Patriots, 63–64
Temperance movement, 66
The Tempest (Shakespeare), 97
Tennyson, Alfred Lord, 126
Testosterone effects on aggression, 120,
    180–181
Thornton, Omar, 206
Thunderbolt publication, 261, 263
Tiger, Lionel, 10, 129–130
Tocqueville, Alexis de, 18–19
Todd, Evan, 79
Tolstoy, Leo, 168
Tom Brown's School Days (Hughes), 48
Tom Joad (character in *Grapes of Wrath*), 251
Torre, Joe, 197–198
Torture. *See* Bullying and torture
Town meetings, 23, 43, 44, 247
Trondone, Sarah, 215–216
True Believers in the American Dream,
    11–12, 112, 202, 278
True Lies movie, 70
The Turner Diaries (Pierce), 256, 261–262,
    278
Tuusula, Finland school shooting, 96
Two and a Half Men television program,
    105
Tyler Durden (character in *Fight Club*), 59,
    218–220, 221
Tyree, Andrea, 192–193

Unemployment
    of men in recession, 209–210
    as predictor of domestic violence, 194
    rates for African American men, 155
    and suicide, 214–215
    White Power's position, 263
Unforgiven movie, 62
Union membership
    assaulted by corporate elites, 281–282
    betrays American Dream, 202
    decline impacts white working class, 13,
        15

    enables men to support families,
        249–250
    and unemployed angry men, 25
University of Montreal rampage shooting,
    171, 197
University of Virginia killing by Huguely,
    173
Upward mobility of the American Dream,
    13, 19–20, 23, 113, 251
US Postal Service (USPS) workers, 201

Victimhood
    introduced, 116–117
    channels hurt into outrage, 37–39
    emasculation claimed, 256–257
    as manhood threatened, 40
    and men's rights movement, 104–106,
        111–112, 118, 125, 138
    of white men by family-court system, 158
Video games/violent video games, 5, 45, 59,
    70, 218, 219, 238
Vietnam war veterans, 243–244
Violence
    applauded against women, as sense of
        entitlement, 171–173, 180–183
    female-victim homicides and attacks,
        173–176, 190–194
    as form of conflict resolution for boys, 75
    as learned, 93–94
    in pornographic media, 115–116
    threatened, encouraged, by men's rights
        groups, 109–110, 117–118
    viewed as restorative, retaliatory, 77, 92,
        176–179, 277–278
    See also Domestic violence
Violence Against Women Act (VAWA), 101
Violence by women against men, 101,
    119–121, 190–194
Violence-prone schools, 88–92
Virginia Tech shooting, Blacksburg, Virginia,
    84–87, 91, 94–96
The Virginian (Wister), 50
Virtual social movement of Angry White
    Men, 37
Voting bloc of American white men, 10

Waco, Texas Branch Davidian–ATF raid, 233,
    249–250
Wales, Rebecca, 65
Wallace, Glen, 247
Walt Kowalski (character in *Gran Torino*),
    61–62
Ward Cleaver (character in *Leave It to
    Beaver*), 224–225
Washington Post newspaper, 91–92
Weaver, Randy, 233

Webster, Stephen, 62
Weiner, Michael Alan. *See* Savage, Mike
Weise, Jeffrey, 74–75
Wesbecker, Joseph, 205, 248
Westward expansion to America frontiers, 19, 20
What's the Matter with Kansas? (Frank), 14, 38
White Aryan Resistance (WAR), 229, 249, 266, 269, 270
White Ribbon Campaign, 197
White studies, 128
White supremacist dating website, 272
White supremacists
    introduced, 233–238
    domestic terrorism of Sikh temple shooting, 227–229
    emasculation politics, 255–257
    on gay men, 260
    manhood reclaimed through racism, 264–267
    patriotism with hatred for government, 253–255
    portrayals of Jewish men, 257, 262–263
    procapitalist ideology with hatred of corporate iterations, 252, 255
    profiled, 239–244, 251
    race politics of lower middle class, 23, 244–251
    rage fueled by aggrieved entitlement, 276–278
    social lives, 265–266
    women's role in, 267–276
    See also Neo-Nazis
White Wing. *See* White supremacists
White women. *See* Angry American women
William Foster (character in *Falling Down*), 60–61
Williams, Andy, 74, 82–84
Willis, Bruce, 239
Willy Loman (character in *Death of a Salesman*), 133, 161, 202, 218
Wimpification, 14, 102
Winfrey, Oprah, 39

Wisconsin Militia, 262
Wister, Owen, 50
Women
    attacked by Limbaugh and Savage, 42–43
    blamed by rejected rampage shooters, 169–173
    feminizing clutches of, 49–50
    as immigrants (nativists' perceptions), 54
    as masculinized, 46, 122
    in military, politics, as inversions, 260–261
    with mission of having babies, 52
    perceived sexy yet contemptuous, 17
Women for Aryan Unity (WAU), 270
Women of the extreme Right
    motivations, 270–271
    refeminized, 276
    required to remain in prescribed sphere, 267–276
Women's and gender studies (WGS) programs, 101, 121, 125, 126–129
Women's anger. *See* Angry American women
Women-victim homicides, 173–176
Woodham, Luke, 69, 74, 78–79, 93
"Working Class Hero" song (Lennon), 218
Working-class white men
    betrayed by corporations, unions, 202–203, 209, 234–235
    changing involvement in family lives, 144–145
    endure discrimination, 124
    rampage murders, 201, 205–207
    as right-wing extremists, 244–245
    suicides spike, 215
Workplace discrimination, 17, 121
Workplace shooters profiled, 207–212
Workplace violence, 179–180, 204–211

YMCA (Young Men's Christian Association), 50
Young, Katherine, 131–133
Youth violence, 70
Youth Violence: A Report of the Surgeon General, 71

Michael Kimmel is distinguished professor of sociology and gender studies at Stony Brook University in New York. An author or editor of more than twenty books, including *Manhood in America*, *The Gendered Society*, *The History of Men*, and *Guyland*, he lives with his family in Brooklyn, New York.

NATION
BOOKS

The Nation Institute

Founded in 2000, **Nation Books** has become a leading voice in American independent publishing. The imprint's mission is to tell stories that inform and empower just as they inspire or entertain readers. We publish award-winning and bestselling journalists, thought leaders, whistleblowers, and truthtellers, and we are also committed to seeking out a new generation of emerging writers, particularly voices from underrepresented communities and writers from diverse backgrounds. As a publisher with a focused list, we work closely with all our authors to ensure that their books have broad and lasting impact. With each of our books we aim to constructively affect and amplify cultural and political discourse and to engender positive social change.

Nation Books is a project of The Nation Institute, a nonprofit media center established to extend the reach of democratic ideals and strengthen the independent press. The Nation Institute is home to a dynamic range of programs: the award-winning Investigative Fund, which supports groundbreaking investigative journalism; the widely read and syndicated website TomDispatch; journalism fellowships that support and cultivate over twenty-five emerging and high-profile reporters each year; and the Victor S. Navasky Internship Program.

For more information on Nation Books and The Nation Institute, please visit:

www.nationbooks.org
www.nationinstitute.org
www.facebook.com/nationbooks.ny
Twitter: @nationbooks